THE LURE
OF AFRICA

**american interests
in tropical
africa, 1919–1939**

winner of the
**allan nevins
history prize**

EDWARD H. McKINLEY

asbury college

THE LURE
OF AFRICA

american interests in tropical africa, 1919–1939

the bobbs-merrill company, inc.
indianapolis and new york

Library of Congress Cataloging in Publication Data
McKinley, Edward H
  The lure of Africa: American interests in tropical Africa, 1919–1939.
  Bibliography: p.
  1. Africa, Sub-Saharan—Relations (general) with the United States.
2. United States—Relations (general) with Sub-Saharan Africa. 3.
Americans in Sub-Saharan Africa.   I. Title.
DT38.M33   301.29′73′067   73-1789   ISBN 0-672-51736-1

To my father,
who made the scholar's life
possible for me

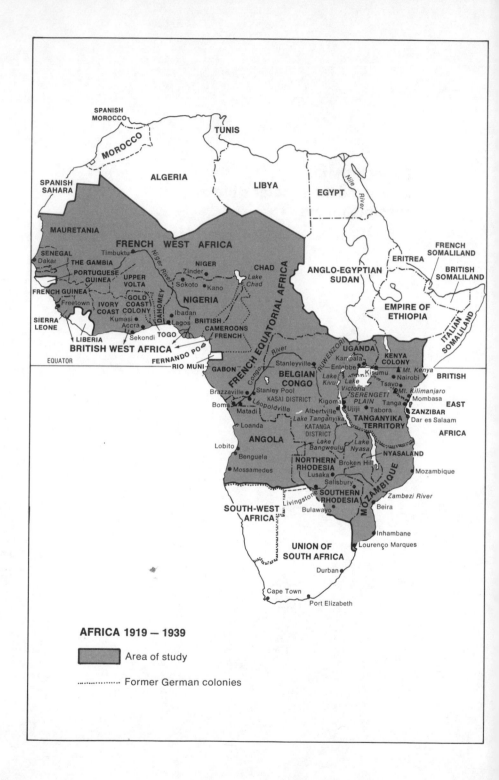

SPANISH
MOROCCO

TUNIS

MOROCCO

SPANISH
SAHARA

ALGERIA

LIBYA

EGYPT

MAURETANIA

FRENCH WEST AFRICA

SENEGAL
Dakar THE GAMBIA
PORTUGUESE
GUINEA
FRENCH GUINEA
Freetown IVORY
SIERRA COAST
LEONE
LIBERIA

Timbuktu

UPPER
VOLTA
GOLD
COAST
COLONY
Kumasi DAHOMEY
Accra
Sekondi TOGO

NIGER
Zinder
Sokoto
Kano

NIGERIA
Ibadan
Lagos
BRITISH
CAMEROONS
FRENCH

CHAD
Lake
Chad

FRENCH
SOMALILAND
ERITREA
BRITISH
SOMALILAND

ANGLO-EGYPTIAN
SUDAN

EMPIRE OF
ETHIOPIA

ITALIAN
SOMALILAND

BRITISH WEST AFRICA
FERNANDO PO
RIO MUNI

EQUATOR

GABON

FRENCH EQUATORIAL AFRICA

Nile
River

RUWENZORI UGANDA
Stanleyville Kampala KENYA
Entebbe COLONY
Congo River Kisumu Mt. Kenya
Brazzaville Lake Nairobi BRITISH
Stanley Pool Kivu Lake Tsavo
Boma KASAI DISTRICT Victoria Mt. Kilimanjaro EAST
Matadi SERENGETI Mombasa
Léopoldville Albertville PLAIN Tanga ZANZIBAR
Kigoma Ujiji Tabora Dar es Salaam AFRICA
BELGIAN Lake Tanganyika TANGANYIKA
CONGO KATANGA TERRITORY
Loanda DISTRICT
Lake
Bangweulu Lake NYASALAND
ANGOLA Nyasa
Lobito NORTHERN Broken Hill Mozambique
RHODESIA
Benguela Lusaka MOZAMBIQUE
Mossamedes Salisbury
SOUTHERN Zambezi River
Livingstone RHODESIA Beira
SOUTH-WEST Bulawayo
AFRICA Inhambane
Lourenço Marques
UNION OF
SOUTH AFRICA
Durban
Cape Town
Port Elizabeth

AFRICA 1919 – 1939

Area of study

············· Former German colonies

contents

acknowledgments

A larger number of persons assisted me on this book than can be practically named individually. Special thanks must go to the fine staff of research assistants and archivists at the National Archives of the United States, and particularly to Albert Blair; Mary Johnson; Kenneth Hall, who superintends the United States Shipping Board records and related materials; and Stanley Brown, who superintends the Bureau of Animal Industry materials in the Federal Records Center, Suitland, Maryland.

The staff of the Field Museum of Natural History was extremely helpful, but I must extend my deepest gratitude to the distinguished Chief Curator of Zoology, Dr. Austin L. Rand, who placed at my disposal the files of his own department, guided me through introductions to all the other departments, and provided me with invaluable personal information on the Chicago museum. I want to thank as well Dr. Donald Collier, Chief Curator of Anthropology; Mary Hagberg of the Registrar's Office; and Mrs. Marilyn Kurland, Dr. Rand's very pleasant secretary.

I also had occasion while doing research to make inquiries of a number of persons in disciplines other than history, and in all instances they received me hospitably and offered their complete cooperation. At the California Academy of Sciences in Golden Gate Park, San Francisco, I was greatly assisted by Associate Director Dr. Robert T. Orr; by Ray Brian, the Librarian; and by Mrs. Jean Firby of the Exhibits Department. Mrs. Firby was in the process of cataloging the Simson osteological collection, and provided me with much useful information.

Mrs. Nydine Snow Latham graciously consented to an interview in her home in Oakland, California, on the subject of her father's expedition to British East Africa in 1919–1920.

Above all, I extend my thanks to Professor John A. DeNovo of the Department of History at the University of Wisconsin.

x   acknowledgments

Professor DeNovo was my friend and mentor through my graduate school years, and he guided this project with painstaking care. I have benefited from his thorough erudition and kind personal attention at every turn.

And a final and special word of grateful appreciation for William Hoth of Bobbs-Merrill, my kind, patient, and very thorough editor.

THE LURE OF AFRICA

american interests in tropical africa, 1919–1939

introduction

The band of the Nigerian Regiment of the Royal West African Frontier Force was playing a lively march. The white wooden grandstand at the racecourse was crowded with people chatting idly, fanning themselves with their programs —the Europeans in white stock suits, straw skimmers, and pastel summer dresses, the Africans in a rainbow of flowing finery. Squares of black soldiers in red fezzes and khaki uniforms stood rigidly along the grass, while young English officers struggled with their nervous mounts. At the far end of the field, a maroon touring car was driven onto the turf. There were tiny Union Jacks on the front fenders, gold crests on the rear doors. In front were two black soldiers, dressed like the others in khaki and red; in the back seat sat a white officer in an elaborate blue uniform, a confection of glittering decorations, white plumes, and a gold sword. The band stopped playing, the car rolled to a stop before the stands, and a sustained drum roll was sounded. From the back of the car the governor nodded to the bandmaster, the first familiar chord brought the crowd to its feet, the straw hats came down, and the uniformed men snapped to their palm-out salute:

> God save our Gracious King,
> Long live our noble King,
> God save the King. . . .

It was Empire Day, 1925, in Lagos, Nigeria.[1]

In Washington, D.C., on August 10, 1927, the Secretary of State, Frank B. Kellogg, took time from his daily schedule to concern himself—briefly—with tropical Africa, a region of the globe in which neither Kellogg nor anyone else in the State Department showed much interest in the regular course of administering the foreign affairs of the United States. As it was, Kellogg was acting in the interest of old friends who were planning a trip to parts of tropical Africa: any little kind-

3

nesses that he could arrange would be appreciated. The secretary was glad to oblige. He did not, of course, send his letters of introduction to Africa; there was no one in Africa who could respond to such high-level correspondence. He wrote instead to London and Brussels, where the power over much of tropical Africa lay. In 1927 the imperial sun was at high noon, bright in the sky. In the last quarter of the nineteenth century, Americans had watched it rise, and by the late 1920s, it seemed a permanent fixture in the sky. It had not once gone backward nor started downward in nearly fifty years; perhaps it never would.[2]

Since 1960—The Year of Africa, when the French Colonies, Nigeria, and the Belgian Congo became independent —sub-Saharan Africa has been part of the Third World. It has become a geopolitical force of sovereign states with votes, policies, armies, resources, and national aspirations. In the eternal maneuvering of modern international combinations, the newly independent nations of tropical Africa have come to possess importance, as a potential power balance, to one side or the other in the cold war. Such, of course, was not always the case with tropical Africa. What is more important, and more to the point of this study, is that it was not the case in the relatively recent past. The entire geographical area examined in this book, with the exception of the Portuguese territories, moved from a colonial status to full independence in the five years after 1957.

Whether or not the American public has reacted with the proper understanding and sympathy to the new African states is not the concern of this book, which closes on the eve of these changes. That the United States was not *prepared* for an independent Africa can be deduced perhaps from the sorts of information reaching its shores over the seemingly tranquil period between the two world wars. Africa has never been, nor is it now, a prime interest of most Americans. During the 1920s and the 1930s they looked upon Africa not as a threat or an ally or an international counterpoise but, in almost abstract terms, as a landscape, a place of animals and people, a place of gold and copper, cocoa and palm oil, a market and a treasure-house totally unencumbered by the political complexities involved in dealing with sovereign powers.

What then was the image of Africa that Americans formed

in those years and that persisted through the new war to serve, for good or ill, as the basis of their reactions to a new Africa? In the absence of direct radio or television broadcasts, most information on Africa was brought home by Americans whose business or pleasure had carried them there. In 1922 Walter Lippmann observed in *Public Opinion* that "the world that we have to deal with politically is out of reach, out of sight, out of mind. It has to be explored, reported, and imagined." My objective is to apply this mode of inquiry to American relations with tropical Africa.[3]

A recent study by Clifford H. Scott of what Americans imagined Africa to be like in the first forty years of this century has suggested that the American conception of African Negroes was largely inaccurate, based on previous misconceptions about American blacks. If the American image of Africa was not correct, what was it? In discussing the elements contributing toward this image, Scott refers, though only briefly, to the numerous scientific and hunting expeditions that entered Africa in these years. In fact, however, a significant part of American relations with Africa pertained to these expeditions. They were perhaps the single most important factor in the formation of American ideas about Africa. To a generation of American youth, motion-picture and magazine accounts of those expeditions, and the specimens carted home by them, *were* Africa. Observers on both sides of the Atlantic recognized at the time the extent to which safaris supplied Americans with their view of sub-Saharan Africa. Phillip Percival, one of the most famous of the English safari managers, or "white hunters," wrote for the magazine of the American Museum of Natural History in 1927 that "probably most of what the great American public has learned of Africa has been communicated by the screen and by the reports and collections of museum expeditions."[4]

In New York City, Chicago, and San Francisco, crowds totaling millions filed spellbound through special exhibits— African Halls—in natural history museums. There under glass and artificial light was poised the life of Africa, pinioned against "scientifically" painted backgrounds, frozen with glass eyes and treated skins, muzzles in brown glass water, claws in plaster blood, snarling, rearing, almost menacing. The visitor to the American Museum of Natural History in New York was told that "transplanted Africa stands before you"; in 1936 alone, two and a half million persons believed it. In 1933, the year of the World's Fair in Chicago, the Field Museum of Natural History in that city received 3,269,390 visitors, the largest annual attendance ever recorded by an American museum. A taxidermic structure of two elephants in mortal combat stood in the main arcade, a Chicago landmark, and the Field Museum's African Hall was one of the finest in the country. Up in the Bronx, the New York Zoological Society offered its patrons a view of Africa similar to that of the taxidermists, though somewhat less dramatic. Seedy and decidedly nonferocious though they were, "Simba" and "Khartoum" were at least alive, and a little imagination could correct any deficiencies in their appearance. Between its opening in 1899 and 1929, some forty-eight million persons, mostly children, peered through the iron railings at Africa in the Bronx.[5]

To a great many Americans before the Second World War, then, Africa was more a land of animals and scenery than a land of people—most of them black. Authors today, reflecting concern with both domestic race tensions and international rivalries, discourse almost exclusively on the people of Africa. But only a few years ago travelers to Africa seldom thought of Africans, except as servants. Scenery, animals, the bustle of American cars, the vagaries of colonial social life—these were what interested most American travelers, and, consequently, their readers—not the indigenous population and its problems.

That African life engaged the attentions of missionaries might be considered an exception. In 1936 one of their journals, the *Missionary Review of the World,* carried twenty-seven different articles on tropical Africa (excluding South Africa, Liberia, and Ethiopia). But missionaries, some of whom were active writers, were seldom interested in Africans as they found them; they much preferred to describe their converts, who never appeared in the journals unless they had made considerable progress toward straw hats and monogamy. When the indigenes were described in their natural state, it was in such horrified and deprecating terms as to emphasize the need for immediate evangelization, which usually required more missionaries, more money, and another Ford.[6]

The reader may wonder why the American missionary

does not figure more prominently in these pages. It is true, for instance, that during the interwar years the majority of Americans in tropical Africa—in some colonies, nearly all— were missionaries. The missionaries' contribution to the public's image of Africa, however, was not proportionate to their numbers; most of them wrote nothing for publication, and those who did wrote for periodicals of limited appeal. Nonetheless, the missionary is included as an important, though not crucial, factor in the American image of tropical Africa.

No better proof exists of what interested Americans in Africa than the pictures they took and selected for publication. In an article entitled "Uganda, 'Land of Something Now,'" published in the *National Geographic Magazine* in January, 1937, Jay Marston included twenty-two illustrations, of which eleven were of Africans. Of these eleven, five were of the Europeanized court ritual of local kings, two were of the King's African Rifles, two were of natives working in a salt excavation, one was of an overloaded native bus, and another was of a "Watusi" chief, who was six-feet five-inches tall. The other eleven pictures were of wild animals, railroad bridges, and waterfalls. When Dr. A. S. Hitchcock of the United States Department of Agriculture attended a botanical convention in South Africa, he made a side trip up the beautiful East Coast. His pictures, accompanying an article in the *Scientific Monthly* for December, 1930, show that the botanists had been typical tourists, even in Africa. They had photographed each other, their train, the hotel, government buildings, nature hikes, plants, the American consulate in Nairobi, and an occasional native—always a woman.[7]

Woodbridge Van Dyke, the American motion-picture director, warned readers of his account of the filming of *Trader Horn* in Kenya in 1930 that he was not presenting an objective study. "Please let me say that I am not describing Africa, its natives and its animals as they really are," he wrote. "I am merely telling of those with which I came in contact and of how they appeared to me." And as the people and the animals appeared to Van Dyke and others like him—Dr. Hitchcock or Marston, the Martin Johnsons or the Carl Akeleys —they appeared to the American public. And as they appeared to the American public, they will appear in these pages.[8]

I have been forced, as the reader will be forced, to bear

constantly in mind that the changes that have affected Africa in the last dozen years were almost undreamed of a dozen years before. One recent traveler commented that "by most measurable criteria, there is a greater contrast between the West Africa of 1962 and that of 1934 than between that of 1934 and the Africa seen by Mungo Park at the end of the eighteenth century. . . ." [9]

Mungo Park, in 1795, was the first European to see the Niger River, but he was neither the first nor the last of the great explorers of Africa. Three hundred years earlier Portugal had carried Europe's war against the Moor to the shores of Africa. During the fifteenth century her navigators circumnavigated the continent, opening its coasts and the sanctuary of the Cape of Good Hope to the Western world. Three centuries elapsed, however, before the European powers turned their full attention to Africa. Except for the bustling trade in African slaves and competition for a convenient spot at which to provision ships bound around the cape to the fabled Orient, Europe showed little curiosity about Africa. Until the pioneer discoveries of the late eighteenth century, Africa below the Mediterranean littoral was indeed the Dark Continent.

In the peace that followed the Seven Years' War, which ended in 1763, new humanitarian and scientific impulses combined with what passed at the time for commercial acumen to draw attention to the neglected continent. A series of discoveries on a grand scale began in 1770 when James Bruce, a former British consul at Algiers, located the source of the Blue Nile. To encourage the exploration of the interior of Africa, the African Association was formed in London in 1788; Mungo Park was an agent of the association. It was also in 1788 that English opponents of slavery organized a settlement of freed African slaves at Sierra Leone on the western coast of Africa—an experiment soon followed by the American Colonization Society, a group of prestigious American abolitionists who could imagine no greater impediment to their cause than the problem of what to do with large numbers of free blacks in America. The society's colony adjoined Sierra Leone, and after a fitful and uncertain history emerged in the mid-nineteenth century as the struggling Republic of Liberia.

As the nineteenth century progressed, a few more Americans began to evince an interest in tropical Africa. Their interest, however, during the first two-thirds of the century, was confined to slavery. Both slave traders and abolitionists concentrated on the West African coast, from which the slaves were taken and to which the colonization humanitarians wished to return them. Official interest was slight, and touched only Liberia, which a reluctant American government only gradually and tacitly accepted as a kind of protectorate. Missionaries from America were neither the first nor the most numerous in any part of tropical Africa, and early hopes for commercial gain wilted at the first exposure to the coast. American trade with tropical Africa practically ended with the end of the slave trade; it was not revived for fully a century. The growing American seaborne empire lay half a world away, on the shores of the Pacific.

The number of Americans who concerned themselves in any way with tropical Africa does not seem to have increased noticeably until the last quarter of the century. In the closing decades of the nineteenth century, several influences combined in that burst of energetic partition among the European powers that has been accurately if unceremoniously styled the "scramble for Africa."

It began, so far as the American public knew, in March of 1871, when Henry Morton Stanley, an amazingly resourceful Welsh adventurer who began life in a workhouse and ended it in Parliament, embarked on a mission for the *New York Herald*. Stanley had spent a varied youth in the United States, where he had earned, among other distinctions, a reputation for intrepid exploring and even more intrepid journalism. Stanley proved the perfect choice for the *Herald*'s publisher, James G. Bennett, who dreamed of finding and rescuing, with appropriate publicity, the missing David Livingstone.

Livingstone was the century's best-known missionary, an honor that rested securely on both his evangelical zeal and an amazing series of geographical explorations in central Africa, beginning in 1849. Among a myriad of African rivers, mountains, falls, and populations first brought to light by Livingstone were the Victoria Falls and most of the Zambezi River system. On several occasions in the course of his adventures, designed as he often said to open the unknown parts of Africa to the Gospel, Livingstone not surprisingly got lost, in 1870—so feared the world—for good. Bennett sniffed a story and sent Stanley on the hunt. Bennett was right: in a memorable scene in the fall of 1871, Stanley, having located the heroic doctor at Ujiji on Lake Tanganyika, marched into the camp beneath a large American flag.*

The rescue of David Livingstone began Stanley's career as one of the most remarkable explorers of modern times. In subsequent expeditions, beginning in 1874, he sailed around Lakes Victoria and Tanganyika; he struck overland for the Lualaba River, and in 1877 followed it to the sea, discovering as a result that it was part of the great Congo. The potential of one of the largest watershed basins on earth was laid before a suddenly open-eyed Europe and a proud America.

Several factors in the late nineteenth century excited an interest in Africa on the part of a growing number of Americans: Stanley's lecture tours; a flood of popular books on African exploration, such as those by the French explorer Paul Du Chaillu; and the desire of more and more American missionaries to share in the work of evangelizing the tropical African population. The total number of Americans who shared an interest in African exploration or evangelization was never large, yet when augmented by the hopes of optimistic businessmen who envisioned a healthy trade in tropical products, it was large enough to prompt an official American presence at the Berlin Conference on Africa held in 1884 and 1885 and a similar congress held in Brussels in 1889 and 1890, both called by the European powers to ratify results of the partition of Africa and to set rules for the new imperialism.

The causes that led to the rapid partition of Africa were many. Stanley's discoveries in the Congo basin had finished setting the stage for the scramble for Africa by confirming

---

* The immortal story of Stanley approaching Livingstone with "Dr. Livingstone, I presume," is, alas, apocryphal. Livingstone's diary for the day of his discovery, Oct. 24, 1871, does not mention it. Livingstone did record Stanley's safari trooping into camp behind an American flag; his version can be found in Thomas Hughes, *David Livingstone* (London, 1889), 140-141. The "I presume" version, however, is standard. E. Alexander Powell wrote in "Drums on the Lualaba: A Journey Across Africa," *The Century Magazine* 109 (1925): 627-628: "The new-comer lifts his topi ceremoniously, as though accosting a stranger in Piccadil[l]y. 'My name is Stanley. And you are Doctor Livingstone, I presume.' " The 1939 movie *Stanley and Livingstone* had Spencer Tracy greeting a stunned and grateful Cedric Hardwicke with the great line, accompanied by the strains of "Onward! Christian Soldiers."

hopes raised through earlier explorations, including those of Livingstone. Suddenly, the teeming millions of inner Africa were exposed to the businessmen and missionaries of Europe, men whose energies and resources heretofore had often exceeded their opportunities and who now saw the masses of Africa lying before them, unspoiled, unclothed, and unsaved. The European powers were ready for just the sort of imperial adventure that beckoned south of the Sahara. France had not recovered from the humiliation of her disastrous defeat and occupation by Prussia, a war which made France yearn for an easy and glorious victory. The German Empire, newly united, strong and bombastic, sought markets for its expanding industry and colonies for a growing population that otherwise would drain off to America. In the mind of Germany's chancellor, Prince Bismarck, these considerations were less pressing, however, than the simple fact that African colonies would be a useful and inexpensive way to divert France's attention from her plans for revenge. Both Britain and Portugal, long ensconced on the coasts of Africa, had regarded the interior of the continent as somehow destined to fall within their respective colonial orbits, and both powers were determined to secure in fact a domination they had always claimed in theory. The recently formed Kingdom of Italy, eager to acquire an empire anywhere on the least discreditable pretext, also hovered on the African outskirts.

The catalyst that prompted the imperialistic stampede came from an unexpected source. Leopold II, King of the Belgians since 1865, offered in his character a distasteful mixture of sensuality, vanity, and greed. His high-sounding royal pronouncements were so obviously unrelated to his intentions that his people had forgotten the genuine idealism that had motivated the king in his youth. Constricted by the rigid Belgian constitution and the surveillance of his sober and thrifty subjects, Leopold was nonetheless one of Europe's wealthiest men. He had been king only a few years when he determined to seek in Africa that field for personal endeavor and despotic power that was denied to him in his tiny homeland. Stanley's explorations confirmed the scheme in the king's mind, and he financed, under Stanley's leadership, a large-scale expedition of the Congo River Basin. After a series of complicated negotiations with African rulers and

European and American financiers, Leopold claimed the entire watershed as a sovereign state with himself as absolute monarch.

The Congo Free State, as the new state was called eventually, proved to be one of the richest areas on earth, in terms of fertility and mineral resources. Initial—and partly specious—arguments in favor of an international consortium over the interior of Africa came to nothing—and the rush was on. Each imperial power sought to establish a claim while there was still some territory left. Operating from ancient coastal enclaves or pushing boldly up every unexplored river into the vast interior, the trading companies and military expeditions of the competing powers laid out the imperial map of Africa: France claimed the great hinterland that lay beyond her West African coastal stations, while her agents sped to the region adjoining Leopold's Congo basin and added those equatorial regions to her empire; Britain used her bases on both coasts to move inland, while dreaming of expanding from the southern cape all the way to Cairo; Portugal secured her aged claims to Mozambique and Angola; and Germany obtained rich areas on the coasts—Togoland and the Cameroons on the West and German East Africa on the East—along with an enclave near the southern tip of the continent. Meanwhile, the King of the Belgians, by playing one power against the other, escaped with his share of the grab more or less intact. The partition of Africa was well advanced when the imperial rivals responded to an invitation in 1884 from Germany for a conference on recognizing each other's conquests and setting the ground rules for the new imperialism.

Bismarck's motives for calling the Berlin Conference were soon revealed. He wanted to divide France and Britain over their African claims, a question of far more importance to them than to Germany—and he wanted to secure ratification of Germany's own new dominions in East Africa. These new colonies, by no small coincidence, were being created by the ruthless Karl Peters during the very months that the Congress was meeting.

The American delegation, headed by an experienced and determined trade expansionist named John Kasson, supported the claims of King Leopold, who promised, with minor qualifications, an open door into what Kasson and everybody else was sure would prove to be the boundless wealth of the Congo Basin. The Americans had no sympathy for rival British claims, and thus with French, German, and American support, Leopold was confirmed as sovereign over the Congo Free State.

The conference produced inspiring resolutions condemning the Arab slave trade, promising free trade in the basin, and requiring effective local occupation of an area before the other powers were obliged to recognize an annexation. Kasson figured prominently in the meetings on trade rights, but the United States Senate, preferring to protect the Monroe Doctrine by the hopeful expedient of recognizing the special spheres of interest of other nations, refused to ratify the treaty that came out of the discussions. The Brussels Conference, called in 1889 by Leopold himself, enacted a series of restrictive agreements that forbade the importation of arms and certain distilled spirits into most of tropical Africa, that again denounced slavery, and that confirmed a free-trade policy for the conventional Congo River Basin.[10]

American admiration for both Leopold and the Congo Free State, however, was rapidly extinguished by the Belgian monarch's even-handed rapacity. He made no pretense of being able to develop this vast resource single-handedly; in exchange for a huge percentage of the profits, he sold off concessions on highly advantageous terms, while retaining much of the best land for himself. American interests, which were considerable from the moment Leopold made his schemes known, centered on the mining industry being developed deep in the interior. As a reflection of these interests, President Chester A. Arthur appointed a commercial agent for the Congo as soon as formal recognition was completed. The king, however, gradually became an embarrassment; his sole objective was money, and he was a total failure at disguising it. The bicycle craze of the late Victorian era was then at its height, and rubber was in constant demand. Leopold's agents met this challenge directly—either by rounding up squads of helpless Congolese and forcing them to collect rubber or by setting outrageous quotas for individuals and villages with severe penalties for failure to produce the required amounts. Atrocities occurred, and enraged and frightened missionaries carried the stories of them to the outside world. Prim and proper cyclists were shocked to learn that they were pedaling through life on the "red rubber of the Congo," stained with the blood of the hapless Africans who had gathered it. Though certain stories were unfounded, it was obvious even to the Belgians that Leopold's personal rule had to end. After an international investigation and several years of negotiation, mostly designed to insure that the king kept a fat share of the revenues from the colony, Leopold relinquished his control in 1908 and sovereignty over the Congo passed to the Belgian government, which created for the new Belgian Congo what in those days was considered a legitimate colonial regime.

As the new century began, American relations with Africa continued to expand. Americans remained active in the extractive industries of the Belgian Congo, both as investors and as field technicians. American missionaries to Africa increased in numbers and influence, both in Africa and at home, stimulating among Americans what there was of a popular and sustained interest in the people of Africa. The exploits of Du Chaillu and Stanley and the showmanship of P. T. Barnum made Africa famous for its animals. The big-game hunting craze began with no less a light than a former President of the United States, Theodore Roosevelt, whose hunting trip through British East Africa in 1908 and 1909 placed that region in the mind's eye of hundreds of American sportsmen and naturalists. Roosevelt's account of the expedition, *African Game Trails,* retained much of its popularity for decades after its publication in 1910. By 1910, indeed, certain aspects of the popular image of Africa were becoming fixed in the American mind.

By 1910 the European occupation of Africa was nearly complete. Partition had taken place and the colonial powers, or at least such "progressive" ones as Britain and Germany, were on the eve of large-scale, systematic organization and exploitation of their colonial resources. Their plans, however, were interrupted by the outbreak of the First World War.

Although military engagements did occur in tropical Africa, these were more exciting than crucial. The fate of the African colonies was determined on the battlefields of Europe, and with the collapse of Germany the final partition of Africa took place. Togoland and the Cameroons were divided between the adjoining colonial empires of France and

Britain, with the largest part of the Cameroons going to France; except for the Ruanda-Urundi district, which went to Belgium, German East Africa passed to the British, who renamed it Tanganyika Territory; German South-West Africa was handed over to the Union of South Africa. For the victorious Allies, the end of the war brought a period of renewed effort in colonial Africa. Medical services were increased; educational programs, largely conducted by Christian missionaries, were standardized; and a more broadly based administration helped to create a stable government in each colony.

Methods and results differed from colony to colony, but American observers generally found progress satisfactory. The size of the areas and populations under European rule was impressive. By the end of the 1920s French Equatorial Africa and French West Africa had a total population of almost 19 million people; Kenya, Uganda, and Tanganyika had nearly 12 million; the Belgian Congo had 9.3 million; British West Africa about 25 million; and the two largest Portuguese colonies had more than 7.5 million between them. Excluding only Liberia and Ethiopia, all of Africa below the Sahara was under the legal and effective sovereignty of European states: Britain, France, Belgium, and Portugal had the largest areas; a small coastal strip north of Kenya belonged to Italy, and Spain held Rio Muni, an ancient and inconsequential enclave entirely surrounded by French Equatorial Africa.[11]

On this enormous mass, an area twice that of the United States, fortune, except on a few notable occasions, seemed to turn a smiling face in the interwar years. The incipient nationalism and labor unrest of the 1920s and 1930s, so significant in retrospect, seemed unimportant at the time.

The chronological and geographical limits of this book are easily explained. The years 1919 to 1939 form a distinct period in African, no less than in world, history. One world war ratified the colonial map of Africa; another brought the "end of an epoch" to Africa. One scholar in West African history calls these years the "period of colonial rule proper." With the exception of Portugal Overseas, World War I strengthened while World War II destroyed the western European empires in Africa.[12]

Tropical Africa has always appeared forbidding to the outside world. Its long, regular coastline down both sides of the continent is almost devoid of harborages and landings. The rapid ascent of the continental terrain causes Africa's magnificent rivers to plunge to the sea in falls and rapids, rather than in gentle navigable streams; the Congo, for instance, falls eight hundred feet between Stanley Pool and the sea. The climate along the coast has been extremely unhealthy to white men; Sierra Leone was known in the 1880s as "the White Man's Grave." All these factors helped put much of Africa beyond easy access from the outside. Only with the end of World War I could the imperial powers begin the development of tropical Africa. This was the work of the two decades after the armistice.[13]

In these two decades the orderly extension of colonial administration was accomplished in regions still untouched by its benefits. The map of Africa no longer contained glaring blank spaces; only scattered regional surveys remained to finish the task of African cartography. The standard indexes of colonial progress all registered steady gains: more schools and more hospitals were built; railway and road construction was extended; more insect pests were eradicated; the value of new crops rose (one of them, sisal, had been brought from Florida in 1892); more swamps and forests were opened to agriculture; and harbors were cleared and shored up against the weather, adding to their capacity.

Other developments there were, too—some of them, had they been taken seriously, less likely to encourage the friends of empire. The effect of exposing Africans to European culture was not always precisely what had been intended. Even before the First World War, self-styled prophets and separatists were gathering sizable numbers of apostate, missionary-trained African Christians. Many of the resulting new churches offered a synthesis of Christianity, indigenous religious traditions, and nascent African nationalism. One particularly important leader of these new churches was Simon Kimbangu, who was active in the Belgian Congo; for creating disturbances and undermining church authority, Kimbangu was sentenced to life imprisonment by the Belgian authorities in 1921. The Watchtower movement, with its emphasis on apocalyptic egalitarianism, was introduced into Nyasaland as early as 1907, only shortly after the Jehovah's Witnesses sect had been founded in the United States. The movement gained a few strongholds in Nyasaland, Northern Rhodesia, and the Katanga province of the Belgian Congo.

Similar religious developments occurred throughout British and French Africa; in 1922 and 1923, for instance, the entire town of Douala in the French Cameroons paraded around in a short-lived religious revival in which "hymns" of a distinctly anti-European character were featured. In most cases these events were regarded by the colonial officials as typically "native" aberrations—further proof, if such were needed, of the absolute necessity of careful white control over religious activity in Africa. The Belgians were willing to resort to harsh methods when the situation could not be passed off; in 1926 they hanged the man who introduced Watchtower doctrines into the Congo. The Portuguese placed the blame for all their civil difficulties on Protestantism, and were often reluctant to allow any but Roman Catholic evangelists into their colonies.

A sporadic rise in labor organizations also took place during the 1920s and 1930s. Most of these organizations were more or less conspiratorial, but they instituted a few labor strikes of considerable proportions, particularly those on the railroads of Sierra Leone in 1919 and 1926 and in the Northern Rhodesia copper mines in 1935. These outbursts were usually regarded before World War II as illegal seditions, instigated by foreign agitators. The unrest, consequently, was forgotten almost as quickly as it was repressed.

There were other portents, like the political associations of British West Africa and French Senegal. But these, like the occasional black in the French National Assembly, seemed almost respectable by the interwar years. Such political organizations were controlled by a small African elite, mostly lawyers and journalists, that had been filling a subordinate position in the colonial administration since late nineteenth century. The attempt by Marcus Garvey to establish a "republic" in Black Africa with the support of many black Americans completely collapsed in the mid-1920s, and the African youth movements that swept through Nigeria did not become a recognized political force until the eve of the Second World War. To the majority of observers, nonetheless, the decades between the two wars were marked by unshaken imperial tranquillity and prosperity.

Midway through these decades an editor for the *Saturday*

Review commented that Africa was a subject that in America was "steadily increasing in popularity." She was right; these years produced a steady rise in published information on tropical Africa. Yet, as we shall see, little of it touched on African nationalism or African political agitation.[14]

Geographically, this study is confined to French West Africa, British West Africa (the Gambia, Sierra Leone, the Gold Coast Colony, Nigeria, and the British Cameroons), French Equatorial Africa, the Belgian Congo, Angola, Northern and Southern Rhodesia, Nyasaland, Portuguese East Africa (Mozambique), and British East Africa (Kenya, Uganda, and Tanganyika). Most of the research materials deal with British West Africa, French Equatorial Africa, the Belgian Congo, British East Africa, and the Portuguese possessions.

This group of territories is essentially what historian George Louis Beer, in preparing himself as the colonial expert in the American delegation at Versailles in 1919, termed "Middle Africa." Beer rightly considered it a unit, distinct by racial and geographical factors from both the Mediterranean littoral and "White Man's Africa" south of the Zambezi. Most contemporary writers on Africa followed this division. The territories that Beer called Middle Africa were the same as those included in two fine studies of tropical Africa, Raymond Leslie Buell's *The Native Problem in Africa* of 1928 and Lord Hailey's classic *African Survey* of ten years later.* Both works, however, devoted considerable attention to the Union of South Africa, which Beer excluded and which is excluded here.[15]

It was commonly believed in Victorian times that the "tropics" were a circumterrestrial band of forty-eight degrees in width between the Tropic of Cancer, twenty-four degrees north of the equator, and the Tropic of Capricorn, twenty-four degrees south of the equator. Modern geographers are not in agreement on a definition of the tropics, except to say that the Tropics of Cancer and Capricorn are unacceptable as limits. Whatever the precise demarcation of

* Hailey admits that his line was chosen "largely as a matter of convenience. . . ." A tripartite division of Africa along these lines was a well-established practice. See, for instance, books by Parker Thomas Moon and Marion I. Newbigin. Newbigin separated Africa into a "very rough division" of northern, central (equatorial), and southern plateau zones for study.

the tropics may be, the choice of territories for study here was based only partly on geographical considerations.[16]

South Africa is excluded because of its own unique and well-documented set of problems. Africa's then sovereign states, Liberia and Ethiopia, are almost completely excluded on two grounds: American relations with them have been exhaustively researched; and, unlike the rest of tropical Africa, neither country contributed to the image of a dependent and passive Africa. In addition, the interwar decades do not form a distinct unit in the histories of these two nations to the extent that they do for their colonial neighbors. South-West Africa and Bechuanaland are relegated to the sphere of South Africa. Portuguese Guinea and Spanish Rio Muni are ignored here because they were ignored at the time; I encountered not a single reference to either colony in nearly two years of research. Italian Somaliland and the extracontinental regions are excluded because of complete lack of American interest in the former, and, in the case of the latter, because of profound racial and historical dissimilarities between the offshore regions and the main areas under study.

A final caveat is in order. Again, what follows is not intended as a portrayal of Africa as it was in reality, but of how it appeared to a generation of Americans. If we are to understand the processes of exchange and dissemination that took place in the context of the past, if we are to recreate the mental baggage that Americans carried into the postwar world, if we are to try to understand how this baggage was acquired through American contacts with Africa, and if we are to begin to understand American reactions to tropical dependent peoples, then we must see the past as it was seen. The images of those years were the result and cause of politics that have continued into the present. Some of the images themselves have not faded and in still-discernible outline dance in our heads today.

> Like trees, great historical events spring from a soil enriched by the remains of earlier growths. The to-days of our lives, and the tomorrows, arise from the yesterdays. The infant present cannot deny the parent past.[17]

one:
europe in
africa

**Since the end of the fifteenth century . . .
Africa has been the food of the empire makers,
its 11,500,000 square miles of jungle, gold,
diamonds, copper, and Negroes cut into juicy
slices for the benefit of European powers.
—*Fortune* (November, 1935)**

The weather was perfect, with a noonday sun in a crystal sky providing that remarkable visibility for which so much of tropical Africa is noted. The lake, in submissive tranquillity, offered not the slightest resistance to the tiny gunboats that glided over its surface with self-important puffings. Nor was human enthusiasm wanting. Thousands of excited black Congolese lined the Belgian bank, thrilling like the crowds of ancient Rome to a mortal struggle imported at enormous cost for their diversion.

The battle that opened on the glassy waters of Lake Tanganyika just before noon on December 26, 1915, however, caused hardly a ripple in the European states that had painstakingly prepared to wage it. The disposition of every African colony was being determined not on African waters but on the battlefields of northern France, more than four thousand miles away. That fact notwithstanding, man and nature had cooperated to supply every detail for a successful battle scene in the middle of tropical Africa.

The occasion for the battle was simple enough, and in a tactical sense, the results might be considered important. The English officers and sailors who had struggled for seven long months to freight two small motor launches down the West African coast from England, up the Congo River, and overland to the German lake were filled with a powerful sense of imperial moment. They were sure that the fate of empires hung on the Admiralty's plan to sweep the three German gunboats from Lake Tanganyika so that British and Belgian forces could cross the water and land on the German coast at Kigoma. Kigoma was the last outpost of German East Africa, pride of the Kaiser's colonial empire and key to its defense in the rear.

The British forces had been encouraged by the preliminaries—a round of national anthems rendered by a native brass band, salutes, toasts, and Belgian kisses—which everyone agreed had been carried out flawlessly. The thought of actual battle prompted some reservations, however. One serious defect in the Admiralty plan was the fragility of the English boats, either of which could be sunk by a single well-placed shell. The keys to success were surprise and speed, and as it turned out the Germans were nothing if not surprised. On their first sortie, the British caught one of the German boats alone. Before the Germans could get the range, the English boats were on them. The Imperial German Navy got off a shot or two before a lucky hit from one of the British boats exploded the German armored screen, killing three of the four Germans aboard and leaving the fourth, a seaman, understandably dazed. Interest in the Kaiser's plans for world domination suddenly vanished among the black crew, one of whom hastily took command and hauled down the German flag.

The whole affair ended quite delightfully for the British. The other two German boats were trapped in their turn, one blown up in harbor by its crew, the other set afire by another fortunate shot while the English were still out of her range. Her German captain was captured wearing an Iron Cross, and proved to be of the literate, gentlemanly sort so inspirational of wardroom reminiscences. The victorious Britons returned to the cheering throngs on the Belgian shore, the brass band, additional kisses, and the black Congolese "simply falling over each other in their hurry to reach the beach in order to pay their homage to the new Great White Chief, our Commander." Soon there were medals for the officers, promotions for everyone (there were twenty-eight

British), and a telegram from King George V himself, in which His Majesty was pleased to "express his appreciation of the wonderful work carried out by his most remote expedition."[1]

The scene was as instructive as it was entertaining. White men were susceptible to bullet wounds and drowning no less than mortal men. And when white men were fighting among themselves, there was no white man to stand the watch over the black man. But these were lessons whose full implications were absorbed gradually, almost unconsciously, in Africa. In faraway Washington more immediate lessons, lessons still for white men, were to be learned from the imperial explosions on Lake Tanganyika.

That Britain and Germany should send fleets to do battle for the lakes of Africa did not surprise some Americans. Students of international relations had followed imperial rivalries in Africa since before the great Berlin and Brussels conferences of the Victorian era. There were influential Americans who believed that the competition for colonies had made inevitable a world war that might otherwise have been avoided. During the war, sentiment grew among Americans for a general revision of the imperial systems as part of the grand world resettlement to be delivered with victory and peace.

When the United States entered the war, Walter Lippmann, a leading advocate of "international commissions" to superintend the colonial areas in the postwar world, joined Colonel Edward M. House's special study group known as the Inquiry; its purpose was to prepare the American delegation for the peace conference. Convinced that Africa was likely to be a field of "detailed negotiations" in which the United States would be called upon to act as negotiator or arbiter, the directors of the Inquiry searched for specialists on Africa. None were forthcoming. Lippmann complained in May, 1918, that there was a "real famine in men" and that the American delegation would have to "train and create our own experts"; Africa was an area that had been "intellectually practically unexplored."[2]

George Louis Beer, an expert on the British Empire, was eventually selected to head the African Section of the Inquiry, and it proved to be a sound choice. Beer admitted his lack of knowledge about Africa, but wholeheartedly devoted himself to his new subject. By the fall of 1918 his intensive studies had convinced him that some form of international administration for tropical Africa was a necessity. The Germans, now regarded in Allied circles as incompetent brutes, could not be allowed to regain their African colonies; the Africans could not be left to themselves; and redistributing the German colonies among the victors would only lead to the same rivalries that had prefaced the late war. The welfare of the indigenous peoples, Beer declared, depended on a "liberal and humane labor regime and an equitable land system," and the records of none of the colonial nations invited close scrutiny on these points. The interests of the natives must take precedence over imperial demands for markets and raw materials; the civilized world must act as trustees for tropical Africa. It was Beer who put the idea of mandates in its final legal form.[3]

The Peace Conference that opened at Versailles on January 18, 1919, stumbled immediately over the disposition of the enemy's colonies. The vanquished had nothing to say on the matter, because he did not participate in the negotiations; the victors had a great deal to say, but the only point on which they agreed was that not a square inch of colony should be returned to the defeated Central Powers. It was quickly apparent that the Machiavellian secret wartime treaties and the lust for spoils were not going to be overridden by the goals of any Labor or Socialist coalitions in Europe, or by the liberality of America's President Wilson, whose principles had been expressed before Congress and the world in his Fourteen Points address. In the midst of the impasse, General Jan Christiaan Smuts of South Africa offered a compromise based on the mandate idea, and using data supplied to him by the Inquiry, Wilson developed the concept. The mandate settlement was accepted in nearly its final form in January, leaving only minor details to be worked out. It was the first real issue to be resolved at Versailles.[4]

To be sure, tropical Africa was not first in importance among the many problems the Peace Conference had to consider. And so far as mandates were concerned, even the interest of the United States, according to a contemporary student of international law, was concentrated not on Africa but on Middle East oil and the cable station on Yap Island in the Pacific. Beer himself was concerned not only with tropical Africa, but with the entire mandatory system as it was to be applied throughout the world.

The mandates were classified according to the speed with which the colonies were expected to proceed toward self-government and a place in the family of nations. The late Turkish provinces of the Mideast were already nearly sovereign polities; these were Class A mandates. Germany's African colonies were expected to remain in a colonial status for an indeterminate period; they thereby constituted Class B mandates. Of these, France and Britain divided the two on the West Coast, Britain and Belgium shared the one on the East Coast, and South Africa took its neighbor to the west. Areas too small or sparsely populated to be considered capable of self-rule under any circumstances were categorized as Class C mandates; these were located in the South Pacific, where a number of islands had been brought under the German flag in Bismarck's day, and they were divided among Australia, New Zealand, and Japan.

The mandatory, according to Article 22 of the League of Nations Covenant, was required to adopt humane labor laws, end military conscription, and grant religious and commercial access to nationals of other League powers. Beyond submitting an annual report, however, the responsibility of each mandatory to the League's Permanent Mandates Commission was not defined, and the question of sovereignty over the mandated territory was left conveniently vague. In fact, in no time at all Secretary of State Robert Lansing came to regard the mandate system as poorly disguised annexation. By the end of the 1920s, most Americans agreed with him.[5]

The United States did not ratify the Covenant of the League of Nations, Wilson's cherished Fourteenth Point. Professor Beer, who had been head of the Mandates Section of the League Secretariat, had to resign. Despite its disavowal of the League, the United States nonetheless insisted on sharing whatever benefits might adhere to League membership. After all, Americans had shared in the cost of victory, and Congress could see no reason why America should be denied a share of the benefits, even in Africa.[6]

As part of the African settlement at Versailles, the Allies, Japan, Portugal, and the United States signed three conventions on tropical Africa. These conventions controlled the liquor and arms traffic into the area and revised the enactments of the Berlin and Brussels conferences to accommodate them with the new mandates arrangement. Signed on September 10, 1919, at the Chateau de Saint-Germain-en-Laye, these conventions also extended to members of the League the same privileges enjoyed by the mandatory power itself over access to markets and resource concessions. Although the United States never joined the League, she insisted on her right to the privileges as long as these conventions remained in force.[7]

From the beginning of the Versailles peace talks, the United States had applied the "open door" principle as broadly as possible in the negotiated settlements. In May, 1918, Beer had suggested that foreign merchants should have "unrestrained access to all dependent and backward countries" of the world, and equal access with the metropolitan powers to resources, public-works contracts, and markets. He believed it mattered "comparatively little to the world" which flag flew over the former German colonies, so long as the Africans were protected "and the *open-door* will always be kept wide open." The day before the final disposition of the African mandates in May, 1919, President Wilson insisted that the open door be applied to them, calling attention once again to Article 22 of the League Covenant.[8]

When it developed that the United States was not going to join the League, it became necessary for Washington to further define its position toward the mandates. Its legal position was that (1) the defeated enemy had relinquished his rights to his overseas territories to the "Principal Allied and Associated Powers"; (2) American consent was required for the disposition of those territories, and for any subsequent alterations in their status; and (3) whether in the League or not, the United States had a legal right to all the privileges that a mandatory enjoyed in territory won in the common war effort. Throughout the early 1920s the United States negotiated a series of treaties with the African mandatories—Britain, France, Italy, Portugal, and Belgium—thereby securing the benefits of the Saint-Germain-en-Laye conventions as well as a "most-favored nation" status in the mandates. The United States refused to concur in any mandate in which these privileges were not forthcoming. The last of these treaties, signed on February 10, 1925, by Great Britain and the United States, related to American rights in the British mandates of Togoland, the Cameroons, and Tanganyika, the former German East Africa.[9]

That Africa was a European domain was accepted as a fact by Americans. Government officials, scholars, and travelers who thought of Africa could not but think as well of its European rulers. Most American commentators saw England and France "the great arbitrers of African destiny"; to these writers, "the road to Africa" lay "through London and Paris." Secretary of State Kellogg wrote his letters in behalf of his traveling friends not to Africa, but to the American embassies in London and Brussels. It was, he explained to his friends, "all I can do," because "we have no ministers or ambassadors" in tropical Africa. American businessmen wishing to sell their products in West Africa dealt only with European home offices. Consuls in Africa could do little to adjust local trade disputes in the 1920s, since complaints were handled directly between Europe and the United States. "The domination of the world by European powers . . . seems so natural," commented international-relations scholar Parker Thomas Moon in 1926, "as rarely to provoke the student's curiosity. . . ."[10]

Yet there were some Americans in the interwar period who were especially curious about European imperialism in Africa. The continent had been drawn under European control so rapidly and so extensively that the imperialistic process itself had attracted considerable attention. A dozen years before Versailles put sub-Saharan imperial domains in their final form, Richard Harding Davis could still make out the remains of the wagons Stanley had used to haul boats past the Congo rapids to Stanley Pool. And now, less than a generation later, the African territories of France and England were each thirty times the size of the mother country; the Belgian Congo was eighty times the size of Belgium.[11]

The imperial system did more than inspire curiosity among a few American critics. Many black Americans despised the whole concept. Halford L. Hoskins of Tufts College declared in 1930, in a pioneer study of African imperialism by a black, that "the benefits of European control to the peoples of

Africa are problematical." Whatever the supposed benefits
of imperialism, they were largely offset by "all kinds of
forced labor, oppressive taxes and levies, and cruel punish-
ments," the expropriation of the "best lands" for European
use, and the spread of various unnamed European vices and
diseases. A host of black writers and teachers agreed. Many
white critics of the imperial system also noted the widespread social displacement among Africans, forced labor,
and exploitative economic policies imposed by the colonial
powers.[12]

The writings of English anti-imperialists like John Hobson
and Leonard Woolf were widely available in the United
States. Albert Shaw, the founder and editor of the *Review
of Reviews,* was highly critical of both French and British
imperialism in Africa. Professor Nathaniel Peffer delivered
a series of bitter attacks on the whole idea of imperialism at
the New School for Social Research in New York in 1926
and 1927. An American social worker, after a West African
voyage in 1927 and 1928, and an anthropologist, after ten
months in Tanganyika in 1931, returned to denounce imperialism for enslaving the black people of Africa with taxes
and pitiful wages.[13]

Such condemnation was, however, exceptional; most
American travelers and writers found little to criticize in
either the premise or the application of imperialism—except
in the Portuguese colonies. The British fared best. American
visitors enjoyed the pomp, domestic fastidiousness, and
courtesy of their English cousins in the colonies. Life in
British Africa was in fact thoroughly British, not merely on
official occasions, but in as many of the routines of daily
existence as determination and patience could provide.
"Truly the British are a remarkable race," observed Julian
Huxley, whose attempts at detached analysis of his country's
African empire were often choked with chauvinism. "No imperialists save perhaps the Romans have ever exported their
domestic habits and their recreations so whole-heartedly
all over their Empire." "Freetown's excitements," noted
Graham Greene, "are very English," though to explorer Sir
Harry Johnston, Lagos was "the most British post in West
Africa, with clubs and European comforts." Evelyn Waugh
said of Mombassa that "the English have converted it into

a passable reproduction of a garden city." Nairobi, according to Carveth Wells, a civil engineer, surveyor, and professional explorer who led a large expedition into Central Africa for the Chicago Geographical Society, was "even more English than British Columbia."[14]

The social conventions, the very entertainments, were British. All of them appealed to Americans. Colonials considered that careful dress and "quiet, unobtrusive service" at dinner were "as essential in Africa as in Mayfair or Upper Fifth Avenue"; newcomers to the Gold Coast were officially warned to bring a dinner jacket, with "old gold cumberbund" and "the usual supply of evening collars." A San Francisco woman bent on exploring the African interior with twenty men and convinced that the key to British control over the natives was "presence," arrived in Nairobi in 1928 and announced she would eat with damask and silver and wear an evening gown every night at dinner. An American missionary urged her colleagues to be as careful in their dress as the British officers were; it was the certain way to preserve one's self-respect, to hold the respect of the Africans, and to lead others to a "better life." A writer in *Harper's* warned prospective African explorers in 1932 that "on the whole, he will find well-cut evening clothes more useful in Africa than a formidable arsenal."[15]

Recreation in British Africa was as little related to local conditions as possible. That their homes happened to be in Africa seldom intruded upon the white community, except in the alluring form of their servants. Few settlers or colonials hunted game, except for meat or as paid guides to American sportsmen. Sharing a trait with their countrymen everywhere in the empire, the British in Africa were a hard-drinking lot. Americans who languished at home on the illicit poisons of Prohibition found liberal supplies of Scotch whiskey in the African colonies. "Probably the most important event of any day in Africa," approved one tourist, "is the sundowner."[16] The term referred to the first socially acceptable drink of the day, taken at sunset.*

* The convention that it was improper, or even dangerous, to drink before 5 P.M. was well-established, but apparently colonials were quite flexible in their definition of sundown, and regarded any little shadows as encouraging. When a majority considered that the sun was indeed down, obligations to lost time were quickly discharged.

Diversions in British colonial Africa were essentially those of the English suburbs and public schools. Village bands thumped at picnics and garden shows, and at evening concerts on East Coast promenades. Garden parties and flower shows dotted the calendar. Football and cricket matches were exciting affairs. When the Royal East Indian Squadron visited East African port cities during Navy Week, elaborate matches were arranged and played with "great keenness." In all the British colonies, noted Consul Karl MacVitty in Nairobi in 1930, "there are many excellent clubs," and in Kenya, nearly every white male adult was a member. Consuls were pleased to accept membership in English clubs. In Kenya the settlers' houses were "mostly . . . English" in design, a fact that had cost their owners dearly in architects' fees and imported building materials. The effects were deliberate.[17]

"Suburbia unrestrained," railed Huxley, "exalted to feudal domination over an African population. . . ." The French, too, felt that their dominion was "feudal," but it was far from suburban. Only in British colonies did American consuls find willing entrants in the International Home Canning Contest of 1933, conducted by the Ball Brothers Company of Muncie, Indiana. Reflecting admiringly on a luncheon party at Government House in Nairobi in 1926, an American lady commented that "the scene might have been anywhere in England. . . ." Indeed, many travelers noted that "in Kenya it is easy to forget that one is in Africa. . . ." So engrossed was the American adventurer and novelist Stewart Edward White in the pleasant illusion that he was in Surrey that he found the intrusion of a file of natives, or a pair of rhinos, "startling." Huxley, for his part, imagined himself in Gloucestershire or Somerset as his car eased through pleasant woodlands near Mount Kenya.[18]

Not just East Africa but other parts of Africa had their European earmarks. One American traveler found the African coasts "about as wild as the Riviera in the tourist season." Central Africa had its attractions as well. Bulawayo in Southern Rhodesia had a new community swimming pool and, reputedly, twenty thousand automobiles in 1937. The Belgian Congo provided a modern hotel in the Kivu District, near several of the colony's major tourist attractions. The Portuguese proposed as early as 1922 to make Lourenço

Marques the "leading winter resort of South Africa," with a new hotel, a racecourse and casino "on the lines of Monte Carlo."[19]

It was, nonetheless, British East Africa with which most Americans were impressed. They felt at ease among the British and, for the most part, they approved of the ways of British imperialism. The Martin Johnsons met the Duke and Duchess of York in Kenya in 1925 and were charmed and flattered that the royal couple should relax enough in their presence to catch a crab and put it in a box as a "mascot." As the royal visitors departed, the duke declared to Johnson that "Kenya is the gem of the Empire." A writer might caution that there could be "no generalizing about the British record in Africa," but most Americans reacted favorably. Travelers praised and scholars studied the British system of "indirect rule" in Africa, by which peace and order were made compatible with quaint native political authority.[20]

Indirect rule was a term that covered a wide range of British colonial policies. Many variations existed on a common theme, drawn from the time-honored and happy experience of the British in ruling the Princely States of India. In general, indirect rule in British Africa meant the maintenance, or in some cases, the creation, of some kind of local "native" political authority over which the British could exercise sufficient influence to control the affairs of the indigenous population. In a sense, it was a classic example of muddling through.

In London this system conjured up pictures of His Majesty's shrewd and farsighted officers deftly manipulating whole populations from the elbows of local potentates who had been rendered suitably suggestible by pensions, orders of knighthood, and touring cars. The idea received its most effective application in Northern Nigeria, where pioneer colonial officials like Sir Frederick (later Lord) Lugard demonstrated that each of the large feudal monarchies of that region could be administered almost single-handedly from a cooperative court. A form of indirect rule functioned adequately, from the British point of view, over the unitary monarchies that had ruled much of Uganda and Tanganyika Territory before the colonial period.

The British liked to contrast their form of indirect rule

with the French system of colonial administration, which was based on the direct administration of a region by a French officer and the subordination of local political structures to an overall long-range developmental scheme. The contrast, however, was often only apparent; the British were far more fond than the French of the ceremonial forms of traditional rule, but all real power in a British African colony was in the hands of the governor and an efficient, well-trained bureaucracy responsible to him alone. The governor was, in his turn, responsible to the Colonial Office in London. He shared his authority in Africa with a local legislative council, representing the more substantial of the permanent European residents, only to the extent that the smooth functioning of the colonial administration required their interest and cooperation—such as in the raising of local taxes or the outfitting of a local military unit. In West Africa the legislative councils admitted to membership an occasional distinguished African who had found employment in some subordinate capacity in the colonial structure, usually as a lawyer. In Kenya a single Christian missionary was appointed to represent the entire African population; elsewhere, this slight token was deemed unnecessary.

The council in Kenya was dominated by long-term residents of British stock who numbered about seventeen thousand in a total population of more than three million, thirty-eight thousand of whom were East Indian artisans and shopkeepers. The white settlers controlled the temperate and lovely Highlands around Nairobi, and resisted every attempt by the wealthier Indians to penetrate their beautiful enclave as vociferously as they resisted every attempt by London to make some empty gesture toward recognizing the validity of African participation in the political process.

To bolster their position, the "White Highlanders" pointed out to every visitor the advantages brought to Africa by white rule, not only in Kenya but throughout Africa. And, indeed, even the most determined opponent of colonialism could not gainsay that certain advances, mostly of a material sort and mostly poorly shared, were made under the system. First among these was peace. The spread of effective colonial administration over tropical Africa brought an end to the incessant inter-village and inter-"tribal" warfare that in some parts of Africa consumed generation after generation of young men. Better agricultural techniques and rudimentary medical facilities came later, and brought improved standards of living to those Africans with access to the new benefits. Thousands of Africans were exposed to at least the basics of western-style education and to the Christian religion, and many thousands more profited from the widespread agricultural prosperity brought, particularly in West Africa, by opening tropical Africa to the markets of the world. Many rare forms of wildlife were at least partially protected against the cupidity of both whites and blacks, especially in British East Africa.

British East Africa received more of America's attention in the interwar years than any other part of tropical Africa. It drew a majority of American tourists, hunters, and animal collectors. It contained not only the much-disputed White Highlands of Kenya but Tanganyika Territory—the Class B mandate that had been the prize of the old German African Empire and the main object of an increasingly determined effort by Germany to regain its former place in the sun. Game laws, settler problems, and international squabbling made Kenya something of a storm center between the wars. So much discussion over Kenya took place after the war that by 1926 "the single word 'Kenya' " evoked "a whole complex of controversies."[21]

In July, 1920, the Protectorate of British East Africa was annexed to the British crown as Kenya Colony, and the white settlers, who had been living in growing numbers on farms in the Highlands since the opening of the Kenya & Uganda Railway, were confirmed in their possession of the land. The thousands of Indians who had come to the colony as laborers on the railroad and as petty traders demanded political and social equality with the British settlers and access to farms of their own in the beautiful white reserves. The Africans feared both groups of aliens. The British colonial secretary, Lord Milner, offered no "definite policy" on the Indians in East Africa, and the passage of time aggravated the situation. The white settlers, led by Lord Delamere, demanded more and more land and more and more representation on the legislative council; some settlers even spoke openly of responsible self-government for Kenya with dominion status. The Indians, with far greater numbers, opposed the settlers on every demand; they insisted on an end to the white domination of the council and the civil service, a proportionate franchise, equal access to land in the temperate regions, and an end to urban residential segregation. Whitehall steadfastly resisted settler demands for home rule, but beyond that, under a succession of governments, the Colonial Office equivocated. In 1923 it issued an official statement that the British government regarded the interests of the indigenous populations in Kenya as "paramount"; in fact, however, the White Highlands were confirmed and occasionally extended at the expense of neighboring "Native Reserves." The Indians won an end to residential segregation in the towns, but they were permanently excluded from the white settlement reserves; they also received more but not proportionate representation on the legislative council.[22]

Many Americans found in the settler regime one of the few aspects of British Africa that was subject to censure. To the large body of travelers' accounts describing the charm and beauty of life in the Highlands must be added the criticisms of observers like Raymond Leslie Buell, research director of the Foreign Policy Association. Echoing the reaction of other visitors, Buell remarked that the settlers in Kenya were "as representative Englishmen as are to be found in the Empire." It was not their "fitness" that was in question; it was a "matter of conflicting interests." The "fate of the native population," he declared, "cannot be intrusted to self-interested settlers; responsibility for their welfare must rest with the British government at home." English writers like Lord Lugard and Llewelyn Powys, a former settler, urged in the American press that the Colonial Office resist the demands of a "noisy minority" for home rule. A Princeton scholar in a study of the British Empire declared that it showed itself at its worst in Kenya. Even friendly visitors like Daniel Streeter, author of a witty travelogue of a type popular with the "smart set" of the 1920s, noted how much land the settlers insisted on expropriating, and how little of it they cultivated; Buell, Moon, and Mary Townsend, professor of history at Teachers' College, Columbia, commented on the same aspect of the settler land economy.[23]

The basis of the controversy, as so often in colonial frontier economies, was land. Whatever form the arguments assumed, at heart was the issue of land, and who should control it. The wealthy Indian traders who represented their people in demanding the franchise in Kenya Colony did so as much to gain legal access to land purchases in the Highlands as for anything else. Their agitations had antedated the war, but grew to such furious pitch in the 1920s that American officials in Africa felt considerable concern. Consular officials did not consider the possibility of black Africans succeeding to actual political power in Kenya. The two alternatives, as most Americans saw them, were rule by the Colonial Office and rule by the white settlers. Either alternative would have served America's limited interests in the region, and the Indians, not the Africans, were the only threat to either.[24]

To the black African, land was essential not merely for wealth or social prestige: land was the basis of his entire life, the home of his sacred dead. Charles W. Coulter, professor of sociology at Ohio Wesleyan, said after a research trip to Kenya in the early 1920s that to Africans deprived of their tribal lands the entire world was turned "upside down." Black American leaders like Carter G. Woodson lamented that the colonial powers had "deprived the Africans of the best lands." Ralph J. Bunche, a young political scientist at Howard University, portrayed the plight of the now landless Kikuyu in the pages of the *Journal of Negro History.* Few Americans concerned about the black Africans in the controversy felt that they could expect any real protection from London against white settler encroachment on their lands. In 1933 the *Christian Century* applauded the protests of British clergymen over the abrogation of a land ordinance favorable to native Africans when traces of gold were discovered on protected land in Kenya.[25]

The map of Africa was "dominated by two colors": British red and French blue. The two imperial systems were often superficially compared in the interwar years. The cheapness and smooth efficiency of the British indirect-rule system, which seemed to work so well on the surface that even anti-imperialists were disarmed, appealed to many Americans. To those few Americans who gave it any attention at all, the sprawling French empire in Africa was less impressive.

On the surface, French holdings in Africa suggested an endeavor of Napoleonic proportions: French West Africa alone was nine times the size of France and French politicians boasted of a France of "one hundred millions." Yet the thrifty and practical French valued their African colonies chiefly as a source of national pride and exotic exhibits at trade fairs. Most Frenchmen were unwilling to sink money into anything so extraneous to their interests as a colony in tropical Africa. Boulevardiers might be inspired by an occasional reflection that the sun was always kissing the *tricolore* somewhere or other, but beyond that few Frenchmen, other than colonial officers and settlers, cared overmuch for the African empire that had seemed so strategically and economically indispensable to their fathers in the bitter days after Sedan.

The logical French believed that however glorious colonies might be, they should pay for themselves. While various forms of centralism were imposed on the innumerable ethnic and linguistic groups in French tropical Africa in an attempt to make colonial administration more efficient, the French National Assembly regularly refused to grant subsidies to the colonies to underwrite adequate European staffs, a refusal that made the cooperation of indigenous rulers absolutely essential to the functioning of the French colonial empire. The distinction between early dreams of "assimilating" Africans into a kind of international citizenship with the French themselves and the practical policy that later evolved of "association" or collaboration between the French and a westernized colonial elite has not been easy to draw. Local rulers always seemed a trifle more artificial, more obviously the employees of the colonial officials than did those in the British colonies. The black Africans under French control, however, often had a far better opportunity to acquire the rights of metropolitan citizenship. Excluding the colony of Senegal, which was an exception to many colonial principles, all actual and most apparent power in French Africa was held by local district officers who supervised everything from public works to mission-school grammar lessons. There were no legislative councils in French Africa, again with the exception of Senegal. Senegal enjoyed effective elective councils in each of the four communes into which it was divided, and it sent a deputy—the only one from black

Africa—to the French parliament. Elsewhere the French colonial officers, most of them recruited from the *petit bourgeois* and equipped with a technical education from the famed *Ecole Nationale de la France d'Outre-Mer,* were supreme.

Whether despite or because of the colonial administration, parts of French Africa experienced enough progress after the war to confirm American belief in the necessity of white rule. Coastal areas able to produce and market cash crops like palm oil and kernels, coffee, cocoa, and bananas prospered. Railroads and especially motor roads were pushed inland. Elemental medical services were provided over a large area by specially trained African doctors and midwives in poorly funded dispensaries. The colonial governments aided the development of new strains of cash crops and encouraged the expansion of elementary education and Christian evangelism by missionaries, most of whom were French Catholic. There were population booms in a few coastal towns like Dakar, capital of the much-favored Senegal.

The vast majority of Africans under French rule, however, continued to live on subsistence agriculture. Their lives were punctuated occasionally by periods of forced labor on one of the few public-works projects or for cash wages to pay the yearly taxes. Many Africans, particularly in the enormous, untraced jungle tracts of French Equatorial Africa, the "Cinderella of the Colonies," passed decades without so much as a glimpse of the tricolored flag.

The French colonials, whether official or settler, did not instill admiration in the average American visitor, who found them officious, narrowly attached to the interests of "their" district, and, worst of all, occasionally indifferent to the smug social conventions and racial protocol so flattering to Americans in British colonies. Many Americans felt that France had carried her national penchant for efficiency and economy too far when she raised whole regiments of black Africans to fight for France in Europe. Black Americans, on the other hand, found reason to praise French colonial policy, which, particularly in Senegal, held out to an educated African elite the hope of full French citizenship and political equality. The bitterest black critics of European colonialism in Africa made a concession to the promise of "French Negrodom"; Hoskins himself wrote in 1930 of the "thriving and contented native populations" of French West Africa.[26]

American reaction to Belgian administration in the Congo varied. Some Americans had not forgotten the bloody rule of the Congo Free State. William Edward Burghardt Du Bois, perhaps the most prominent black American publicist, founder of the National Association for the Advancement of Colored People and editor of its journal *The Crisis,* execrated the memory of Leopold II—"a bearded roué"—and Vachel Lindsay thundered at lecture audiences in the 1920s with "Listen to the yell of Leopold's ghost/Burning in Hell for his hand-maimed host." Journalist May Mott-Smith complained in 1930 that Belgian administration had softened little since Leopold's day, and that local officials did not care for visiting American reporters.

Nevertheless, Americans were drawn to the Congo, primarily because of its wildlife. And most of those who went were not displeased with the Belgians. One expedition leader witnessed in outspoken approval a series of floggings of African men administered by a Belgian officer for minor breaches of discipline. An article written in 1919 for high-school geography teachers, entitled "Progress in the Belgian Congo," praised the "indomitable spirit of Belgium" in the Congo. Nineteen years later an American writer could praise the record of Belgian success in the Congo, based on "native respect for an authority remote but powerful. . . ." In 1937 the colonial reputation of Belgium was sufficiently rehabilitated to bring a request from the Disabled American Veterans for an old Congo Free State flag for its Hall of Nations; the governor-general in Léopoldville was delighted to donate one.[27]

It was Portugal's image in tropical Africa that was, in American eyes, most susceptible to improvement. Her survival as a colonial power struck one analyst as "one of the anomalies of modern history," and another reported that Portugal had been so weak, inefficient, and corrupt in the administration of her African territories that Britain and Germany had brazenly signed a treaty in 1913 dividing Portuguese Africa between them. The partition of the Portuguese

African colonies, or their forced donation to Germany in the 1920s to satisfy her resurgent colonial demands, was discussed regularly in the interwar period.[28]

For Portugal, the outbreak of the world war was fortuitous. Her colonial economies boomed—albeit temporarily—on wartime demands for tropical products, and after 1914 neither Britain nor Germany was free to press her demands against Portugal for colonial cession. The Portuguese were grateful for the respite, but they were not surprised; it was not the first time Heaven had exerted its benign influence on the affairs of the devout Portuguese, and it would not be the last.

Portugal had been a colonial power for centuries. Her flag still flew over forts on the African coast that had saluted the caravels of Prince Henry the Navigator, and four hundred years had come and gone since Bartholomeu Dias rounded the southern tip of Africa to pierce the seas of Asia. While other empires rose and fell and rose again, tiny Portugal, poor in everything but pride, maintained a precarious clutch on her African colonies. This remarkable feat was due in part to dogged determination on the part of the mother country, in part to a conscious desire by each of Portugal's potential rivals to maintain her in Africa as a harmless makeweight against the others, and in part to incredibly good luck.

Portugal's colonial holdings in Africa consisted of Guinea, a small enclave on the coastal flank of French West Africa, several islands in the Gulf of Guinea, and two great territories in Central Africa, Angola and Mozambique (Portuguese East Africa). By the end of the 1920s the latter two colonies contained a total population of some eight millions; less than 1 per cent were European, and these almost entirely Portuguese officers and settlers. Fiercely proud and nationalistic, the Portuguese had from the beginning regarded the smallness of their homeland and the enormity of their imperial responsibilities as a divine challenge. God had willed that Portugal should carry the message of the Catholic Church and the blessings of civilization to the darkest recesses of a savage world. The spread of imperial authority, therefore, was essentially a crusade. No disaster was so great that it could not be explained away as a mere temporary setback, over which Portugal's civilizing mission must inevitably triumph.

There was little room in the Portuguese scheme for such concepts as "indirect rule" and "association." At home the Portuguese revered a long tradition of executive domination by their government, a tradition that they could not be expected to soften in far-off colonies. Their mystical sense of mission did not encourage the Portuguese to nurture African ways of life where these could be extirpated. Legislative councils did not exist. Whether under a crown, a transient republic, or, after 1930, the Corporative State of Antonio de Oliveira Salazar, the Portuguese were determined to rule their African colonies with an iron hand. The difficulty, however, was that there were never enough iron hands to go around. Portugal's control remained more or less confined to a few trading and administrative centers while the vast unexplored hinterlands were either turned over to concessionaires with nearly sovereign rights or left altogether outside the limit of civilizing influences.

Portugal's record in her African colonies won a grudging admiration from a few visitors for its longevity alone. But aside from endurance, there was little to praise. Port facilities at Lourenço Marques, Beira, and Loanda were improved and rail lines begun. The profits from the wartime colonial boom were quickly dissipated, however, and many projects came to a halt; only the vitally important Benguela Railway was completed, in 1929, opening Angola and the southern part of the Belgian Congo westward to the sea. The Portuguese escudo began a rapid decline; homeland investors refused to export precious capital to the colonies, which languished more visibly as the years passed. Faced with serious financial difficulties at home, the Portuguese government did nothing more for the African colonies than demand balanced budgets. By the mid-1920s the escudo had completely disappeared, and American investment handbooks no longer carried Portuguese colonial trade figures in terms of the dollar.[29]

Undermanned, provided with inadequate funds in the best of times and none in the worst, charged with the maintenance of an antique illusion everywhere without the means of realizing it anywhere, generation after generation of Portuguese colonial staffs had either exploited or neglected their African charges. From the earliest days of colonial rule both the local governments and the concessionaires had resorted to ill-disguised forced black labor on both public works and private plantations. Yet in many areas of Portugal's colonies, some Africans never saw a white man, and sizable numbers of them encountered the ruling race only in the form of an occasional missionary or tax collector.[30]

In 1925 the University of Wisconsin sociologist Edward Alsworth Ross caused an international uproar with his report on Portuguese labor policy in Africa; the so-called Ross Report equated Portuguese labor conditions with slavery. Following publication of the report, American missionaries were continually harassed by Portuguese officials, who apparently intended to discourage both the spread of the Protestant version of Christianity and the use of the native vernacular in instruction. Americans doing research in the field had to be wary of offending sensitive and overbearing Portuguese administrators. "It is essential," wrote one, "that any publicity respecting the expedition shall be favorable to Portuguese authority and administration." American consuls in Loanda and Lourenço Marques were sometimes appalled at the malfeasance of local government officials. Portugal allowed the sale of alcoholic beverages to Africans, in order to insure a market for home industry. The worst of it was, lamented the American consul in 1919, that not even the Portuguese denied the "disastrous" effect that European hard liquor had on the Africans. Other consular reports bemoaned the inactivity of local governments, the lack of reforms, the frequent pointless disputes with neighboring colonies over tariffs and customs, and the ruinous financial policies.[31]

Relations between Americans in Africa and local colonial officials differed from colony to colony—from generally friendly in the British territories to generally unpleasant in the Portuguese. The British Foreign and Colonial offices promised that "all proper facilities" would be afforded to individual scientific investigators like Coulter and ethnologist Wilfrid D. Hambly, and to large-scale excursions like the Smithsonian-Chrysler African Expedition of 1926. Privileges that London could not guarantee were often provided by local officials. Kenya, for instance, allowed the agents of

American museums to obtain baby elephants and giraffes, animals otherwise absolutely protected, if the Game Department were satisfied the museum had the facilities for the proper care and display of such large animals. Local British officials often took a "close personal interest" in American projects, and placed invaluable facilities and personnel at the disposal of the Americans; zoologists, anthropologists, archeologists, sociologists often received "cordial cooperation" from local administrators. The governor of Uganda sent a British officer to serve as general aide to W. S. Van Dyke during the time his movie company was in the protectorate, and placed a squad of the King's African Rifles, the famed East African soldiers, under Van Dyke's personal command when dissension arose among the safari blacks; naturally, the director "welcomed them with open arms."[32]

American consuls occasionally complained that French authorities in Dakar were uncooperative. In the 1930s the officials of French West Africa apparently resented the fact that the American consulate for western Africa was in Lagos; they pretended to believe that the American consul was only "accredited" to British officials and either refused to answer his inquiries or sent the replies to the French Colonial Office for transmission to the consul through Washington—six months later. The French government itself, however, was officially cordial to Americans approaching Africa through channels in Paris. The French were usually willing to grant extensive collecting privileges to legitimate scientific expeditions, and some French field officers went far out of their way to be helpful to Americans. In 1929 a Field Museum truck sank into the sand near Agades, and the French governor sent forty horsemen dashing to the rescue.[33]

Ever since Carl Akeley of the American Museum of Natural History had worked closely with the Belgian government in establishing a gorilla preserve near Lake Kivu in the Congo in 1926, relations between American scientists in Africa and the Belgians had been excellent. Journalists might complain of rebuffs from administrators with long memories of exposés of the old Free State regime, but representatives of American museums received generous cooperation from Brussels and local officials in Africa. A key figure in building rapport between American museums and the Belgian government was the Baron Emil de Cartier de Marchienne, Belgian ambassador in Washington in the 1920s, who developed a warm personal affection for both Akeley and the project for a gorilla reserve. Throughout the interwar years the American Museum conducted what amounted to its own diplomatic relations with the Belgian embassy.

Although genuinely solicitous of the fauna of the Congo, the Belgians often granted expanded licenses to American collectors. Only the most unreasonable requests were denied: "Altho' we are in the 'Heart of Africa,' " grumbled a collector for the Field Museum who had been denied two gorillas over the limit as trophies, "our troubles are all on the outside (at Brussels)." American missionaries were usually welcome in the Congo; the Belgians alone could not begin to provide educational or medical facilities for their huge African population spread over such a vast area. American medical missionaries were sometimes employed by the government to attend to villages far from their own hospital compounds. American travelers of any sort were a happy diversion for lonely Belgian officers in the field, and the Belgians did what they could to make the United States consulate in Léopoldville a congenial post.[34]

The Portuguese, on the other hand, frequently made life for American missioners, hunters, scientists, and travelers as unpleasant as they could. Although an animal collector or hunter might be attracted to Portuguese Angola and Mozambique by the laxity of the game laws, he was not won over by the Portuguese officials who extracted such export tolls as suited them. Animal collector Wynant D. Hubbard was allowed to hunt freely through a district in Mozambique, but he had to present the government with nine head of large game for every elephant he collected. The officials wished an inexpensive way to rid the country of marauding game and the tsetse fly, which housed itself on the larger animals. One collector for several American zoos in 1929 had to present to the government officials at Lourenço Marques a living pair of every kind of animal captured. When Arthur Vernay was in Lisbon in 1929 making arrangements for his expedition to Angola for the Field Museum, he found the Director General of the Colonies of the West "favorably inclined" only when that official learned the expedition would bring 1 million escudos into Angola's languid economy. The colonial administration in Lisbon was generally willing to act on petitions from the American embassy and "request" local officers to grant American museums "all facilities compatible with the law"; their requests, however, meant that all decisions were made on the local level.[35]

Local officers very often proved uncooperative. The non-political activities of animal collectors provoked nothing more than rapacity, but when travelers became interested in the lot of the natives, that was a different matter. Directly responsible for their country's colonial regime, and unable to control the criticism it engendered in the foreign press, Portuguese officials in Africa fell back on interfering with any outside investigations not warmly endorsed by Lisbon. The Ross Report, published in 1925, was a disaster for Americans in the Portuguese colonies; a year later, the United States consul in Loanda described Ross's investigation as "exceedingly unfortunate." "It certainly has been detrimental to American interests in Angola—to trade, to missions. . . ." When Buell, collecting material for a book on tropical Africa, requested the consul at Lourenço Marques in 1926 to inquire about native labor laws, the latter refused. He replied that he wished Buell had been the first American to investigate Portuguese labor laws, and not Ross. As it was, the consul could make no inquiries; the United States government was "somewhat suspected" of having had "some connection" with Ross, and the slightest consular interest in native labor would "increase suspicion." In 1929 Hambly complained that the "unfortunate actions of an American named Ross" had made the Portuguese authorities "less enthusiastic towards strangers." Hambly felt that Angola was "such a profitable field of research" that the Field Museum should include in the publicity of the expedition "some acknowledgment of the cooperation of the Portuguese authorities," whom he observed to be "a proud sensitive people, easily offended, but most responsive to courtesy and a little flattery." The museum reacted with orotund tributes to the Portuguese.[36]

Portugal was not the only nation against which the charge of colonial incompetence was raised. The Allies in the war had justified operations against German Africa, and their later retention of the colonies, with the statement that Germany had been brutal and cruel to her African charges, and unfit to shoulder the "White Man's burden." The Germans, however, did not simply withdraw from the African scene; between the wars, Germany remained one of the European nations whose interest in tropical Africa was often brought to American attention. Indeed, the postwar controversy over the African mandates, no less than the turmoil in Kenya, made East Africa one of the trouble spots of the world.

The United States had been involved in every aspect of the mandates settlement at Versailles. The trusteeship program was in no small part an American scheme. The United States, however, had brushed aside British proposals that she accept the mandate over German East Africa; most Americans regarded imperial rivalries as an important factor in causing war, and would have been glad to see them laid to rest. America, therefore, watched with a mixture of interest, understanding, and anxiety efforts by Germany in the interwar period to regain the colonies she had lost at Versailles.

The month the peace treaties were signed an American editorial observed with relief that "the story of Germany's attempt at colonial expansion is definitely closed." Throughout the early 1920s, much of the American press followed the implementation of the new mandate system in Africa as though the decisions were final and the matter had been "definitely closed." The Germans, however, did not regard the matter as closed at all. Even the most moderate politicians in the new republic, men like Matthias Erzberger, who had criticized the excesses of the old regime in Africa, urged the Allies to allow Germany to become the mandatory for at least part of her old African empire. The same forces within Germany that had inspired the prewar drive for colonies continued their propaganda throughout the interwar years, strengthened by the opinion of an increasingly militant public and by the fact that a succession of governments was ever more willing to urge their proposals upon the Allied mandatories. National organizations to press for colonial restitution began forming, or re-forming, in 1920; in 1924 the first of the great annual Colonial Congresses was held; and by 1926 most imperialist lobbies had joined together in the *Kolonial Reichsarbeitsgemeinschaft,* which claimed thirty thousand members in that year. The old colonial journals were revived.

Translations of works by Martin Johnson and Carl Akeley were published, and in the United States German atlases appeared with Tanganyika marked *Ehem.* (for *ehemaliges,* "former") *Deutsch Ostafrika.* After the National Socialists came to power in 1933, demands for colonial restitution became so strident that many Americans feared another European war if Nazi demands were not satisfied.[37]

There was some sympathy in the United States for the German position long before Adolf Hitler threatened war to regain the African colonies. America's high hopes for the mandates solution were jeopardized almost immediately by the blatant manner in which the Allies divided the German colonies as the spoils of war. Writers began to praise the valiant stand by the Germans in East Africa during the war, and British encomiums for German colonial administration in the old days of Anglo-Saxon camaraderie were recalled. Legalists like Alpheus Snow denounced as absurd Allied claims that Germany had acquired her African empire illegally. Students of imperial relations like Mary Townsend dispassionately retold the story of Germany's colonial expansion. In 1904 and 1905, for instance, German General Lothar von Trotha had punished a rebellion by the Herero people of South-West Africa by massacring or driving out of the colony so many of them that in three years the population of Hereros fell to less than one-quarter of its level in 1903. Yet Townsend observed that following the fierce debates in the Reichstag caused by the Herero war, stupendous results had been accomplished by the reforms in the German colonial service. Many Americans were embarrassed by Germany's claim that she had agreed to the armistice partly on the basis of Wilson's promise of equitable treatment in the colonial settlement. American tractability toward Germany's African cause grew to such an extent that by 1932 the New York *Journal of Commerce* was recommending a restoration of the German colonial empire.[38]

German arguments for a return of the *Kolonialreich,* as presented to the American public, fell into two broad categories: those having to do with economics and those having to do with prestige. What Germany had to have was a source of raw materials, overseas markets, and a place under her sovereignty in which to locate her excess population. For decades, these had been the classic arguments for imperialism, but they seemed to gain strength after Germany lost her colonies. Critics, however, pointed out that the Germany of Kaiser Wilhelm II had acquired only one-half of 1 per cent of her raw materials from her empire, that should the old colonies now be forced to purchase *all* their goods from Germany it would raise German exports by only 0.7 per cent, and that few Germans had ever settled in the colonies.

The real reason Germany wanted her colonies back was prestige—the thrill of imperial dominion and the status of a Great Power. The *New York Times* editorialized in 1937 that the inspiration for the German demands was "the prestige of the Third Reich," and that the economic arguments were specious. The leader of the colonial movement within Germany agreed, in an article in an American periodical, that the issue was primarily a matter of "national honor and national prestige." Parker T. Moon was among those who attempted to demonstrate that the intensified imperial rivalry of the 1920s was based on a desire to secure an independent supply of certain materials for strategic purposes, that economics had almost nothing to do with German demands. Nevertheless, some Americans, including *Business Week* magazine, continued to urge a redistribution of colonial resources in favor of Germany in the interests of peace and prosperity. Germany played successfully on American fears of another war. In a major article in *Foreign Affairs* in January, 1937, Hjalmar Schacht, the respected president of the Reichsbank, hinted darkly: "A nation which is cut off from the essential necessities of life must be a source of unrest in the world."[39]

In all this discussion, Africa was regarded as putty in the hands of Europe. The only question in American minds that turned to Africa was which European power should rule it. Sovereignty over mandates lay somewhere between the mandatory and the League of Nations—just where was not altogether clear; what was clear, however, was that the indigenous population of Africa did not share it. Africa continued to be, in 1939 as in 1919, "a continent owned and operated by Europeans." Since the fifteenth century, observed *Fortune* in 1935, Africa's resources and its peoples had been "cut into juicy slices for the benefit of European powers." The status of the Africans as "wards of the society of nations" and of Africa as territory "in which no national consciousness exists" was established in international law, and remained unchallenged after it had been laid down at Berlin, Brussels, and Versailles.[40]

This is not to say that Americans were completely indifferent to the fate of the Africans should Germany regain control over them. Beer had spoken of "Germany's unsympathetic and contemptuous government" under the old regime, and travelers occasionally commented on the lingering effects of German discipline. One American geologist in Tanganyika in 1937 drove past Africans on the road who still clicked "their bare heels together" and gave the "military salute." It is rather to say that the mandates were considered by all concerned to have become colonies of the mandatory powers, and that the only impediment that stood in the way of their outright transfer to Germany in the interest of peace was the doubt that colonies would satisfy Hitler for long. To many Americans in the last half of the 1930s, Tanganyika seemed a small price to pay to prevent another world war. Some even voiced sympathy for the several schemes involving the donation of Belgian and Portuguese territory in Africa to placate the omnivorous Germans.[41]

In the years between the wars, Americans could still see evidences of the old German regime in the mandates. Cities like Tanga on the Tanganyika coast carried a well-scrubbed German look. The German consul at Lourenço Marques was still using stationery marked *Kaiserlich Deutsches Konsulat* in 1924, with the *Kaiserlich* inked out by hand. Monuments to the heroic defenders of German East Africa of 1914–1918 stood in several towns in Tanganyika. The hulk of the cruiser *Königsberg,* sunk by British monitors in 1914, rested in the mouth of the Rufiji River. American travelers in Tanganyika often had transactions with German colonists, mostly settlers who had moved to Africa long before the war. These settlers were sympathetic to the requests of the Weimar Republic for a share in the administration of the former German colonies. British settlers throughout East Africa, meanwhile, were increasingly uneasy, and eyed both their German neighbors and Whitehall for signs of an alteration in the new arrangements in Africa. An editorial in the *Tanganyika Times* in 1927 and an incident between British officials and the crew of a visiting German cruiser in 1930, both dutifully reported by American consuls, suggested that tensions could run high between the two settler communities.[42]

In 1933 the situation of Germans in Africa changed abruptly. Local agitation, spearheaded by new Nazi immigrants and geared to Berlin's aggressive foreign policies, became shrill. German consuls began to display swastika flags on their official cars, and local Germans were coerced into supporting the party's uncompromising stand against the mandates with threats of retribution against relatives and investments in the fatherland. The ranks of resident Germans were swelled by persons of suspicious intent thinly disguised as "planters."[43]

In 1936 Hitler openly declared his support for Germany's colonial demands, and restoration of the German colonies became official policy. By 1938, the year of the Austrian and Czechoslovakian crises, the Nazis had exported their political and social structure to Africa. Germans could approach their consul only through party officials; Jewish refugees were assessed a share in the fines imposed on Jews in Germany in the persecutions of 1937; Germans were forbidden to associate with Jews, or to listen to foreign radio broadcasts. Five German schools were opened in Tanganyika, which all German children were obliged to attend. Immigration from Germany increased until by August, 1938, the Germans were the largest European group in Tanganyika. The newcomers brought the same daily round of bund picnics, rallies, and parades they had known in Germany; even the *Kraft durch Freude* program came, offering low-cost excursions to the Ngoro-Ngoro crater to loyal Nazi settlers. The *Finanzamt* in Berlin sent assessment bills to Jewish refugees blatantly mailed in care of "Nairobi, Deutsch Ost Afrika"; the American consul could not understand why the postmaster delivered them. In 1939 Germany became the second nation with a full-time consul in Nigeria, and armbands and swastikas began to appear among local Africans. The old-time German communities were overwhelmed by the militant, disciplined newcomers of the 1930s; many German settlers who had come in prewar times sold their farms in Tanganyika and moved to Kenya.[44]

American interests were sometimes involved directly. Nazi

activities in Kenya were coordinated and financed for awhile in 1937 by a Ford agency in Nairobi, which was partly owned by the German consul. In the spring of 1939, the American consul at Nairobi found it "most embarrassing" to be told by the colonial authorities that an American Seventh-day Adventist mission at Musama, Tanganyika, was a front for a Nazi spy ring; one missionary, a German-American named Rudolph Helbig, was district leader for the Nazi Party. Mortified, the consul informed Washington and requested an immediate investigation of the denominational headquarters at Takoma Park, Maryland. The General Conference of the Seventh-day Adventists sharply disapproved of the mission's activities, and warned the leaders at Musama that another complaint to the consul from the governor of Tanganyika would result in their instant recall to the United States and disgrace. As Nazi activities increased in Tanganyika during 1939, American consuls began sending reports on them to the highest State Department officials, including Under Secretary Sumner Welles and Secretary Cordell Hull.[45]

The rise in Nazi activity in Africa after 1936 and the passive reaction of Britain and France to Hitler's take-over of Austria and Czechoslovakia threw non-German colonials in tropical Africa into a panic. Many feared along with Mary Townsend that Hitler would penetrate Africa, regain Germany's empire, and disrupt the continent as painlessly as he had rolled into Vienna and Prague. It was known that Neville Chamberlain had discussed colonies with Hitler at Munich, and settlers feared the worst. In October, 1938, the British cabinet examined appeasement proposals that ranged from returning the German colonies to coercing Belgium and Portugal into allowing German capital access into their colonies as part of a Central Africa "colonial pool." In Africa rumors spread of secret German troop movements and the smuggling of arms into African hands. Every newcomer who was not a Jewish refugee was regarded as a German spy. Settlers in British East Africa formed the Tanganyika Defense League to lobby in London against cession of the colony, and for armed defense if necessary. The Belgians, Portuguese, and French staged encouraging military reviews, drew up mobilization plans, and congratulated themselves on the adequacy of their African defenses. To avert hysteria among whites and blacks alike, the governors of British West Africa cabled London for permission to issue categorical statements that colonial transfers were not being contemplated.

After the German seizure of Czechoslovakia in March, 1939, appeasement collapsed, and the fears of local defense leagues were quieted. With the attitude of the British and French stiffening, the Nazis in Africa could not be quite so certain they would have their own way. The shoe was, in fact, on the other foot. The hopes of the German community had rested on a peaceful transfer of the mandates to German control; war between Britain and Germany could only mean confiscation and ruin for Germans in Africa.[46]

The interwar period ended as it had begun: Africa was still the property of Europe. German demands for an African empire were once again settled in Europe, not in Africa. The last dispatch on colonial transfer from the United States consul in Nairobi was placed in the Department of State files with the following note stamped on the margin: "FILED September 20, 1939." The war that was to destroy African imperialism came to Africa in European terms. The governor of Nigeria was "composed" at the declaration of war on September 3; the governor of Kenya left to rejoin his Royal Air Force group. Ladies' auxiliaries, the Home Guard, and the Boy Scouts were mobilized; the King's African Rifles and the Royal West African Frontier Force were hurried to hostile borders and an obstruction was sunk across the Lagos roadstead. Most young Britons volunteered for service with the army at home. The Belgians and Portuguese proclaimed their colonies neutral territory, and the French did nothing. All eyes looked outward, toward Europe, where the destiny of colonial Africa would be decided—for the last time.[47]

two: america in africa

In a sense, we were King
and Queen in our own right.[1]
—Martin Johnson (1928)

The number of Americans living in tropical Africa in any one year during the interwar years was never large—one thousand at most. The long-term residents—mostly missionaries, with a handful of salesmen, commercial agents, engineers, and consular officers—far outnumbered the Americans who paid relatively brief visits to Africa in the interests of science or for their own amusement. The activities of the transient Americans, who seldom remained longer than a single dry season and who confined their sojourns almost exclusively to British East Africa, provided the major part of the publicity on tropical Africa for home consumption. It was the permanent population, however, that represented what there was of a sustained American interest in Africa.

Few Americans were willing to abandon the certain benefits of life in the United States for the exigencies of an extended residence in Africa. No land grants, no enabling acts, no free new society awaited Americans beyond the coastal jungles. Employment opportunities were scarce. Service in a United States consulate in tropical Africa was not considered the zenith of a Foreign Service career. A commercial agent now and then came out to beat the drum for the Bureau of Foreign and Domestic Commerce, but the markets did not swell, natural resources came no cheaper, and Afri-

51

can shirts did not drop the golden inch. The few American sales agencies that did exist met the needs of European communities no larger and not much richer than the clientele in a small American town.

Driven thus by motives, and under circumstances that themselves suggest the nature of American-African relations, Americans living in all of tropical Africa fell into two loose residential categories: urban on the one hand and decidedly rural on the other. Those engaged in commercial agencies for American manufacturers or shipping services and those serving as U.S. consuls lived in the Europeanized cities, usually the colonial capital. Christian missionaries sometimes operated churches or schools in the cities—the American mission at Lourenço Marques was the most striking example—but for the most part these Americans, a few engineers and a rare settler, lived and worked "in the bush," often a considerable distance from the centers of business and administration.

The only colonial city with a self-consciously American community was Nairobi, the capital of Kenya Colony, and of all African cities the best-known in the United States. On several occasions the American consulate in Nairobi prepared a list of the Americans in the city for inquirers back home, and, with the exception of the missionaries, these lists give a clear indication of the permanent American residents' scope of interest in tropical Africa.

Two lists compiled by the Nairobi consulate—one in May, 1932, of contributors to a fund to help a destitute American transient, the other a year later of guests at a Fourth of July reception—suggest that they included all the Americans in the city. Most names appeared on both lists, which together contained the names of eighteen Americans inscribed as permanent residents of Nairobi. This little group both stimulated and reflected a considerable part of the interest that the American public showed in tropical Africa.

The most prominent names on the lists were those of Martin and Osa Johnson, who divided their time between a fieldstone mansion in Nairobi and several permanent "camps," and professional safari manager, photographer, and publicist A. J. Klein and his wife of Muthaiga, Kenya. Aside from the Johnsons and the Kleins, however, the group was far from glamorous. Mr. and Mrs. R. C. Gilfillan, assisted by the L. D. Browns, ran one of Nairobi's leading automobile agencies. U. S. Jestes operated the Motor Mart & Exchange, agents for the General Motors Export Corporation. Samuel H. Wallace, with his wife and son Bill, lived on the commissions of the Texas Oil Company of South Africa, Ltd. Both A. Liversage (or Liversedge—the lists differ) and his wife worked for the Kenya Department of Agriculture. A Mrs. Dennis was listed as employed by the British Colonial Broadcasting Company, Ltd., of Nairobi; Robert N. Bergsten and his wife operated the International Harvester Company agency; and one E. P. Firth, whose form of employment, if any, was not specified, listed his address as Fort Ternan, a settlement near the city. Later the American manager of a newly opened Nairobi agency for the Caterpillar Tractor Company would join the group.[2]

Other territories did not sport well-organized American colonies in the capitals. In 1932, for example, Congressman Sol Bloom informed the American consul at Lourenço Marques that the official Memorial Volume on ceremonies around the world celebrating the two-hundredth birthday of George Washington was still awaiting reports from several consulates, including his. In fact, the great event had passed unnoticed in Lourenço Marques. Two of the city's three American citizens (the consul being the third) were away at the time, and the consul had been reduced to raising the "large flag" and closing the office as part of the worldwide festivities. In a rather tardy response to the congressman's inquiry, he was able to include the irrelevant but inspiring account of the successful gala given at the consulate on Independence Day, attended by many local officials and the entire consular corps.[3]

In the Portuguese colonies, in British West Africa, in British East Africa (except Kenya), in the French colonies, and in the Belgian Congo, all but a handful of the permanent American residents lived "in the bush," alone or in small groups scattered some distance from major settlements. It was often difficult for the American consuls to maintain an accurate account of these citizens, since the consular districts in Africa covered territories of almost incredible size, and communication with the interior ran from troublesome in the dry season to impossible in the rainy. When submitting a list in 1922 of American residents within his huge district of some 480,000 square miles, Reed Paige Clark, the American consul at Loanda, warned that it was "subject to amendment by every mail."

United States consuls discouraged Americans from taking up permanent residence in Africa unless they had the backing of an established missionary society, were the representatives of an American firm, or had sufficient capital to invest in a profitable business or farm. Jobs were scarce and salaries low by American standards. For the most part enterprising persons, like the army captain discharged after World War I who wanted to bring his whole company to Africa to cash in on the "vast opportunities," were advised by American officials in Africa not to make the move.* A few American engineers were employed in the field, concentrated in the mining industries of the Katanga District of the Belgian Congo and in Northern Rhodesia, and a very few—perhaps half a dozen—settled on farms in British East Africa. The great majority of Americans living in Africa, however—and these were welcomed by American consulates—were Protestant missionaries.[4]

National records show that in 1922 there were 281 Americans living in the Belgian Congo, 122 in Angola, and 9 in the "French Congo," the southern and coastal parts of French Equatorial Africa. These Americans were registered at the consulate by the mission society that sponsored their station, or by employer. In 1924 there were 365 Americans living in the Belgian Congo, almost all of them missionaries. "With occasional exceptions," the State Department was advised in 1925, the entire American population of Portuguese East Africa consisted "only of missionaries living in the interior and near the coast some distance north of Lourenço Marques." Of 42 Americans living in the colony ten years later, 32 were listed at the U.S. consulate as engaged in "educational work, sectarian." In 1937, 36 of the 39 Americans living in the colony were missionaries.[5]

Although the proportions were not always so lopsided, the preponderance of Americans living in British East Africa were also missionaries in these interwar years. In 1938 the

* The captain's letter was addressed to the U.S. consul, Zanzibar, "German East Africa." Zanzibar, of course, was not in "German East Africa," called Tanganyika after the war; with no consulate in Zanzibar, the letter was forwarded to Nairobi.

consul at Nairobi listed 350 Americans living in the three territories of British East Africa, two-thirds of whom were missionaries living "up-country," most of them for many years. The consul, asked by the State Department to submit a "plan for emergencies" on the eve of World War II, made no provision for these missionaries, explaining that they were "thoroughly at home" in the bush, with automobiles they could service on their own and surrounded by "friendly natives." In fact, the consul made no emergency plans for any Americans in his district; he considered the Kenya Highlands among the safest places in the world.

The figures for Tanganyika alone are revealing. Of 156 Americans registered at the consulate in Nairobi, 143 were missionaries, 4 were listed as farmers, 5 represented the Texas and Vacuum oil companies, and 4 were engineers employed by British companies. Americans owned property in the territory valued at $1,013,500, $866,500 of it belonging to the missions. The remaining $147,000 represented the investment, most of it in stocks, of the two oil companies.[6]

Permanent American residents engaged in the daily affairs of a mission station or business had little time or opportunity to pursue the spectacular activities that drew the American visitor to Africa. There were exceptions. The Martin Johnsons, residents of Kenya since 1921, produced motion pictures of African wildlife; the Johnsons were the best-known Americans in Africa on either side of the Atlantic. Safari manager Klein, a native of New Jersey, was in an occupation otherwise monopolized by British colonials. Resident engineer Leslie Simson collected the entire African Hall, group by group, in 1931 for the San Francisco Natural History Museum. Missionaries, like J. D. Pointer of the Methodist Mission at Inhambane, Portuguese East Africa, would collect a specimen or two for a museum back home. An American living in Freetown, Sierra Leone, listed his occupation in 1938 as "animal collector." Wynant D. Hubbard and his wife arrived in Central Africa just after the war, hoping to make a fortune in an asbestos mining scheme. When the project failed, the stranded Hubbards, steeped in the lore of Africa, decided to recoup their losses by rounding up some of the wild animals they saw all about them and selling them to American zoos. Financed by a Rhodesian, the

Hubbards lived in Rhodesia and Portuguese East Africa for years, collecting animals, writing articles, and petitioning local authorities for exemptions from the game laws, so as to keep themselves constantly supplied with fresh merchandise. African animals, however, were highly susceptible to every imaginable hazard when removed from their natural habitat, a fact that not only accounted for the high prices per head in New York that had lured the Hubbards into the venture in the first place, but also gave the business of collecting live animals for profit a highly speculative reputation. When Hubbard's original backer withdrew, he could find no others, and his operation quickly folded.[7]

In Kenya, some American residents, like the Johnsons and the Kleins, also became important members of the European community. An American named William Northrup McMillan settled in the Highlands long before the war, and renounced his citizenship to become a British subject. Knighted for service to the empire, he lived in baronial splendor on his estate at Juja. Sir William prided himself on his hospitality to visiting Americans, the most famous of whom would always remain Colonel Theodore Roosevelt. After her husband's death, Lady McMillan established as a memorial the finest public library in Nairobi.[8]

Despite the prominence enjoyed by a few resident Americans, however, visitors from the United States often made a far greater impact in a few weeks than did most permanent American residents in many years. This was particularly true in the interwar period, though several notable Americans had been to Africa before the First World War—Stanley, for example, in 1871, and Roosevelt in 1909–1910. Roosevelt was almost venerated in British East Africa. A gentlemanly sportsman with a keen sense of trail etiquette, brave and impulsive, a late-Victorian imperialist without a trace of self-consciousness about it, he represented all that British colonials found admirable in a man, even an American. His classic account of his expedition to Kenya, *African Game Trails,* was widely read on both sides of the Atlantic after the war and continued to draw American sportsmen to "British East." For many years after Roosevelt's death in 1919, guides reverently pointed out his campsites to hunting parties.[9]

For decades after the war, African game trails lured hundreds of Americans to Africa: big-game hunters after trophies, professional collectors after merchandise, naturalists and taxidermists after specimens for museums. They formed a steady stream through tropical African ports and capitals into the bush in search of those distinctive wild animals that were synonymous with Africa in so many American minds back home. Along with a few journalists, movie directors, and anthropologists, these visitors brought money and publicity to colonies desperately anxious for both—and considerable variety into the lives of the American consuls.

For the American visitor and resident in Africa, as well as for the United States government itself, the most important American was the consul. Embassies and legations were assigned to the capitals of foreign powers only; for the imperial powers, these were in Europe. In tropical Africa the official representatives of the United States were the consuls. The State Department was as conscious of its obligations to provide for American citizens In Africa as it was desirous of tapping the potential markets and resources of a largely unknown region. These impulses, however, had to be balanced against steadily decreasing appropriations, with the result that personnel were assigned to tropical Africa only very sparingly. In 1920, the United States had but four consulates and two poorly staffed legations (in Liberia and Ethiopia) to serve all of tropical Africa; during the Depression of the early 1930s, even one of these consulates was closed.

Central Africa—that enormous area of which the Congo River Basin formed the heart—was the most difficult consular assignment for an American. The United States had little traditional interest in the European states—Belgium and Portugal—that were sovereign over Central Africa, and few commercial ties with them; also, American trade with Central Africa was slight. In the case of Portugal, there was the added problem of a language unfamiliar to most American Foreign Service officers. American missionaries and engineers scattered throughout the backcountry were all inconveniently equidistant from Africa's principal cities. Furthermore, parts of the Congo River Basin really *were* "darkest Africa," some of it a charmless, unhealthy region of fever-inducing swamps and jungles. American consuls sent to the regional post at Boma, then capital of the Belgian Congo, quickly became exasperated and began agitating for a transfer, or to have the entire consulate transferred, to some—any—less uncongenial place.

The United States had maintained a consulate at Boma, sixty miles up the great Congo River, until 1916, when it was closed. In 1920 young Reed Paige Clark was sent out to transfer the post south to Loanda, on the Angolan coast in the "Portuguese Kongo." A year earlier the U.S. consulate at Mombassa, on the coast of Kenya, had been transferred to Nairobi. In 1920, then, there were American consulates at Loanda, Nairobi, and Lourenço Marques in Mozambique. Along with a post at Dakar in Senegal, and the legations at Monrovia, Liberia, and at Addis Ababa, Ethiopia, these consulates were expected to look after Americans and American interests in almost all of tropical Africa. One American expert on African affairs termed these provisions insufficient, and urged their expansion.[10]

In an action widely hailed by local officials and the business community, the United States opened a new consulate at Lagos, Nigeria, in March, 1928.* In October, 1929—a month of ominous portent for commercial enterprises—the consulate at Loanda was transferred back to the Belgian Congo, this time at Léopoldville, its new capital, though a few months later the department gave up altogether on finding the right location. Faced with drastic reductions in appropriations during the Great Depression, however, the State Department had to close the new Léopoldville office almost immediately. The order to reopen it in 1934 marked the last alteration in the location of American consulates in tropical Africa until after the Second World War. As the war began, American missions were in operation at Dakar, Addis Ababa, Monrovia, Léopoldville, Lourenço Marques, and Nairobi.[11]

These consulates acted in the capacity of unofficial American embassies for the resident populations, most of whom made but infrequent use of their official services. They also

---

* The new consulate at Lagos was expected to administer the affairs previously handled by the one at Léopoldville, and, before that, at Loanda; consuls at Lagos, however, declared this an impossibility, and advised the State Department to either reopen the Léopoldville office or transfer what had been its share of the work to Brussels.

catered to a small and well-financed transient population, and processed the negligible American commerce.* When ships flying the American flag later began calling at African ports in greater numbers, the duties of the consuls increased —as did the loudness of their requests for assistance.[12]

It is probably fortunate that the volume of business transacted by these consulates was modest, because they were hopelessly understaffed, and forced to administer districts so enormous that even the consuls themselves had only a vague idea of their extent. Distances in Africa, complained one, were "not the same as distances in other parts of the world. . . ." Never did consuls attempt to enlarge or even preserve their domains; on the contrary, their efforts were usually bent toward shuffling some unwanted hinterland onto a colleague. Places like Fernando Po, Ruanda-Urundi, the Rhodesias, and Nyasaland were particularly subject to repudiation. At almost the same time the consul in Lagos was grumbling about "trying to limit my District to British West Africa," his colleague in Nairobi was trying to saddle him with Ruanda-Urundi. A few months later the Nairobi consul attempted to unload the Rhodesias and Nyasaland onto the Johannesburg district. French Equatorial Africa, which always seemed to be something of a consular no-man's-land, was especially distasteful; consuls invariably referred inquiries concerning it to some other consulate, or, with a fresh demand for more help, to Washington. Communications with the Interior were none too reliable even in good weather in a well-administered colony like Kenya. In bad weather, or in Portuguese territory, travel was impossible, and consuls dreaded the thought of a sudden need to establish emergency communications with Americans in the interior.[13]

While the consul at Nairobi might consider it unnecessary to make emergency evacuation plans for the missionaries in Kenya's interior, the consul at Lourenço Marques, responding to the same prewar inquiry from the State Department,

* For instance, total exports from The Gambia to the U.S. in 1936 came to $80, and there were no residents, no investments, and no missionaries to register. T. C. Wasson to State, Lagos, Dec. 8, 1937, DS 811.5031 Near East/203. Matters relating to The Gambia, of course, are often properly relegated to footnotes, for they can hardly be said to demonstrate any point not confined to merely Gambian affairs. The classic stepchild of imperialism, The Gambia is nothing more than two river banks and the water in between.

prepared a full report. Although neither complicated railroad schedules nor secret wireless codes existed to reas-
sure the State Department, Consul Samuel Ebling felt compelled by the dictates of bureaucratic efficiency to point
out that there was a weekly freight train between Lourenço
Marques and the Union of South Africa, as well as telephone
service. The consul, however, deemed communications in
Portuguese East Africa so fragile even in the best of times
that in any sort of emergency he would have to send a
messenger by car, horse, or bicycle overland to use the
telephone in Swaziland. Or he could ask a passing ship to
drop off a message at the next port. Ebling was confident,
nonetheless, that the Americans in Portuguese East Africa
could still be collected for evacuation. After all, only twenty-
five adults and fifteen children of American citizenship lived
in the whole colony, and nine of them were already in
Lourenço Marques. The remainder was divided among three
Protestant mission stations in the southern part of the colony, and these Americans, under the consul's plan, would
gather at the Methodist Episcopal Mission at Inhambane,
from which Ebling would rescue them a few at a time in a
plane borrowed in advance from the Lourenço Marques Flying Club.[14]

Like Ebling, most American consuls in tropical Africa were
sensitive to their responsibilities as deputies of the American
government. In 1926, for instance, an American missionary
near Lake Victoria spotted an African clad in a loincloth
made from two small American flags stitched together. True,
the American flag was so little seen in tropical Africa that
many Africans did not recognize it. But Consul Avra M.
Warren in Nairobi was properly horrified, and prepared to
make an international issue of the incident. He got the names
of the local flag dealer and the London manufacturer, and
demanded an instant cessation. Refused, he expressed "indignation" at the "reprehensible practice" to the colonial
governor, who promised to issue a proclamation on the
subject in the next Official Gazette.

Far from satisfied by the languid pace of retribution, Warren informed Washington of his "vigorous" action, and asked
the State Department to secure the cooperation of the
British Foreign Office in stopping the practice. Having heard
rumors that the publisher of the New York World was plan-

ning to visit Nairobi in the near future and might give "publicity" to the flag scandal, the consul was perhaps understandably agitated. He was soon informed that the chief native commissioner had issued instructions to prevent the "misuse of our National Emblem." The Foreign Office later informed the American embassy in London that the exporter of the flags had been "approached" on this delicate matter, and would contact his Nairobi outlet as soon as possible. The blacks, however, were attracted to the brightly colored breechcloths, and were, consequently, an irresistible temptation to the local dealer, who proved unscrupulous. It took several further vigorous protests from Warren and two more official remonstrances from the chief native commissioner before the flag affair came to a close. In pressing the flag controversy to its happy conclusion, Consul Warren was acting, and was recognized as acting, in the capacity of an official representative of the United States government.[15]

No matter how zealously they might pursue their duties, however, it was fairly obvious to the consuls that the State Department did not overvalue American interests in tropical Africa. Lacking clerks, messengers, and translators, American consulates were badly understaffed for even the limited business required of them. The consulate buildings themselves were sometimes in bad repair. A 1925 photograph of the American consulate at Nairobi reveals a single office over an auctioneer's showroom, a location unenhanced by the fact that the showroom was "To Lot" at the time. In 1920 the new consul at Loanda found a note from his predecessor warning him to have a boy go over all the office furniture once a week with gasoline to stave off attacks by white ants. When the American minister to Portugal visited Angola in 1928, he commiserated with the consul on the shabbiness of the consulate: "It is a damn shame that the American Government has made no better provisions for the American Consul at Loanda than it has."[16]

Washington's lack of interest in tropical Africa in these years was also revealed in decisions to curtail consular appropriations, reduce staffs, and even close one consulate. The Division of Western European Affairs, which in those high imperial days included in its purview the African colonies of the European powers, expressed no objection to closing the consulate in Léopoldville; it prepared a memorandum in August, 1930, for the Personnel Board of the Foreign Service, expressing the opinion that should a career Foreign Service officer spend one month in Léopoldville every two years, it would "adequately take care of our interests in [the] Belgian Congo." Catching the sentiments of their superiors, consuls sometimes felt a little shamefaced in even referring to their districts. When in 1932 the chief of the Western European Division asked the consul at Lagos for the privilege of informal correspondence on certain aspects of his district, the latter accepted agreeably, but added sheepishly that the information "might not be of much value to you."[17]

American consuls were forced to rely on local American residents for help. Where transportation facilities were primitive, as they were in Angola in the early 1920s, consuls were completely dependent on missionary assistance in traveling through the district. Consul Clark relied on the accommodations of missionaries during a five months' tour through Angola to outlying American mission stations, copper mines, and a small American diamond mine. He rode in their steamboats, refreshed himself and replenished his camp kit at their stations, and used their converts and workers to carry his baggage. In the cities, too, contact between consuls and missionaries, often the only American citizens in the vicinity, was helpful—at times, indispensable—to the consuls. When Robert Fernald was sent to open a consulate in Lagos, he counted on a local Southern Baptist missionary to help him find a building; the missionary, perhaps wishing to help two worthy causes at once, suggested Fernald get in touch with the Salvation Army, whose building on Kakawa Street was for rent. Consuls could usually rely on local American residents to provide pictures, curios, and lodging for guests in response to requests reaching the consulates from home. When a penniless American traveler was stranded in Nairobi in 1932, the consul had no funds with which to provide relief and had to depend on an emergency collection taken up by resident Americans.[18]

There were others who relied on the consuls for unofficial assistance. The National Geographic Society consistently sought to establish working relationships with American consuls in Africa. By advertising in the *Foreign Service Journal,* the society attempted to solicit stories and pictures of native life for its magazine. Editor Gilbert Grosvenor offered consuls "generous honorariums" for material accepted for publication. The society provided U.S. consulates with free subscriptions to its magazine and map service. Museums and travelers often called on consuls to perform personal favors not related to the official assistance rendered as a matter of course to American expeditions. There always seemed to be a bundle of special oat grass needed for a display or a small animal that somehow got left on the dock or, through an oversight, had never been collected. Most museum officials claimed a handy friendship with a consul or two, who would be "quite willing" to pick something up as a favor.[19]

Occasionally, consuls would be called upon to provide assistance to a congressman who had turned his attention to some aspect of Africa long enough to plan a junket, usually to one of its more attractive spots such as Nairobi. Congressmen were always careful to see that the State Department was informed of their project, so as to insure a royal reception on the scene. Using the official stationery of the House Committee on Appropriations, Congressman James P. Buchanan of Texas was not above asking the consul at Nairobi for information on how one might obtain three or four horns from a Roosevelt gazelle, "if they do not cost too much." By return mail the congressman was informed that the Kenya game warden already had a man in the field to shoot a pair, and did the congressman want two nice heads for trophies, or just the horns? Consuls also participated directly or indirectly, with other agencies in a number of cooperative projects of the United States government. The projects demonstrated the sorts of technical data on a wide range of subjects pertaining to tropical Africa that were reaching interested persons in the United States—at a time when broad policy planning on Africa was nonexistent and routine official relations were handled almost cavalierly.[20]

Consular cooperation was evident, for example, in many services requested by the Department of Agriculture. Would the consul send some mafura seeds from Kenya? Would the consul gather information on the Karakul sheep industry in Portuguese East Africa? Can the consul arrange a regular exchange of soil erosion bulletins between the American and Ugandan departments of agriculture? The department once asked for samples of East African gum arabic, frankincense, and myrrh, classical African treasure. In 1926 the American consul at Lourenço Marques helped the Portuguese governor hire a Department of Agriculture expert to study the possibility of raising cotton in the province; results of the survey turned out rather badly when the expert, James A. Evans, offended Portuguese sensibilities by declaring Portuguese East Africa unsuitable for cotton cultivation. When the Bureau of Entomology and Plant Quarantine wished to send an expedition to Central Africa to find a natural enemy to the Mediterranean fruit fly, the consul at Léopoldville secured the complete, almost extravagant, cooperation of the Belgian governor, who placed practically his entire scientific staff at the disposal of the American research team.[21]

Much of the consular correspondence with Washington was with the Bureau of Foreign and Domestic Commerce in the Department of Commerce. Consuls were ever busy in the interests of American business. Divisions within the bureau required a continuous stream of detailed statistics on the volume and price of all imports into and exports out of each consular district. Consuls also submitted reports for the Commerce Department's *World Trade Directory,* the *Commerce Year Book,* and a number of trade bulletins. Shortly after the New Deal began, the Departments of State and Commerce agreed that information about local investment and sales opportunities from American consuls should go to the addressee in the United States, a decision that brought many American businesses into direct correspondence with consulates in Africa.[22]

Many other government agencies besides the State and Commerce departments received information from consulates in Africa. The American Merchant Marine Library Association of New York was sent data for its *Seaman's Handbook for Shore Leave.* The Interstate Commerce Commission received the official tariff book of the Kenya and Uganda Railways and Harbors, plus corrections. The *Nigerian Handbook* went to the Tariff Commission; the Public Health Service was kept informed on the progress of the plague in Nigeria; the United States Weather Bureau was given the monthly meteorological observations taken at Entebbe, Uganda. Coins from the Belgian Congo and the Cameroons went to the Smithsonian Institution, and the Library of Congress was supplied with a yearly set of the official publications of Kenya Colony.[23]

To the extent that they were able, American consuls assisted federal regulatory agencies in preventing the flow of narcotics from several African ports to the United States. Most of the drug traffic came through Portuguese colonies, where governmental administration was regarded by its supporters as charmingly flexible, and by its calumniators as nonexistent. U.S. consuls at Loanda and Lourenço Marques kept a wary eye on ships stopping off at either port from British India. Every local development pertaining to drugs was reported to Washington.[24]

The United States Navy was supplied with port directories and harbor information, although there were few visits to African ports while Congress, during the interwar years, begrudged every gallon of oil that went into the bunkers. Nevertheless, the visit of a warship, all flags flying and a band on the quarterdeck, was a colorful and impressive sight in a sleepy African port. Until the early 1920s, it had been many years since an American ship had shared the scene with the British and French navies. The United States Navy, however, had seen its horizons extended by the First World War, which removed Germany as its chief rival for world runner-up. Anxious to maintain its new prestige at home and abroad, the navy decided in the first years of the decade to allow its new light cruisers to take advantage of their "large radius of action" on shakedown cruises. The decision thus enabled the navy "to show the American flag in ports that have not been visited by our vessels for many years."[25]

Original plans to send the whole Atlantic Fleet to South Africa in 1921 were not consummated, and the Atlantic and Pacific fleets were combined the next year under one command. But three new cruisers—the U.S.S. *Richmond, Concord,* and *Trenton*—visited tropical African ports on their shakedowns in 1923 and 1924, the first and last such visits for many years. The *Richmond,* commissioned July 2, 1923, fired her first salute off Dakar five weeks later. The ship dropped down the coast, exchanged salutes with the battery at Freetown on August 22 and steamed into the harbor with the British ensign at the main, to be ceremoniously received by the colonial officials. The *Richmond* went no further down the coast, spending the rest of August at Ascension Island and then sailing for Montevideo.[26]

The shakedown of the *Concord* was a cruise in the grand style. The vessel took a full year after being commissioned in November, 1923, to complete a cruise through the Mediterranean, down the East Coast of Africa, around the Cape, across the South Atlantic, and up the West Coast of South America. Elaborate ceremonies took place at Zanzibar, where the Sultan received his accustomed salute aboard the royal yacht, and the *Concord* shared the ways with H.M.S. *Hood* and *Repulse* with full-dress exchanges. At Lourenço Marques the *Concord* filled the harbor, Portuguese official-dom scurried on board, and the American consul was given a gratifying seven-gun salute on his departure. The ship laid at anchor a week, took on provisions, and part of the crew responded to the Portuguese governor-general's invitation to participate in a local military review. The *Concord* sailed for Port Elizabeth on January 29, 1924, the last American naval vessel to visit a continental port in tropical Africa until the Second World War.[27]

The *Trenton*'s much-heralded circumnavigation of Africa in 1924 was for the most part an affair of charts and sea-lanes. The cruiser sailed from the West Indies to Cape Town, thence to Durban, and from Durban directly to Zanzibar, where she spent five days before steaming through the Suez Canal. Consuls continued to report the visits of French frigates and British sloops-of-war, but their hinted requests for another American naval visit went unheeded.[28]

Official relations conducted as disinterestedly as those between the United States and Africa hardly affected the lives of Americans in either place. Americans in Africa experienced and reported life as it was determined by the conditions surrounding them. Whether in Africa to gather treasure of a spiritual or more tangible nature, Americans living there found hazards and pleasures unrelated to flags and naval visits, the proportion varying with the person and the place.

Hazards there were even in the best of places. Much of the popular image of tropical Africa as a land of danger and wild adventure resulted from conscious stereotyping, a process warmly resented by the settlers in British East Africa, who prided themselves on how closely their new home had been made to resemble the Sussex countryside. Yet even in Kenya there were discomforts, and in less hospitable regions, like the Congo River Basin and long stretches of both coastal belts, there was an element of truth in even the most gruesome distortion.

Not surprisingly, American travelers arrived in Africa with confused ideas about its physical geography. Permanent residents might know better, but American tourists were forced to rely on the scanty information available in the United States, where the average American's factual knowledge about Africa was exceedingly slight. Atlases and geography texts were often of little help; they did nothing to offset the impression created in the twenties and thirties by a seemingly endless succession of lurid motion pictures, comic strips, and missionary-in-the-pot cartoons in the *New Yorker* and the *Saturday Evening Post*. Except for *Trader Horn,* Metro-Goldwyn-Mayer's extravaganza produced between 1927 and 1931, none of the African features was filmed on location, and none mirrored any genuine relationship between the United States and Africa. The popularity of some of these pictures, however, requires brief mention of them.

Several silent matinee serials—*With Stanley in Africa* in 1922, the *Green Goddess* in 1923—ran absent-mindedly around a jungle setting. *Stanley and Livingstone,* a major Twentieth Century-Fox production in 1939, contained some distant outdoor scenic footage shot on location in Kenya under the direction of A. J. Klein. Throughout the 1920s and 1930s, of course, there were the *Tarzan* potboilers, loosely based on Edgar Rice Burroughs' fantastic plots and filmed on Hollywood back lots, first by a series of independents beginning in 1918. Universal Film Manufacturing Company was the first major production company to film a Tarzan episode, in 1928. In 1932 both Paramount and M-G-M made Tarzan pictures, and in 1933 Sol Lesser began his series of Tarzan films. Far and away the most popular and profitable of the Tarzan movies were M-G-M's, featuring Johnny Weismuller, Maureen O'Sullivan, and stock shots filmed on location in British East Africa. Van Dyke had filmed thousands of feet of distance shots for *Trader Horn,* and M-G-M decided to cash in on the extra footage in the form of Tarzan movies, directed by Van Dyke. The *Trader Horn* scenes appeared as scenic intercuts—the same scenes, in fact—in each subsequent Tarzan epic. M-G-M cheerfully sold stock shots from its African footage to competitors, at the regal price of ten dollars per foot.[29]

After twenty-three Tarzan novels, all of them elaborations of the 1912 original, and sixteen movies, the character Tarzan was well established by 1940. A syndicated comic strip based on the novels appeared in 1929; drawn by Hal Foster, it was the first modern illustrative strip. All this material—a mishmash portraying mortal combat with various beasts; comical chimpanzees; savage, simple-minded "natives"; and a tree-swinging, speed-swimming Tarzan who could outsmart any ivory poacher or foreign agent—presented "Africa" to millions of Americans.[30]

In 1929 the *New Orleans Times-Picayune* stated that a national election might give Tarzan as many votes for President as Herbert Hoover. The films were box-office gold, the books were a top item even in Montgomery Ward's scanty national line of books in the 1920s, and Tarzan songs, gags, and skits were collegiate favorites. One nine-year-old New Yorker, reading about the Field Museum's proposed 1934 West African expedition, urged his services upon the museum; after all, he could "climb trees and vines the same as Tarzan."[31]

By the late 1920s American film producers were writing directly to consuls in Africa for factual information. And well they might—there was little enough of it at home. As late as 1936 the noted missionary Emory Ross considered it perfectly reasonable that Americans should think of Africa as "mysterious," so incomplete was available knowledge. Americans seemed particularly weak in African geography. A Nigerian colonial traveling in the United States was somewhat startled when a "prominent professor" asked him to look up a friend living "just south of you near Capetown!" The trade commissioner for South Africa in the United States was "surprised" every time an American businessman asked him for information on Algiers, the Belgian Congo, or Mauretius.[32]

This geographical ignorance is less surprising when one considers how difficult it was to obtain the information that would have corrected it. Persons planning overland trips in Africa wrote an "endless number of letters and inquiries," after which they might lament that "Africa was still the 'Dark Continent!' " The director of the Swarthmore College Expedition of 1925 to study an eclipse off the coast of Kenya could find "absolutely nothing" about the area. J. Russell Smith, professor of economic geography at Columbia and the author of several geography texts, wrote in 1929 for climatic information to the consul at Lagos. Smith complained that in the United States material was "so meagre that the books are very inadequate."[33]

Most American geographies and maps were indeed very poor. Many schoolbooks and texts contained only brief and superficial treatments of sub-Saharan Africa, and even within that brief compass retained some outdated spellings. At least one reference work gave a population figure for Africa based on a guess made by Stanley before 1881.[34]

Although the continent held no enormous geographical mysteries by the end of World War I, American travelers often encountered localities that had "never been mapped in detail." Hubbard wrote to the consul at Lourenço Marques in 1924 that he was lost somewhere in Southern Rhodesia; his map failed to show a river he was supposed to locate. Maps used by Wilfrid D. Hambly, a pioneer African ethnologist for Chicago's Field Museum, contained disconcertingly large blank spaces. Writers had to designate locations for their readers by describing the relation of those points to obvious landmarks. Van Dyke grumbled in 1931 that there was "no such thing" as a reliable American map of Africa.[35]

American atlases were of little help. Many supplied nothing more on Africa than simplified physical and political maps of the entire continent. Firms like Rand McNally and C. S. Hammond corresponded directly with consuls in Africa for local statistics and spellings, but the final product often contained little information. A simple colored outline map of Africa by C. S. Hammond was in wide use in atlases published in the interwar period; it appeared in Funk & Wagnalls' *Atlas of the World* in 1923, in the 1926 *Literary Digest Atlas of the World,* and in Hammond's own *Our Planet: The Blue Book of Maps* published in 1935. The Williams Engraving Company of New York produced a clear, more detailed set of African maps in the 1920s for geography texts, but one of the few American maps of real use to African travelers and scholars was that published in 1935 by the National Geographic Society—detailed, precisely accurate, and beautifully produced.[36]

Serious students and travelers relied heavily on European maps. German atlases, the finest in the world, graced college reading rooms. Colonial maps were available from local governments, colonial automobile clubs, and American consuls. Van Dyke used the "very accurate" maps and surveys of the Royal Geographical Society. British and German steamship lines offered good regional maps in their African guidebooks. The 1934 African geography by the British scholar Walter Fitzgerald was a recognized standard. An American geographer found in 1923 that the best study of Angola was German, and Carveth Wells, planning his assault on the Ruwenzori in 1929 relied on the directions in the Duke of the Abruzzi's 1906 account.[37]

Amid what books there were on Africa, the American student was often confused. Each "had a different tale to tell," and collectively they were dumb on a thousand details. Was Africa the land of jungles, or was it not? An African library, like Scripture, would reflect in sacred authority whatever prejudices were carried to it. Homer L. Shantz, a Department of Agriculture botanist who conducted extensive field research in Africa, was joint author of what should have been regarded as the definitive work on jungles as early as 1923. The tropical rain forest was "not as extensive as one might suppose"; it covered but 7.8 per cent of the total area of the continent, confined to parts of the Belgian Congo, French Equatorial Africa, and the Guinea Coast. Many leading geographers agreed, and travelers' articles often confirmed the scarcity of "jungles" in large sections of Africa; in three years of capturing animals in Rhodesia, for example, the Hubbards never saw a jungle.[38]

Yet other geographers emphasized the forest covering when discussing Africa. J. Russell Smith referred to the interior as "this unhealthful tropical jungle," and the *Wonder Book* volume on African animals described the terrain around Nairobi as "essentially a mixture of jungle and plains, wild and untamed." *Van Loon's Geography* spoke of "the lightless tropical forest which has put its dreadful stamp upon the whole African civilization." R. H. Whitbeck and V. C. Finch divided Africa into "vast inhospitable deserts" and "sweltering jungles," and Parker T. Moon referred to Central Africa in his notable study of empires as "an equatorial land of drenching rains, dense jungles" and "tropical fevers."[39]

As many travelers ignored the parklands as spoke of them. Carl Akeley wrote of "the great mysterious jungle," and explorer E. A. Powell prowled, pen in hand, through "the mysterious black forest of the Congo." Never was a theme more congenial to the literary imagination. Joseph Conrad's characters wilted in a black, damp, silent forest where lurked nameless terrors. A biographer of Stanley evoked the "gloomy walls on either bank" as his hero proceeded down a stream, "black depths which the eye cannot penetrate." And the indomitable *African Queen* maneuvered its readers through "a wild tangle of trees of nightmare shape."[40]

There was a fascination about the image of Africa as the "Dark Continent" that did not owe its influence to novelists alone. Americans were, in the words of a writer in 1923, "in the habit of thinking of Africa as the great Dark Continent." It was a habit that was reinforced at every turn. "You can predispose the world to any desired thrill," observed an explorer in 1927, "by suitable advance publicity."[41]

Americans, then, arrived on the coasts of Africa ready to believe anything, and the coasts did not disappoint them. Their first impressions of tropical Africa were almost invariably bad — so bad that many early-day travelers never returned for a second look. The uninviting nature of the coastline had fended off large-scale penetration of the interior until Africa became the last continent to retain sizable regions unexplored by westerners. The West Coast in particular had earned a nasty reputation, which neither casual travelers nor long-term European residents did much to correct in the interwar years.

The oppressive heat was often the first and most unpleasant aspect of the continent to strike American visitors. The climate along the coast had not changed from the prewar days when the river port of Jebba, Nigeria, was described as "like living in a Turkish bath." To the author of *Trader Horn,* the African coast in 1928 was still "the White mans [sic] Grave." Dropping down the East Coast in 1929 on his way to produce a much-publicized sound movie of African wildlife under the auspices of the Colorado African Expedition, Paul

D. Hoefler was so afflicted by hot winds coming off the land that his entire supply of wing collars melted in the course of the evening's dancing.[42]

The climate of some regions of equatorial Africa was traditionally regarded as "none too healthy a place for the white man," even by such a robust white man as Theodore Roosevelt, who was just passing through. Exposure of the uncovered head to the vertical rays of the equatorial sun was considered a fatal error. The topee—the venerated pith helmet—was standard equipment, and colonial officials warned newcomers to wear it at all times between 8 A.M. and 4 P.M. Medical technology had of course improved since the slave-trade days, but travelers did not feel that science could provide infallible protection against all the effects of a tropical climate. Contemporaries believed that remaining in the humid regions for a few weeks was an ordeal and that living in them could permanently impair the health. American elementary-school geography books flatly declared that the white race could not live for long periods in tropical Africa. A University of California political scientist stated that physical labor in the tropics was "fatal to the white man." The entire machinery of government and economic exploitation, therefore, had to be supported by a "servile native population" working under an imported "ruling class." The crown agents for Nyasaland, hardly witnesses who could be accused of trying to discourage interest in the territory, warned of the climatic perils in a semi-official document issued in 1922: "Nyasaland cannot be said to be altogether a healthy country for Europeans. . . . The average European not only feels the need of alcoholic stimulant, but experience shows that he cannot maintain his efficiency without recuperating his health every few years in a temperate climate."[43]

"Africa," observed an exasperated Van Dyke, "is the bug's paradise." Their variety, their number, and their aggressive habits appalled the uninitiated. Skins itched at C. S. Forester's account of an attack of river flies assaulting the heroic pair on The African Queen; for those on the spot, more than itching was involved. R. L. Garner, an American animal collector living in the French Congo, was resigned to turning over his windowless shack to periodic invasions of driver ants, consoling himself that the other insect pests were cleaned out in the process. Garner was remarkably adept at making the best of a bad thing. He also reconciled himself to the tsetse fly on the assumption that only one bite in "a great number of times" brought the dreaded sleeping sickness. The tsetse fly was indeed a menace. Vast tracts of Africa, not otherwise made uninhabitable by the "fever-laden jungle," were still beyond the field of white endeavor because of the fly, whose sting infected and destroyed every large mammal within its range. Protection for whites was not impossible, but without horses, cattle, and African men there would be no one to work for them.[44]

Besides sleeping sickness, the list of diseases endemic to the tropics, or to which white men were particularly susceptible while living in them, was forbiddingly long. It included dysentery, beriberi, tetanus, malaria, leprosy, typhoid fever, syphilis, yellow fever, and the bubonic plague. A light case of malaria seemed unavoidable. Sir Harry Johnston admitted that the beauties of Uganda, a land he had first opened to the world, were spoiled by "an infinity of diseases." The party of Americans traveling through East Africa filming the movie version of *Trader Horn* in 1930 were incapacitated for days and weeks by malaria and dysentery; the picture's star, Edwina Booth, later died of what she insisted to the end was a mysterious African malady. Many Americans living alone for protracted periods were in genuine peril during epidemics; without medical or dental attention, the occasional infection could prove fatal, particularly to children. American consuls took furious precautions to protect themselves, requesting special funds for "disinfection" of their quarters, but they, too, had periodic bouts with fever.[45]

Most dread of all diseases was yellow fever, endemic to West Africa, a deadly disease for which previous infection provided the only immunity. A violent and painful affliction, it struck suddenly. A few fresh cases were enough to terrorize the foreign community. American consuls were quick to note every case. Colonial officials, however, were not eager to have every case reported, and attempted to prevent news of outbreaks from being circulated in the white community.[46]

At times the crowded and unsanitary native quarters in colonial African towns were breeding grounds for that medieval nightmare, the plague. Some Americans adjusted to conditions in Africa quickly. The indomitable Reed Paige

Clark in Loanda returned a dispatch in 1921 that read simply: "Send by mail form #225A. Bubonic plague abating." Other consuls, less nonchalant, reported cases of plague from many points in Africa throughout the interwar period. The region around Lagos suffered a serious outbreak in 1926, which raged among the native population for several years. In 1928 the Lagos Infectious Diseases Hospital reported 399 cases of plague—and only three recoveries.[47]

As for the African jungle, it could overwhelm even the acclimatized traveler or resident. From outside, its miles and miles of sameness could become tiresome. "Among travelers on the Congo River steamers the 'monotony' of the forest is proverbial." From within, the jungle could be terrifying, especially at night. A lover of Africa like the naturalist Delia Akeley wrote from a camp in the Congo that "the solid wall of trees surrounding the pitiful little clearings where we camped changed to prison walls." Joseph Conrad's famous lines might well have been describing the apprehensions of many Americans as they forged up an African river or trail for the first time: "We penetrated deeper and deeper into the heart of darkness."[48]

A sojourn of any length in these regions could produce feelings of desperation. American missionaries, traders, and colonial officers not infrequently found themselves alone for long stretches of time. This was particularly true in the equatorial regions under the French flag, areas with sparse European populations where a colonial officer was separated by hundreds of miles from his nearest colleague. Writers spoke of "the horrors of solitude in the forest." Whites in the interior lived for the mail and cherished their phonographs as a link with the world they had left behind. The gramophone, wrote one American missionary, "is a kind of hero of my little piece —a kind of David with five tunes to do battle with nostalgia."[49]

Over large parts of Africa the postal service proved rather a weak reed. Hambly estimated in 1929 that it would take eight to ten weeks for a letter from his camp in Angola to reach his superiors at the Field Museum. Mail service between the United States and coastal cities in Africa was in itself amazingly slow, but even in the late 1930s, surface communication between the coast and parts of the interior was impossible except by foot. Consuls were seriously hampered in their work by a mail service that delivered many departmental instructions and inquiries long after the fact. Business correspondents in the United States complained of delays of six months on inquiries, and suggested that perhaps American consuls were diddling away on taxpayers' time. Consuls blamed the mail service, which Consul Clark told the American Telephone and Telegraph Company was "poor." Telegram service, especially to Portuguese territories, was worse. Sent to consuls in Angola, telegrams went through Lisbon, where they were consigned to the vagaries of the Portuguese mail service. Those that finally reached Loanda were "garbled or in some way mixed up."[50]

Climate and disease were sometimes hazards, but for the person who did not diligently search it out, there was little danger from either animals or "natives." It was always possible, of course, to disregard the carnivores in their own habitat, which was carrying insouciance too far. When three American Boy Scouts won a trip to Africa with Martin Johnson in a national contest, the photographer arranged for the boys to get all kinds of thrilling game pictures. Once he allowed them to camp out with a truck in the midst of lion country, with a tripod camera and flash equipment, to snap any passing lions. Morning found seven lions climbing over the truck, chewing up the camera and gnawing on the tires. The boys were huddled together in the wire-cage body of the truck, not even trying to look brave. The camera-chewing lions were an exception; animals were usually no threat. One American traveler dryly observed in 1930 that "in the course of an ordinary African journey, . . . there is no more danger from animals than there is from being hit by a stray meteor."[51]

As for the "hostile savages," there was even less danger from them than from the animals. The present-day reader may feel that some of the little inconveniences inflicted on the white community by their cooks and porters were of wider significance than mere stupidity. An English big-game hunter on safari near Lake Bangweulu in Northern Rhodesia, for instance, was served sheep-dip instead of mustard by his cook. Yet many Africans risked their lives to rescue white men who had blundered into some predicament, and physical attacks on white persons were an almost nonexistent sacrilege before World War II. Commented one writer in 1928: "So far as the native is concerned, the white visitor to the Dark Continent is amusingly safe. . . ."[52]

The main drawback to a life of African service was not so much the danger as the lack of it. Life was not only uncomfortable in some places, it was dull. In response to a cartoonist's inquiry for "odd facts" about life in Africa, A. D. Cameron, U.S. consul at Lourenço Marques in 1932, complained that "nothing particularly startling" had occurred in Mozambique since the time of Vasco de Gama. Cultural life was thin. Julian Huxley admitted that "anyone to whom music and the visual arts have much to say makes a real sacrifice in coming to the tropics." Difficult travel conditions and small potential audiences kept tropical African cities off the colonial theatrical circuits, and even the American movies, upon which local residents relied for entertainment, were silents "of an ancient vintage" long into the 1930s. The social whirl sometimes stalled for lack of personnel: the white community in Lagos, for instance, had to pass up an invitation to the World Bridge Olympics in 1932 because there were not enough players in town "to make up eight tables."[53]

The colonial system itself sometimes added afflictions to the boredom and the bites. British East Africa experienced a wild inflation after the First World War. Local businesses profiteered shamelessly. In 1920 a dozen eggs cost $1.30 in Nairobi, a pair of shoes $21.09, and a house that had rented for $19.47 a month before the war brought $64.89. Consul Stillman Eells estimated his bare monthly expenses at $279.34, and bare it was, excluding recreation, clothing, transportation, and medical costs.[54]

Window screens in the British colonies were nonexistent, refrigerators were rare, and electrical service was limited to the largest cities. In the Belgian Congo there was not a single refrigerator in 1930. In Portuguese Africa the difficulties of maladministration were added to the repulsive climate in some parts and the primitive conditions throughout. Even before the Depression destroyed their feeble economies, Portuguese colonies had suffered from currency systems based almost entirely on wishful thinking. Daniel Streeter noted drolly that the chief point of interest in Lourenço Marques was the currency: "It fluctuated so rapidly that every time you changed a dollar into escudos you owed yourself money." The Portuguese also burdened Protestant missionaries, most of whom were Americans, with discriminatory educational requirements that the clerics believed were designed to discourage their work. During one of its frequent tariff disputes with the Union of South Africa, Portuguese East Africa levied a residence tax on all foreigners; its purpose was to harass the British, but Americans suffered as well.[55]

Life anywhere in tropical Africa, then, was not an unmixed delight; in some places it was virtually impossible. On a flight over Africa for the American Geographical Society in the winter of 1937–1938, Richard U. Light meditated somewhat fancifully on the one-thousand-mile Limpopo River far below him:

> Above regions like this the airplane fails to acquaint one with the full nature of one's surroundings. The Limpopo appears a lazy stream, it is true; but who can interpret from this the buzzing mosquitos, the bites and itches, the sweaty heat, the lurking saurians, or the utter hopelessness of its isolation? Conjure up a shudder if you can: this is a river that, from one end to the other, is known by fewer than half a dozen living men.[56]

Hazards notwithstanding, the attractions of Africa lured many Americans. Returning travelers again spent huge sums on transportation. Even some who did not find it particularly beautiful were nonetheless attracted. "Although Africa is harsh and ugly, with very few places of real scenic beauty, there is a subtle appeal which draws the traveler back to it again and again," wrote May Mott-Smith. In commercial fields, many Americans in Africa could have earned an equally good salary in the United States. Missionaries, completing the home furlough permitted after five years in the field, boarded their children and returned to Africa, often displaying a willingness only partially explained by a passion for souls. And despite their complaints, many consuls enjoyed their African service.[57]

The paradox is apparent only. Even the inhospitable zones offered certain compensations for whites, and in the regions of middle Africa not covered with fever-inducing jungles, life could be delightful. On the East Coast, the journey itself from the coast to the temperate Highlands was an attraction. From Mombassa up into the Highlands to Nairobi, rail passengers traveled through a pleasant countryside teeming with herds of game. The Kenya and Uganda Company clung to Victorian woodburners with high stacks and screaming English whistles, and it was common for a trip to include a derailment or two and a half-dozen unscheduled stops. Yet not a newcomer failed to be impressed by the landscape and the animals. The company catered to especially prestigious clients by fitting the engine fender with a bench, from which the view was not obstructed by smoke, sparks, and the cars ahead.[58]

Some places in Africa were among the most beautiful on earth. Favorite scenes included the broad savannas of British East Africa, dotted with baobab and acacia and covered by a blanket of Thomson's gazelles; the thundering Victoria Falls; Kilimanjaro; the snow-capped Ruwenzori, reputed to be Ptolemy's "Mountains of the Moon." The brilliantly blue sky was reflected everywhere by lakes and pools; so completely did they seem to shimmer in the color of the sky that going "into the Blue" was a local term for traveling into the backcountry. And along both coasts, the fresh sea breeze rolled a gentle surf against white sands and old stone forts.[59]

One of the great charms, the one almost irresistible attraction in colonial Africa, however, was not the beauty of the scenery but the cheapness of the labor. Jean Kenyon Mackenzie, a Presbyterian missionary in West Africa whose articles reached a far broader public than was usually the case for missionaries, stated openly that she lived in "luxury" in a beautiful country tended by "the wonderful servants of the white man." When the necessity arose to leave her permanent station and go on circuit, the lady was ported from village to village in a sedan chair, living handsomely on the food and labor obtained in exchange for an occasional fishhook. A domestic servant as a routine feature in more modest homes in the United States had disappeared by the early 1920s, as the supply of farm girls and Irish lassies dwindled. A maid in an American home was becoming an accouterment of wealth, and only persons of legendary riches had real butlers. The newly arrived American in Africa, however, discovered almost at once that he could command a platoon of retainers beyond the means of a corporation president back home.[60]

The Africans, hungry for the artifacts of an alien and novel civilization, obliged to obtain cash for a variety of taxes, and forced from the land or game fields by new laws, crowded the labor market of every colony. Men were available in such numbers and at such low wages that raw materials gathered by their hands in Africa were cheaper when sold in faraway Western ports than the same resources produced in the importing country itself. Of far more consequence to the average white resident or tourist, however, was how readily the local economics of colonialism could be translated into a regal style of life. For few white men were so poor that they could not employ a "boy" or two; all African men under any sort of white supervision were called "boys," and the term was used almost unexceptionally. Everyone had servants, noted one amazed American: "They get under foot, in your hair, and between your teeth."[61]

Martin and Osa Johnson abandoned their nickelodeon in Independence, Kansas, for a life of adventure. On their first endeavor, a low-budget motion-picture expedition to Melanesia, they traveled light and worked hard. "And then," said Osa, "we went to Africa." They had not been in Nairobi an hour when they were besieged by applications from prospective servants. Despite their limited funds, in 1921 the Johnsons' life of drudgery was over. Their first, admittedly modest, household consisted of seven men and a child, who carried Mrs. Johnson's market basket for her.[62]

The disabilities of a hot climate were more easily endured when one was fanned by one man, sponged with cool water by a second, and handed an iced drink by a third. The absence of modern sanitary facilities was no more annoying to a colonial than to a duke, who also had a servant to carry out the waste. The discomforts of a high stiff collar were somewhat alleviated by a man who unobtrusively slipped up from behind and snapped a fresh one in place at fixed intervals during the evening. The roads were frightful, but boys were in plentiful supply to wash the dust or mud off the car. There were no telephones, but someone could always run across town or over to the next farm with a note.

"That Africa requires and affords an indefinite number of servants, personal and general, I well knew," said the wife of naturalist Carl E. Akeley in 1926.* Indeed, so well did she and everybody else know it that permanent residents some-

---

* Carl Akeley had two wives, Delia J. and Mary L. Jobe, both of whom wrote numerous articles in Africa during the 1920s. He was married to Mary at the time of his death in 1926.

times took their princely staffs for granted. While lamenting in 1920 the wretchedness of his living allowance, Consul Eells at Nairobi blandly admitted that it allowed him to maintain seven personal servants. A fixed wage scale for servants was rare, and employers paid as little as the market would bear. Osa Johnson recalled that on arriving in Nairobi she could hire ten servants for the wages of one in the United States. Her statement is tinged with noblesse oblige, for it suggests that Mrs. Johnson paid her Africans an unnecessarily high wage. Fully sixteen years later, for instance, trained domestic servants in the Gold Coast, a colony that provided considerable opportunity for profitable native agriculture, received the equivalent of $12.50 a month.[63]

Service in the home required training, both in domestic sciences and in courtly deference. When their servants took to wearing the *konza,* "the flowing, nightshirt-like garment that is the livery of Kenya Colony," American residents noted it with lordly pride. The wife of the last U.S. consul at Boma recalled boastfully that her chief Congolese steward, or "head boy," had "surpassed many a Park Lane knee-breeched doorman."[64]

Outside the home, the casual labor required by most transient Americans required little or no skill, and if there did happen to be some kind of wage scale, it never lasted for very long. After disembarking on the Lagos roadstead in 1930, journalist May Mott-Smith was picked up and carried to the Bonanza Hotel by a white gentleman in a passing Ford roadster, who simply commandeered five black men on the spot to carry her baggage. In those instances where some pay was required for unskilled labor, it was so trivial that it encouraged projects on a grand scale. Until 1925 the American consulate at Nairobi found it cheaper to maintain a "Government ricksha" and three full-time "boys" to pull it than to buy a car.[65]

If life indoors seemed regal to the American, on the safari it was positively Byzantine. It was in the field that the full potential of the African labor economy was realized. "The natives are paid so little," noted James L. Clark of the American Museum in 1928, "that sometimes you permit yourself to hire a host of personal servants, or 'boys' as they are called." Insofar as wages were concerned, animal collector Garner was correct when he noted in 1920 that the worldwide rise in the cost of living had "left Central Africa untouched." His safari men received fifteen francs a month,* plus seven and one-half francs in rations.[66]

Martha Miller Bliven, who had acquired a taste for Africa as Carl Akeley's secretary, hired sixty men in French Equatorial Africa in the mid-1920s to carry loads of fifty-five pounds apiece for fifty cents each a month, or two cents a day for periods of less than one month; each man had to provide his own food and "looked out for himself." The manager of the Straus West African Expedition for the Field Museum in 1934 paid two men thirty-six francs to tend the camp in Senegal for twelve days. In British East Africa Stewart Edward White, who established an honored reputation both in Africa and in the United States as an explorer and writer, paid fifty-four men in the early 1920s a total of the equivalent of $250 a month. These wages must have seemed munificent to Martin Johnson, who sometimes paid his porters only in rations. "Accustomed to a state of semistarvation, they were happy to be assured a daily ration of two small dried fish and half a dozen sweet potatoes," Johnson explained. For nothing more strenuous than photographing lions, Johnson required fourteen servants. So elaborate did the staff become that Osa was forced to divide her time between standing guard over Martin with a double-barreled elephant rifle and seeing that the safari servants kept "the home fires burning at dinner time." Looking back over her years in Africa, Osa recalled that on "so many occasions," she had been grateful for their "small army of well-trained blacks."[67]

Under these circumstances it should not be surprising that Americans, like Pharaoh, found regiments cheaper than wheels. During his big-game hunt in Kenya in 1934, Ernest Hemingway learned that porters were cheaper than gasoline; he was immediately tempted to leave the truck and take a safari of porters on a side trip. Long after automobiles were available, Americans still indulged their childhood fancies and hired long lines of porters to tramp behind them on the hunt. Mr. and Mrs. Frederick Dalziel required 170 "servants" for their party of five whites on a trek over the plains

---

* It is difficult to state with precision the value of these sums in American currency; Garner, like many authors, is impossibly vague about what years he refers to, and the French franc fluctuated in value throughout the early 1920s. In 1916 it was worth just over nineteen cents.

of Tanganyika in 1922. Since his boyhood visit with Stanley, E. A. Powell had dreamed of visiting Ujiji, the site of the great explorer's historic meeting with Livingstone; when the opportunity came, in the early 1920s, he insisted on going "as Stanley did, in a *machilla,* a hammock slung from a pole and borne by relays of sweating porters."[68]

Many white persons, from the wives of French officers to American missionaries, were ported or pulled about on black shoulders in a variety of sedan chairs, hammocks, and carts. One vehicle popular among missionaries was a "chair-cart." "In the shafts of this little vehicle, fore and aft," observed the wife of a geologist in French Guinea, "there is a man to push and a man to pull." Whites would sometimes eschew the river steamboats and engage a dozen or four-teen men to paddle them upriver in a huge canoe, while they lounged beneath a thatched cover "with the ease of Cleo-patra on the Nile." The added speed, convenience, and re-liability of the automobile gradually caused many Americans, especially those who traveled regularly, to adopt the motor car for routine transportation; many safaris also used trucks to carry the baggage. But life in camp continued to be pleasurable on a scale unprecedented even for wealthy American sportsmen. "It is extraordinary," observed the wealthy Mrs. Dalziel on a lion hunt, "how comfortable these primitive savages can make the luxurious white man." Re-marked another American, on safari in French Equatorial Africa in 1927:

> In fact, it was camping *de luxe* compared with the 'rough-ing it' trips one takes in America. There were plenty of personal servants—boys of various ages and sizes and tribes—to wait upon us, to prepare warm baths in portable tubs, to clean boots, to keep the tents neat and to prepare and serve meals.[69]

On motorized safaris, it was the practice of the Africans to drive ahead of the white group and prepare camp. Carveth Wells, on a long publicity tour of East Africa in the late 1920s that later included a hike to the Ruwenzori snow line, drove his touring car into camp each night to find the tents neatly stretched, hot baths waiting for each white, and "boys" set-ting out dinner and the bar. George Eastman, the camera magnate who financed one of the American Museum's most lavish African expeditions in 1926, also returned to camp each evening with his party after the day's hunting to find a hot bath waiting—and a Scotch highball; soon everyone was once again "fresh as daisies for dinner." To W. S. Van Dyke, it seemed that the whites on safari did nothing for themselves; at night, the Africans even tucked the mosquito netting around each bed. Said Van Dyke: "It is the camp boys of Africa that really keep the whites alive."[70]

Labor was so cheap that Americans could hire African servants to wait on their pets. Delia Akeley hired a nine-year-old Swahili in Nairobi in 1926, bought him a khaki uniform and a red fez, and made him "companion and valet" to her pet monkey. Woefully low wages for the black man in Africa remained in effect throughout the interwar period. Thirteen years after Mrs. Akeley hired her monkey's companion—on the eve of the ruin of the colonial system—a geologist wishing to photograph volcanoes in the Belgian Congo could still hire three Africans to assist him for almost nothing. As he explained in an article in the *National Geographic:*

> But when one realizes how truly comfortable and luxurious it feels to go around with never less than three porters—one for the camera, one for the tripod, and the third as a spare—a fresh outlook is gained. Then this part of Africa seems no longer such a backward place, and the advantages of civilization become less obvious.[71]

For the vast majority of Americans touring and visiting in colonial Africa, their pleasure at being surrounded by Africans did not represent any real interest in the blacks themselves or in their future. Delia Akeley prided herself on how well she got along in Africa not knowing a single word of any African language. "She maintains," observed a writer for *St. Nicholas* in 1930, "that an intelligent sign language and a smile never fail one, even in the most uncivilized regions of Africa." To most Americans, "tribal" distinctions were of no concern beyond the fact that it was commonly thought best on safari to mix men from several different language groups (contemporaneously called "tribes") in order to avoid any possible concerted action against the white leaders. Stewart Edward White made it a fixed rule to "mix in four or five tribes," because, as he put it, "no one tribe will help another." Wynant Hubbard, whose unsuccessful efforts to corner the wild-animal market had made him an expert on all things African, was appalled to hear of a missionary preaching racial equality. "The Negro *in Africa,*" he affirmed loftily in the *Nation,* "occupies at present a very distinct place. And most certainly that place is not a place of equality on earth with the white man." Writing in *Harper's* in 1934 about a flight from Cape Town to Cairo, one author stated that "at either terminus the white man, Aryan or Semite, dominates even when he is outnumbered; in between he is merely master."[72]

Some Americans had a genuine concern for the "natives' " welfare, which, of course, is not the same as an interest in them as people. Regardless of his sympathies, however, every American in colonial Africa was made aware of his unassailable position in a rigid social structure. To be white was to rule. And most Americans were delighted with their regal status in African life. Osa Johnson described the pleasures of camp life to the readers of *Good Housekeeping* in 1924, and how anxious she was to return to Africa, where she could again "feel myself queen of all I survey . . . with a tatterdemalion retinue of negro servants for attendants." "In a sense," exulted Martin Johnson, "we were King and Queen in our own right."[73]

In *Green Hills of Africa,* supposedly a true story, Hemingway encountered an Austrian expatriate living in Kenya as a farm manager. Because he had fought on the German side in East Africa during the war, his estate had been confiscated, and he had been ruined. Yet he remained in Africa, and was glad to explain his reason:

> Then, too, in reality, I am king here. It is very pleasant. Waking in the morning I extend one foot and the boy places the sock on it. When I am ready I extend the other foot and he adjusts the other sock. I step from under the mosquito bar into my drawers which are held for me. Don't you think that is very marvelous?[74]

"Bwana" was the usual title of address in this arrangement so full of charms to Americans newly introduced unto empyrean heights. This term was in ways more prestigious than "Your Majesty," for even reigning African monarchs apologized to U.S. consuls for imagined social slights.

"Bwana," as hackneyed as it was to become, recognized and perpetrated in a single word the deference due an accident of birth, and it was insisted upon and its use defended with ardor. The blacks were quick to utter it, particularly for newcomers like Daniel Streeter: " 'What's this "bwana" stuff,' I interrupted. 'It means worshipful master,' said Gregg. 'He's hired,' I said."[75]

American tourists and residents alike were pleased and grateful to be included in colonial society. They were delighted by the British, who in their turn were officially and privately hospitable and gracious. The number of American tourists and sportsmen who visited French colonies was very much smaller, but relations were cordial with the French, despite cultural differences and the laxity of French colonial social standards, which offended a few Americans. The Belgians were civil, if sometimes suspicious of journalists; their national sensibilities had not recovered fully from the opprobrium drawn upon them by King Leopold II and the "Red Rubber of the Congo." The enormity of the Congo and the scarcity of Belgians to administer it made it possible to travel extensively in the colony without encountering any Belgians at all. Except in Léopoldville, there was little "society," in the sense that there was throughout the British, and to a lesser extent, the French colonies. Americans did not admire the Portuguese, whose administration they regarded as oppressive, petty, and incompetent.

Into whatever colonial society Americans were introduced, however, they were quick to learn that colonial rule rested on racial prestige, not armed power. Prestige, like fear, is an unreasoning and unquestioning reaction, dependent for its controlling power on the acceptance of a hypothesis, which may or may not be true, but which all the concerned parties must accept as true. In colonial Africa this hypothesis stated that it was the eternal and inevitable order of things that the white race should rule, however indirectly, and that the black race should obey, in however royal a capacity.

The maintenance of authority based on this hypothesis required the tacit acquiescence of the masses of the population, which could be encouraged by the ceremonial displays of power so congenial to the European, and by instant retribution for infractions. Acquiescence required as well the active cooperation of persons holding important positions in the indigenous political order, a cooperation that the British, above all nationals, were adept at securing in a variety of ways. But most of all, colonial authority depended upon the close cooperation of the members of the ruling class in perpetrating the myth of their own superiority.

These general truths were most easily demonstrated in British colonies, where they seemed to receive their most resolute application. The other imperial powers were more practical, and to that degree less fascinating to Americans, who continued to wonder at British muddling through. The French colonial budgets were heaviest in the military columns, and Belgian and Portuguese officials often relied directly on terror. In British Africa, however, the regions to which Americans most often turned their interest, rule seemed, to many travelers, to rest more gently on the illusion of a rigidly ordered and absolute hierarchy of human relations, an illusion that allowed no betrayals. The French, with their *tirailleurs,* could occasionally marry native women and forget to shave. The British could not, although there was no reason to suppose, even at the time, that clandestine interracial liaisons were less frequent among the British than among any other colonial ruling classes. The system that provided them comfort and reward and fulfilled their wildest aspirations for their country required that the British live naturally in Africa, at least on the surface, as though their presence there was unexceptional, as though they lived in England.

Critics of this system, including an occasional Englishman, pointed out that it contained illogical elements. The body of similar opinion has swelled greatly in recent years, but long before World War II Parker T. Moon, a leading American student of international relations, wished to free the study of imperial systems from what he termed "a fog of mid-Victorian misinformation, accumulated in the form of prejudice and venerable sentiment." British colonial experts were able to admit later that the colonial empire had been "too long and too deeply rooted in the traditions of a bygone age. . . ."[76]

There was indeed a self-consciously old-fashioned element in British colonial life. Colonials acted upon interpretations of what constituted the best arrangement of the social order that had long since been challenged successfully at home. The empire had reached its protracted zenith in the great queen-empress's last years, and a Victorian aura pervaded the libraries and clubs of the empire under her son and grandsons. Even a colonial far removed from the centers of power could thrill with the heroine of *The African Queen* to "all the glamour and romance of imperial dominion." In the heart of hearts of every Britisher in Africa there dwelt the prideful knowledge that they and their countrymen ruled so much of the Dark Continent, and a quarter of the globe besides, because the British did not depend so heavily upon armed force as upon adhering rigorously to a myriad of little conventions, regardless of where they might be. Great Britain is the only country in the world that has made a tradition of her soldiers fainting on dress parade.[77]

For the same lordly reason that they insisted upon crystal and fresh linen every evening, Englishmen in the colonies, ordinarily proud of their national sense of fair play, would persevere in an unjust course rather than appear ridiculous before blacks. Llewelyn Powys, a Kenya settler whose articles on life in that colony appeared regularly in the American press, once confiscated the goats of a "witch doctor," whom he admitted to be legally in the right, and lashed him down a path, because the man had made Powys look bad in front of other men. "It had evidently come to a struggle between their superstitious dread of the witch doctor and my prestige as a white man."[78]

Into this little imperious world Americans plunged with a cooperative spirit. Educated Africans were not received socially. Expedition leaders took pains to insure that the safari porters were properly cowed. Stewart Edward White, on a pathfinding journey into the game fields of Tanganyika, stated that when a man was insubordinate his "usual procedure" was "to knock him down on the spot." Once, a case of "rank insubordination" occurred—a Wakamba refused to fetch water—when White was too ill to strike the man. White cowed the man by sheer "will force . . . much as one would compel a reluctant dog." When the man returned with the water, White had him beaten, and when he tried to run away, he was dragged back and fined the whole month's wages. James L. Clark knew the importance of gaining the ascendancy on a safari at the outset. "Once under way with such a party, the hunter must, in the beginning, be extremely uncompromising. Then is the time to impress upon his natives the fact that he is boss." For being drunk, W. S. Van Dyke humiliated his gun bearer, a member of the proud Masai, before the entire camp by threatening to cut off the man's ears and flog him forty lashes.* Seldom was it necessary, however, to strike or even to threaten an African. It was better, in fact, to avoid doing so, for retribution that was implied was far more effective in encouraging deference than actual force, which when unleashed might be exposed as more pomp than circumstance. What the modern reader would call "confrontation," in other words, rarely occurred.[79]

Most Americans were able to contribute to white prestige in Africa in more subtle ways than the exercise of brute force. The U.S. consul at Lagos, for example, warned American motion-picture distributors in 1934 against sending films to the district that "might discredit the white race in the eyes of the natives"; the majority of audiences in "British East," the consul at Nairobi declared grandly, were "refined and well-to-do people, and they appreciate high-class pictures." It was, in fact, the American consuls who contributed so much to the sustenance of white prestige.[80]

In all the colonies American consuls participated in official ceremonies, and there was a deliberately courtly air about many official functions in the colonies. At L'Eglise Léopoldville-Est in June, 1930, on the occasion of the forty-fifth anniversary of the founding of the Congo Free State, a "special place" in the front of the church was reserved for the consul of the United States. Prominent places on reviewing stands and platforms were reserved for American

* Sociological studies of African peoples, which might have shown how deeply they resented such treatment, were extremely rare in these years. Professor Charles W. Coulter undertook a long trip through South-Central Africa in 1929, partly to collect small fauna, partly to study native conditions. His conclusion, based on four hundred life histories, was that the Africans felt white people cared less for them than for their horses, and had less regard for their welfare. Unfortunately, Coulter's study was confined to regions with conditions radically different from those in areas most frequented by American travelers. Coulter, "Problems Arising from Industrialization of Native Life in Central Africa," *AJS* 40 (1935): 582–592. See Chapter 6 below for American reactions to the Africans.

consuls when a new Belgian governor arrived in Léopoldville in 1934, when a review was held on the anniversary of
King Albert's birthday in 1930, when the governor of Kenya
dedicated another war memorial in 1926. The consul at
Léopoldville was naturally invited to the select and prestigious reception given by the governor to celebrate the
marriage in 1930 of Princess Marie-Jose of Belgium to
Prince Umberto of Savoy, heir to the Italian throne. In the
round of exchanges, American consulates were hosts at
"formal receptions" on Independence Day, to which local
officials and the consular corps repaired in full regalia.[81]

Yet as exciting as this swirl of white gloves and plumed
helmets seemed to be, such official ceremonial was only a
small part of an American's life in Africa, even for a consul.
On every hand Americans in Africa actively supported the
less spectacular conventions of colonialism, which singly
reflected and collectively confirmed the illusion that tropical
Africa would forever be a white man's domain. Proper black
noncoms, waiters, headboys, and chauffeurs, ingratiating
beggars, pathetic mimics in cast-off European clothes, be-
mused pastoral chieftains, and shy wide-eyed village girls
played their roles in the imperial pageant—a kind of half-
hidden, almost silent background. Charles Burke Elliot, one
of America's eminent international lawyers, observed in
1919 that "the most liberal interpretation of the right of self-
determination cannot make it applicable to African savages." Few Americans who had been to Africa challenged
such statements in the interwar years, and many of them
added similar statements of their own to the rising chorus
of imperial praise.[82]

Tropical Africa, then, was a strange combination of menace and charm for Americans. There they experienced the
contradictions of discomforts and dinner by candlelight,
loneliness and scores of willing servants, white ants and
military march music, unavoidable malaria and unassailable
prestige. Most Americans found that the royal style of life
provided by cheap and docile labor and the pleasure of
membership in the highest society were compensations for
an uncomfortable climate. In the hospitable regions, the
attractiveness of life in Africa, where all the comforts of
Somerset were combined with armies of retainers and a
beautiful and unspoiled country, was almost irresistible.

three:
american commercial penetration of africa

Old 'Darkest Africa' is lightening fast. Its present commerce is relatively small, but a much more active future is promised as a result of the new transportation routes now being opened in all directions.'—J. Russell Smith (1925)

The last Te Deums had scarcely finished sounding at Franz Ferdinand's funeral when American businessmen began to appreciate the twin advantages of productivity and neutrality. The boom ushered in by the European war, once the early disruptions in wartime shipping were settled, must have seemed too good to be true. European competition shrank with every week the war continued, and the markets of the world clamored for American goods. With their factories turned to war production and their dwindling merchant fleets carrying supplies from the United States, the European powers could not hold even those colonial markets long bound to home industry by imperial preference. Africa, a market and treasure trove of unknown but tantalizing proportions, was suddenly vacated by European enterprise, and onto this unguarded vein pounced the Yankee claim jumper. American trade with Africa leaped from $47 million in 1914 to $325 million in 1920. And this, it was confidently stated, was only the beginning. Africa was no longer a continent of mystery; it had become, suddenly, "the Continent of opportunity."[2]

Africa had lured American businesssmen for decades; long before the Berlin Conference of 1884–1885, the United States government had become officially responsive to that sector of the business community that envisioned in tropical Africa heady possibilities of exploitation. The United States adopted, for Africa and for the rest of the colonized world, the refreshingly direct policy of demanding the "open door," by which America meant that her citizens should have the same commercial access into any European power's sphere of influence as that enjoyed by the citizens of that or any other power. From this policy the United States never wavered, and the American delegation to the Versailles Peace Conference of 1919 insisted upon the open door with a fervor strengthened by a now sacred tradition, by strong fears that with the war over the imperial powers would again clamp their colonial domains under exclusionary tariffs, and by the equally strong conviction that only America's intervention in the war had made possible the very victory the conference had been called to ratify. The Americans had their way: the omnibus peace treaties and the Convention of Saint-Germain-en-Laye provided that each member of the proposed new League of Nations would enjoy equality of commercial opportunity with every other League member in the new African mandates. Later, when the United States failed to join the League, the State Department busily set about securing the open-door privileges in the African mandates anyway, on the basis of America's contribution to the Allied victory, and by the mid-1920s the imperial powers had grudgingly granted these privileges in a complicated series of negotiations.

For the rest of the interwar period, America kept a watchful eye on the commercial policies of the imperial powers in tropical Africa. Concern for the open door remained an integral part of official American policy toward the region. Neither the urgent needs of European home economies for protection in the worldwide trade depression of the 1930s nor metropolitan strategic considerations that demanded colonial exchange and export controls on the eve of another European war discouraged the United States State Department from pressing inquiries on its African consuls as to whether or not the "Open-Door principle" was being "scrupulously maintained" in their districts.[3]

Nor was the effort of U.S. consuls in Africa in behalf of American business confined to merely watching that the open door was left ajar; they were eager that such an inviting portal should be put to use. In the months after the armistice, the consuls sent back encouraging reports on local markets. At Nairobi the new consulate was officially opened with an "At Home" on the Fourth of July, primarily to interest the local public in the "Commercial Library" of American trade manuals and catalogs. In the United States, the president of the American Manufacturers' Export Association set the tone for the 1920s when he demanded direct selling: follow the English example of getting orders locally in every market of the world, and the temporary gains of the war would become permanent. A New York steamship line, eager to start service to West Africa to carry the expected increase in trade, sent one of its ships on a trial run in 1919; the agents reported that American ships had "a wonderful opportunity to take over old business, and to build up new," in the unsettled conditions at the war's end. The American consul at Lourenço Marques was sufficiently enthused by these and similar indications of business acumen that he requested an extra clerk, since "considerable American shipping may reasonably be expected at this port from now on."[4]

Until the Great Depression, the United States government never slackened its efforts to stimulate American trade with Africa. The series of treaties guaranteeing the open door in Africa were jealously maintained, and the Department of Commerce was determined to see that no opportunity to encourage trade with Africa was wasted. Its Bureau of Foreign and Domestic Commerce was furiously active. It provided publicity material on African market possibilities; it sent out special agents to promote trade in places like Accra, capital of the Gold Coast Colony; and it published an extensive array of trade bulletins and optimistic articles in *Commerce Reports* urging American businessmen to get in on a good thing before the rush. By 1929 the bureau had a special fund of $106,000 for "Promoting Commerce, Africa." In that year Fred Morris Dearing, the American minister to Portugal, visited the Portuguese Empire in Africa in the interests of promoting trade; he pronounced Portuguese Africa to be "an almost unknown and undeveloped field for American effort." On the scene in Africa, consuls were indefatigable in their efforts to interest American companies in their local market—and to generate sales in the United States of African products; they dispatched a continual stream of wood chips, hide samples, and assorted unknown plants to Washington to be investigated for potential commercial value. In 1926 the enterprising consul in Nairobi went so far as to suggest that if zebra hide could be used to cover baseballs, "this country could furnish an inexhaustible and a cheap supply."[5]

All public and private American exertions to penetrate the African market, to transform the continent into a land of unlimited commercial opportunity proved, nevertheless, to be unavailing. In terms of total American or colonial foreign commerce, U.S. trade with tropical Africa in the interwar years remained negligible. At the end of World War I, the imperial tide washed back over Africa with renewed force, and American enterprise, with a few notable exceptions, was unable to stop it. American observers noted that European capital was pouring into Africa at a rate "unequaled" in history. The predictions of European Socialists and American businessmen that the war would shatter Europe's economic control of Africa proved unfounded. The European powers were determined in the 1920s to rebuild their devastated domestic economies on an imperial basis; in the 1930s they expended greater and greater efforts to secure independent and reliable sources of strategic raw materials. Commercial geographers in the United States were soon referring to Africa as "the Continent of European Exploitation," and writers were unabashedly suggesting that only if American investors recognized European primacy on the Dark Continent would there be "honor and profit for all in that vast kidney-shaped treasure house of material wealth. . . ."[6]

Where it flowed at all, therefore, American trade with tropical Africa flowed inevitably into imperial channels. The alluring black African markets did not materialize, except on a small scale in British West Africa and Uganda, where indirect rule and successful native agriculture created elite classes with purchasing power. Most American sales went to white colonial communities, a tiny market in terms of total American export figures. As it had been for decades before, most of America's African commerce throughout the interwar period was with the Union of South Africa.

American products that did find an African market were those of use to either the settlers, the government officers, or the administrators of exploitative economic systems: heavy machinery; petroleum; building materials like lumber and cement; a host of small, mass-produced household items; tobacco; motion pictures; sporting goods; arms for government troops; and, above all, automobiles and trucks. "Fords, Flit and flyswatters," declared the Yale historian Ulrich B. Phillips, "are America's contribution to Sudan comfort. . . ."[7]

One reason for America's failure to penetrate the African market in any substantial way was because the United States was not, but for a few products, dependent on Africa for the major part of its supply. Nor was the United States the continent's major customer for these few products. Palm oil, used in the manufacture of soap and in milling tin, was the staple item in American trade with Nigeria; spices, peanuts, cashews, plants, and cabinet woods sometimes formed a part of American-bound cargoes; manganese, used in making hardened steel, and cocoa came from the Gold Coast; and before the war scares of the late 1930s, the Belgian Congo was the source of much of the radium needed by American scientists. For a time, iron and copper ore from southern Central Africa was transshipped through Lourenço Marques to American ports, but the Depression ruined this trade—and Portuguese East Africa at the same time. The United States was not a customer for the Belgian Congo's rubber, for much of Kenya's expensive grades of coffee, or for Uganda cotton.

Throughout the interwar period, many Americans lamented the "insignificant part" played by the United States in the "economic regeneration of this vast continent." Only in the independent states of Africa—Liberia, the Union of South Africa, and Ethiopia, where a New York contractor built the Blue Nile Dam in the late 1920s—could any claim be made that the United States had been able to secure an economic foothold. In total tonnage, United States waterborne commerce in 1924 with Portuguese East Africa and the Gold Coast, the two colonies with which America carried on her greatest trade, was less than her trade with

Java. In 1927 American trade with all of East and South Africa was less than that with Uruguay, New Zealand, or the Lesser Antilles. In 1929, the last boom year of American foreign trade, all of Africa accounted for only 2.5 per cent of the total, and American trade boosters were gamely admitting that "the major economic interest in the United States in Africa lies in the future." The Bureau of Foreign and Domestic Commerce still insisted that reports on African trade prospects would be "keenly appreciated by forward-looking exporters in the United States." More disinterested counsel, however, declared tropical Africa to be "the part of the continent that yields least to commerce, and much of it affords little prospect of yielding much more in the near future." The "near future," unfortunately, brought almost complete collapse; by World War II American trade with Africa had not regained its low pre-Depression levels.[8]

Numerous obstacles were in the way of large-scale American economic development in Africa: imperial preference tariffs; the smallness of the real, as opposed to the potential, market; the market's unshakable preference, with a few exceptions, for imperial products; the distance between the United States and Africa. One of the most serious obstacles was the lack of adequate American flag shipping services to Africa. No commercial air traffic existed between the United States and Africa before World War II; passengers and freight reached Africa by ship, usually by way of Europe. The British and German steamship companies that monopolized the service between Europe and Africa were organized into "conference lines"—shipping cartels that set common rates and divided the trade among the members—which blandly discriminated against American freight. American shippers, or their intermediaries, were charged all the traffic would bear, which usually averaged between 25 and 30 per cent more than the rates on European goods. "Our matchless supplies of raw material," said one British expert on imperial economics, "must be jealously safeguarded from the insidious wiles of peaceful penetration." The United States, however, was not entirely without competitive resources of her own. Despite imperial and customs preferences, American exporters were in a position to export certain products of such obvious superiority that they were in demand even at high-tariff prices. And despite the shipping discriminations of the imperial powers, the United States could and did sail its own African lines.[9]

A long history of governmental encouragement and sub-sidizing of American merchant shipping had culminated in the Shipping Act of 1916, which created the United States Shipping Board and authorized it to build and operate a huge fleet of merchant ships either directly or under private lease or sale. The result was the largest shipbuilding pro-gram in history. Apparently convinced that the European war and, with it, America's new monopoly of the world's carrying trade would go on interminably, the board con-tracted for some 1,700 steel vessels, in addition to smaller, wooden ones, at a cost of nearly $3,250,000,000. The armi-stice of November, 1918, left the government heavily bur-dened with most of the ships and all of the bills, and the Shipping Board eagerly sought customers for hundreds of freighters in all shapes and sizes. Demand for the ships steadily declined, and after 1922 most of the board's mer-chant fleet was idle; hundreds of ships were junked and hundreds more were sold at a fraction of their cost (with payments deferred) or leased to American shipping lines on the charitable basis of two long-term, charter-purchase plans, which usually included generously subsidized oceanic mail contracts. In the early years of the interwar period, when hopes still ran high that American advances in African trade could be made permanent, the Shipping Board found willing agents to take over and service steamship lines to Africa. Such lines were expected to bring a double benefit; they would open a rich trade to American industry on a competitive basis, and they would unload a number of other-wise useless ships onto paying customers.[10]

The first of these enterprises, the A. H. Bull West African Line, began operations in 1921. It soon encountered a dis-couraging list of difficulties. The schedule of sailings, ports of call, and shipping rates was set by the board, which pro-vided the ships and subsidized their maintenance. The government schedule, based on the wildly enthusiastic pre-dictions of the company's agents who had taken a trial voyage down the West African coast on the freighter S.S. *Beatrice* in 1919, required one sailing per month between several American ports and most West African ports from

Senegal to lower Angola. Operation of the old-fashioned coal-burning freighters was costly even on the high seas, while each of the numerous stops along the West African coast extracted more money for salaries and for harbor and lighterage fees.

The West African Line, beset as it was on all sides by financial problems and government interference, received considerable encouragement from its potential customers, who were only too glad to be free from conference-line discrimination. The Pensacola Chamber of Commerce, for instance, declared itself "much interested" in the Bull service, which opened "practically virgin territory to our shippers," and enabled them to build up "a nice business, that is steadily increasing." Unfortunately, American shippers in the African trade were few in number, and the West African Line's steamers often put out for Africa more than half empty, to plod through the monthly circle in the frequently vain hope of a homeward commitment of cocoa, manganese, or palm oil.[11]

In Africa, meanwhile, the conference lines were enjoying their revenge for having been forced to lower their rates on American traffic to the board's level. It became impossible to challenge the conference monopoly on the limited dock and lighterage facilities in West Africa, and American ships were the last in the lists to be serviced. Lighter crews and stevedores would even stop unloading an American vessel if a conference-line ship appeared on the horizon. Such unpredictable delays, combined with the increasingly pathetic meandering over the sea-lanes in search of cargo, introduced a certain unreliability into the West African Line's shipping schedules. As a result, trade between the United States and Africa began to pursue more predictable channels. By July, 1927, the A. H. Bull West African Line was losing an average of $10,041 per voyage, and operations for the year lost $378,442.

Understandably, the United States government was dismayed by these revelations. Apparently sending a fleet to capture the West African trade was like hunting ducks with a battleship. When its contract with A. H. Bull expired in 1928, the Shipping Board eagerly offered the West African Line for sale—ships, good name, and all. The new owner, the Barber Lines of New York City, recognizing that the

West African trade was "conceded by experienced steam-ship men to be the most difficult trade in the world," proved equal to the task. By shortening schedules, redesigning the vessels, sailing only on consignment and offering trans-shipments to the conference lines, the new service, the American West African Line, established itself in the trade and has survived to the present day.[12]

The story of a single ship engaged in the American flag service to West Africa in the interwar period serves as a kind of brief case study on the trade. The S.S. *West Lash-away,* 5,637 deadweight tons (DWT), was a small general freighter built in a final and superfluous burst of wartime energy in November, 1918. Her chances of performing pa-triotic service being so quickly ended, the freighter passed through the Shipping Board charter lists into the vagaries of the West African trade. At the time the Barber Lines pur-chased the Bull company's line, in 1928, it wanted a small tanker with which to compete in the growing palm-oil trade. To forestall the charter of a foreign vessel, the Shipping Board agreed to fit the *West Lashaway*'s holds with special tanks at government expense and to offer the ship on a yearly charter at twenty-five cents per DWT per day of actual service; the palm-oil trade was as yet too uncertain to warrant the ship's outright purchase by the new line. From 1929 to 1935, when the *West Lashaway* passed into private hands, the freighter was the last Shipping Board vessel engaged in the West African trade. Since the days of James Monroe, the potentials in West African trade had periodically lured the United States government. One cen-tury later, however, the government's dwindling interest finally came to rest on a single, aging makeshift tanker ploughing the South Atlantic.[13]

Outfitted with new deep tanks and heating coils for the palm oil, the *West Lashaway* made her first voyage in the summer and fall of 1929. The ship worked laboriously down the coast from Dakar, often carrying a few hundred tons of cargo from one port to the next, taking samples of palm oil at Matadi, the Belgian Congo, and full consignments of the oil at Port Harcourt, Nigeria, and at Cotonou, Dahomey. Operations were simple; the ship could not be worked in heavy surf, which even at a large port like Accra prevented lightering; the palm oil was simply dumped into the open tanks from casks. The long voyage was nonetheless a huge success. A contract was secured with the mammoth United Africa Company, Ltd.—the British combine that dominated West African trade—to carry all its trade with the United States, and the American West African Line took out a five-year extension on its charter of the small tanker.[14]

Both the *West Lashaway* and the West African palm-oil trade, however, were not quite equal to the confidence lavished upon them. On her second and subsequent voyages, the ship encountered various mechanical "mishaps." On a single voyage, in the summer of 1930, her windlass was damaged at Accra, she ran aground at Port Harcourt, and on the return voyage the crew detected a "heavy vibration" that turned out to be caused by a lost propeller blade. On a sailing in the spring of 1935, the *West Lashaway* lost her steering gear in a heavy sea, developed disconcerting leaks, and was towed into collision with another ship in the Brooklyn yards. The palm-oil trade in the meantime had collapsed, due to the "extreme depression," and the American West African Line not unnaturally asked for permission to lay up its floating disaster at a greatly reduced monthly charge. The *West Lashaway* was idled for more than two years through the worst of the Depression; altogether, she made only twelve voyages in the six years after her charter began in 1929. Although the Barber Line's freighter was the only American ship available for charter that was specially fitted for palm oil, a staple in the West African economy, the American West African Line admitted in 1935 that during "the past few years there has been no need for the regular employment" of the vessel. The government had lost steadily on the ship, and finally sold her to the West African Line in 1935 for less than her palm-oil tanks alone had cost.[15]

Operations on the East Coast were somewhat more successful. For the first few years after the war, the American service ran at a loss, caused primarily by antiquated and inefficient equipment, and the Shipping Board initially had to maintain the service at a loss simply to end conference-line discrimination against American trade. From Cape Town to Suez, however, the prospects for profitable American steamship connections were far better grounded in local conditions than they were on the West Coast. The ports were fewer, larger, and better equipped. Commerce with the Union of South Africa was well established; vessels were also able to carry expensive manufactured freight and building materials to the settler communities of Mozambique and British East and at the same time be assured of full homeward consignments of iron and copper ore— loaded in the beautiful Portuguese harbor at Delagoa Bay. The United States Shipping Board was in the comfortable position of receiving steadily increasing bids for its South African service in the 1920s. The result was that operation of the service was taken over in 1922 by the Mallory Transport Lines. In 1924 A. H. Bull, not yet discouraged by the results of his West African operations, assumed control of the service, now named the American South African Line. Both Mallory and Bull managed the line on a Shipping Board account, as lessors. Business was good, and a combination of shipping interests headed by James G. Farrell, son of the president of the United States Steel Corporation, entered the next year's competitive bidding and took the line from Bull by outright purchase. Under Farrell's management the shipping company continued to be called the American South African Line.

From the start, the South African service looked promising. When the first of its ships, the S.S. *Eastern Glade,* arrived at Mombassa in October, 1922, the American consul reported that it was a "source of great satisfaction to many members of the commercial community." The satisfaction was not shared by the agents of the conference lines; faced with direct American competition, they were forced to lower their rates on American freight from twenty-three dollars to ten dollars per ton. This cheery news helped American shippers to overlook the fact that the Shipping Board had begun its operation in East African waters with what one consul called a "distressing display of mismanagement": it sent out during the first few years its usual selection of antiques that only an "unusually able staff of engineers" could keep afloat. Under private ownership the condition of the ships did not invite the same criticism, and after 1925 the South African Line had a healthy share of the East Coast shipping trade.[16]

Indeed, relations between the American company and the conference lines on the East Coast seemed remarkably cordial. The Shipping Board had come to an understanding with the conference, as an "experiment," by which the American line carried only American freight trans-Atlantic—leaving anywhere from 93 per cent to 98 per cent of the colonial export trade to the foreign lines at their rates—and the conference charged American shippers the board rate. A. H. Bull had been eager to participate in this arrangement, but the firm began to complain that these relations were sinister and unpatriotic after Farrell won the bid for the line in 1925. Farrell undoubtedly represented a cosmopolitan collection of interests, among which was the staid old firm of Norton, Lilly & Company; by no small coincidence, Norton, Lilly was the American representative of every British line in the East and South African conferences. The American South African Line suddenly began showing a profit, to the great relief of the Shipping Board, which was operating on steadily decreasing appropriations; the board chose to give no "official recognition" to the Bull protest, and the American South African Line continued through the interwar period.[17]

Two other American shipping companies were also engaged in trade along Africa's southern and eastern shores during the interwar years. In June, 1935, the Robin Line began what its owner described as a "regular dependable monthly service" between New York and both South Africa and East Africa with five freighters. A subsidiary of the large and powerful Seas Shipping Company, the Robin Line immediately raised a storm of protest over the American South African Line's contract to carry the United States mail. Robin claimed that the South African Line was in league with the foreign conference lines and was trying to "drive" it out of the trade. The complaint was not, however, accepted; even without the mail it prospered, and is still in business. In 1929 the South African Dispatch Line of San Francisco began operations with three Shipping Board freighters. Advertised as the "Only Direct Freight and Passenger Service Between Pacific Coast and South Africa," the line was enjoying a handsome profit by 1931. Its ships included Portuguese East African ports on its schedule, but went no farther up the East Coast.[18]

At no time between the two world wars did these American lines threaten the dominant position of the leading British, German, and Dutch lines. Because of the direct intervention of an agency of the United States government, American ships were enabled to carry a small portion of their nation's

102 	the lure of africa

trade with Africa. But the European lines continued to maintain connections between Africa and the United States, and their vastly more convenient and reliable schedules and competitive rates insured their control over most of the American trade and over all of the rest. American merchantmen remained something of a curiosity in some African ports in the interwar period. In 1929, for instance, the tonnage of American shipping engaged in carrying trade to Latvia, Estonia, Lithuania, and Finland was slightly higher than that serving all of East and South Africa. In 1936 there were four American flag services to sub-Saharan Africa, with a combined fleet of only twenty-three medium-sized ships. Even in a peak year, the port signal for "American Ship in Sight" seldom flew over Delagoa Bay.[19]

European lines also nearly monopolized what little passenger traffic there was between the United States and Africa, a circumstance not too difficult to explain in view of the fact that of all the American ships engaged in the African trade, only one, the South African Line's S.S. *City of New York,* was designed to carry passengers as well as freight. The Shipping Board insisted that its chartered lines to Africa offer passenger service, and the board included this stipulation in the sales agreements under which private commercial companies took over existing board services. But there were few customers. The board might have its requirement, but the passenger cabins were makeshift at best. And while the American lines offered the only direct connections between the United States and Africa, the few passengers who did wish to make such a voyage were "deterred by the inferior accommodation and the uncertainty of time and place of arrival in the States. . . ." In addition, the board's rates were higher than the total fares charged by the conference lines for the trans-Atlantic voyage with a stopover in Europe. Furthermore, despite the direct connections on the American route, the trip took longer. Passengers on the Union-Castle Line or the revived German East Africa Line sailed down the African coasts in unstudied ease, befitting the companies' long familiarity with the imperial channels of commerce. Travelers to West Africa in the 1920s were still reminded to take a portside cabin out to face the gentle night breezes off the coast. Passengers on European ships dressed formally for dinner and were attended by stewards, orchestras, and ship's doctors; all that an American ship could offer was the friendliness of the captain, who was sometimes the only American aboard and anxious for company. The American consul in Portuguese East Africa in 1927 observed that of the 8,375 passengers departing by ship from Lourenço Marques during one three-month period of that year, American ships carried away 2.[20]

Once in a while an American traveler chose an American ship in a high spirit of adventure. Two American journalists, on their way to begin a trans-African motorcycle trip, sailed on the American West African Line's S.S. *West Humhaw.* May Mott-Smith, whose journalistic project required stopping at many ports, traveled on the same ship and observed that a single word of praise for it would be "excessive." The leader of the Field Museum expedition of 1933–1934 investigated the accommodations on the West African Line's S.S. *Zarembo.* He lamely volunteered to his wealthy patroness that the cabins were "passable," and that she "might enjoy it as a lark." He was coolly informed that she and her maid had booked on the regal *Champlain,* and would meet the party in Africa. Some Americans, apparently, preferred to have their adventure begin after the voyage to Africa. The American West African Line finally gave up altogether and abandoned even the pretense of a passenger service in 1938.[21]

A typical list of items deposited ashore by an American ship plying its way along either African coast in the interwar years would have included three to six loose or crated automobiles, a few small cases of manufactured household items, a case or two of motion-picture reels, some drums of gasoline, perhaps a load of lumber or tobacco. The list would not include a passenger. In exchange for its cargo, the ship would have taken up a bulk cargo like cocoa, palm oil, or manganese on the West Coast, and iron or copper ore, spices, coffee, or sisal on the East Coast. The outbound U.S. cargo is a significant selection of items. Never more than a very small percentage of total colonial trade, certain American products, nonetheless, had so pervasive an influence on colonial African life that the face of the continent was altered by their presence.[22]

Though the audiences were never large, American motion pictures monopolized the African market. Theaters were small, part-time affairs, with antiquated equipment; one theater in Angola was described as a "large hut." The films shown in colonial Africa were supplied almost exclusively through two South African agencies, the International Variety & Theatre Agency of South Africa and the African Films Trust, Ltd. About the latter, there was "an unconfirmed rumor" that it was "largely backed by American capital." It was in any case not a big operation. In 1935 the Union of South Africa imported American films valued at $37,395, a fraction of the industry's export sales. The films themselves must have presented a somewhat bizarre view of the United States; one theater operator in Nigeria was "much interested in comedies of Chaplin, Harold Lloyd, Buster Keating [sic] . . . ; age of films is immaterial." The U.S. consul at Lourenço Marques noted that "practically all" the movies shown in the colony were American, adding that they were "neither high-class nor recent" and were "usually badly worn." And, throughout Africa, old and worn they continued to be long into the 1930s.[23]

American musical instruments also dominated the African market, and made a considerable contribution to colonial life. The Portuguese in Africa were "particularly devoted to music," and the American consul at Lourenço Marques alerted manufacturers to the possibilities of the market in Mozambique: every town had a band, and many homes had American phonographs. American phonographs and records were, in fact, heard everywhere in Africa. Traders, officials, and missionaries were devoted to the instrument. A few resolute turns of the crank, and out of the morning-glory horn came a link with home—"a kind of David with five tunes to do battle with nostalgia"—everything from a Beethoven adagio to Charlie Kellogg's evangelistic bird whistles. Isak Dinesen wrote lovingly of the phonograph that brought "new life" to her farm in Kenya. Travelers were particularly fond of describing the awe-inspiring effects the instrument had on the Africans. A writer in *Travel* observed that "this phonograph which the white man has brought into the heart of British East Africa is the source of great mystery and high amusement to the simple-minded Kikuyu." After playing a few numbers by Paul Robeson and the Fisk Quartet, one missionary modestly allowed his congregation to conclude that the race that had invented the phonograph was capable of unlimited wonders, such as raising the dead.[24]

Africa had joined that growing list of places that inspired the American tourist's lament: "No matter into what remote region he may travel," declared a distinguished international lawyer to college audiences in 1928, "an American can scarcely get away from his own civilization. Even in out-of-the-way villages where the language is unfamiliar and the roofs are still thatched it follows him like a spectre. . . ." Like a specter, maybe—like a host of specters—but not silently. "Everywhere in Africa the petrol-driven car is working a quiet (or perhaps not altogether quiet) revolution in travelling and transport of goods."[25]

The automobile burst upon the Dark Continent "as suddenly as its own tropic sunrise," and with effects no less inspiring, both to local residents and to American manufacturers. The war had barely ended when General Motors was writing to consuls in Africa about hotel accommodations for a "large number of travelers." American motor vehicle manufacturers deluged Africa with agents, catalogs, trade letters, and franchises. Many companies established special African divisions, and the Department of Commerce obligingly assigned a special trade commissioner for automobiles to sub-Saharan Africa. These efforts were not in vain. American companies captured the market, speeded on the paths of conquest by a comfortable margin of competitive advantage in their product and by the perversity of their European rivals.[26]

The extent of the triumph was wondrous to behold even by the most outspoken believer in Yankee ingenuity and the free-enterprise system. By 1923 the number of American cars per capita of the white population was higher in Kenya than in the United States; in that year the Royal East African Automobile Association estimated that 93 per cent of the cars in British East Africa were American.* In the French tropical African colonies, there were more Fords than "all French makes of automobiles put together." In Portuguese

* The American consul at Nairobi apparently thought the excitement over the African car market in the 1920s provided a golden opportunity to drop the old consular ricksha and purchase a car.

East Africa, almost 80 per cent of the cars and 90 per cent of the trucks were American; ten of the eleven automobile dealers in Lourenço Marques were agents for American cars. In British West Africa Reo trucks and Ford cars led the registration lists.[27]

Trade figures alone are always a little dull, however, and never more apt to be misleading than when they refer to Africa. The market so thoroughly captured by the American car was, after all, not large. By the mid-1920s American consuls in British East Africa were offering "precautionary advice" against overestimating the demand. Most of the fifteen thousand English settlers, the rich Indians, and the African kings already had cars, and few ordinary Africans could afford to buy a car. By January, 1930, 6,352 motor vehicles were registered in Nigeria—more than the total white population; here, too, the consul warned that future demand would perforce be "small," since so much of it had already been met. In terms of overall car production in the United States, the demand was infinitesimal: in 1923 the Ford Motor Company manufactured and sold 1,850,000 cars. But in terms of the effect of the American automobile on Africa, words like "magic" and "revolution" sprang readily to the minds of proud American observers.[28]

It was no time until the jungles and veldts of Africa echoed to the sounds of wheezing springs, backfires, and Klaxons. The problem of African transport that had retarded the continent's development since the days of Prince Henry the Navigator was solved at last; Africa was on wheels—reliable spoke wheels and wire wheels from Detroit, Flint, and Lansing. American missionaries and big-game hunters, Belgian elephant trainers and the Royal West African Frontier Force bounded over the grasslands in Fords. The King of Bukwimba in Tanganyika was given a "magnificent" Buick by his grateful subjects on the occasion of his twenty-fifth year in the royal hut. Steamers on Lake Victoria were crowded with "Fords, Overlands and Dodges," most of them for African chiefs "grown rich on Uganda cotton." One pair of pioneers on the Cape-to-Cairo route—a route so often pioneered that a hotel in Arusha, Tanganyika, advertised itself as the "Half-Way Station"—pushed their way up the "practically impossible" roads in a 1929 Chrysler "72" sedan. The Royal Italian Cape Town–Roma Expedition rolled northward in a

Buick touring car and a Model A Ford truck with little Italian flags flapping on the fenders. One of the numerous allurements offered by the Belgian government to encourage colonization in the Congo was "une auto Ford"; the Hotel des Volcans in the Kivu District of the Congo was well served with Chevrolets. At Dakar in French West Africa, the taxi stand was comprised of "a line of Ford touring cars." In Nairobi, the visitor trod carelessly if he did not keep an eye out for Highlanders roaring into, around, and through town in their Lincolns and Packards. Small wonder that one of the few passengers on an American ship to Africa noted that it carried "three Buicks and five thousand gallons of gas" for Freetown, Sierra Leone.[29]

Missionaries were quick to recognize the automobile's usefulness. What the Ford had meant to rural America, it could mean to Africa. Remote mission stations could be visited more often, and isolated villages could be reached with the Gospel, doctors, and medicine for the first time. The Lord's vineyards were wonderfully expanded, due to His beneficent intervention through the agency of Detroit. One missionary doctor in French Equatorial Africa declared that the same new roads that were suddenly planned in all the colonies could become "the highways along which the Church militant advances to the evangelization of Africa's last frontiers." Missionary journals ran articles that contrasted the vastly superior "New Way" of traveling in Africa with the "Old Way": dug-out canoes and machillas. Congregations back home were reminded that "every missionary needs a motor car as much as, or more than, a typewriter." When the first Model T reached the famous Southern Methodist station at Wembo Nyama in the Belgian Congo in 1924, the natives took it for a "black monster"; the missionaries, however, "bubbled over with joy" at the thought that the Africans' lives of drudgery were over. So touched were clerics to receive one of these clattering angels that they endowed them with names and personalities. A missionary in Angola for the American Board of Commissioners for Foreign Missions named his new Ford "The Swallow" when it arrived from the Beloit, Wisconsin, Missionary Association; another christened his Ford "Queenie," and maintained that "she assumed the role of a full-time missionary." The staid *Missionary Herald* ran a special "Automobile Section" in its

June, 1929, issue "Dedicated to the Proposition that the modern missionary is motor minded in 1929 A.D." In 1930 a delegate at the fiftieth anniversary celebration of the American Board's mission in Angola returned convinced that "a trustworthy Ford multiplies a missionary's efficiency many times over and gives him a range incredible twenty years ago."[30]

"A range incredible twenty years ago" did not appeal to missionaries alone. Big-game hunters and scientific expeditions increasingly used motor vehicles in the 1920s, after the idea was first tested under dubious but fascinating circumstances by an animal collector from Oakland, California. Henry A. "Del" Snow, a man of widespread and profitable interests that included collecting birds' eggs and managing the Newark, California, Giants, arrived in Kenya in 1919. Africa was to be his bonanza. He had arranged financial backing to make a big-game hunting feature film—a subject just coming into vogue—and to acquire specimens for the Oakland Natural History Museum, which he proposed to establish upon his return. Snow had planned to use his hunting experience in the American West, and apparently was surprised to discover the absence of pack animals in Kenya. If his oversight seems strange, it is no less strange that the local residents somehow had not yet thought of using their automobiles for camping and safari purposes. The idea occurred to Snow instantly; he purchased several Fords, painted "Oakland Museum Expedition" and his own name all over them, and disappeared into the Blue.

Snow had "decided to pin his faith on the flivver, and he was not belied." He was, in fact, amazed at his success. The Ford car, it seemed, revealed a remarkable aptitude for this new work: not only was it immune to the tsetse fly, it was as fast as most game animals and practically indefatigable. Snow could course over the veldt, running animals for hours until they were in a properly subdued condition for filming, or he could shoot them from the car at ranges that encouraged the best marksmanship. The operation even provided some adventure: once a warthog charged the car, knocking it into reverse, but the New York papers informed an anxious public that "the brave Ford met the charge undauntedly." At another time, a leopard jumped into the back seat of Snow's touring car while Lizzie sailed over the scrub; fortunately, the "brave Ford" had proved its mettle already, because Snow momentarily lost the composure that was otherwise so reassuring a feature of his film and fumbled hysterically for his revolver as the car careered into a tree. The leopard, not surprisingly, was temporarily stunned, giving the rattled Snow time to retrieve his gun and collect another specimen for Oakland. Such risks did not discourage man nor Ford. The hunter immediately covered his open cars with wire cages and the expedition continued. The Oakland Natural History Museum was duly opened to house Snow's numerous specimens, and the motion picture, released by Universal in 1922 as *Hunting Big Game in Africa,* was a financial success of enormous proportions. "Snow's revolutionary method of collecting specimens by flivver," affirmed a publicity booklet, "was one of the novel features of the film."[31]

As "novel" as his techniques were, it cannot be said that Snow's sporting qualities were widely appreciated. The world's first motorized safari was soon under a cloud. Practiced hunters and naturalists on both sides of the Atlantic were appalled by Snow's methods. The Kenya Game Department described them as "unsportsmanlike, unscrupulous, cruel and illegal." The American consul at Nairobi lamented that Snow had earned the "most unenviable reputation" of any American ever to set foot in the colony. The *Kenya Observer* ran an article entitled "Game Slaughter by Motor Car: Or A Western Yankee in Africa." The Society for the Preservation of the Fauna of the British Empire, a noted British animal photographer, and the directors of both the American Museum and the New York Zoo registered public protests, the latter declaring that Snow was unequaled in "bloodthirstiness and in brutality." The colonial government declared that Snow would be prosecuted if he attempted to return to Kenya.[32]

The furore over the first use of the motor car in big-game hunting did not die down. For years afterward American hunters in Africa apparently felt that Snow had to be denounced. Snow's film, which in addition to the automobile chase sequences contained views of tame lions photographed on the governor-general's lawn and labeled as ferocious wild animals, was the first American big-game picture to be shown in the United States, a blow from which

Martin Johnson took some years to recover. It was easy, Johnson declared loftily in 1927, to shoot animals from a car, "picturing the process and its excitements." Ernest Hemingway was still sufficiently exercised in 1934 to growl manfully that the practice of hunting lions from a car was a "cowardly way to assassinate one of the finest of all game animals." It is, of course, inexcusable to pursue game in a car," recorded Stewart Edward White in 1925, "and since a certain motion-picture man ran beasts to death from exhaustion it has also been illegal."[33]

Happily, the new law forbade only the actual shooting of animals from a moving car, or their pursuit in a car for that purpose. Running among animals to photograph them was allowed, and became increasingly popular. Indeed, the practical advantages of the car over foot travel in the backcountry had been amply demonstrated by Snow, whose exploits received wide attention in the United States, Britain, and Africa, and the rush was on. Soon explorers, hunters, and photographers were chugging over the landscape, demanding new roads or forging their own. One intrepid Englishman in Kenya drove off into the bush in a Ford car in 1919, penetrating ninety miles beyond the farthest point of previous automobile traffic. He wrote to the U.S. consul in Nairobi that "this car is doing his excellent service day in day OUT especially on several occasions in going through virgin country of uncut thick Bush." The man planned to start a "mechanical transport fleet," a prospect that so encouraged the American consul that he spontaneously produced a glowing report on "The Use of Motor Vehicles in British East Africa." The Englishman for his part established a business, carrying hunters on automobile safaris.[34]

Martin and Osa Johnson began their first explorations in 1921 in Fords purchased from Nairobi's leading safari outfitter, who had been quick to adapt. Later the couple used Willys-Knight touring cars with special camera platforms fitted over the back seat. World-Wide Photo Service issued a picture of one of the Johnsons' Willys-Knights covered with Lumba warriors in full regalia. The splendid Akeley-Eastman-Pomeroy African Hall Expedition of 1926 moved through British East Africa in thirteen vehicles—five Chevrolet trucks, several Overland and Willys-Knight cars, and

George Eastman's seven-passenger Buick touring car, with which the inventor of the Kodak camera busied himself chasing impalas, topi, and lions across Tanganyika. Paul Hoefler's Colorado African Expedition of 1929 covered Africa in two Durant trucks. An American Museum team searching Angola for Giant Sable antelope traveled part of the way "in Ford cars, which proved very useful." One American photographer took an interesting series of pictures of running giraffes and elephants from a "converted Ford car, built to cope with the worst of roads"; Julian Huxley's party moved reverently through the incredible variety of game in Tanganyika in "our Chevrolet lorry"; several parties from the *Trader Horn* movie expedition chased game in cars, and as a partial reward for their depredations, one of Van Dyke's touring cars was charged by a rhinoceros.[35]

The automobile offered real advantages: speed, comfort, and convenience. And it extended the distances that could be covered within the limits of available supplies and water. The famous Serengeti Plain, lying in the shadow of Mount Kilimanjaro, had been discovered by Stewart Edward White when the Kaiser's flag still flew over it. Yet the great game herds that fed there on the grass and each other had not been molested by hunters until the motor car was introduced. Distances between water were so great on the Serengeti, Hemingway noted, that the region had not been hunted in "the old foot safari days, and that was what preserved it." Indeed, by the late 1920s the foot safari had become a memory in many areas of Africa and in most of British East. Game on the plains had become so accustomed to the "rattle and bang of the automobile" that the animals would run along with the cars and cross the bows playfully, supposing that the strange intruders were in some way living things like themselves.[36]

In all these activities—hunting, missionary work, scientific expeditions—and in the employment of motor vehicles in less spectacular ways, American cars dominated. If a European car was ever used for fieldwork in Africa during the interwar years, it escaped notice. British governors clung to their dark red, crested Rolls, and in the late twenties the Morris gave the Ford close competition for first place in the cities of Nigeria and the Gold Coast. Otherwise, Africa moved on American wheels, because to the general advantages of the motor vehicle had to be added the particular advantages of the American product.

American cars were the world's most efficient on gasoline consumption, in terms of horsepower and weight, and gasoline remained in critically short supply in tropical Africa during the interwar years. It had to be imported, stored, and then shipped to distributing points in five-gallon tins. As a result, gasoline was expensive throughout tropical Africa, and in some places prohibitively high. A merchant in Abéché, French Equatorial Africa, had a new Ford brought out from Khartoum in the early 1930s, only to discover that gasoline cost two dollars a gallon. In 1923 gasoline cost 88 cents a gallon in British East Africa.[37]

Good gasoline mileage was not enough. A car had to be sturdy, have enough horsepower for speed over discouraging terrain under a full load, carry heavy springs, and have a durable transmission, preferably one with three forward speeds. European cars sometimes rated fairly well on gasoline consumption, but otherwise their manufacturers seemed determined to squander the colonial markets that ties of custom and sentiment might otherwise have set at their feet.

Frail and underpowered, most British and French motor vehicles literally fell apart under the strain of colonial service. "It is a regrettable fact," complained Huxley in 1931, "that even the so-called colonial models of British makes will not stand up to African conditions like the American cars." In 1925 and 1926 surveys of the market conditions in Portuguese Angola and the Belgian Congo revealed that colonists wanted black, open, five-passenger cars with magneto ignition (the arm-operated crank starter, as opposed to the battery-operated self-starter) with high road clearance and demountable rims—a description comfortably suggestive of the Ford car, which of course had already captured the trade.[38]

The most popular American makes in tropical Africa were the Buick; the Chevrolet; the Dodge; the Overland "Four," a light, well-built car noted especially for its good springs and excellent mileage; the Willys-Knight, with the remarkable Knight-patent sleeve-valve engine that actually improved with use, sometimes running 200,000 miles without major repairs; the Packard, Lincoln, Cadillac, and Chrysler in the settler communities of British East; and the Ford—above all, the Ford, the "Ubiquitous Ford," the most popular car in Africa. In many colonies the Ford outnumbered all other makes combined. In Africa, as in the United States, the Model T had made automobile transportation widely available. American visitors praised the Ford's wondrous effects, and one American observed reverently that the "influence of Henry Ford" had "fallen like a blessing on these vast wilderness spaces of Central Africa."[39]

One reason for the popularity of the Ford car was its awe-inspiring durability. The machine was not only the world's least expensive automobile, and one of the easiest on gasoline (or, in a pinch, kerosene), it was practically indestructible, no small consideration in a country where the aggressions of motorists consistently outran the roads.* In 1930 an unnamed English sportsman rattled into the *Trader Horn* Serengeti camp in a 1912 Ford, which he had found abandoned in the bush on the Congo border. James Chapin of the American Museum sold a "battered" old Ford to a Belgian at the end of an expedition in 1926; when Chapin returned five years later, he found the car "still rolling around the Ituri" forest in the Belgian Congo. Explorers thought nothing of driving blithely off the end of roads into unknown country in their Fords, pushing ahead the frontiers of science, Christianity, or the free-enterprise system. Hambly penetrated a completely unknown country in Angola in his Model A in 1929, using the car as a traveling camp in uninhabited regions.[40]

There remained quarters, of course, in which the "influence of Henry Ford" and his cohorts was not regarded as a "blessing" at all. French and British manufacturers watched in dismay as American cars took over their colonial markets. They fought back with several attempts designed to demonstrate in a practical fashion that, in the words of a writer in the London *Sunday Times,* "this alleged superiority of the Yankee car is all bunkum." The French took no chances. For the Citroën Central African Expedition—Algeria to Madagascar—of 1924, the cars were completely rebuilt into formidable-looking rolling boxes with caterpillar treads, sug-

---

* The Fords sold in Africa were made in a wholly owned subsidiary plant in Ford City, Ontario. See *Moody's Manual of Investments: Industrials, 1927,* 2394.

gestive of Rommel's half-tracks that would later roll over some of the same route. Someone thoughtfully remembered to replace the "Citroën" insignia, but no one was fooled; the company continued to lose ground in the colonies to American cars.[41]

The British, as so often in their industrial operations, refused to make adaptations that were suggested by nothing more pressing than practicality. One group of hardy souls determined to prove the reliability of the unadorned Crossley in 1924 by driving a pair of them from Cape Town to Cairo. The trip, which finally took sixteen months, was an unending succession of ripped-out bottoms, flooded engines, and broken springs and axles. The party left a trail of camp beds, Gramophone records, and dispensable accessories—like the cloth tops from the cars—thrown overboard to lighten the load, but the cars were still unable to pull through adversities, and had to be carried bodily over most of them. The publicity from the trip gained a wide reputation for the pioneer motorists who made it, and so depressed Crossley sales in Africa that the car vanished altogether from the colonial scene.[42]

Fourteen years later, after an excellent system of motor roads had been laid down in colonial Africa, a British party sponsored by the London *Sunday Times* set out again to prove that the "typical modern British car" could "stand up to really tough colonial going just as well as an American car." Even under the improved conditions, these efforts— there were three—were not an unqualified success. The Rolls Phantom III performed well enough over the flat Sudan, but the Morris was "terribly overloaded" carrying three men on a trip in Nigeria, and the 1938 Wolseley saloon ended up in a crocodile-infested river in the Belgian Congo. Aside from these specially arranged sorties, French and British pioneering continued to be done in American cars. The modified "colonial models" of British makes never caught on. One such, the Trojan, did not impress Americans who saw it: "It is an English attempt to produce a Ford," sneered one in 1931, "and it makes you proud of Lizzie by contrast."[43]

The far more serious threats to the predominance of the American automobile in Africa were the attempts of colonial governments to restrict its use. In 1922, in one of their periodic fits of perversity, the Portuguese passed a law to restrict the operation of automobiles in Beira, Mozambique. The introduction of American cars, "driven rather recklessly," had caused a storm of protest because of several near collisions with the city's famous black-powered personal trolley handcarts. Several governments in 1928 toyed with the idea of enforcing an antique law against four-wheel brakes in order to restrict the importation of certain American makes. In 1932 Kenya Colony prohibited commercial carriage in motor trucks within twenty-five miles of the railway; the Kenya & Uganda had lost £65,000 to truck competition the year before. Almost every truck in the colony was American, and the U.S. consul at Nairobi wrote the Department of State for instructions.[44]

There were certain other difficulties in a motorist's life in Africa, which, while they did not impede the progress of the American conquest, kept it from being an unmixed delight. Shipments from the United States could occasionally take an inordinately long time. Parts were not always available. When the magneto went out in the Field Museum's new 1929 truck in Sokoto, Nigeria, another had to be brought from Lagos, a thousand miles distant. One American had to melt his partial denture over a campfire to fashion a breaker hearing for his motorcycle, after the original had fallen off somewhere near Lake Chad. A miscalculation on gasoline consumption could leave a party stranded amid the roars and snarls of an aroused animal population.[45]

Nor was the country always accommodating. One American woman became so unsettled whenever her husband attempted to float the family car across a river on a fragile reed raft that she hid in nearby huts and counted to a thousand. When the rivers dried up they became dongas, and one game hunter was tempted to adopt as "his motto, Life is Just One Donga After Another." The veldt was "an ideal coursing ground" only to "the superficial glance"; in actuality, it was a mass of warthog dens, hummocks, ditches, stones—just "one damn puncture after another." While in headlong pursuit of a buffalo, George Eastman's Buick went sailing over a low hill in Kenya into a donga. The discouraged Eastman had the car carried bodily back to Nairobi for a new set of springs, and departed in it for safer ground. A Catholic missionary driving a Ford through Rhodesia in 1931 was jarred from his meditations on Saint Paul by a crocodile, which clamped its jaws onto a front tire and held on for two hours. In Kenya Stewart Edward White found that cranking his Model T, not a surefire operation under the most favorable conditions, acquired a certain added excitement when the car became an object of interest to surrounding lions.[46]

The scene is the sort of convenient juxtaposition of symbols so dear to photographers, and a charming one upon which to close: a noble African lion staring cross-eyed into the snout of a Model T Ford on the plains of Kenya. Thus it was that an American presence came to Africa between the two world wars. Trade did not follow the flag, which fluttered from a random freighter and remained something of a conversation piece. In only one major manufactured product—the automobile—did the United States predominate, and with that product the continent was transformed. By 1935 the construction of roads in Africa had "gone forward at an astonishing rate," and tens of thousands of American cars sped over them, welcomed even by the animals, whose instincts for once failed them.[47]

Perhaps Lizzie and the lion are yet preserved in opposite corners of some museum, dusty relics of a time when both automobiles and lions excited curiosity and fired the imagination. And if a hunter's Ford recalls the penetration of Africa by American enterprise, the lion suggests the purpose for which most Americans came. For Africa was the Land of Wild Animals, and the 1920s and 1930s were years of expeditions great and small, the activity that drew more American visitors than any other.

four:
americans and
the animals
of africa

**The idea that Africa is the 'world's zoo'
is indelibly impressed upon the general
mind.'—Mary L. Jobe Akeley (1929)**

On a bright mid-April morning in 1926 the S.S. *Llan-stephan* of the Union-Castle Line, a star British member of the conference line, put out from Genoa for the East Coast of Africa. Passenger facilities on the eleven-thousand-ton vessel were limited, but the line was proud of the service on its African run, and by the time the ship passed Corsica the passengers were agreeably settled for the long voyage eastward across the Mediterranean, south through the Suez Canal and the Red Sea, around the Somaliland horn and halfway down the coast to Mombassa, chief port of Kenya Colony. Aboard by happy coincidence were no less than four different American zoological expeditions. Two were groups of wealthy sportsmen planning big-game safaris, one of which would be guided by A. J. Klein. The other two were scientific expeditions, among the largest and most expensively furnished ever sent to Africa from the United States: the Akeley-Eastman-Pomeroy African Hall Expedition for the American Museum of Natural History in New York, and the Smithsonian–Chrysler East African Expedition for the National Zoological Park in Washington, D.C. The four groups had arrived separately in Genoa, but the same attraction had drawn them all there and on to Africa: animals. The animals

117

of Africa had been the lure—for them and for hundreds of other Americans, while millions of stay-at-homes followed their exploits and admired their trophies.[2]

The spectacular wildlife of sub-Saharan Africa, which, according to a long-standing zoological convention, was classed as the "Ethiopian Region," had intrigued the American public ever since the graphic accounts of explorers Henry Morton Stanley and Paul Du Chaillu were published in the latter half of the nineteenth century. The reports of the prewar field observations of Theodore Roosevelt and Stewart Edward White continued to reach wide audiences in the 1920s. Roosevelt's two works on African wildlife, and those of the old-time British hunter Frederick Courteney Selous, were standard reference works throughout the interwar years.[3]

By the late 1890s, both the Chicago and the New York museums of natural history had dispatched their first major zoological expeditions to Africa, and prior to World War I the United States National Museum in Washington, D.C., had accomplished extensive fieldwork. Before the war, the largest American zoological parks had also acquired handsome African collections, and clamored for more; by the end of the war, zoos faced a shortage of African animals. So, too, did the circuses. Led by Barnum & Bailey, whose African elephant "Jumbo" was a national fixture, a score of lesser shows hauled African menageries, some of them fairly shopworn, through awestruck clapboard towns. In 1922 the first of many American big-game films flickered in dark halls across the country, and throughout the decade popular accounts of the many safaris and expeditions ran into the dozens.

Most Americans, when they thought of Africa at all, thought first of its wild animals. One naturalist observed in 1928 that when the "average thinking person" in the United States conjured up pictures of Africa, "the image of a country . . . teeming with game" was "probably the dominant one." Books on missionary endeavor, educational reform, anthropology, and railroad construction succumbed to the demands of the public. "It would be a strange book on Africa," confessed a missionary in 1926, "that would make no mention of wild game." Writers spoke of Africa as "Noah's Ark," and, like him, concentrated on "every living thing of all flesh"—except, of course, people. A leading American geography text offered a full-page "Animal Map" of the "important" and "useful" animals of Africa, and half as much—a single column—on the "black race." Of the four illustrations of tropical Africa in the book, three depicted animal life; the fourth was a picture of Victoria Falls. The tendency to overlook the humans for the lions was so far advanced at the end of the interwar period that a prominent American historian of African imperialism declared that the many "vivid descriptions" of animal life in equatorial Africa had "obscured the picture of its human inhabitants."[4]

The emphasis on African wildlife—in contradistinction to any major interest in African people—brought considerable benefits to the imperial governments. Persons attracted by a colony's wildlife made the best visitors: they were rich, and therefore able to pay the astronomical fees for hunting and collecting licenses and for exporting specimens and trophies; and they perpetuated the convenient idea that Africa was a nonpolitical land of scenery and wild animals, whose incidental human population had been brushed aside and subdued in the interests of civilization. Furthermore, these visitors came into repeated contact with the efficient and courteous colonial game departments—humane and self-effacing agencies that even in long retrospect put a good face on imperial government.

Unfortunately, not all imperial powers were equally endowed with zoological treasure. The British, as so often was the case in imperial history, seemed to have the best of Africa. The Belgian and French Congos had many different kinds of wildlife and were particularly noted as the home of the gorilla. Angola was the last remaining habitat of the beautiful and rare Giant Sable antelope. But in all the world, no place could compare with British East Africa for the variety and quantity of game or for the convenience of hunting it. Roosevelt had called British East "a naturalists' wonderland"; in his day, too, it had been "the best-known big-game field in the world." A tropical climate and the absence of thick jungles and swamps had caused an incredible diversity of animals to proliferate over the wide, temperate savannas. A stable government and congenial climate encouraged the sojourns of hunters and scientists who might have collected the same animals elsewhere but with considerably less ease. Tanganyika in particular, which had not been hunted before the introduction of the motor car, became in the 1920s the world's most important single source of wild animals. "Game in Tanganyika is thicker than ants," quipped W. S. Van Dyke, "and that is saying something." Arranging and outfitting hunting safaris became a "regular profession" in Nairobi. American zoos officially put British East Africa at the top of their list of countries "most fruitful in supplies."[5]

British colonial governments gave official sanction to the image of Africa as a natural zoo by adopting indigenous animals as official colonial symbols for use on flags and seals. In the British Empire, the government of a non-self-governing colony flew the Union Jack with the colony's badge set centrally in a white disc. The badge of Tanganyika was the head of a giraffe, and that of Kenya a red lion. Uganda's was the "Great East African Balearic Crane," and those of The Gambia, Sierra Leone, and the Gold Coast, an elephant under a palm tree. Nyasaland's badge was a leopard "in full colour," and Northern Rhodesia displayed a view of Victoria Falls surmounted by an eagle and a fish, "these being symbolical of the fauna of the country." The Tanganyika giraffe stamp, printed in a wide range of denominations and depicting a giraffe's head against various background colors, was a great favorite of American collectors. In New York in the mid-1920s, mint giraffe stamps sold for twice their issue price; by 1932 even a used 1922 giraffe stamp commanded sixteen dollars.[6]

Even colonies not as richly endowed with animals as British East Africa tapped the trade in zoological postage stamps. Stamp collecting, after all, was "one kind of adventure and one kind of exploring and one kind of hunting." The Belgian Congo, French Equatorial Africa, and the Portuguese African colonies produced many stamps depicting everything from aardvarks to zebras. In the rush to portray the national wildlife at a tidy price per stamp, Liberia—undiscouraged by its lack of sizable animals—bravely issued a series of stamps showing local snakes and lizards.[7]

Not only on flags and stamps, but in the minds of many travelers, particular animals came to symbolize Africa. None was more famous, more typically African, than *Felis leo,* the black-maned African lion. "The lion," declared a typical

commentator, "has always seemed to me to typify Africa—
serene, majestic, inscrutable, like the soil from which he
springs." But the lion was not the only symbol in the bush.
"Few animals," observed a writer in the *Wonder Books* series,
"appeal to the imagination as does the ponderous African
bull elephant," the largest land animal on earth. The giraffe,
too, was described as uniquely "an African form," an animal
"at once beautiful and truly African," the tallest living thing.
Giraffes were the most prized of zoo animals, but their delicate natures and susceptibility to injury and illness when
removed from their habitat made live specimens almost un-
obtainable; a pair of grown animals was worth twenty thousand dollars to an American zoo in the 1920s. To some, the
gorilla was also a symbol of Africa. Ever since Du Chaillu's
hair-raising account of the mountain gorilla, that "hellish
dream-creature" had fascinated Americans; few jungle stories or movies were complete without a ferocious gorilla
dragging off a fainting white lovely. Carl E. Akeley made the
study and preservation of the creature, which proved in fact
to be shy and inoffensive, the last of his life's work as an
African naturalist.

There were other animals symbolic of the continent, too
—other uniquely African animals much valued by museums,
zoos, and circuses: zebras, hippopotamuses, chimpanzees,
and an array of less famous but equally curious forms.* Also
prized were the antelopes, like the eland, the spiral-horned
koodoo, gazelles, impala, gerenuk, the tiny dik-dik, wilde-
beest, klipspringer, and that favorite of limerick and pun, the
gnu. The shy, russet bongo, a forest antelope, was among
the rarest of zoo and museum specimens. The okapi—the
only known relative to the giraffe—with its black-and-white
legs and blue tongue, was a "living fossil" much in demand.
The aardvarks, the lemurs, the civet cats, and that "feathered
legion" of tropical birds also captivated animal collectors.[8]

Americans were particularly keen about tales featuring
what was in truth an extremely rare phenomenon—the man-
eating lion. "Naturally, where there are lions, they will roar
at night," an article in *Harper's* pointed out. "But in the travel
books such happenings are menacing, ominous." Naturalists
like the Akeleys and serious sportsmen suggested in vain

---

* Rhinoceroses are not confined to the African continent and cannot be considered typically African, any more than can leopards or eagles.

that lions were dangerous to man only when wounded or cornered, and that stories to the contrary were "exaggerated." Many writers preferred to relate dramatic stories of the rare man-eaters, certainly the most famous being that of the man-eaters of Tsavo. No less than 135 Indian and African laborers working on the Tsavo River Bridge in Kenya were carried off by two lions, finally necessitating stoppage of all work on the Kenya & Uganda Railway. That the tragic episode had occurred in 1893 did not keep it from the public eye; practically every American traveler who visited Kenya in the 1920s re-created for his reader the story of the "screaming victims" and "gruesome remains." In 1924 Stanley Field, president of the Field Museum, seized upon a visit by Colonel J. H. Patterson, who had shot the two Tsavo killers thirty years before, to purchase the ancient skins. The Museum mounted them in a "splendid group," which is still on display.[9]

Not only certain animals, but the whole process of survival of the fittest was taken as symbolic of Africa. "Kill! Kill! Kill! that was what one had to do to keep in tune with the African rhythm," declared Llewelyn Powys. "Aye," warned the author of *Trader Horn,* "whenever you lose a fight in Africa you're lost. There's no softness about Nature." Frank Buck, the well-known animal collector, ridiculed the idea of a "code" of the jungle: "Life in the jungle is a free-for-all fight, no fouls recognized, and no weight limits." Some American tourists in Africa began to fancy themselves succumbing to savage impulses. One thirteen-year-old boy startled his father, an industrialist from Buffalo, New York, by shooting a reedbuck and dramatically plunging a knife into its throat, only to have the creature bound away, knife and all. This was too much for the father, who wrote in consternation that Africa's effect on his boy "was becoming horrible."[10]

The traveler's effect on Africa was often worse. Stewart Edward White had discovered the Serengeti game field on the eve of the First World War; it was the last "virgin game country" in Africa to be opened to the "sportsmen of the world." In twenty years it acquired what another American sportsman, Ernest Hemingway, called a "picked-over, shot-out feeling." Some hunters, like White himself, were inveterate game slaughterers. In 1925 he declared that "in any fair and dispassionate argument we ought to feel it our duty to

shoot every lion we get a chance at. . . ." Prestigious hunters like Teddy Roosevelt and Prince Vilhelm of Sweden, who
prided themselves on shunning what Roosevelt called the
"barbarity" of "game butchery," shot almost incredible numbers of animals, in order to select one or two specimens of
each species for a favored museum. Many lesser visitors
shot game indiscriminately. Carl Akeley's secretary whiled
away the hours on a slow steamboat on the Congo by shooting crocodiles sunning themselves on the riverbank. Van
Dyke's movie expedition shot up the countryside for diversion, trophies, and to attract carnivores for the film; at one
time, according to the director, the camp looked "like a
Chicago stockyard." Hunters who took only one or two trophies made up in numbers what they lacked in individual
rapacity.[11]

Added to the carnage of hunters was the continual spread
of settled communities. The very attractiveness of British
East Africa, both as a game field and as a permanent home,
was a menace to its wildlife. Between the hunters and the
settlers who steadily encroached on the grazing lands, the
animals were literally set upon from all sides. One hunter
returned in 1928 to a place where he had shot a kongoni
buck in 1919 only to find "the second largest hotel in Kenya"
on the spot. Stewart Edward White declared loftily that
"game and settlers cannot live together." Several officials of
the American Museum of Natural History and William T.
Hornaday, director of the New York Zoo, believed that it was
the spread of "civilization," not the sportsman, that imperiled
African game. Farms and towns would end the African herds
as they had ended the American bison. "Not a year passes,"
warned one American observer, "but what British East Africa
comes closer to the situation, in regard to game, that Ne-
braska and Kansas are in today."[12]

American naturalists joined in demands for "drastic laws"
against the "wanton orgy of slaughter" by hunters; simul-
taneously, they urged the creation of animal reserves against
the encroachment of settlement. Americans participated in
the creation of colonial Africa's first national park, and were
active in continuing conservation activities throughout the
interwar years. The single most important American engaged
in African conservation during his lifetime, which ended ap-
propriately if prematurely in 1926 on a camp cot in the Belgian

Congo, was Carl E. Akeley of the American Museum. The preservation of African wildlife for future generations became a genuine passion with Akeley. It was Akeley who developed the process for preparing taxidermic exhibits with scientific precision; his projected collection of habitat groups, finally gathered together in the African Hall of the New York museum, became one of the world's major museum exhibits. Akeley's other important conservationist activity centered on a gorilla reserve in the Belgian Congo. During an expedition there in 1921 to make a pioneering film on wild gorillas, he became convinced the creatures were in danger of extinction from white hunters, Africans, and Belgian settlers. He conceived the idea of a government reserve in the Congo's Lake Kivu District, and enlisted the crucial support of the Baron Emil de Cartier de Marchienne, Belgian ambassador to the United States. In two royal decrees of 1925 and 1929, King Albert I set aside a half-million acres for the project, under the direction of an international commission. The Parc National Albert was Africa's first national park. It was operated on lines suggested by Akeley: the gorillas were absolutely protected, even against unlicensed photography, which alarmed them. The Baron de Cartier was "adamant on the subject of shooting gorillas" even while planning proceeded for the new park. He convinced the Belgian minister of colonies to refuse requests for gorilla specimens from the most important museums in the United States. The baron became one of the world's few genuine gorilla lovers, and for Akeley's part in their preservation, he compared him favorably with Saint Francis.[13]

The British colonial governments had been the first to respond to the requests of American and British naturalists. Long before the war they had made considerable efforts to protect their larger fauna from wholly indiscriminate slaughter. The protection was far from complete, but the region between Mombassa and Nairobi was already a game preserve in Roosevelt's day; he was the first American to comment on the "literally unique" train ride through the herds of game on a cowcatcher. Throughout the twenties and thirties, all of British Africa had game laws that placed rigid limits on the more popular kinds of game and made hunting them expensive. A visitor's license to hunt any kind of animal in British East Africa cost £100 (the equivalent of twice the

price of a new Ford roadster back home), and another expensive permit was needed to export trophies from the colony. Many species, like the giraffe, and the young of almost
all species were absolutely protected. In 1935 the Uganda
game laws were amended to prevent even the photographing of animals if it were done in such a way that they became
alarmed and had to be shot by the camera party in self-
defense. British colonial game departments heartily cooperated with such important American conservation groups as
the American Committee for International Wildlife Protection, headed by the Harvard zoologist Harold J. Coolidge, Jr.[14]

It cannot be said, of course, that these enactments seriously discouraged big-game hunting. The British laws were
designed to prevent wanton destruction of wildlife; the
hunter with ample funds and a steady eye could get his
"bag" readily enough. Many animals, notably the lion, were
covered by a limit, but they were not otherwise protected.
Local safari outfitters assured the world that "Kenya will for
many years to come offer some of the finest big game shooting in the world." In the Portuguese colonies, the game laws
were enforced only spasmodically, and then merely, as the
American consul warned Professor Coolidge, "for pecuniary
reasons." At other times officials seemed indifferent even to
the financial possibilities of their zoological resources. In
1922 the American consul at Loanda made inquiries to the
local government about the game laws for an American
sportsman. He discovered that the officials somehow had
never heard of the Giant Sable antelope, the most prized and
beautiful game animal in Angola. The consul was offered a
nonresident hunting license for the equivalent of four dollars;
it entitled the bearer to shoot, among other things, ten of
each kind of antelope, five eland, six hippopotamuses, ten
rhinoceroses, and fifteen zebras—*per month.* A few years
later, on the other hand, the government of Mozambique,
anxious to attract wealthy hunters, took the cavalier position
that any trophy in the possession of a hunter with a valid
license had been, as the chief of the civil cabinet explained
it, "acquired in accordance with the particular local regulations, if any." The generosity of Portuguese game laws, however, was not enough to entice sportsmen and collectors
from the comfort and security of a well-planned hunt in British East, where, after all, firms like Newland & Tarlton and

Safariland, Ltd., made advance preparations for a successful and leisurely expedition—with trophies guaranteed. The professional safari guides were able to make such guarantees by inducing lions to come to a spot where they had left dead antelopes for several weeks. The eager sportsman was conveyed to the baited spot, accompanied by a sure-shot employee in order to avoid any nasty little slipups.[15]

The preservation of examples of African wildlife for the American public became an important endeavor in the 1920s. Officials of museums and zoos in the United States came to believe that wildlife in Africa was doomed. Only the British and Belgian colonial governments had made any real effort to slow its extinction, but these were the colonies that encouraged immigration and the spread of settler agriculture, processes that discouraged prospects for establishing any further game preserves. Writers predicted that the time was "not far distant" when an American could study African wildlife only in zoos or "stuffed, in the natural history museum." A sense of almost apocalyptic urgency gripped these naturalists. In every edition of the *Official Guide* to the New York Zoological Society's zoo in the Bronx, Director Hornaday warned that the day was coming when the African lion would "be without a home outside of zoological collections." Akeley believed in 1923 that it would "not be many years before . . . museum exhibits are the only remaining records of my jungle friends." To him the American Museum of Natural History's African Hall was "one of those projects which cannot be delayed. Now or never must it become a reality."[16]

To insure that African Hall, and numerous other similar projects, became a reality, zoological expeditions were dispatched to tropical Africa under a variety of arrangements. These endeavors were the classic African expeditions, the fabled penetrations into darkest Africa with gun and camera that dominated American-African relations for a decade, in the public imagination if not in trade statistics. The most common type of expedition was that of the natural history museum, which now and then financed, but more often merely sponsored, the collecting of specimens for taxidermic preparation and display. Museums would encourage photographers to accompany the expedition in the hope that the sale of still pictures or motion pictures would help defray the enormous expense and bring valuable publicity to the institution.* The hunting of animals was usually guided by local professionals, much in the same way in which private trophy hunters were guided.[17]

A notable American museum expedition—one that included many typical features in its planning, and the most number of untoward incidents in its execution—was the Smithsonian African Expedition of 1919–1920. As an official agency of the government, the United States National Museum was the object of special attentions from the State Department, foreign ministries, and colonial officials. The venture was one of the few African expeditions to receive the official patronage of the federal government in the interwar years.

In the spring of 1919, while the Versailles Conference was still in session, the Universal Film Manufacturing Company developed a plan to make a motion picture of an African expedition. Through its Washington attorney the film company approached the Smithsonian Institution, offering in return for its prestigious endorsement the privilege of naming the director of the expedition and sending along a team of scientists. The film company also offered to submit the motion picture to the Smithsonian for its approval before it was shown to the public. This arrangement was to become standard. The National Museum approved the idea, and secured on its own the patronage of wealthy friends like Andrew Carnegie for a major expedition. Homer L. Shantz, a botanist for the U.S. Department of Agriculture recently returned from work for the peace-conference Inquiry, and Henry C. Raven, an assistant curator on the museum staff, were to do the actual scientific collecting of animals. Edmund C. Heller was suggested as director. Heller was one of the most interesting

---

* The *New York Times,* for example, obtained exclusive rights to photographs of the Field Museum's Rawson West African Expedition in 1929. It paid ten dollars to the FMNH for every picture used in the paper's rotogravure section; the museum got full by-line credit. The paper endeavored to sell the pictures through its photo service, and split the take with the FMNH. W. D. Hambly was so excited by the extra picture-taking assignment that he took ten rolls of film *before* reaching Africa, which he eagerly submitted for "the purpose of publicity." He was advised that pictures of Antwerp and shipboard personalities were "of little or no interest to the public," and that it was hoped that "hereafter better ones will be sent on."

characters in a profession that attracted colorful personalities. A Stanford graduate in zoology, he had worked with Roosevelt in Kenya, where he acquired an enviable reputation for both fieldwork and scholarship. His career as an African hunter and collector was stellar, and despite what many might consider curious defects in his personality, he passed through disaster after disaster unimpaired, going from the Smithsonian to the Field Museum, from there to the Milwaukee Public Museum, finally ending his career as director of the San Francisco Zoological Gardens.[18]

The expedition was lavishly outfitted, and the Smithsonian had high hopes for it. With its collection of specimens, the National Museum staff hoped to work into public displays the material brought home by Roosevelt and Paul J. Rainey, another prewar American sportsman. "The experienced collectors," announced the museum secretary, would "undoubtedly send back to this country much material of value concerning the little-known parts of the 'Dark Continent.' . . ." The British Foreign Office and the Belgian Foreign Ministry offered the warmest cooperation, United States consuls were alerted to help smooth the path, and the expedition set sail for Cape Town in the summer of 1919. One group, comprised of Universal technicians and actors, was to travel up into the Congo for filming; the second group, including the scientists and Heller, was to move up the East Coast to collect specimens. The two groups were to meet later in British East Africa for extensive joint operations.[19]

The first suggestion that all was not to go well with the expedition came with news in November that the Congo wing had been knocked out in a railroad accident in the Belgian Congo. A run-away water-wagon had smashed into the party's railroad car, killing the business manager-medical director and the film director, and sending two photographers to Johannesburg to recuperate. The governor-general informed the foreign minister at once, and the latter requested that Baron de Cartier de Marchienne convey the minister's "heartfelt condolences" to the Smithsonian. The Belgian government had promised every assistance to the expedition, which all foreign officials took to represent the United States government—in 1919 still regarded by the Belgians as their liberator from the German heel and currently their major creditor. The Belgians were disconcerted by the "terrible railway accident" within their jurisdiction. All observers agreed that the expedition was definitely off to a poor start.[20]

One of the injured Universal employees, Henry N. Kohler, recovered and joined the East Coast contingent, whereupon it rapidly became apparent that the Universal Film Manufacturing Company had little scientific curiosity and was determined to make a profitable film at minimum expense. Kohler quickly usurped real control from Heller, a task rendered somewhat easier by the latter's unhappy fondness for alcoholic stimulant, the bane of colonial society. Raven and Shantz, in the meantime, were busy in the bush collecting botanical and zoological specimens.

The British welcomed the party with a formal banquet, at which Heller fell asleep and Kohler himself became drunk and picked a fight with the game warden. Heller was given to wandering away, and at one point even the British Foreign Office had to exert itself in order to locate him and get him into communication with the rest of the Smithsonian party. Kohler, who later openly bragged that he could pull "the wool over the eyes" of local British officials, avoided payment of import and export duties by every possible subterfuge. The two scientists, awakened to the situation, appealed to the American consul, who was hard pressed to put a good face on the affair to the British, whose cooperative spirit had begun to flag. At last, Heller and Kohler drove off in a drunken stupor and got stranded in the backcountry during one of Nairobi's periodic gasoline famines. The humiliated consul had to coerce the British into releasing gasoline for a rescue by dropping unpleasant hints about the consequences of allowing official representatives of an agency of the United States government to starve in the field.[21]

The British, the American consul, and the Smithsonian scientists centered their criticism on Kohler. Around Heller still shone the aura of his association with Teddy Roosevelt; Shantz declared that he and Heller were on the "best of terms," and that he, Shantz, was doing all he could to keep the "thoroughly rotten old ship afloat." As effectual director, Kohler had gained control of the expedition's funds, and his interest in the selfless pursuit of science being low, he gave no money to Raven and Shantz, who were forced to work at their own expense; Kohler went so far as to refuse to develop their purely technical film for them. The two scientists besieged the American consulate with complaints, which naturally reached Washington. The Smithsonian, thoroughly embarrassed, acknowledged that the "present management" of the expedition subjected the institution to "very severe criticism," and was liable to ruin its ability to secure official British cooperation for future expeditions. Heller sent in a rambling defense, claiming to be the victim of an "intrigue," in which the two scientists—"unreasonable plotters"—had convinced a "weak-minded and officious American Consul" to submit damaging reports. The Smithsonian rejected his charges in "very plain language," and decided to sever its connection with the expedition. In June, 1920, Heller was ordered to turn the project over to the film company and to send the two scientists home. The Smithsonian then thanked the State Department in warm terms for the consul's yearlong efforts to "safeguard the interests of this Institution."[22]

The film that was finally put together added to the gloom at the National Museum. In an official report to the museum's director, the chief curator of biology regretted that an "expedition so lavishly fitted out and with such possibilities . . . should not have brought home pictures of more intrinsic and permanent value." The views of scenery and animals were generally undistinguished, and the titles were "flippant and undignified besides lacking in information worthwhile." Tame animals filmed on Cecil Rhodes' farm were labeled wild, and the comments about natives were "about as educational and slangy as the texts of the comic supplements in the Sunday papers." The secretary of the Smithsonian informed the Universal Company that the institution could not "afford to be mentioned with any affair which is not of the first class in every respect," and refused to endorse the film. The company in its turn treated Heller shabbily, refusing to pay him for his expenses. The affair ended with the Smithsonian and the film company politely attempting to blame the other for selecting Heller as director.[23]

Despite its largely unfortunate consequences, the expedition was not an unmitigated disaster. Much of the film retained by the Smithsonian was quite good, some of it the only film views of several African subjects in the United States. The film company's other cameraman, George Scott, continued on good terms with the Smithsonian; after the controversy had settled down in Africa, Scott wrote proudly to the Smithsonian's secretary that it had been "a wonderful journey," and that he was bringing home 120,000 feet of film. Shantz had somehow managed to collect 2,600 different botanical specimens; some of his expedition photographs appeared as illustrations in American geography textbooks for years. Raven brought home 697 mammal specimens, many from regions of Africa "hitherto very imperfectly represented in the Museum's collections"; he also found time to gather up 567 birds, 206 reptiles, and 193 fish.[24]

Far more successful in every way was the great expedition sent to East Africa and the Congo by the American Museum of Natural History in 1926 to collect specimens for Carl Akeley's African Hall. Bountifully financed by George Eastman and Daniel Pomeroy, a Detroit industrialist, the Akeley-Eastman-Pomeroy Africa Hall Expedition was the most elaborate American museum expedition ever to penetrate Africa. United by common devotion to Akeley's dream of preserving Africa and by congenial and mutually attractive personalities, the party rolled leisurely across Africa, hunting choice specimens, painting scenery for backgrounds in displays, and collecting molds of plants and trees for the habitat groups. Martin and Osa Johnson were the court photographers, British officials and American consuls hovered in attendance, and the scientific world waited eagerly for reports. Unfortunately, Akeley perished of a mysterious fever in the Belgian Congo on the eve of his triumph, but by then the success of the Africa Hall project had been insured. The expedition's specimens, films, and field records were of superb quality.[25]

Museums did not often encounter such munificent patrons as George Eastman. Far more commonly institutions, in return for their official patronage, interested sportsmen in donating their best specimens, or in collecting certain specimens at their own expense. The patronage enabled the sportsman to claim his safari as a scientific expedition, entitling him to exemption from colonial game laws and import duties on guns and camp equipment. The Field Museum entered into such an arrangement with two New York sportsmen for the collection of its southern Sudan "waterhole group"; the sportsmen paid their own expenses, the museum sent its own taxidermist and paid his expenses, and the institution received the best of the animals shot for its display. Photographs and publicity were mutually controlled, and the museum cloaked the enterprise in its renowned auspices. The Cleveland Museum of Natural History had what amounted to a standing contract with Dr. George Crile, founder of the Cleveland Clinic and one of America's foremost big-game hunters. Wilbur D. May, the department-store tycoon, furnished trophies to the Los Angeles Museum of Natural History in return for its assistance in securing "special courtesies" for his big-game hunt in 1929. Occasionally, returning missionaries and persons on expeditions to study native life were asked to collect a desired specimen.[26]

At least two American museums owed their entire African collections to single individuals: the (Henry A.) Snow Museum of Natural History in Oakland, and the California Academy of Sciences Museum in San Francisco's Golden Gate Park, whose benefactor was Leslie Simson, an American mining engineer. Simson graduated from the University of California School of Mines in 1901, and moved to British South Africa with his mother. He eventually became superintending engineer of the vast Consolidated Gold Fields Company, Ltd., amassing a fortune along the way. He was a game hunter of some repute, a close friend of Stewart Edward White, and one of the first to recognize "the wonderful shooting opportunities" in northern Tanganyika. When his mother died, Simson became a "nomad," retiring with his fortune to become a full-time hunter. In 1925 he conceived of an African Hall for the new California Academy of Sciences, and offered to supply it with specimens at his own expense—a stroke of unparalleled good fortune for the academy. Simson had unlimited time and money, and was a superb shot. Year after year he collected specimens, continually upgrading the habitat display groups and carefully measuring and preparing the animals, and sent them on the long voyage to San Francisco. Simson wasted not a shot, and every specimen had scientific value. The museum staff had only to stroll through some rival institution, spot an interesting display, and write to Simson, who followed all museum instructions to the letter. It was a remarkable tour de force. The academy's African Hall of twenty-four groups was among the nation's best, and to this day the remaining unmounted Simson material—skeletons, hides and headskins, and field notes—is the finest osteological collection in the western United States.[27]

Simson, unlike many hunters and museum collectors, was one of the few in Africa who did not call upon the assistance of the United States government. As a longtime resident of Africa and an experienced and respected sportsman, his own contacts were probably superior to any that could be provided by the U.S. Foreign Service. In some instances, traveling scientists did not contact American consulates because they preferred to rely for assistance on the big commercial firms in the region. Dr. Austin L. Rand, chief curator of zoology at the Field Museum, recalled many years later that on his trips to the Dutch East Indies and Madagascar in the 1920s, his party regarded it as foolish to contact incompetent American officials, who, he said, worked entirely in a narrow social stratum and were of limited use to scientists hoping to work in the field. Nevertheless, many American hunters and collectors relied on the State Department. Arranging for American scientific expeditions was a common activity of the U.S. consulate at Nairobi, and the other consulates in Africa were often engaged in similar efforts.[28]

Far from the protection of their government, in an alien and mysterious environment, members of American expeditions were often anxious to arm themselves with authorizations and permits from their own and imperial governments before setting foot in Africa, and to have American consuls informed of their plans. The State Department was willing to cooperate with expeditions "under the auspices of" or "sponsored by scientific institutions," and for such legitimate projects, American ambassadors abroad secured invaluable permits and letters of introduction to colonial officials from the imperial colonial and foreign ministries. For persons who could not secure scientific endorsement, or did not seek it, American Foreign Service officers would offer to make introductions to local officials, as a "convenient channel of communication," but they assumed no official responsibility for the expedition's actions. For all American expeditions institutional endorsement was convenient, since colonial game laws, railroad freight rates, and import-export duties were liberalized or waived for scientific projects. For some expeditions, endorsement was an absolute necessity. The

Belgian government, for example, was "always very reluctant" to permit armed parties to visit the Congo, and would in no case consent to it without having been approached through the highest diplomatic channels. When an expedition had been officially endorsed as legitimately scientific by the American ambassador and presented by him to the colonial minister, the government of the Congo cooperated fully, providing personal letters of introduction from the governor-general that were "extremely useful" to Americans in the field.[29]

The Portuguese, ever alert to any possible affronts to their national pride, also insisted that all prospective American expeditions approach their colonies through the American legation in Lisbon. The colonial high commissioners were periodically subject to fits of devotion to the game laws, during which throes the laws were suddenly and rigidly enforced, necessitating the good offices of the U.S. State Department to secure exceptions in the name of science. The Portuguese in Africa were inordinately suspicious of foreign interest in the Africans, and after the Ross incident it became necessary for American applicants to emphasize that their anthropological expeditions were neither political nor humanitarian but "purely scientific." By 1929 the requests made to the Portuguese government through the American legation for permission to send expeditions to Angola and Mozambique had become "so numerous" that the American minister warned that the Portuguese might "become weary"; we "must have a care," he suggested, "not to overburden our Portuguese friends."[30]

Ordinarily, the State Department refused requests from expedition leaders for official letters of introduction or for special endorsement from high American officials. There were a few notable exceptions. The Smithsonian Institution was presented abroad as a government agency; Secretary of State Kellogg, in wiring instructions to the American embassy in London to arrange for the Smithsonian animal-collecting project in British East, was specific: "In presenting these requests to the British authorities you should point out the governmental character of Smithsonian Institution." Official letters of introduction were also obtainable for persons with the right connections. In 1934 the secretary of the Guggenheim Foundation secured the active interest of the

Department of State's economic adviser, Dr. Herbert Feis, in the zoological expedition of Professor Harold Kirby of the University of California. A friendly note from Ralph Pulitzer of the New York *World* to President Hoover about a projected collecting trip for the Carnegie Museum of Pittsburgh brought an even friendlier note in return from Acting Secretary of State Wilbur Carr, who was only too glad to provide Pulitzer with a personal letter of introduction to American field officers, in which he was willing to "cordially bespeak" for the publisher and to invite from the reader such "courtesies and assistance" as might seem appropriate. This note, however, did not seem quite "personal" enough to Pulitzer, and Carr produced another, a circular to the whole Foreign Service: "I shall greatly appreciate your doing whatever may be feasible to contribute to the success of Mr. Pulitzer's expedition." Many Americans carried letters of introduction from state and municipal officials, which while impressive to the bearers were not always so on the scene in Africa. In 1926 three Colorado photographers calling themselves the Denver African Expedition arrived in Nairobi bearing letters from the governor of Colorado and the mayor of Denver; the colonial government sent a puzzled inquiry to the American consul, who gamely replied that the signatures were entitled to "full faith and credit." Del Snow was able to produce letters from an imposing array of Americans, ranging from Teddy Roosevelt and Woodrow Wilson to the mayor of Oakland. Snow unfolded these letters so many times before leaving Kenya that they disintegrated. The letter from Roosevelt had the effect in Nairobi of unveiling the Holy Grail, until Snow sped away from public esteem in his Model T.[31]

American consuls were sometimes sorely pressed in the interests of science. In April, 1927, the consul at Nairobi interceded in a complicated litigation involving the Field Museum, whose Conover-Everard Expedition was stalled in Uganda by a run-in with the law. One Major F. A. B. Nicoll, commanding the Arua Detachment, Uganda Police, arrested the museum's assistant curator of birds for shooting a white rhinoceros, which looked "immature." The major soon discovered what he thought was a second dead rhino, and was so outraged at this further disregard for His Majesty's game laws that he dragged the entire expedition into court, breathing threats of fines, confiscation of trophies, and jail. The consul finally straightened out the matter—after it developed that the first rhino had just been small, not young, and that the second rhino had either been the first or a figment of the major's imagination. The High Court at Kampala threw out the case, and the governor of Uganda hastened to apologize. The expedition lost so much time, however, that its funds ran out, and it had to return to Chicago. In another incident, Professor Kirby, Feis's friend, had to be extracted from the clutches of a Nairobi used-car dealer. Now and then even official forms proved inadequate; in 1937 the exasperated consul at Léopoldville had to write for instructions on the procedure for invoicing one okapi from the Belgian Congo to New York.[32]

The purpose of these expeditions for the museums that sponsored them was the collection of zoological specimens for taxidermic preparation and display. The process from hunting, selecting, and shooting the animals to unveiling them frozen in a ferocious posture in a museum display case was time consuming, exacting, and prodigiously expensive. The entire mounting procedure had been developed by Carl Akeley, who, according to *Life,* had "revolutionized taxidermy" during his years at the Milwaukee Museum and the Field Museum in the 1890s. When Akeley began his career at Ward's Natural Science Establishment in Rochester, he found that taxidermy served only to preserve trophies for hunters and sideshow menageries. The procedure was roughly akin to upholstery; skins were merely stuffed with rags and straw; Barnum's famous "Jumbo," one of the last major trophies prepared in the old way, looked surprisingly like a giant footstool.[33]

Akeley's method, which has never been surpassed, required the taking of anatomical casts, measurements, and sometimes photographs in the field, followed by careful removal of the hide, skull and headskin, and all major bones. These materials were then shipped to the museum, whose preparation department had been "visited with the Jehovah-like function of breathing life into dead bones and dry skins." On the basis of field notes and casts, an exact duplicate of the animal was fashioned by a complicated artistic process, and the skins were fitted over it. At the same time, artists and craftsmen, who had made sketches in the field, were at work painting scenic backgrounds and modeling imitation trees, bushes, and ground coverings out of paper, wax, and celluloid. Veteran taxidermists took an undertaker's pride in their work, gravely warning that the carcass must be "regarded with due respect," since their purpose was to "immortalize" the fortunate creature "by all the means that art and scientific skill can command."[34]

A considerable number of African animals were "immortalized" in this way during the interwar period. The largest American museums prided themselves on the completeness of their African Hall collections. Nothing on four hoofs or paws was safe when a museum expedition was in the field, bent on preserving Africa. Catalogs made up in camp listed specimens taken by the hundreds and thousands, everything from lions, elephants, and zebras to rare birds, bats, and chimpanzees. Even the lovely bongo, one of the shiest of animals, was not safe; its very coyness made it the more desirable. In November, 1930, the leader of a Field Museum expedition wrote excitedly from Kenya that he had shot "the finest group of Bongo ever taken out of Africa." Using Akeley's methods, now long since adopted by major museums, the bongo family was painstakingly prepared in Chicago and placed in the museum's Akeley Memorial African Hall in 1934, where it can still be viewed.[35]

For the big museums, those well endowed with foundation bequests and ready lists of patrons, these efforts to preserve Africa for generations of admiration and study were remarkably successful. In the nation's capital, the United States National Museum housed many groups collected by Roosevelt. The Carnegie Museum of Pittsburgh also had a fine African display. Stewart Edward White predicted accurately that Leslie Simson's African Hall project in San Francisco would allow the "man on the street" to "stand actually on the African veldt or in the African jungle, gazing with almost no necessity of imagination at all upon so near the real thing as it is possible to conceive." In Chicago, the Field Museum's lavish Akeley Memorial African Hall was the finest African zoological collection between the coasts. It contained specimens obtained from the museum's major African expeditions, beginning with Akeley's first, in 1896. His pair of African elephants, which stood in the main entrance of the museum, were famous. By far the most elaborate and expensive collection, however, was the Akeley Memorial African Hall in the American Museum of Natural History in New York. Originally planned by Akeley as a memorial tribute to Theodore Roosevelt, and representing the work of as many as one hundred men over a dozen years, the African Hall was the most expensive group of exhibits ever mounted by an American museum of natural history. *Life* called it "Africa transplanted," an "exhibit unique among the world's museums." Visitors passed through an elaborate Roosevelt Memorial foyer, decorated with murals symbolically depicting, among other things, the great game hunt of 1909, into the unsettling presence of a charging elephant herd, obtained by Akeley and by a later museum director, F. Trubee Davison. Akeley's elephants were, in fact, his pride and joy. It was no easy matter to prepare a tiny dik-dik; to mount an elephant, or a whole herd of them, was a task that literally absorbed the taxidermist for months. Akeley's were so well done that those in the Field and American Museums were used to illustrate scientific textbooks. To all these displays came many millions of visitors, representing one of the largest groups of Americans to give their attention, however briefly and superficially, to the Dark Continent in the years between the wars.[36]

It cannot be said, however, that all zoological interest in Africa was taken up with bringing home bones and hides. Many conservationists and naturalists pointed out that these museum projects, however well motivated, were from the animals' point of view indistinguishable from the depredations of trophy hunters and settlers. And while some kinds of zoological research could be conducted on museum specimens, many kinds could not. Both science and ordinary human interest coveted living animals, and supplying the demand became a major business between the wars.

American zoos emerged from the war years with their stock of African animals badly depleted. The war had completely disrupted the flow of traffic in the animal trade. German steamship lines, which had been "most liberal" in their treatment of animal shipments from East Africa to American zoos, had been ruined. The British, Dutch, and fledgling American lines, lacking the pride of the Germans in their country's traditional monopoly of the wild-animal trade, were grudging and uncooperative. To obstruct further the recovery of American zoos, animal diseases—particularly hoof-

and-mouth disease—ravaged most of the war-torn world. The Bureau of Animal Industry in the Department of Agriculture clamped a series of restrictions on live-animal imports. It required that an import license for every animal be sent from Washington to the port of exit before the local American consul could authorize shipment to the United States. This regulation effectively ended the friendly amateur imports of crew members and passengers that had been an important source of supply. In addition, since Africa was at the distant end of lengthy and unreliable connections, the import permits could not easily be coordinated with legitimate shipments. The worst blow of all was the bureau's blanket proscription of ruminants from everywhere except England and Canada. Fully half the collections of the New York and Philadelphia zoos consisted of ruminants—animals that chew their cud—a classification that included all kinds of antelope. Zoo directors complained bitterly that this striking off of whole continents with "one stroke of the pen" spelled "sweeping disaster" to American parks. They urged that some discretion be given to American consuls in securing local veterinary inspection, and that animals from places free of disease, such as British East Africa, be allowed into the country.[37]

Under pressure from American zoos, the bureau relented, and late in 1919 it issued new regulations. Wild ruminants could now be imported provided they were accompanied by a local veterinarian's certificate stating that the animal had been quarantined in a disease-free area for sixty days prior to exportation. The bureau waived the requirement that an import license reach the exportation point in advance of shipment. A spokesman for the zoo directors said they were "greatly indebted" for these major concessions, which would "greatly facilitate" the supply of animals. The Bureau of Animal Industry, which also inspected all incoming ungulates— hoofed animals, including the ruminants, giraffes, zebras, elephants, rhinoceroses, and hippopotamuses—continued throughout the interwar decades to be the government agency most intimately concerned with the importation of wild animals. The Bureau of Biological Survey controlled the importation of carnivores, but since these did not carry contagious livestock diseases, little direct interference in the traffic came from this quarter. In the government's view, the difficulty with most African animals was their biological similarity to ordinary domestic animals like cattle (ruminants), horses, sheep, and swine (all ungulates) and the susceptibility of these animals to the same unwelcome diseases.[38]

The new importation rules and the speedy restoration of normal communications with tropical Africa enabled American zoos to fill their long-standing needs for African animals. The animals were supplied by professional collectors and dealers, by special expeditions sent by the zoos themselves, and by an occasional private donor. The Martin Johnsons, for instance, ceremoniously handed out gorillas to zoos in San Diego and Washington, and rubber magnate Harvey S. Firestone once presented a pygmy hippopotamus to a startled President Coolidge, who silently passed it along to the National Zoo.[39]

Most animals were supplied professionally, however, and it quickly became the practice "for every zoological garden or park" to patronize responsible animal dealers, whose resident collectors had sufficient experience and knowledge of local conditions to fill almost any order. Prices were high in the 1920s; a pair of healthy giraffes sold for $20,000 when a new Ford cost $290, and $1,200 was considered a handsome year's wages for skilled factory work. Throughout the interwar period Chapman's zebras steadily brought $750 each, and in 1925 mature male lions were priced at $800 each. As a result collecting animals was a "big, well-established business," in which a number of Americans were engaged, several of them doing the double work of collecting and selling the animals. The most famous of these was Frank ("Bring 'Em Back Alive") Buck, who confined his activities to the jungles of southern Asia and the East Indies. Wynant D. Hubbard and his wife attempted to corner the African animal market, first from Rhodesia and later from Portuguese East Africa, not by filling orders as Buck did but by anticipating a market by rounding up hundreds of animals and putting them on sale. Hubbard tried to extract practically unlimited collecting privileges from the Portuguese by offering to donate a long list of animals to the Lisbon Zoological Gardens. The governor in Lourenço Marques smiled on the project, but illness, sunstroke, the mutual greed of Hubbard and the Portuguese, each of whom continually raised the price the other was to pay, and the withdrawal of a financial backer ruined the endeavor. In October, 1924, Hubbard, complaining that he had had "very bad luck" in Mozambique, released three hundred captives. The American consul, who had spent considerable time and effort extricating Hubbard and his furry charges from Portuguese animal-nappers, breathed a sigh of relief; Hubbard was, he said, "quite right" in getting out.

Buck and Hubbard were among the very few professional American animal collectors. Ivan T. Sanderson, who gathered small animals around Mamfe in the British Cameroons was another. Most Americans engaged in the animal trade, however, did so in the United States as dealers, or as the agents of European dealers. The foremost American agencies were Ansel W. Robinson of San Francisco (Buck's partner), Horne's Zoological Arena Company of Kansas City, John T. Benson of Nashua, New Hampshire, Meems Brothers and Ward, Inc., of Oceanside, New York, and Henry Trefflich, Louis Ruhe, Henry Bartels, and Ellis S. Joseph of New York City. These agents solicited and accepted orders from American zoos, forwarding them to such European principles as G. Bruce Chapman Zoological Company, Ltd., of London and the giant firm of Carl Hagenbeck & Sons of Hamburg, or to resident collectors like Christoph Schulz of Arusha, Tanganyika. The American firms guaranteed safe delivery, and conducted all transactions with American consuls and customs officials.[40]

For many years Benson was in the enviable position of representing the world's largest and most famous firm of animal dealers: Hagenbeck. Greatly assisted by German steamship companies, the Hamburg company had all but monopolized the supply of animals from East Africa since the German flag had flapped above the Serengeti herds. Hagenbeck worked hard after 1919 to regain its old dominance in the trade, which it succeeded in doing. Until the Second World War, its animal park—the *Tiergarten*—in the suburb of Altona-Stellingen, was thought of as the Hamburg Zoo. Hagenbeck acclimatized and quarantined the animals in its luxurious Tiergarten and, through Benson, supplied the most prestigious zoos in the United States. Benson, who rapidly rose to a commanding position among American animal dealers, even opened his own little Tiergarten, "Benson's Wild Animal Farm, Nashua, N.H., The Wonder Place of New England," where he displayed his consignments to an admiring, paying public. The complaint of a competitor, Ruhe, that Benson's was a "German house" and thus ineligible for a government importer's permit was technically unfounded, and lost much of its force when it later developed that, strange to say, Ruhe himself had intimate connections with an animal firm by the name of Ruhe in Hanover. More unfortunate for Hagenbeck—and Benson—a hoof-and-mouth epidemic struck Germany in 1931, forcing the Hamburg firm to move all its animals onto a barge in the Elbe to insure quarantine. This raised the overhead and the retail price of the animals just at a time when the Depression was causing a collapse in demand in the United States, Hagenbeck's primary outlet. Benson, who for years had been a spokesman for animal lovers in the country, suddenly revealed a practical side in the crisis. "About 80% of the animals right here on my place that I imported this spring [are] eating their heads off," he screamed. "What chances have I of unloading any of the stock to city zoos." Such was the ungracious welcome for a party of African antelopes and zebras for which American zoos had only too recently been clamoring.[41]

The collection of live African animals by special expedition was not common; even relatively large consignments could be handled more easily by experienced professional collectors. By 1926, however, the National Zoological Park in Washington, D.C., found itself lacking so many African animals that it was impossible to purchase the necessary additions at dealers' prices. The need for these animals, "considered essential to a zoological collection," was brought to the attention of Walter P. Chrysler, who contributed fifty thousand dollars to finance an expedition. The Smithsonian-Chrysler Expedition, led by Dr. William M. Mann of the National Zoo, departed in March, 1926, for Dar es Salaam, complete with camp equipment lent by the United States Marines and a cameraman from the Pathé-Review, a popular newsreel. The State Department pressed the expedition at London as an official government endeavor, the London Zoo lent its auspices, and the governor of Tanganyika provided "very generous" licenses, which, according to Mann, enabled the party to collect "practically all the game in Tanganyika." The assistant chief game warden joined the group when it arrived on the coast, and

the expedition rolled out to Dodoma in a gift Chrysler touring car and proceeded to collect animals.[42]

There were a few minor setbacks: the impalas proved to
be "great leapers" and sailed over the net, twenty-two rhinos
charged back and forth through camp four times without a
single one being captured, and the only giraffe that the party
caught, a baby, although rushed to the ship in the back seat
of the Chrysler, died of pneumonia. All in all, however, the
trip was a roaring success; one of a few special American
excursions in two decades made for the specific purpose of
collecting live animals, the Smithsonian-Chrysler Expedition returned in triumph with seven hundred prizes. A part
of the American public, which was kept informed of the expedition's progress by a series of reports on WRC Radio,
Washington, was on hand to watch the unloading of the
cargo, which included everything from two giraffes—the
gift of the Sudan government—white-bearded gnus, and
koodoos to a red-nose leaf bat and four kinds of skinks.
Mann later gave more than fifty lectures on the expedition,
using the Pathé film, and there was enough left from the
Chrysler gift to purchase a gorilla in 1929 and a "very rare
saddle-bill stork of West Africa" in 1930.[43]

Zoos were extremely popular in the 1920s and 1930s,
attracting millions of visitors, most of them children. Children or not, the visitors represented the largest single group
of Americans exposed to the results of contacts between
their nation and tropical Africa. In 1921 alone, 2.4 million
persons visited the zoo in Washington, where they viewed
an exemplary group of African lions and "Jumbina," one of
the two African elephants in American zoos. The other was
"Khartoum," the pride of the Bronx Zoo, whom the keepers
had been instructed to stuff with vitamins in a shameless
attempt to push him over the ten-foot nine-inch height record
left by Barnum's departed "Jumbo," the most famous wild
animal in American history. In Chicago's Lincoln Park, in
San Diego, Milwaukee, Wichita, Cleveland, and Philadelphia,
on Staten Island, at New Orleans and Dallas, an unending
stream of curious gawkers filed by captive Africa: elands
and koodoos, giraffes and cheetahs, chimpanzees, hippopotamuses, rhinos and zebras, pacing behind iron fretwork or
lounging in the sun, bedraggled perhaps, and subdued, but
unmistakably alive with the mystery of the remote Dark Con-

tinent. The Bronx Zoo even housed a living bongo, snatched from its cool forest home in the Aberdares of Kenya in 1933, at the time the only one of the shy creatures in an American zoo.[44]

Not only in zoos, but in a score of dusty traveling menageries Americans could view African animals. Gentry Brothers, Barnes, and Sells-Floto, and the sprawling Ringling Brothers and Barnum & Bailey circuses featured African lions and leopards, giraffes, zebras, chimpanzees, antelope, and warthogs. Circus posters depicted terrified natives being charged, trampled, and devoured by snarling African beasts. Nowhere in America was the image of Africa as a land of zoological freaks and frights more unqualified than in this world of whips, calliopes, and tawdry gilt. The elephants were from India, the African species being regarded as too difficult to train; the chimpanzees, however, were African. In 1938, having regained control of the family circus, John Ringling North set about to revive its popularity by dressing up the acts and adding a new feature—"Gargantua," a 490-pound gorilla from the Belgian Congo. Billed as "The World's Most Terrifying Living Creature," the disagreeable ape was hauled around the ring in an air-conditioned glass cage drawn by six horses. Circus posters portrayed "Gargantua" as terrifying, indeed—several times the size of man with huge fangs about to rend a helpless African warrior held high overhead.[45]

Africa was brought to the United States in another exciting way as well: on film. The interwar period had barely begun when the cameras started spinning. In October, 1919, a news agency asked whether any motion pictures had been taken of the war against the Germans in East Africa; it was advised that the only films of Africa known to the American consulate in Nairobi were some big-game pictures taken by A. J. Klein. Also in 1919, Del Snow arrived in Kenya to begin filming *Hunting Big Game in Africa.* Soon thereafter the cameramen of the ill-fated Smithsonian expedition came unsteadily on the scene. In the Belgian Congo in 1920 Carl Akeley managed to make the first movies of living gorillas in their natural state. Thus, the camera came to Africa, to record its wildlife for both science and entertainment. In the next decade African big-game and animal pictures proliferated so rapidly that Julian Huxley complained in 1931 that "Africa's big animals have been photographed almost *ad nauseum.*"[46]

Certainly the best-known figures among American big-game photographers were Martin and Osa Johnson. Carl Akeley had seen the Johnsons' South Seas picture, a disjointed but promising first effort; convinced that "his" Africa was about to vanish, Akeley prevailed upon the photographers to make a record of its wildlife. The couple required little convincing that destiny had called them to preserve on film African animals that in "another generation, perhaps . . . will be all but extinct." Johnson did skillful, tasteful work. His first picture, *Trailing African Wild Animals,* fortuitously arrived in New York just as local naturalists were recovering from Snow's extravaganza. The American Museum approved Johnson's titles to accompany the silent footage, after he had an interview with Akeley, who regarded the movie—the first ever endorsed by the American Museum—as a "great step" toward "disseminating natural history through motion pictures." Johnson's films had the happy faculty of enjoying the best of two worlds: they were shown at the Field Museum as part of the Saturday afternoon science program, while at the same time they "made a mint" on the Fox and Keith circuits. *Simba,* a 1928 feature film on the lions of Serengeti, and *Congorilla,* a pioneering attempt at a jungle picture with sound, released in 1932, were the most notable of the four Johnson films after the first. *Congorilla,* which "brought the reality of inner Africa many degrees closer to us," also inspired a song for its debut: "Congorilla, The New Dance Craze." After the numerous times Martin Johnson had faced charging elephants and rhinos with his camera, until Osa shot them practically at the tripod, his accidental death in a plane crash near Burbank, California, in 1937 seemed almost anticlimactic.[47]

Photography in the African bush was not as painless as Johnson's smooth products suggested. The tropical climate caused emulsions to deteriorate, while heat waves, shifts in wind and light, and the sudden appearance of clouds spoiled many shots. Animals of a ferocious nature would appear unexpectedly and make a rush for the camera, making it difficult for the operator to remember to turn the crank at an even speed. At other times, animals would not appear at all.

On the great American Museum expedition of 1926, Johnson spent thirteen days with six cars and forty men vainly attempting to photograph the rhinoceroses that were supposed to be everywhere in the vicinity. The introduction of sound equipment in the late 1920s made an already tricky process more complicated. No one had noticed it in the days of the silent film, but African animals did not make much noise, except at night. Johnson spent days watching hippopotamuses to catch one bellowing. "And at that," he said, "nineteen times out of twenty, we prepared for a bellow and found ourselves cranking away on a water bubble or a yawn."[48]

Despite these difficulties, or perhaps partly because of them, conservationists welcomed African animal pictures for their scientific value as a record of vanishing species, and commercial news services found wild-animal pictures profitable copy. African films and still photographs were in constant demand, and wire-service picture syndicates were constantly on the alert for new material. Professional wildlife photographers included in their books friendly tips on equipment to enable novices to get good results. The distinguished British cameraman, Major A. Radcliffe Dugmore, was asked to give special lectures at the Field Museum. Periodicals like *Nature* and the *National Geographic Magazine* published many beautiful African animal pictures. The major purpose of several small expeditions, and a secondary purpose of the large ones, was the production of a motion picture that would be accurate enough to salve scientific consciences and exciting enough to make money. The only real result of Paul Hoefler's Colorado African Expedition of 1929 was *"Africa Speaks"—First All-Sound Film of African Adventure.* In the late 1920s an American consul in Kenya suggested that all the publicity East Africa was getting in the United States was confined to films made by Martin Johnson and by "numerous" American "hunting parties."[49]

Excursions into Africa that had as their sole purpose the manufacture of a feature film did not require a huge initial outlay of funds, but the big institutional expeditions that depended on economic prosperity, leisure, and the taste for ostentatious personal philanthropy did. With the prospects of profit high, motion-picture ventures into Africa continued throughout the interwar years, but institutional expeditions were curtailed by the Depression. The steady decline in the value of endowment-fund securities, such as those left by Marshall Field in Chicago, and the near evaporation of gifts, memberships, and paid admissions meant the end of expeditions, invariably the first items cut from dwindling budgets. "For reasons of economy," reported the Field Museum, "the Museum conducted no expeditions during 1935." Even completion of habitat groups, for which the animals had already been collected, came under fire because of the enormous costs involved. American zoos also ceased to launch expeditions, and transactions with individual collectors and animal dealers were cut back sharply. As Benson's exotic merchandise ate up his profits, American zoos pooled their extra and captive-born animals to avoid any cash expenditures through the Depression. With the Crash of 1929 came the end of one era in American-African relations: the classic African expedition.[50]

An expert on American museums declared in 1939 that the large zoological displays in museums were "things of the past"; the attempt to preserve African specimens forever through the expenditure of vast sums would prove futile. "Time will do its corrupting work despite the best efforts of the taxidermist," he added. Yet today the visitor may still stroll through the same darkened halls and illuminated cases that drew crowds in President Harding's day and see the same exhibits—preserved, if not for immortality, at least beyond the time when Africa could be regarded as little more than the world's zoo. Time has done its work, not so much upon mounted specimens as upon a system that could in so many ways encourage Americans to think of Africa as a place of real animals instead of real people. Nonetheless, despite the disproportionate publicity given to the animals, there was interest in the people of Africa between the wars, some of it scientific, a great deal of it incidental, almost all of it patronizing and evangelical. At bottom, it remained the animals that received the disinterested admiration of the American people.[51]

five:
americans and
the people
of africa

As for the rest of our equipment, mostly porters, they were proper good howling savages— Yafoubas—a superb, grand gang.'—William B. Seabrook (1931)

When the staff of the American Museum was readying the Akeley African Hall for its long-awaited unveiling in 1936, Museum Director F. Trubee Davison was pleased to accept one additional gift for the display. A patron wished to donate a bronze figure of an African drummer, the work of Malvina Hoffman. A nice thought, observed Davison pleasantly; it would "add a human touch to the African Hall."[2]

That Africa had a human side seemed to strike many travelers as an afterthought. When the *Trader Horn* movie expedition returned to Hollywood and learned that the African "tribes" in the film would need names for a sound picture, it was discovered that no one could remember any African names. White writers who would "see Africa develop into a major power or Continent" noticed the indigenous population on occasion, but only, as Wynant D. Hubbard described it, as "the greatest source of worry and speculation." A writer in *Living Age* gave the oft-repeated warning that American tourists and residents alike in Africa could be thoroughly familiar with their own African laborers and servants "and yet be entirely ignorant of the natives." Julian

148

Huxley lamented that his countrymen in England and Africa were "lamentably ignorant of both the racial and social anthropology of the African," and one American journalist admitted to beginning a study of African life in Rhodesia with a lack of knowledge that she frankly declared to be "complete."[3]

To American scholars engaged in the still relatively new studies of human life and social groups—anthropology, ethnology (defined at the time as the study of races and their relations to one another), and sociology—the wide gaps in public and academic knowledge of African people were an invitation. Expeditions by Americans to study the life of Africans began after the war and were one element in relations between the two peoples during the interwar years. These expeditions seldom involved more than a few members, who often had to carry home animal trophies to help pay the freight on the entire trip. The projects did not receive nearly as much publicity as did the animal-collecting trips, but being less elaborate and less expensive than zoological expeditions, they were able to continue through the Depression years.

Harvard University led the way in several aspects of African studies in the postwar years; the Peabody Museum's *Harvard African Studies* seldom referred to sub-Saharan Africa, but the school was joint sponsor in 1925, along with the Rockefeller Foundation, of an important series of field investigations in that region by Raymond Leslie Buell of the Bureau of International Research of Harvard and Radcliffe, and, after 1927, research director for the prestigious Foreign Policy Association. Buell's journey throughout Africa in 1925 and 1926 took fifteen months, and was designed to collect material for a "study of financial and political questions" relating to Africans as they were forced to adapt to the economies of Imperial control. Buell shared the preconceptions of his era and found little to criticize in the presumed necessity of prolonged white rule. Not blind to the faults of European colonial governments that failed to help their African subjects adjust to the new demands of an industrialized society, Buell nevertheless reserved his most unfavorable comments for the government of the independent Republic of Liberia. In Africa Buell encountered few difficulties from the colonial authorities and from these the

American consuls on the scene easily rescued him, assuaging the suspicious Portuguese in Lourenço Marques and tracing the four packages of notes that the professor absentmindedly left in Nairobi. The results of Buell's inquiries, *The Native Problem in Africa,* published in two volumes in 1928, covered historical developments, labor policies, agriculture, ethnology, and colonial government. Besides his months in the field, Buell had read almost every relevant colonial document; his bibliography ran to sixty-six pages (with only a very scattered reference to an American author), and his book became a standard reference on Africans under colonial rule.[4]

Two years after the appearance of Buell's book, two anthropological studies were launched in tropical Africa—one by Wilfrid Hambly of the Field Museum, who penetrated Angola and Nigeria, and the other, of far greater importance, by Professor Melville J. Herskovits of Northwestern University, whose research took him to the French colony of Dahomey. Sponsored by the Rockefeller-funded International Institute of African Language and Culture, the studies by Herskovits were the first modern anthropological surveys of an African state made by an American. The work was of such high quality that it has yet to be superseded. *Dahomey: An Ancient West African Kingdom* was published in 1938, after years of analysis of the materials gathered on the trip, years in which Herskovits and his wife Frances established themselves as the leading American Africanists, and made Northwestern a major center of nascent African studies in the United States. The trip through French West Africa was facilitated by the French Colonial Office after proper diplomatic representations were made in Paris, and by the American consuls at Dakar and Lagos. Even the U.S. trade commissioner at Accra, the Gold Coast—the only other representative of the American government on Africa's West Coast—offered his services to Herskovits.[5]

Herskovits' interest began with the old world origin of the American black. His doctoral work in 1926 had been done on East Africa, but his first African field research five years later was in West Africa, which he believed to have been a major source of the American black population during the slave trade. The Herskovitses returned to Chicago laden with Dahomean wood cuts, appliqué cloth, carvings, cast-

ings, and sound recordings, all of which they scattered about
their rooms at Northwestern, to the great joy of Chicago art
students. Although the bulk of their analyses produced results that appeared only in scholarly journals, the Herskovitses joined almost at once in the popular current controversy over African art. In an era that wished above all else
to be avant-garde, African art had special appeal; pieces of
merit were expensive, daring, and "primitive"—sufficiently
expensive, daring, and primitive, in fact, that some art critics
blandly discounted the possibility that the pieces were
genuinely African. The work must have been inspired by
contact with the superior colonizing white or Arabic races.
In the same way, other critics debunked the African influences in those darlings of the twenties: jazz and spirituals.
The Herskovitses stoutly maintained the African origin of
the disputed works, and contributed a stream of sympathetic
pieces to a wide variety of liberal, artistic, and black periodicals. To the American black intellectual community, the
controversy was of far more than academic interest; proof
of African origin for the popular artworks bolstered crucial
ideals of racial capacity. Blacks were delighted by the Herskovitses' constant assertions that their mounds of African
materials contained irrefutable evidence that the "inner life
of the natives" had been but little affected by European
contacts.[6]

Hambly's West African expedition for the Field Museum is
an interesting case study of such projects in the interwar
years. The American public did not share the anthropologists' interest in African life, and its more affluent representatives much preferred to support zoological expeditions,
the kind that invariably produced large, colorful, and exciting trophies. Museums found it difficult to scrape together
enough money to finance even the most modest anthropological field trips. In 1929 a Chicago philanthropist, Frederick H. Rawson, president of the Union Trust Company,
donated ten thousand dollars to the Field Museum, without
specifying its use—a sort of last benefaction of the Roaring
Twenties. The museum seized upon this unexpected gift to
send forth its first anthropological expedition to Africa.
Hambly, a member of the museum staff, was selected to
direct the operation, which consisted largely of himself. The
State Department was asked to prepare the way; the Portu-

guese, as usual, were suspicious and caused a delay by requesting more information. After American consulates at Lagos and Loanda were informed of the project, and the Portuguese had relented, Hambly set sail with a shotgun, a dictaphone, two cameras, and "a set of instruments for anthropometry."[7]

Once safely arrived in Angola, Hambly secured the permission of the *alto commisario* to move into the bush. He made his base at an American mission station in Elende in south-central Angola, the center of Ovimbundu territory. Most American students of African life were in one way or another dependent upon American missionaries in the field, and Hambly was no exception. In this case it was veteran evangelist Dr. Merlin W. Ennis who was of invaluable service. Ennis provided Hambly with porters, a dark room for developing films, hospitality, and, most importantly, Ngonga, an "interpreter and chief informant" who providentially proved to be the only man in the district who spoke English, Portuguese, and Umbundu. Hambly measured 54 adult males with his anthropometric calipers, gathered up 1,239 artifacts, took 2,000 feet of film, and recorded 50 cylinders on the dictaphone. He also sent back rolls of "human interest" pictures for Wide World Photos, which depicted market scenes and Africans gawking into the horn of the dictaphone, which Wide World captioned "The 'Black Magic' of the White Man."[8]

Hambly pressed on from the scene of these triumphs to Nigeria, where he ranged over most of the colony, from Benin to Sokoto, collecting bronzes, dictaphone rolls, movies, stills, and small artifacts. His acquisitions in the area of Ibadan and Ilorin were particularly extensive, and added vast amounts of new material to the Field Museum's resources. In the interests of peace, the British did not allow Christian missionaries into the large Moslem areas of northern Nigeria, and on the last stage of his expedition Hambly was without the assistance of any other American. He was able to purchase a new Model A Ford truck, into which he piled an ever-growing mound of specimens, but the truck became mired once too often in the sandy roads around Lake Chad and had to be abandoned. Hambly put the little expedition on horseback and proceeded in an ungenerous frame of mind; most of the cultures he encountered from then on he styled "not rich."[9]

He did have the good fortune once, near Katsina, to stumble onto some real cannibals, but the British, who had just raided the place, "specially requested" him not to "make publicity photographs dealing with these barbarous practices." Hambly, who shared the interest of the wire service in profitable publicity, was severely disappointed, and complained that "such matters are the only anthropological information really appreciated by the public." In the end he had to content himself with two skulls. The rather vivid nature of Hambly's tastes, in fact, were not fully admired by the Field Museum, and although he produced several transient monographs on his work in Africa, Hambly did not become a leading figure in American African studies. One of his articles appeared in *Scientific American* in 1937, accompanied by lurid photographs of snake worshipers, and he edited a popular *Sourcebook for African Anthropology.*[10]

Among several American ethnologists to investigate African peoples in the period were Charles W. Coulter of Ohio Wesleyan, in 1929, and Henry Usher Hall of the University of Pennsylvania, in 1936. Although Coulter, a sociologist and an expert on American race relations, was still obliged in Africa to collect small animals on the side, his ethnological investigations were of lasting usefulness. Research among African peoples gained stature with every passing year. Seven years after Coulter's trip to Central Africa, Hall luxuriated in a handsome grant from Penn that enabled him and his wife to spend six months in Sierra Leone in pure research among the Sherbro and Bulloro peoples, unencumbered by demands for animal trophies or the necessity of relying on local missionaries.[11]

The observations of American missionaries, for decades the main source of information on African life, continued to enjoy circulation in popular scientific journals, but serious scholars entered the field after World War I, and they eventually captured it. In the early 1920s such American scholars as Robert H. Lowie, at the time an assistant curator of anthropology at the American Museum, and Alexander A. Goldenweiser of the New School for Social Research began using objective illustrations from African cultures in their books. By the time George P. Murdock of Yale wrote *Our Primitive Contemporaries* in 1934 the practice was standard; even such a general work as Ruth Benedict's *Patterns of Culture* touched upon scientific observations of the Nandi in British East Africa and Zulu medicine men. American field-work began in earnest with Herskovits' research in Dahomey in 1931. G. Gordon Brown's study of legitimacy among a tribe in Tanganyika the next year was an indication of things to come. By the end of the decade, a number of notable field projects had been completed in West Africa by Hers-kovits, William Bascom, Jack Harris, and Dr. Lorenzo D. Turner, while Joseph Greenberg, a young doctoral student at Northwestern, had started the investigations in Northern Nigeria that opened his career as America's most distin-guished expert on African linguistics. In a slightly more popular vein, photographers like the geographer Richard Upjohn Light were portraying their subjects with precision and objectivity, producing useful scientific records, free from the dictates of a wire-service public.[12]

It cannot be said, however, that the American scientific and academic communities showed the same interest in the people of Africa that they showed in its wildlife. Nor was the paying public's curiosity about Africa gratified with the results of ethnographic investigation to anywhere near the extent that it was with zoological prizes. Anthropology was not, like zoology, a settled discipline in the interwar years, combing the last recesses of its province for specimens. Most leading American anthropologists concentrated their investigations on the native peoples of North, Central, and South America and, to a lesser extent, the South Pacific. Herskovits for years remained the most eminent figure in American African studies, and one of the few of major aca-demic stature, although he was consistently encouraged in his work by the great men of American anthropology. But Herskovits' work was unique. Most of the information on African peoples that was laid before the American public in these years was the result of rather offhand observations. By and large, what Americans read were the comments of travelers who had gone to Africa for purposes other than the study of African life, or those of domestic academicians distantly applying a theory based on the study of maps, museum artifacts, travelers' accounts, and the physical measurements cataloged in scholarly journals in that hey-day of physical anthropology.[13]

All commentators were agreed that the indigenes of Africa, members of the black race with various admixtures, were different from whites. But to the dispassionate and often antique records of "cephalic indices" and measurements of "prognathism" were added the combined value judg-ments of generations of travelers. The distinguished Vic-torian anthropologist Sir Edward Burnett Tylor, whose works were reprinted into the interwar years, noted that the Afri-can Negro compared unfavorably in point of anatomical de-tail with the Apollo Belvedere, that "ideal of manly beauty." It was commonly believed that the anthropometric measure-ments of the Negro indicated a sort of physical primitivism, a retarded evolution from the common animal ancestor of man. *Carpenter's Geographical Reader,* a prewar school text in wide use, informed its readers that the Namas of South-West Africa were "as ugly as any people we have yet seen." And they were not the only ones. Murdock of Yale was not overly impressed with the features of the Ganda of Buganda: "In general, the features are not unprepossess-ing, even according to European standards." Not only were the Africans regarded as ugly, they were condemned for their lack of concern over the fact. One writer for *Atlantic* complained of "the indifference of natives to human physical beauty."[14]

"Savagery" is an illusive concept. Some persons intend the term to have a favorable, even a complimentary con-notation; at least a hint of this is found in several important American writers on Africa. Roosevelt and Akeley were among several Americans who were considerably moved by the lion-spearing ritual of the Nandi Masai of Kenya, by which the young men of the tribe proved courage and man-hood. Akeley preserved the scene in a notable group of bronzes, in two sets—one each for the African Halls of the Field and American museums. One American was so im-pressed by the courageous Masai that he abandoned a profitable lecture circuit—devoted largely to this subject— and went to British East after the war to film the ritual. Martin Johnson, in *Simba,* and Paul Hoefler devoted extensive footage in their African movies to the gallant, be-feathered Nandi, and their stills of the lion spearing were sold by Wide World.[15]

Most writers, however, viewed the African in his natural state as an unwelcome adjunct to an otherwise pleasant journey. To these visitors, "savage" referred to any African not in the paid employment of a white. The term carried the most unpleasant connotations. Lord Lugard warned in *The Dual Mandate in British Tropical Africa,* which for twenty years wielded almost Scriptural authority on African affairs, that "some corners of tropical Africa . . . resemble the conditions of predatory warfare which is characteristic of animal life in the ocean's depths." Carpenter's geography book, by way of counseling generations of African explorers, declared: "We have our guns with us. Most of Africa is inhabited by savages, some of whom are cannibals. . . ." Indeed, a writer in *National Geographic* assured his readers in 1919 that "cannibalism" was "an everyday occurrence." The memoirs of a British police official in Nigeria carried a photograph of a "Typical Group of Cannibals (The Leopard-Skin Bag Contained Cooked Human Hands)."[16]

In 1931 a New York free-lance writer named William Seabrook published an account of his investigations into the practice of cannibalism by certain Africans in French West Africa. A compendium of clubroom gossip, barroom reminiscences, and playroom imagination, Seabrook's *Jungle Ways* even contained the author's description of the taste of human flesh, to which extreme his journalistic curiosity had purportedly driven him. In a moment of unintentional self-revelation, Seabrook described the scene in one village: "All the bad fiction-traditional stage props were there—night, torchlight, superstition, crowds hysterical, and mumbo-jumbo raised to the nth power."[17]

The scene had been a "traditional stage prop" since Paul Du Chaillu's steel engravings had been opened to a fascinated juvenile public, showing Africans wildly dancing around a pot-bellied idol by torchlight. This was a picture, said a writer for *Century,* "that time can never fade: black figures, bounding, crouching, whirling, inconceivably grotesque, silhouetted against the leaping flames; . . ." "The black man's a fearful savage we say," remarked Trader Horn, "when we see him crucify a man head down." The movie based on these reflections showed a "ju-ju and witch-craft" hut in one scene, filled with skulls and crocodile skins; the effect of the scene was not lessened by the director's incidental admission that the skulls were, alas, papier-mâché. The public was quite keen on skulls. The solemn demand of the British at Versailles for the return of a totem skull long held by the Germans in East Africa as an aid in controlling a certain people aroused such curiosity in the United States that the National Geographic Society issued an explanatory bulletin. Skulls on poles and piles of bones were a familiar feature in a long succession of jungle matinees. *Tarzan Escapes,* a typical number released in 1936, contained several fetching scenes in which the "fiend-ish Ganeoloni tribe" achieved "sadistic revenge" by flinging the villain into a cave of giant lizards; another "good shot" showed these same men "ingeniously tearing a captive limb from limb."[18]

The *Foreign Service Journal* published an article by the American consul in Mozambique entitled "The Witch of Lourenço Marques"; it told of an old woman driven from a nearby village to starve in the bush on the questionable pre-text that she had been turning herself into a hippopotamus at night and eating the village corn supply. The ritual killing of twins, who were considered extremely bad luck, the "curious" custom among the Mangbuttu of wrapping little girls' skulls to distend them; the "horrible and inhuman practice" in which the Kikuyu, believing death to be con-tagious, took their aged and dying far from the village to die in the bush; the ritual serpent worship; and ceremonies of circumcision—all were the subjects of exciting popular ac-counts. A respected anthropologist filled many pages with a grisly description of the sanguinary rites that traditionally had attended the coronation of the King of Baganda; the royal kraal ran red with the blood of whimsical slaughter. The author did not dilute the effect by mentioning that such practices had largely disappeared a half century before. May Mott-Smith was among several writers to dwell on the "leop-ard men," a secret West African sect that supposedly skulked about disguised as leopards, tearing victims to death with iron claws.[19]

At times the accounts of native savagery reached such florid heights that even their authors used words like "fantastic" and "the phantasm of a disordered brain" to describe them. The manner in which the Africans stripped a dead elephant after the white sportsman had removed the trophies made particularly bloodcurdling reading. "It was naked savagery," harrumphed Daniel Streeter. "Not a single element of humor relieved its dreadfulness." The area was "an inferno filled with things that had once been men, covered with blood and sweat." "It became a Bakst poster," wrote another, "of black and browns against the dripping red." "Is it any wonder," asked Martin Johnson, "that the African elephant has also remained a savage, when the members of the human race that reside near him fall so low in the scale of man?"[20]

"So low in the scale of man"—a revealing phrase. For if there was a scale of man, few disputed that the African fell somewhere near the bottom. He was not only savage—and the missionaries railed against "the brutality of the raw African native"—he was a child. Africans were among "the child races of the world, declared Maurice Delafosse, the French ethnologist who wrote one of the best general surveys of West African culture: to him the "Negroes of Africa" were "children with respect to the majority of European peoples of our time." The Akeleys thought of their "black boys" as "just overgrown children." An art collector affirmed that the African's artistic conceptions "resemble those of children." Children—but only mentally; not young, but retarded; the African was backward. Reginald Coupland, later to be knighted as a pioneer African historian, called his subjects "that swarming, fecund Negro race, the most backward among the great races of mankind. . . ." Africa offered Paul Hoefler "a journey backward into the neolithic period." The distinguished anthropologist Alfred L. Kroeber of the University of California spoke of tropical Africa as "prevailingly uncivilized," a land of "comparative cultural backwardness."[21]

To those who considered the African "so low in the scale of man," little that was truly indigenous to tropical Africa had value. Scholars confidently asserted that whatever merit African art and culture seemed to possess rested on "external influences." Kroeber declared that any part of African culture that had not yet been "definitely traced to

an extra-African source" would one day "prove to be due to
transmission from Asia or Europe." The most respected
authorities concurred. "New ideas and thoughts, and new
customs, have come from without," stated the librarian of
the Royal Empire Society in the *Yale Review.* "Very little of
value has been initiated in the country." The blood itself
that coursed in the veins of those Africans who seemed the
least primitive was proclaimed by any number of writers to
be alien—a beneficent dilution of the morbid black blood.
Many writers on this subject, scholarly and otherwise, affirmed that the superior African was the "Bantu," technically
a much-abused linguistic term that had come to refer to
any "fundamentally negroid stock with a certain admix-
ture of Hamitic blood." "Hamitic"—originally a reference to
the generations of the second son of Noah—had meant the
Caucasian races of the Mediterranean littoral, such as the
Berbers and Egyptians, with their aquiline features and a
range of coloring. The great Bantu migrations of African
pre-history were made up of "this higher type, intermediate
between negro and Hamitic." These peoples, according to
Roland B. Dixon, a Harvard anthropologist, had brought a
"leavening to the Dark Continent." From this mythical infu-
sion of light blood welled the superb physiques of the noble
Masai, the political sophistication of the Baganda, and the
ancient heritage of the Abyssinians, who, attested Parker T.
Moon, were "not for a moment to be classed with jungle
savages." Such ideas are based on the now-discredited
hypothesis that a basic relationship exists between physical
type and cultural attainment. Yet for decades scholars in
African affairs on both sides of the Atlantic flatly declared
that the entire history of sub-Saharan Africa could be told
in terms of successive waves of Hamitic blood, the great
civilizing impulse of black Africa.[22]

Many travelers and popular writers affirmed in the years
between the wars that the Africans lacked visible political
systems of their own devising. Where the Hamitic infusions
had been at their invigorating work for centuries, as in
Uganda and West Africa, rudimentary native polities had
risen on the inert black substratum of society; even these
polities, however, were declared to need the guidance of a
civilized hand. Under the international law in force after
Versailles, Africans were lumped together as "aborigines,"

described in a United States government publication as members of "uncivilized tribes which inhabit a region at the time a civilized state extends its sovereignty over the region," and the descendants of such tribes. It was not essential that the region be considered a complete political vacuum for it to be legally available for occupation; so long as the indigenous population was "not united permanently for political action," an imperial power had a legal right of "acquisition" or "appropriation." In fact, imperialists considered the existence of some form of native government rather useful; it enabled them to obtain the unimpeachable legal sanction of an aboriginal cession, after which the sovereignty of the local political system was extinguished. This acquisition process so seldom encountered local resistance that texts spoke of European possession of Africa as the inevitable result of the attraction of its rich natural resources on one hand and the "weakness of its political system" on the other. So complete did the African "abnegation of self and possessions" seem that Mary Townsend found that most of the standard "accounts of colonial expansion" available to Americans simply neglected the indigenous peoples.[23]

What history could a people claim, who lacked their own culture and political identity? There are those, W. E. B. Du Bois noted bitterly during the war, "who would write universal history and leave out Africa." His statement was not precisely true; while few Americans acknowledged the fact of African political or cultural history—Daniel Streeter simply declared that Africans "represented the negation of civilization. They had no history"—considerable attention was given in the United States to a remarkable series of archeological discoveries in Africa in the mid-1920s. "Africa," said Julian Huxley, was "a continent almost without a history; but it is rapidly acquiring a surprising prehistory." Charles Darwin had believed that Africa was the home of the earliest progenitor of man, and in the decade after the First World War archeologists working in Africa uncovered strong evidence in support of Darwin's thesis. In 1921 a "highly remarkable and enigmatic skull" was found at the Broken Hill Mine in Northern Rhodesia. Aleš Hrdlička of the Smithsonian Institution was a key figure in the subsequent study and reporting of the "Rhodesian

161   americans and the people of africa

Man." He reported it different from any known type of African, comparable in ways to the European Neanderthal, but perhaps earlier; it was truly the center of a number of "anthropological puzzles." Beginning in 1926 the British anthropologist L. S. B. Leakey opened a series of cave excavations in Kenya, from which he soon produced bone fragments that he confidently declared to be the remains of the oldest known examples of *Homo sapiens* in the world. He occasioned a long and surprisingly warm debate with his conclusion that by the Upper Pleistocene age a number of distinct examples of the human species were afoot in Africa. To prevent a bone rush, British colonial authorities in Kenya soon passed a new "Antiquities Ordinance" that enabled the governor to prevent the removal of "even a portion" of any archeological discoveries.

Yet what was the present-day significance of Darwin's hypothesis? What contemporary value did the discoveries and work of men like Hrdlička and Leakey have? Travelers and tourists might be perfectly willing to accord the African the privilege of being the progenitor of humanity, but what was noteworthy was how little progress he had made since then. Streeter even discovered regression: "Why, from an even start, they had descended the ladder, while we had climbed, was hard to comprehend."[24]

There was an occasional reference in American publications to the great black Sudanic kingdoms of the Middle Ages. Blacks were extremely proud of "this splendid history of civilization and uplift," and they attempted, without much success, to bring knowledge of these states to a broader public. Among professional anthropologists, knowledge of these states was common by the mid-1930s; with the publication in 1938 of Herskovits' research in Dahomey, a wide and interested range of readers learned of a black dynasty that owed "little to foreign contacts." Nevertheless, the bulk of scholarly and popular opinion continued to attribute these highly developed political states, even when they were acknowledged to have occurred, to alien religious and racial inspiration.[25]

A significant controversy centered on the great stone ruins discovered in the mid-nineteenth century at Zimbabwe in Southern Rhodesia. Located in the heart of Central Africa, inconveniently distant from any point at which alien traders or explorers could have easily deposited uplifting influences, the Zimbabwe ruins attracted a variety of treasure hunters, tourists, and partisans. The partisans took up positions fortified by theoretical explanations of how the culture, to which the stones bore witness, could, or could not, have been an indigenous production. The Beira, Mashonaland and Rhodesia Railways, perhaps seeking an antique precedent for its own high-handed labor policies, insisted in its tourist guide that the elliptical temple, acropolis, and circular walls had been built by Bantu slaves under the direction of Asian gold miners. A painstaking investigation by an English scholar on the scene in 1929 found "not one single item that is not in accordance with the claim of Bantu origin and medieval date," but concluded that the history of the Zimbabwe culture would remain a "mystery—the mystery which lies in the still pulsating heart of native Africa." To black Americans like Du Bois, the origin of the Zimbabwe culture was no mystery, and he denounced the then common theory that the ruins had been left by Asian intruders who had come searching for gold—the "usual" attempts, as he called them, to find "an external and especially an Asiatic origin for this culture." Carter G. Woodson, executive director of the Association for the Study of Negro Life and History and editor of the *Journal of Negro History,* joined in the criticism of those who "took up the distortion of the truth in glad refrain of the traducer and exploiter." Mary L. Jobe Akeley was curiously in agreement, but most American tourists, while eager to visit the site and be steeped in the mystery and romance of a misty and largely imaginary past, accepted the alien gold-miner story uncritically.[26]

The African, in short, was regarded as a copier. Having created nothing of value on his own, he was sometimes portrayed as at least perceptive enough to recognize the superiority of the alien cultures to which he was exposed. The most recent and most obviously superior of all of these outside influences was, of course, that of the white European. "The black tribes of Africa are tired. Our force and our scorn have more than half convinced them that all the things which are not ours are lies." An important Methodist missionary reported that in their haste to abandon old ways as a result of white penetration, the African became unhinged, and had "no chart or compass for the new sea of life upon which he has been thrust." Popular writers expressed little surprise at being taken for supernatural beings by the natives; travelers professed to believe that the simpleminded blacks were so amazed by such wonders as steam-traction engines, airplanes, wireless, Chevrolets, phonographs, and flashlights that they thought of the wielder of these marvels as a "Great White Chief from Heaven," or a "White Goddess." The editor of *Africa,* the journal of the Rockefeller-sponsored International Institute of African Languages and Cultures, regularly delivered grand pronouncements on this gratifying phenomenon:

> The European's position as a dominant power in Africa has been made easy by the fact that he was since his first arrival an object of admiration to the African. He was looked upon as a superior being, possessing every desirable object and being capable of doing almost anything, a man by nature a ruler to whom one willingly submitted.[27]

The black expressed this "admiration" in a number of satisfying ways, most notably by adopting European dress. The African attempted to overcome his "feeling of inferiority" in ways that were often "naive"—he copied "the white man to a slavish degree." A few Americans were vaguely annoyed at these attempted imitations, but most were gratified and amused by what they took as the hopeless incongruity of the situation. Certainly no more familiar and genial African stereotype existed in the American mind than that favorite of cartoonists, the top-hatted African king. Paul Du Chaillu had pictured a chief in a stovepipe hat in the 1870s, and there had been little change in the picture since. Osa Johnson was particularly fond of the scene; she sent a view of herself and "her 'high hat' caddy in Tanganyika" to a news-photo syndicate, and included in her autobiography a shot of a "Meru Dandy" of Kenya in a London top hat. The wife of the last American consul at Boma recounted the story of the elevation of her head boy to the village council for giving the local chief the consul's cast-off opera hat. Seabrook, the American cannibal, discovered an African king in a "French fireman's helmet instead of the classic silk hat," and a West Coast chieftain regularly surprised his visitors by mustering a parade of eight men clad in fancy-dress cuirassier uniforms, donated in happier days by the

German Kaiser. Returning from the frosty Ruwenzori, a party of Americans was met at Ibanda, Uganda, by a chief in a white cotton night shirt and a tuxedo.[28]

To some writers, the African could not avoid being funny. One commented on the Kikuyu of Kenya, "the most light-hearted of African tribes, fond of singing and dancing"; although lazy and unreliable, according to another writer, the Kikuyu were "gay, good-natured," and "feckless." Trader Horn recalled an African king who was "always in good humor and always half intoxicated. A regular King Lear." The stereotyped Africans were, of course, wholly given to drink and its evil effects. A regular contributor to the *Atlantic* observed in 1921 that "the whole population of Tropical and Subtropical Africa is drunk after sunset," a failing hardly confined to the black Africans. But drunk or sober, the African was funny, or at least curious, and the native governments were the funniest and most curious, of all. Richard Halliburton wrote off the Abyssinian religion as a thing of incantations and costumes, while the Ethiopian government itself was lampooned in a best-selling novel of 1932, *Black Mischief* by Evelyn Waugh. African rulers were presented as pompous and overdressed buffoons in Broadway productions like *The Emperor Jones* and *At Home Abroad.*[29]

One British colonial officer said he was "puzzled over the dramatic scheme of nature in providing such entertainment as the negro affords, even if only by his very appearance." Streeter thought the earlobe distortions of the Kavirondo women of Kenya "hilarious." The *National Geographic* ran pictures of Africans with captions like "Central African feminine beauty unadorned," and "Dandies of the Kikuyu Tribe, Kenya Colony." The women of the Ubangi of French Equatorial Africa, who distended their lips as a mark of honor and beauty, were "platter pusses" to the *National Geographic,* "Plate-Lipped Flappers" to the *Literary Digest,* and "Flap-Jack Ladies" to *Life.*[30]

Indeed, one traveler complained that the people of Central Africa were "generally misjudged" by whites who knew only blacks corrupted by contact with Europeans; the "negro as he is" was much more interesting. News-photo services agreed. The arrangement between the Field Museum and The *New York Times*-Wide World was typical; S. C. Simms, the museum's director, instructed W. D. Hambly to "make some negatives of human interest" while in Africa, "as these will prove more profitable owing to the greater demand on the part of the public for such illustrations." The demand was not confined to pictures. A man in Parkersburg, West Virginia, inquired of the American consulate at Lagos about taking a family of four Ubangi on tour in the United States. A group of Ubangi were with the Ringling Brothers, Barnum & Bailey circus in the years 1930-1932, and proved the biggest sideshow attraction in the circus's history. In 1934 Robert L. Ripley was "particularly anxious" to obtain a selection of "native warriors" with "striking costumes," such as "Zulus, Masais, Kikuyu, Kavirondos," for his Believe It or Not Odditorium at the Chicago World's Fair; he offered to pay the American consul at Lagos $500 upon the safe arrival in Chicago of any of these "human oddities." The request was eventually forwarded from the consul to Martin Johnson in Nairobi. Tourists in Africa had many opportunities to pick up souvenirs of the "human oddities" all around them. The Native Registration Department of Nairobi gladly sold confiscated Masai shields and spears to tourists. In the 1920s, groups of Africans stood along the roads in Uganda in ceremonial grass headdress and white body clay, ready to "dance and pose" for tourists passing in their open cars, "in return for small change."[31]

The unpleasant conclusion to be drawn by persons steeped in this racial lore of imperialism was not long in coming: the African savage, comical, and bizarre was not quite human. When in 1921 an Oklahoma curio dealer tried to buy "a few skulls of the different tribes and monkeys Apes-Babbons [sic]—any of the limbs" from the United States consul at Loanda, he was expressing a confusion that had been fixed in some American minds for years. Teddy Roosevelt noted of the Africans that some were "ape-like naked savages, who dwell in the woods and prey on creatures not much wilder or lower than themselves." The American consul at Lourenço Marques warned American film distributors in 1924 to expect little from the local market: the "great bulk of the native population" was "still in a savage state" and was "in a number of instances but little above an animal." The imperial army in *Black Mischief* was called a "menagerie," but most writers were more specific. Carl Akeley, not without genuine affection, thought of his favorite gun bearer as a "faithful dog." His wife Delia, however, found the more popular simian comparison more congenial: she thought a group of baboons squatting around an ostrich nest "looked for all the world like a lot of natives at a feast." Other writers described black men for American readers as "like so many erect hairless apes," as "leaping apes," as "grinning black monkeys." Trader Horn declared that the "most amusing native" of his recollection had a face "exactly like that of a good-looking gorilla." One lecturer qualified the identification of men and monkeys by stating that the Congo pygmies lived "as close to the monkey as it is possible for human beings to do," while at least one writer—an Austrian missionary-anthropologist—told the readers of an American Catholic magazine that the pygmies had "nothing whatever in common with monkeys." Ignoring this solitary voice, American observers continued to catalog the animallike characteristics of the African, not the least of which was smell. George Eastman recalled that the arrival of a certain headman added "that dash of local color— and smell"; Trader Horn stated that even animals looked down their noses at blacks: "A gorilla's like humans in that way—can't stand the natural perfume of the negro." W. S. Van Dyke remarked that "of all the smells I ever smelled, the pygmies have the smelliest smell."[32]

An important group of American commentators, including many political theorists and geographers, were willing to accept the African abstractly as a human being, but regarded him in a practical sense as a kind of natural resource, to the dismay of black American scholars like Woodson and Halford L. Hoskins of Tufts. In this regard, the popular conception of the African as a childish and colorful brute was useful. "The natives of Africa," observed an author in the *Atlantic* in 1919, "whether they are regarded as economic assets or as human beings, are in reality children. . . ." The African was, then, "Good Raw Material" to builders and traders no less than to missionaries who shared with Jean Kenyon Mackenzie a fondness for that revealing term. The secretary of the British and Foreign Bible Society commented in the Philadelphia *Public Ledger* in 1926 that "the African's contribution to the human race will . . . be on the practical rather than the artistic side. It is he who will serve humanity by hewing out and digging out the treasures of that rich continent in aid of commerce." A decade later, an American economic geography text pronounced Africa "a promising field for successful exploitation," because of its minerals and rich soil, and "because it has a native population which can be made to serve as an economic asset for industrial projects." Another writer enthused in several articles in the mid-1930s that "Europe's exploitation of Africa has only begun."[33]

The consummation of this exploitation awaited certain developments, however. The Africans at first showed small interest in playing their role in the grand scheme, which role all observers agreed was indispensable. One American geographer laid the problem bare: "The first thing in African trade is to wake the native up and make him willing to work for the things he is in the habit of going without." One of the nation's most eminent international jurists discoursed upon the same difficulty. "In dealing with aborigines, the common experience of civilized states is that they find no inner compulsion of the mind urging the aborigines to secure land and personal property as a means of pursuing happiness, by exchanging their labor for land and commodities."[34]

Many writers suggested that the problem was with Nature herself; she had heaped her munificence upon the African without his having had so much as to wish for it, let alone work. The "complete wants of the average negro," lamented the American consul at Nairobi in 1925, were "provided by a bountiful nature." A missionary with thirty years' experience stated that the Africans dwelt "in the midst of a prolific nature that supplies their vegetable foods with very little exertion, and in such environments that their needs are few and easily met." "To get food," declared a school geography book, "the black man has only to gather the wild fruit or to hunt and fish." And in a "country of continuous summer," why would he not, as a British traveler observed, be "innocent of clothing"? Indeed, few visitors failed to comment on this aspect of the African, particularly the African woman, who so often greeted the eager photographer clad in "brass wire principally." In 1932 the consul at Nairobi nearly despaired of securing a native doll for the Temple School of Alexandria, Virginia; it has "been impossible to find any model of a woman which is properly dressed." Clearly the friendly sun had made Africa a poor market for ladies' ready-to-wear.[35]

Or perhaps the sun was not so friendly. Some Americans believed that the tropical climate had enervated the African; that while providing his basic wants, his environment had sapped his desire to want more. "Tropical climate," ran a typical statement on the subject—this by a Berkeley political scientist in 1933—"tends to relax the mental and moral fibre, induces indolence, self-indulgence, and various excesses which lower the physical tone of the population." On the "World Map of Climatic Energy" in one text, tropical Africa ranked "Very Low." The African races, the "most backward" of all, according to R. H. Whitbeck and V. C. Finch's standard *Economic Geography,* were "essentially the product of the tropical climate which dominates three-fourths of the continent."[36]

Others disagreed on the sun's ability to lessen the vitality of the African. Ralph Linton, a respected anthropologist, stated that the West African far from being enervated by the climate, was the only man capable of hard work amid the malaria and heat. The West African racial type, said Linton, was the classic example of a "human breed" developing distinctive characteristics to meet environmental conditions. Alfred Kroeber declared that it was not "nature" or climate that determined racial attainments, but the general state of advancement and knowledge of the group.[37]

Most travelers and writers were agreed, however, that whether due to climate or constitution, or both, the African was lazy. A standard work on trade routes described the African more genteelly as "the non-productive type," but most writers were more direct. A member of the University of Wisconsin geography faculty declared that the African "dislikes steady work of any kind, lives as lazily as he can. . . ." Anyone who would "conquer Africa," advised one expedition leader, must overcome the "procrastinating spirit" of the inhabitants. Llewelyn Powys described some Africans for the upper-class readers of *Travel* as "a group of primitive misanthropes almost too indigent to provide themselves with the necessities of life." *Living Age* carried an article in 1920 purporting to show that all the black man's failures in Africa were due to his indolence and lack of will. Sir Harry Johnston and L. Haden Guest pronounced the

African "naturally lazy" in their much-reprinted three-volume survey of world affairs. Even Du Bois noted, with considerable pride, that the black man in Africa had not lost "his joy of life. He can be lazy, engaging in work as a pastime rather than for the income it brings."[38]

Few Americans accepted Du Bois' romantic view on the subject: work in the interest of world civilization was definitely not a "pastime." And, as the African seemed disinclined to assume these civilizing burdens spontaneously, most Americans agreed that he must be forced to do so, both for his own good and for the good of the outside world. Professor Beer, the mandates expert, was firm on this point: as "the negro is apparently incapable of advance by his own unaided efforts," he informed the Inquiry in 1918, "foreign guidance was and is essential." The secretary of the Presbyterian Board of Foreign Missions believed that the African was "not lacking in energy or ability when rightly taught and led," and many writers concurred that development of the continent depended on an efficient and dependable black labor force under white supervision. Roosevelt declared in *African Game Trails* that "over most of Africa the problem for the white man is to govern, with wisdom and firmness, and when necessary with severity. . . ." Colonial administrations noted for their firmness frankly advertised the fact. "One of the strongest inducements to undertaking large-scale agricultural enterprises in Portuguese East Africa," reported the American consul in 1925, "is the abundance and certainty of the labor supply"; the natives "rank well for intelligence among the bantu races, and make very satisfactory laborers under proper supervision."[39]

It sometimes became difficult, during descriptions of "raw materials," the "black race," and "labor supply," to think of the Africans as individual people. A writer for *Harper's,* freshly returned from a flight over Africa, stated that Africans "have a group history; they can advance only as an organism, in the mass." Travelers on the ground affected surprise whenever they discovered that the blacks "actually" had different personalities. "One soon ceases to think of the African as so many 'natives' or 'negroes,'" Julian Huxley admitted; "they become just people, as full of individuality as a European crowd. . . ."[40]

For the Africans, after all, were people. Isaiah Bowman, president of Johns Hopkins University and America's most distinguished American geographer, could preface a book of aerial views of Africa in a spirit of near relief: "In the air Africa can be seen and enjoyed without perpetual reminders of the desperate human problems on the ground." Powys might compare the burying of several Kikuyu, dead from dysentery, to "burying black cats: for what chance, what possible chance . . . had these jackdaws of enjoying a blessed resurrection?" But there were still hundreds of Americans who directed their energies to alleviating just those "desperate human problems"—the exploitation, poverty, disease, ignorance—from which the cursory glance turned away, and for whom the possibility that the African could not enjoy "a blessed resurrection" simply did not exist. These were the uplifters, the Christian missionaries, the medical teams, the educators, who, year after year and decade after decade, made up the overwhelming majority of American residents in Africa. If there were few to deny that the African was passive in the hands of the whites, a child to be led, was it not possible to write upon that tabula rasa something of eternal value? If the African had to be led, could he not be led upward? "As we write on the tablet of the hearts of the youth," a missionary wrote of Africa, "we are determining the future of the nation."[41]

six:
americans
and the uplift
of africa

From Greenland's icy mountains,
From India's coral strand,
Where Afric's sunny fountains
Roll down their golden sand;
From many an ancient river,
From many a palmy plain,
They call us to deliver
Their land from error's chain.
—from a missionary hymn,
Reginald Heber (1819)

Ideas of uplift and mission had inspired African imperialism since the heyday of European expansion. The First World War, which brought tropical Africa to its penultimate imperial state, also brought to its rulers a determination to rejuvenate the impulse to humanitarian activity. A shifting combination of political liberalism, evangelical Christianity, and Victorian crusading, this spirit found its perfect exposition in Africa. It had always been difficult to speak seriously of improving the culture of British India or French Cambodia, but Africa was largely regarded as a cultural blank and a political vacuum. In Africa the idea of mission was never divorced from that of exploitation, and these twin guides of traditional imperialism found expression there long after they had been discredited or driven underground in the remaining parts of the European empires.

171

The friendly spirit of western superiority that once had moved freely over the world had been forced to find refuge at last beneath the palms and acacias of Africa, in clubrooms and mission chapels and comfortable automobiles, and could not be driven out by the glare of criticism that seemed unable to penetrate those shadowed confines. Comments about the civilizing mission of imperialism that would have been politically impossible in India and North Africa even before World War I were passed about in tropical Africa as acceptable currency for a full generation after the peace. It was not until 1922, in fact, that the classic statement of the idea that Africa required both exploitation and improvement was given the world by Britain's most famous and successful African administrator, Sir Frederick (later Lord) Lugard. His treatise on *The Dual Mandate in British Tropical Africa* was accepted by the English-speaking world as only an impressive exposition of a familiar and gratifying premise can be. It brought Lugard a baron's coronet, and instilled a glowing resolve in the hearts of thousands of missionaries engaged in a variety of good works in Africa.

> For the civilized nations have at last recognized that while on the one hand the abounding wealth of the tropical regions of the earth must be developed and used for the benefit of mankind, on the other hand an obligation rests on the controlling Power not only to safeguard the material rights of the natives, but to promote their moral and educational progress.[1]

That such an obligation rested on the "controlling Power" was more or less openly admitted at Versailles, where the "doctrine of trusteeship" was written into the mandates system of the League of Nations. By 1919 there was little that was novel in the theory behind the mandates scheme, but the League did manage for the first time to capture in an international statute the familiar and hitherto illusive parallel between children and backward races—wardship. Scholars spoke of the peace treaties as signaling a new day in African colonization. Missionaries noted that "a better spirit" seemed to "be abroad." It was generally agreed, of course, that the parallel between Africans and children was imperfect: children eventually grow up. Most African experts conceded this aspect of childhood only as an abstract possibility, like the Second Coming—for which, indeed, many of them waited with considerably more eagerness. Other aspects of childhood—ignorance, cruelty, dependence—were emphasized, and uplifting remedies poured forth.[2]

The work was embraced by the colonial powers with eager pride, and contemporary periodicals were full of self-congratulatory paeans, describing a continent "advancing out of the dark into the glare of noonday with the speed of the twentieth century." The moral value of the imperial mission seemed so great that countries that had no colonies felt legitimately aggrieved: Chancellor Franz von Papen emerged from the Byzantine labyrinth of German politics in the early 1930s to address the readers of the *Saturday Evening Post* on a familiar point: "To Europe has fallen the great task of bringing [the Africans] the blessing of civilization. Should Germany alone be excluded from this mission?" On the other hand, African states like Abyssinia that had not enjoyed the practical benefits of colonial guidance were pitied, since, as the dean of Lawrence College in Appleton, Wisconsin, observed, such states were "independent of powerful foreign influence with more or less civilizing results."[3]

These "civilizing results" were brought about in many ways—Christian evangelism, education, medical services—and these were not inspired solely by imperial pride. Many of those who carried on these endeavors were Americans, a people as crusade-minded as any in history, yet one singularly free from African colonial entanglements. In some colonies—those of Portuguese Africa and parts of the Belgian Congo—native education was almost completely in American hands. The British also relied on American techniques and ideas in black education. Major research in tropical African medicine was financed by and conducted by Americans. At all times within the interwar period, the great majority of American citizens in colonial Africa were Christian missionaries. Unlike members of the educational commissions and medical-research teams, few of these missionaries returned frequently to the United States. Their proportion was never less than 75 per cent of all Americans within a consular district; on the eve of World War II, fully 95 per cent of the resident Americans in Africa south of Nigeria and west of the Great Lakes were missionaries. All these uplifters—missionaries, teachers, medical researchers—produced a flood of information, and misinformation, on Africa. Their publicity lacked the slick excitement of big-game hunting, but through their sincerity, doggedness, and constant repetition, they impressed their beliefs about tropical Africa upon many American minds.[4]

From the 1880s to 1930, the works of American missionaries were among the "best sources" for the scholarly study of African life, for it was not until the thirties that American anthropologists produced creditable field studies on African culture. Long before that decade, hundreds of studies, histories, reminiscences, and tracts by missionaries on African peoples and their spiritual progress poured from the presses of publishers like Fleming Revel, Zondervan, the Methodist Book Concern, and the Catholic firm of Benziger Brothers. The bulk of this work was on library shelves before the First World War, where it continued through the interwar years to serve as a major source of information in the United States on African peoples. "The literature published on Africa," commented the *Missionary Review of the World* in 1928, "is unusually rich and offers a feast" for anyone interested in the progress of Christianity in Africa. Missionary magazines often ran entire issues, called "Africa Numbers," devoted to Africa in the 1920s and 1930s.[5]

In this vast amount of missionary material there were some fine pieces of reporting. *Among Congo Cannibals* by John H. Weeks, a missionary for thirty years in the Congo Free State, was a collection of careful and objective notes on the Boloki people. Jean Kenyon Mackenzie, a Presbyterian missionary in French Equatorial Africa, produced charming and sympathetic accounts of African life, first in *Black Sheep: Adventures in West Africa* (1916) and then in a series of articles in the early 1920s in the *Atlantic, Forum,* and *Missionary Review.*[6]

Most American missionary writing, however, portrayed Africans in distinctly unpleasant ways, touching upon indigenous folkways only to unload a heap of abuse on them. About the customs of the Buras of Nigeria one American missionary left little doubt: "Ignorance, polygamy and devil worship in their worst form are entrenched as deep as hell itself." Another commented that African drum music, which was just beginning to receive serious attention elsewhere, could serve only to provide music for the "repulsive scene" of "heathen dances," unless it were adapted to call the faithful to Sunday chapel. A lady Presbyterian could scarcely steel herself for the work of "elevating her black sister"; only prayer brought the "grace to stand the dreadful, disgusting, every-day occurrences. . . ." The sainted Albert Schweitzer attacked the "mad delusions" of spirit worship and fetishes in every sermon at Lambarene; "All my savages live with these ideas," he added. The wife of a future Methodist bishop for Africa collapsed in despair at the thought of finding disagreeable adjectives to convey a complete picture of native life; she could only tantalize her readers with the parting observation that "many social customs are too revolting for description." Many Americans sincerely believed that these appraisals were, if anything, too moderate, and missionaries were quick to discover the value of such comments in encouraging the constant stream of volunteers and material contributions upon which their work in Africa was wholly dependent.[7]

In the late 1930s a new, more dramatic method of communication, the motion picture, was added to the evangelical arsenal. The Missionary Education Movement received a small grant in 1937 from the Harmon Foundation to provide a film for a national interdenominational study program of Africa taking place that year in American churches. From reels submitted by ten mission boards, Martin Johnson, and the South African legation in Washington, a three-part film was spliced together and sold in sets of three reels each. These films, which depicted wildlife, native dances, village scenes, and the countless happy effects of colonial rule and Christianity upon the black race, were enthusiastically welcomed by local church missionary committees. The success of this first pictorial effort encouraged another, more ambitious project in the fall of 1938. Representatives of eight major Protestant denominations, the Harmon Foundation, and the Phelps-Stokes Fund, a philanthropic trust dedicated to the betterment of blacks around the world, hit upon a "unique idea." A young Brooklyn cameraman was induced to accept a honeymoon trip to an American mission at Elat, French Cameroons, in return for filming a dramatized version of Presbyterian missionary endeavor among the local Bulu tribe. The film, *Ngono and Her People,* depicted a girl's rescue from polygamy, and her conversion and marriage to her teacher, a previous convert (naturally) now properly attired in collar and tie. *Ngono and Her People* rented to churches for $3.75 and was a further boon to local committees trying to drum up congregational interest in the annual missionary appeal.[8]

It was not precisely true, then, as African nationalist Jomo Kenyatta claimed in 1938, that American missionaries, or their readers and supporters at home, regarded the African "as a clean slate on which anything could be written." To put the slate into that inviting condition required vigorous scrubbing. The dean of missionary education for the Southern Methodist Board of Missions declared that the new African convert "must utterly renounce all immoral heathen practices and all observances inconsistent with Christianity, such as polygamy, slavery, idol worship, sorcery, obscene dances, and the like." Not every missionary distinguished between activities that were incompatible with the teachings of Christ and those that were merely offensive to his own social traditions. A single visit to a witch doctor or "attendance at a beer-drink in a heathen village" was enough to disqualify an aspirant from membership in the Congregational mission at Bailundo, Angola. African dress and implements were regarded simply as relics of "old heathen Africa" and were to be discarded. In June, 1924, the *Missionary Review* proudly carried the story of an African couple married by missionaries without *lobola* (bride-wealth) in Rhodesia; accompanying the article was a photograph of the happy couple, dressed awkwardly in European style, the man in an oversize black suit, Hoover collar, straw boater and cane: to many readers the ideal incarnate of African evangelism.[9]

It must be added, however, that the crucial ingredient raising these zealous endeavors above mere cultural relativism of the worst sort was the sincerity of the missionaries, who were sincere in the true sense of that often misused word; their religion was complete. Not content with finding their own salvation in Christianity, these persons felt compelled to save others by extending to them the knowledge that they needed salvation, and that this most precious of gifts was available in Christ. For those who accepted the New Testament as divinely inspired, the premise upon which the missionaries operated—that Christianity was the single alternative to eternal misery—was unassailable.

With few exceptions, American missionaries were Protestant. For both doctrinal and practical reasons, the Roman Catholic Church in the United States had not been affected by the evangelical fervor that seized the more literal minded among the Protestant clergy in the late nineteenth century. There were few American priests on the African field. Most Catholic missions were operated by nationals of the Catholic imperial powers—France, Portugal, and Belgium—or by Irish, German, and Austrian clergy. This is not to say that the Catholic Church in the United States showed no interest in African missions. The Jesuit school and hospital in Tanganyika were operated by Americans. American parishes conducted extensive fund-raising campaigns for the worldwide efforts of the *Propaganda de Fide* during the forty days of Lent. Yet publicity in the United States concerning African missionary work focused on foreign priests and nuns; the highly publicized campaign of a group of English Franciscan nuns to raise money in the United States in the early 1930s for their leper hospital at Buluba, Uganda, was an example. Most American Catholic missionary literature, however, concentrated on the good work among the peoples of South America, the South Seas, and the Far East.[10]

The case was far different for American Protestantism, which chronicled its triumphant course through the Dark Continent in the most complete and gratifying way. And triumphant it was. By the early 1920s the British authorities informed a local American missionary who wanted an extension on his land grant that "very nearly all the available area for missionary enterprise" in British East Africa was "already allot[t]ed to one Society or another." The Presbyterians had a chain of missions "from the coast to the Congo River Valley" in 1932, and counted 35,000 members in the Cameroons alone. Protestant work in Portuguese Africa was almost completely in the hands of determined American missionaries. The American Board complex of seven Congregational stations in the Umbundu language area of Angola, and the Methodist mission at Inhambane in Portuguese East Africa were among the best-known American missions. The Belgian Congo, an enormous country for which tiny Belgium could not begin to provide adequate medical and school facilities, welcomed American missionaries; according to one Baptist minister, they "practically occupied the Belgian Congo for Christ" during the interwar years. The Methodist Episcopal Church, South, expanded its wide-ranging educational and medical work over central Congo. The largest American mission in the colony was the sprawling Africa Inland Mission, an old and famous interdenominational project at Aba that employed nearly one hundred missionaries. By 1937 forty different Protestant mission societies were working in the Belgian Congo, with more than one thousand superintending missionaries. The total of African church members, catechists, and schoolchildren in the Belgian colony, was estimated by Rev. Thomas Moody of the American Baptist Foreign Missionary Society in that year at slightly more than eight hundred and twenty-five thousand.[11]

Christians were never allowed, however, to rest on their laurels: only 2 per cent of Africa's total population had been converted by midpoint in the interwar period, and missionary societies had to "take courage and press forward to the unevangelized peoples." The ultimate purpose of missionary work was the conversion of all Africans to the Christian religion, and in pressing forward to achieve this objective, missionaries employed persuasive means other than the pulpit and strictly religious activities. The work of leading the Africans "out of the Jungles into the Light" also included educational programs and, often, medical assistance. Few missionaries had a deep interest in the native cultures into which they had been thrust. They believed that the African convert should be made over in as many ways as possible, that even an African who genuinely believed in Christianity was likely to wander off if a place were not found for him within the mission program or the colonial economy, and that if an African did backslide it was doubly regrettable because there was nothing of value in the village life that he had previously left behind. The missionary was there to "replace the world's lowest religion, or one of them, animism, with the world's highest, Christianity. . . ."[12]

In church and out, therefore, missionaries emphasized the standards of deportment that they had carried from home. Straw hats, linen collars, hand-holding courtships, the hymns of Sankey and Rodeheaver, brass bands, Sunday

School contests, and vegetable gardens were regular features in the life of the newly converted African. Religious services, among both Protestant and Catholic alike, were conducted on traditional European lines; the universal liturgy of the Catholic Church rose from thatched village chapels to blend above the jungles with the tones of "Are You Washed in the Blood of the Lamb?" sent aloft by some dusky choir in a neighboring American Board mission station. In the missionary literature sent home, success or failure was measured in terms of the alacrity with which African converts imitated the example of their ministers and teachers.

Colonial authorities welcomed the missionaries, or, as in the case of the Portuguese, at least tolerated them, for the educational and medical services they brought to the Dark Continent, and for the tranquilizing effect of Christian doctrine upon recalcitrant African spirits. With few exceptions, modern empires did not repeat the error of their ancient Roman progenitor by oppressing the most nonpolitical and pacific of religions. The several Bible-inspired black nationalist religious revivals that spread through West and Central Africa in these years were regarded at the time as only temporary aberrations. Progressive administrators recognized the value of native evangelists, thoroughly trained in European clerical skills and imbued with a peaceful philosophy, and of natives schooled in complicated agricultural and home-industry processes. They also saw the advantages of teaching the African to "cooperate," as Lord Lugard put it, in developing the continent. To insure that nothing suspect was transpiring in isolated corners, however, and to maintain something like uniform educational standards, missionary endeavors were closely supervised by colonial authorities.[13]

Relations between American missionaries and the political world around them were regulated when necessary by American consuls. When missions were well-established in the esteem of both the local population and the colonial officers, missionaries had little occasion to contact the U.S. consul; the consul, in fact, was far more likely to need the assistance of the mission. Applications to establish new stations, however, or to renew or extend old grants, were transmitted to the colonial governor through the American consulate, whose duties were otherwise largely confined, so far as the missions were concerned, to validating passports and registering births. In the Belgian Congo, an American mission society had only to demonstrate its legal incorporation in the United States to secure the friendly cooperation of the Congo government, which was authorized to grant all necessary permits, negotiating directly with the missionary and the American consul, independently of Brussels. Portuguese and British colonial officials also had considerable authority over local missionary activity. The French, however, required that American consuls transmit requests for land grants, as well as many mundane matters concerning missions, to the minister of colonies himself, through the American embassy in Paris.[14]

Official relations between American missionaries and Portuguese colonial officers were more often than not unpleasant, alternating unpredictably from strained to hostile. There were several long-standing causes for the friction, which touched all other American endeavors in Portuguese Africa as well. American visitors and journalists had the same ill-disguised contempt for Portuguese colonial administration that the citizens of the other imperial powers did, while the Portuguese, a volatile and sensitive people, seized upon even qualified praise as an insult to the national honor. Portugal's resources, on the other hand, were simply not adequate to provide for the economic well-being of her colonies, which languished in a squalor made all the more embarrassing for local authorities by the prosperous bustle in neighboring colonies and dominions. But Americans did not comment simply upon the poverty in Portuguese colonies; travelers and writers regaled those back home with stories of venal, incompetent, and vainglorious officers, crumbling stucco plantations, and lazy, music-loving settlers—all the standard ingredients for a musical comedy, in which the Portuguese were the perennial straight men.

In addition to their general dislike for foreigners, the Portuguese had, or imagined they had, specific grievances against foreign missionaries, nearly all of whom were American and Protestant. The Portuguese government's brief attempt at anticlericalism had ended in spectacular failure at Fátima, and the country had returned with a rush to the forgiving arms of Mother Church. With extraordinary agility, the government took up the Catholic cause, which very soon became characteristically confused with national prestige. Lisbon dailies and colonial papers began to warn of the "insidious propaganda which the foreign religious missions are spreading" in the African empire, noting that Protestantism, which existed on "an inferior moral level," was certain to bring about "denationalization of the colonies." Colonial land laws concerning foreign missions gradually but perceptibly grew more difficult of speedy interpretation, and long delays, punctuated only by the apologies of local officials, attended the simplest requests. American missionaries became apprehensive. Letters from Angola to the *Missionary Review* made "painful reading" in 1921: "The Portuguese government officials are reported to be openly opposing Christian activity, and are even unsympathetic with humanitarian movements." Late in that year the high commissioner of Angola published Decree 77, which rigidly controlled the activities of foreign missions within the colony; his counterpart in Mozambique revived an antique version of the same law. The decree required that a missionary society prove that all members of its staff were ordained ministers or qualified assistants in the denomination, and that a mission's "program of civilization" be approved by the government. The decree also prescribed that the only foreign language to be used or taught in Angola was Portuguese, and that the native language could be used only in elementary catechism and in Portuguese language classes; native languages could not be taught as a separate subject of instruction.[15]

For a while, the missionaries' apprehensions were dispelled by the new decrees, which had the incidental benefit of granting statutory security to those missions fulfilling the requirements, which was not difficult for most American stations to do, and impossible for none. Portuguese officials in their turn prudently restrained their dislike for foreigners and "heretics"; the colonial government had no desire to drive from the country a large part of its educational and medical facilities. As a result, a sort of truce was established, which the missionaries regarded in a most hopeful light: "Now an excellent spirit of cordiality exists between the Government and our missions because of our effort to make the natives better citizens."[16]

The truce was not to last. Missionaries had been concerned for years that the chronic agricultural depression in Angola and Mozambique, coupled with the demand for labor in neighboring British colonies, would compel the Portuguese officials into using forceful means to prevent the flow of workers out of the colonies: black laborers would be recruited under arms and hired out to local plantation owners at prices low enough to encourage profitable agriculture and in quantities large enough to insure a handsome income for the officers. Though such practices were not permitted under the laws of the Portuguese Republic, the missionaries' fears were confirmed. Incidents of forced recruiting of laborers increased through the first decade after the war, and these activities so clearly violated the trusteeship principles of Versailles that the missionaries were now and then emboldened to send out a protest to missionary journals back home. And it was in 1924 that a group of humanitarians prevailed upon Edward Alsworth Ross, then planning to conduct field research in British India, to stop off in Portuguese Africa and make an informal investigation of the labor situation there.[17]

Ross was an abrasive, self-righteous man who richly enjoyed the role of gadfly, and he went at the work of crusading reporter with single-eyed alacrity. He allowed the American consul at Lourenço Marques and the Portuguese to interpret his presence as that of a tourist, while he closeted himself with a succession of American missionaries. Ross departed, leaving behind the growing suspicion that his visit, as the American consul advised the State Department, had been "more or less under the auspices of the Methodist Episcopal Church," and that he had been collecting "atrocity material" for unspecified "propaganda purposes." The suspicions were soon confirmed. His *Report on Employment of Native Labor in Portuguese Africa* appeared in print in 1925 and was read before the League of Nations.[18]

The *Report,* based entirely on missionary accounts and Ross's own hurried observations, described Portuguese labor policies as "virtually state serfdom." Ross depicted working conditions as an unhappy combination of oppressive taxes, which forced the Africans to earn cash wages, a lavishly corrupt and undisciplined native police force that collected either the taxes or the defaulting taxpayers, and a judicial system that was distant, incomprehensible, and frightening to the Africans. Blacks once recruited into work gangs by government agents were ill-treated and underpaid by their employers. The author cited unnamed missionaries who recounted "many cases of the conscienceless behavior of the authorities."[19]

The Portuguese cabinet responded to the accusations in the *Report* with high indignation—not wholly feigned. Lisbon had attempted reforms in Africa, but the national government traditionally had been separated from control of the colonies by an ancient and lethargic bureaucratic system of mystifying complexity. The republic was subject to periodic bursts of energy in its dealings with Africa, usually provoked by the exposure of some particularly scandalous outrage. The *Report* had such an effect. The minister of colonies dispatched to Africa a special investigator, the secretary for native affairs, while the citizens of the republic raised a chorus of complaints that the national escutcheon had again been blotched. The secretary was a trifle disconcerted by what he found; while he refused to acknowledge the existence of actual slavery, he did admit that some black workers were ill-treated and unfairly paid. He also admitted that the agency law, which allowed compulsory service on private estates, was outdated a "feudalistic idea," as he put it—and promised swift retribution against any official who disregarded Portuguese statutes.[20]

The furore in world circles was stilled by the Portuguese attitude, to the intense displeasure of Ross, whose reaction was not softened when the American consul in Lourenço Marques denounced the *Report* as hopelessly biased. The local officials were not to be mollified. Once again those upon whom the national prestige came so often to rest had been exposed to the world as incompetents, or worse; they steeled themselves for swift revenge. It was not long in coming. Local officials launched an "obstructionist policy" against American missions, which on one occasion resulted in the breaking up of several outstations near Dondi, Angola. Colonial papers called for yet more stringent action in defense of the "national honour and dignity," while the missionaries flocked to a man behind Decree 77. Certifications and building permits granted by once friendly officials were not acted upon by their successors. In 1927 the American consul at Lourenço Marques had to prevail upon the governor-general not to preside at a public meeting at which the Ross *Report* was to be denounced. Finally, in that year, the Portuguese East African Government adopted Proclamation 10, which struck down the sanctuary of Decree 77: all African teachers in mission schools must have official Portuguese credentials, equivalent to those required of grammar-school teachers in Portugal; propagandizing beyond the church building was forbidden; and, worst of all, the use of the native vernacular in any spoken or written form, including the Bible, was forbidden. The missionaries, facing the ruin of their lives' work, put up a spirited defense. They petitioned the governor, offered compromises, and finally declared with the desperate courage of the cornered that if they were not granted the "minimum amelioration" of bilingual instruction and a modification of the teaching-certificate requirement, they would cable their international superiors to press for diplomatic intervention. The Department of State informed the American consul that the Portuguese action was permissible under international law, but authorized him to press the missionaries' appeal on humanitarian grounds. The British made official representations at Lisbon in behalf of a Church of England mission, based on an Anglo-Portuguese treaty of 1891 under which the subjects of each power were mutually guaranteed freedom of religion in the colonies of the other. The American minister to Portugal endorsed the missionaries' case on more informal grounds, but with considerable determination. The Portuguese government, faced with importunities from its ancient and only reliable ally, Britain, and from the United States, decided that the local officials in Africa had gone too far, and overruled them. The governor-general of Mozambique was instructed to "adjust dispute with the Consuls and the missionaries," and that officer announced concessions: Africans already in service could be retained despite their qualifications, and the native vernacular could be used in church services and in printed books. The American missionaries, secretly overjoyed, announced publicly with a certain admirable aplomb that they were "fairly well satisfied," and the matter was laid to rest early in 1930.[21]

Missionaries were, in truth, quite as willing to provide information of all sorts for any inquirer as they had been for

Ross, with results far more agreeable to everyone concerned. Regardless of a traveler's opinion of the value of
religious evangelism—and such opinions among the run of
scholars, consuls, and tourists were low—missionaries could
provide invaluable knowledge of local conditions. Consuls
in Belgian and Portuguese Africa depended greatly on
American missionaries, relaying to them the exotic requests
that often came to consulates for butterfly specimens, photographs of local customs, and schoolgirl penpals. Consuls in
the Belgian Congo traveled on mission steamboats on their
rounds of the district. W. D. Hambly arrived in Angola with
an anthropologist's prejudice against missionaries, determined to avoid them, for their influence must surely have
altered the native culture; the U.S. consul, anxious to
assuage the Portuguese, agreed completely that Hambly
should avoid the missionaries. Yet the anthropologist ended
by relying heavily on an American missionary, who provided
him with every assistance necessary to make the expedition a success.[22]

The spread of useful information was one of the functions
of a mission. All colonial authorities warmly endorsed this
part of missionary activity, and the British incorporated
mission schools into the official educational system in their
African colonies (except in Northern Nigeria, where the
principle of indirect rule forbade Christian evangelism
among the Moslem emirates). Parker T. Moon wrote of the
"heroic endeavors on the part of missionaries and a pitifully
inadequate effort on the part of governments" in African
education. The president of the Carnegie Fund was surprised during a tour of British East Africa at how completely
African education and hygiene were in missionary hands; he
found the results praiseworthy, particularly in view of the
somewhat limited training of many missionaries. Some American opponents of African imperialism were also impressed;
for example, a writer in the *Crisis* endorsed the educational
work of missions in Uganda, although he criticized the
Baganda for being too quick to copy European ways in such
nonessentials as dress.[23]

Most missionary teachers believed the African to be completely normal in learning ability. The course of instruction
in a mission school was practical: personal hygiene, proper
methods of soil cultivation, handicrafts, arithmetic and read-

ing, the Christian religion, the "development of the simple virtues" like moral purity, orderliness and perseverance, and rudimentary instruction in the colonial administration under which the African lived. African history and culture were ignored. The Missao Americana in Loanda was the largest school in Angola, where attendance was not compulsory for Africans. It conducted all classes in Portuguese, and offered instruction in "reading, drawing, writing, Scripture, arithmetic, geography and history of Portugal, sewing and laundry." The usual course in farming techniques was not offered by this city school.[24]

The French government intended that the educational system in its African colonies should integrate the blacks completely into French cultural, social, and political ways of thinking. Of all the imperial powers, therefore, France exercised the most rigid and pervasive control over its colonial school system. American personnel and ideas, consequently, played little part in it.[25]

The British, whose entire colonial educational system in Africa was under missionary direction, possessed both the resources and the will to maintain high standards in instruction. British colonial schools adopted a self-consciously British posture, with "march bands," the *Book of Common Prayer,* and crested blazers to dignify the clerical and farming classes. The school for the sons of chiefs at Tabora was styled "The Eton of Tanganyika"; it, too, was noted for its public-school spirit. The school model sought by progressive administrators after the war, however, was British in appearance only; in substance, the greatest influence on British African education was American.[26]

Even before the war, British educators had regarded the system of black education in the American South as exemplary for the African empire. Officials in increasing numbers had come to the conclusion that the black masses could only be uplifted to a cooperative role in the empire through a practical education adapted to local conditions; to give a tiny minority of Africans a European, "denaturalizing" education was a waste of effort. In 1921 and 1924 the Phelps-Stokes Fund of New York, a socially prominent philanthropy directed at black educational projects in both the United States and Africa, sent commissions to Africa to study the educational needs of the African. Dr. Thomas Jesse Jones, educational director of the fund, led the two commissions, which had a wide and lasting influence on African education.[27]

Jones's first commission traveled along the West Coast, concentrating on British West Africa. The second, more extensive trip, took seven months to complete and included the Union of South Africa, Portuguese East Africa, British East Africa, and Abyssinia. The United States government adopted the 1924 commission, and instructed local consuls to assume semi-official responsibility for the project. American officials secured interviews for the group's leaders with colonial ministers, Prime Minister Jan Smuts of South Africa, governors, and the Ras Taffari, Prince of Abyssinia (later Haile Selassie). The British accorded Jones's commission official status, and the cordial welcome received in British East doubtlessly soothed the wounded feelings of the team after the apparently inevitable run-in with the Portuguese. The education commission paid only a "hurried" visit to Lourenço Marques, but Jones found time to interview a group of "educated natives," whose stories of labor abuses evoked his incidental expressions of sympathy. The Portuguese announced that "a grave indiscretion" had been committed, and gave the consul to understand that since the consul had assumed responsibility for Jones the prestige of the United States and its consulate had been "impaired." A flurry of letters from Jones, the Phelps-Stokes Fund, Washington, and Lourenço Marques cleared up the affair, which the startled Jones blamed from the first on "false statements" about the suddenly notorious interview.[28]

Jones, who had enjoyed extensive experience with black colleges in the southern United States, was convinced by his two field trips to Africa that the greater part of the American Negro educational system could be transplanted to Africa. His program, which American missionaries accepted almost unequivocally throughout British Africa, and in other parts of Africa as well, was fourfold. African education should provide for: health and sanitation; for agricultural, industrial, and elementary-educational training, along the lines of the farm, shop, and school training at Hampton and Tuskegee; for decency and safety in the home; and for healthful recreation ("Moonlight orgies," warned Jones, were sapping the energy of the race that must develop

Africa). School lessons were to introduce such useful maxims as "The 'three R's' become the first plowing in the field of barbarism." The African was to be made a good citizen and an efficient worker, and in this uplifting work the Christian missionary schools, with a few suitable and simple adjustments in the curriculum, were to continue as the driving force.[29]

These conclusions were lauded by American and British educators. One American writer pointed out how neatly Jones's system—the "four walls of the African House of Learning"—dovetailed into the political realities of colonial Africa. But W. E. B. Du Bois, noticing that same feature, denounced the whole scheme in the *Crisis* as a means to render "black labor most profitable to the white exploiter." Melville Herskovits urged "the greatest caution" in applying American educational techniques to Africans. A writer for the National Urban League, on the other hand, called the Jones program "intelligent mass education," an appraisal with which such eminent British observers as Huxley and Lord Lugard were in the fullest agreement. American scholars like Moon relied completely on the two Jones reports for material on colonial education, and the Church of the Brethren, following a suggestion in Jones's *Education in Africa,* established a teacher-training school in northeastern Nigeria.[30]

The American missionary educational program in the Belgian Congo followed the pattern of practical and religious instruction that was being established all over colonial tropical Africa. The work of the Methodist Episcopal Church and its fiery Southern counterpart was typical. The MEC concentrated its efforts upon the newly industrialized regions of the southeastern Congo, where thousands of Africans, drawn together into sprawling tin villages to work in the copper mines and smelters, were allowing the twin novelties of money and leisure to draw them into many "moral disasters." The church tried to "develop a modern type of institutional evangelism," which included medical care; rudimentary instruction in "modern farm methods," to keep some Africans on the land and to provide for the increased needs of the towns; literacy in the vernacular language; and familiarity with the Gospel. The program was designed to enable the Congolese "to take their places as self-supporting members of the new African communities." The Southern Methodists for their part had been ensconced in the heart of Africa since before the war, and by 1929 the Congo Mission was officially proclaimed "the most popular foreign Mission of the Church." All of their missionary projects were in the lands of the Batetela people a few degrees below the equator in the center of the colony, and were divided into four "departments": industrial, which taught simple building and workshop skills (in large part to build and furnish missions); medical, which operated three small hospitals and a leper colony; educational, which permitted a "select few" of the Batetela to "learn to read and write their own language, obtain a smattering of French, the official language of Belgium, and the beginnings of mathematics"; and evangelistic, the most important of all, which conducted the religious services, trained "native evangelists," and exercised "whatever religious discipline is necessary."[31]

Missionaries regarded their educational service as "an evangelistic agency." The purpose of mission schools was to win converts and to provide them with skills. The skills were to render them useful to the mission or to the colonial economy; armed with skills, the new Christians could support themselves and their families without returning to the villages where they were subject to every kind of demoralizing influence. The new converts also helped the Christian cause; even strictly industrial schools produced African evangelists. In the summer of 1933 the entire body of apprentices at the Frank James Industrial School at Elat, French Cameroons, engaged in an enthusiastic religious crusade and brought in 2,332 "lost sheep."[32]

No less welcome to colonial officers than the teaching missionaries were the medical missionaries. Theirs was a genuinely inspiring aspect of Christian missions in Africa. "It is impossible to exaggerate the importance of medical work to advance the Kingdom of Christ in Africa," declared a Baptist missionary in Léopoldville. In the same colony the Southern Methodists cared for some 160 lepers, looked after the orphans left by the disease, and made strenuous efforts to prevent the spread of sleeping sickness. In the terminal stage, the sickness caused a form of insanity, and in such cases the missionaries could only offer a Christian witness by providing "a more humane treatment of patients in the last stages of the disease." An American doctor in Efulan, Cameroon, used "tactful persistence" to win his patients to Christ, praying and speaking gently of God, the source of healing, to every patient. Schweitzer, the world's most famous medical missionary since Livingstone, was a one-man beehive in French Equatorial Africa, dividing his apparently inexhaustible energy between treating leopard wounds, burying sleeping-sickness victims, providing the usual variety of medical services, delivering sermons (some of them accompanied by gramophone records of what he called "solemn music"), writing books, and practicing the organ. In West Africa the Presbyterians set up a series of rural baby clinics, at which religious meetings, medical services and lectures on hygiene and baby care were offered in native Christian churches. For decades throughout tropical Africa, the sufferings of tens of thousands of Africans were alleviated by the work of American medical missionaries. Like all missionaries, medical evangelists often spent their furloughs touring churches in the United States to raise money for their clinics in Africa.[33]

Not all medical facilities in tropical Africa were provided by missionaries or served an evangelistic purpose, of course, and Americans often made a contribution to those services that were not directly sponsored by religious agencies. At times, an American medical missionary was employed by the colonial government to offer medical care only for Africans in the vicinity of the doctor's mission compound, but outside the missionary context; Dr. Henry S. Hollenbeck of Wisconsin worked under such an arrangement in the Belgian Congo. Far more common were the Americans who sponsored or joined medical-research projects conducted under the auspices of the colonial governments in the hope of discovering cures for the host of tropical diseases that literally plagued much of Africa. These efforts ranged in consequence from offhand donations by wealthy tourists to the hospital fund in Nairobi to large-scale research financed by American philanthropy. During the First World War the Rockefeller Institute for Medical Research had produced a sodium salt, tryparsamide, which was found to combat some of the effects of mental deterioration in cases of sleeping sickness. In 1920 the new salt was introduced into the Belgian Congo, with the eager cooperation of the government. Several years of field testing showed, however, that prolonged use of it caused damage to the eyesight. As a result, missionaries and colonial doctors in the Congo were overjoyed when the Guggenheim Fund financed new research on sleeping sickness late in the decade, under Dr. W. K. Stratman-Thomas, a member of the Department of Pharmacology and Toxicology at the University of Wisconsin. The Rockefeller Fund also sent six American scientists to Lagos in 1920 as a commission to study yellow fever along the West African coast.[34]

The industrial and medical missions, which were ably staffed and supplied the African population with services of unquestionable value, had few critics; reaction to and the results of Christian evangelism, however, were far different. Detractors pointed out a number of unfortunate aspects to missionary proselytization. Denominationalism was marked. Christianity had come to Africa "under a score of different trademarks," and to the African this was wholly incomprehensible. The Congregationalist American Board found Angola a "most inspiring" field for its work—because "practically no rivalry of other denominations" existed in that Portuguese possession. Other missionaries were not so fortunate in their surroundings. "Materialism, atheism, Mohammedanism, Catholicism, and nationalism are saluting and beckoning," warned one in 1928. Another stated in 1936 that although "Catholicization" was only a "superficial form of evangelization," it might yet produce a continent with a "Catholic-pagan population." As for the Catholic viewpoint, one missionary priest noted loftily that the religion of the pygmies elevated that people "in a theological sense . . . head and shoulder above our Protestant brethren." Some priests and ministers spent much of their energy stealing sheep from each other's fold, to the complete mystification of the African, a mystification rendered the more pathetic when, as occasionally happened, the local police were enlisted by one side or the other to retrieve ex-converts by force.[35]

Leading Africans and American blacks also argued that missionaries were not "conspicuously zealous" in bringing the Africans those aspects of their European inheritance that could be really useful to the black people, such as material progress and exposure to more of the Western world's culture. The Pan-African Congresses declared that the imperial powers sought only profit, and cared nothing for the "spiritual uplift" of the Africans. Du Bois stated in 1938 that the "educational activities of the missionaries" served only to induce "the acquiescence of Africans in foreign control." Another writer denounced the hypocrisy of American churches that were "strong for missions in Africa," yet did nothing to integrate churches in the United States or stop house-bombings in Chicago.[36]

The effects of Christianity on the individual African produced heated, prolonged, and, in the end, fruitless controversy. Protestants, Catholics, and critics of missionary work were all in general agreement that the number of genuine Christian converts among the Africans was small—"an infinitely small minority." Missionaries, even so, regarded this minority of wholehearted believers as "the hope and guarantee of the future." Protestants prized their native evangelists, Africans who accepted the implications of Christianity so completely that they could not rest while their people lived in perilous ignorance of its saving Founder. Not only did an African preacher represent the kind of commitment that any minister would welcome in his congregation, it was impossible to evangelize without an active native ministry. The Catholic Church, which reserved the prerogatives of the clergy to those who had undergone considerable training at the expense of sacrifices incomprehensible to most African men, was nonetheless not lax in searching for African helpers. And unlike the Protestants, the Catholics could search the next world for assistance as readily as this one. In 1925 a group of African converts who had perished under terrible circumstances in Uganda in the 1880s were beatified with great ceremony in Rome. The *Catholic World* glowed: "The Church that produced Cyprian, Augustine, and Athanasius, had now her young African martyrs in African lands. . . ." Years later, on the eve of World War II, Pope Pius XII appointed three native African bishops, two to Vicariates Apostolic in Madagascar and Uganda, the third to the Prefecture Apostolic of Senegal. Catholics did not fail to note how markedly Mother Church differed on the matter of African church leadership from the southern United States, that incubator of Protestant missionary projects.[37]

Despite the attention lavished by Protestants and Catholics alike upon the small minority of true believers and showcase African churchmen, the great body of African Christians accepted their new religion only superficially, and often for distressingly worldly reasons—a cause of near despair to many missionaries. Evangelists acknowledged that Africans adopted the form of Christianity—and accepted the benefits of mission life—more often than they adopted its spirit. One medical missionary noted a discouraging tendency among his patients to repair to the "witch doctor" when they thought they might be dying. Many visitors and popular writers observed the same sort of tendency, with a hundred variations, but did not share the missionaries' conviction that redoubled efforts at conversion would draw the Africans into the fold in mind as well as in body. On the contrary, Africans were widely held to be incapable of any but a casual reaction to anything. The black man, declared May Mott-Smith, was a "disciple of expediency. He acquires a veneer, a glibness which at first rewards his instructor. But underneath the negro's mind remains the same."[38]

While some travelers denounced the whole idea of education for the blacks, American Negroes deplored the destruction of African culture effected by missionaries who failed to replace the old beliefs with new ones of equal force. Missionaries countered with the argument that the disruption of African society was inevitable from the moment of white discovery, and that Christianity, once it obtained a foothold, would become the sheet anchor for drifting souls. One traveler commented, however, that education for Africans was "so often destructive of Negro character." An animal collector for the Smithsonian voiced what was a surprisingly common American reaction to "mission boys": "An unlearned savage is honest and dependable; an educated Congo negro is more often than not the contrary."[39]

It was impossible for many hundreds of American missionaries and educators to accept the premise that the African could not be truly prepared for a useful place in what was regarded as an everlasting colonial system, or that he could not be induced to accept into his heart the True Religion. Many Americans shared the earnest conviction of European colonialists that African empire had as its ultimate goal the introduction of the African to a beneficial, healthful, and spiritually uplifting way of life. That these uplifters regarded the African as raw material, without a history or culture or religious beliefs of his own, a passive creature to be fitted for life in an alien economic system, is not open to argument. Nor is it untrue that many missionaries presented the African in the most unattractive and subjective light for the American supporters of evangelism in Africa; Africans were savage, cruel, childlike, lustful, unprincipled, superstitious, and insensitive to every decency. The fact remains that the missionaries bestowed upon the imperial system whatever truth lay in its claim to be a trustee for civilization. In so doing, they introduced Gospel hymns and cotton shirts into ancient and delicate cultures, and spoiled forever dark natural songs of a hundred mysterious nuances. Yet they brought as well the knowledge of a thousand years of mechanical progress, of literacy, of medicine, and of a religion that at its best put love, domestic fidelity, and selflessness high on its list of virtues. Far from teaching the African to believe that he was incapable of sharing the knowledge of the West, as so many travelers and writers declared, many missionaries tried to make the African aware that in sharing in Christianity, he was a part of the Body of Christ that had been the center of Western civilization for twenty centuries.

It must be remembered that few men were prescient enough in 1939 to see the doom of the imperial system in Africa. If it is just to claim that American missionaries and educators deliberately encouraged the African to adapt himself to colonization, it is equally just to say that neither the missionaries nor anyone else could foresee the day when the African would have a better alternative, and there were many worse ones close at hand. In helping the African to share at least a part of the benefits of imperialism, in bringing him medicine and literacy, and, above all, in introducing him to the eternal blessings of Christianity, the American uplifters of Africa believed they were doing a timeless work.

epilogue

"Change," declared one Old Boy in fond recollection of his English alma mater, "is a melancholy word." Melancholy, indeed, but how refreshing, how reassuring, to be where such a word was seldom heard—the African empire, for instance, which drew more than its share of public-school men to service. In colonial Africa, change was regarded by most of those who could be brought to regard it at all as a possibility of pleasant remoteness. When and if change did begin, it would proceed toward them with the reassuring imperceptibility of a glacier.[1]

Certainly British bankers, a group of men not known for misplacing long-term confidences, had little reason even in the depths of the Great Depression to doubt the profitable durability of the empire. In June, 1932, the Bank of England offered, at a slight discount, an issue of guaranteed stock of the Tanganyika government, in the sum of £500,000. The stock, a direct obligation against the colonial government of Tanganyika, sold well. Few investors questioned whether Tanganyika stock was a safe harbor in which to weather the storms of a collapsing market, and no one could doubt the reliability of a gilt-edged security founded on the resources of a rich if undeveloped satrapy, especially when the security did not fall due until January 1, 1972.[2]

Africa was regarded as passive, a sort of inert mass in which Providence had placed extraordinary treasures and enchantments for the white race to find and carry home. At the height of the German-mandates crisis of the 1930s, authors typically spoke of Africa as being "on the block." Economically and culturally, Africa was thought of as "raw material," from which western enterprise and missionary zeal might be able to fashion something of value to "mankind." The African was a child, a witless brute, a comical mimic whose ancient political states and artistic legacies were dismissed as copies, almost forgeries, of alien models.

195

Africa was a market, a trifling qualification to its passive status, but only a trifling one, because only the white rulers could buy, and they had to buy the same things in Africa that they bought in Somerset or Kansas. Africa was a vast storehouse of gold and copper, iron and palm oil, chocolate and spices. There lived an endless variety of exotic animals and plants, to be collected for the diversion of the Western world. Over this tropical toy box, the European powers had established imperial dominion in behalf, so they genuinely believed, of the outside world, which could justly claim an interest in the efficient and orderly exploitation of African wealth and of native populations, who needed to be raised from barbarism to a place where they might cooperate in the great work of administering Africa's one-sided economies.

European imperialists regarded themselves as the trustees of civilization, to whom their African colonies had been mandated by some Higher Power. The principle of progressive imperialism, of which the mandates were but a final explicit expression, stated that the African peoples would one day in the misty future be capable of domestic autonomy. Lord Lugard, however, advised patience; such noble ends are not quickly attained. "Perhaps," he cautioned, "that objective can never be fully realized, but the principle of continuous evolution remains." Even though such feeble encouragements were notably absent from the pronouncements of imperial powers other than Britain, it was clear to all but the most prejudiced viewers that the stark and shameless exploitation of King Leopold and Karl Peters was not in fashion anywhere in tropical Africa after the First World War. No one was more critical of such shortsighted rapacity than the White Highlanders of Kenya, who in their turn dreamed of demonstrating their own version of Lord Lugard's evolutionary principle by guiding British East Africa along a course from which it would one day emerge as a "self-contained nation just as any of the other Dominions." The white settler, affirmed Raymond Leslie Buell, had "no intention ever of relinquishing his control" over East Africa.[3]

A wide range of sympathetic commentators postulated the length of time in which European control of Africa would remain vital—from "a hundred years" to eternity. In 1927 Buell praised the "intelligent [that is, British] governments in Africa" who trained their native subjects "so that eventually, even after a hundred years, they may be able to govern themselves." The dean of Lawrence College was less confident. "The African is even yet a child," he noted in 1928; "give him time—five hundred years, or even less, to demonstrate his full-orbed native abilities." The *Review of Reviews,* a digest of current articles, carried the prediction in 1925 that "for our generation, and for many more of our posterity, Africa is to remain a colonial land, an annex of Europe." Isaiah Bowman, president of Johns Hopkins, declared in 1941 that Africa was "one of the ultimate tests of the white man's 'civilizing' power, a challenge to put into long-range and humane synthesis the terrible resources of his will and his science." An American critic of white exploitation of black labor in South Africa, writing in the late 1930s, felt compelled to admit that there was "not much to be gained . . . from discussing an independent Africa." On the eve of the Second World War the *Rotarian* confidently announced that when science and industry finally conquered tropical disease and provided adequate "air conditioning, so that sweltering jungles become habitable for men of energy, the tropical portions of . . . Africa . . . may become the earth's most important producing areas for foods and for many industrial crops." George Creel, Woodrow Wilson's wartime chief of propaganda and later a New Dealer, declared in 1932 that the map of Africa would honor Stanley's name "as long as the world lives." According to a popular writer in the *Atlantic,* however, these questions of time did not press heavily upon the Africans; he commented in 1923 that "natives never bother much about the future, confident as they are that the Government will provide help if it comes to a pinch. . . ."[4]

Even critics of African imperialism—that "reprehensible white invasion"—seemed to feel that it might "yield good results in the course of centuries." A scholar who denounced European exploitation and ethnocentric missionary projects felt that orderly self-development of the blacks could come only under the "tutelage" of the whites. Commentators who recorded centrifugal tendencies in the British Commonwealth and subwars in India, Ceylon, and Palestine saw nothing to indicate that tropical Africa was a likely spot for rebellion. Certainly Americans in London did not encounter discussions of the possibility during the 1920s. Leonard

Woolf, perhaps the leading anti-imperialist writer of the decade of the war and early 1920s, stated that while "non adult races" of Africa were being ruined by exploitation, they could not stand alone; the mandate principle was their last hope. Parker T. Moon constructed a long list of countries that were stirring "in the face of European imperialism," to which he diffidently added "perhaps even parts of Africa" at the bottom. Nathaniel Peffer specifically excluded tropical Africa from his series of strongly anti-imperialistic lectures at the New School for Social Research in 1926–1927. Peffer announced that the "reckoning" of world imperialism was at hand—"excepting those [peoples] which are primitive, as in inner Africa." Peffer went on to say that the decision of the imperial powers as to how best to combat new restive influences "can be postponed for long" in Africa, "as it can wherever there are primitive cultures and an embryonic sense of unity." Melville J. Herskovits recalled years later that in 1931, at the time of his first field research, "not even the most fervent African nationalist—and there were few of them then —would have hazarded a guess that any African territory, much less most of Subsaharan Africa, would be fully self-governing within a little more than a quarter of a century."[5]

Yet there were cracks in this ageless dolmen, faint, almost imperceptible lines across the still-benign face of empire. W. E. B. Du Bois, and the unaccommodating wing of black American intellectuals that found its inspiration in him, grew increasingly daring in their predictions in the interwar years. At the London Pan-African Congress of 1921, which called for "a great black African state, founded in peace and goodwill," Du Bois spoke of a "great, unresting, mighty surge," the "ground swell in the Negro race" that was "feared by every colonial power." In 1925 he announced that "Black British West Africa is out for self rule and in our day it is going to get it." Other writers commented on the "race-consciousness" of the blacks of British Africa. A black professor of history at Tufts College declared in 1930 that "African peoples have been learning apace the secrets of European superiority." Carter G. Woodson put the matter more directly: the force that the Africans would wield in modern Africa "will depend upon how well by training or contact the natives may learn from the interlopers to surpass them at their own game." Du Bois, like most American blacks, looked with unfeigned admiration on the native elite of French West Africa, particularly of Senegal, hoping that in these black leaders "the salvation of black Africa will yet be the gift of France." By the end of the 1930s, after the Italian conquest of Ethiopia, a heart-breaking disaster to many American blacks, Du Bois was posing bitter and dangerous questions: "Who can be certain," he asked in an article in *Foreign Affairs* in 1938, "that the white rulers in Kenya, the Union of South Africa and the Belgian Congo may not some day face the mass of their black subjects in arms . . . supplied by European rivals, or by black America, or even by brown and yellow Asia?"[6]

A disturbing question—if taken seriously. Yet few important white travelers took such suggestions seriously, although on rare occasion they were whispered to Americans as they glided through colonial society on a silent sea of black retainers. Few Americans knew of Jomo Kenyatta, the general secretary of the Kikuyu Central Association in Kenya, who began the first Kikuyu language newspaper in 1928, or of J. E. Casely Hayford, Léopold Sédar Senghor, or of a host of West African parties and newspapers. Kenyatta might denounce "British imperialist robbery and oppression" in obscure black radical corners of Europe; in Africa, he and all similar persons were regarded as the puppets of alien "disturbing elements." Oscar Thomason, the veteran American vice-consul at Nairobi, claimed that Kenyatta had fallen in with unnamed "Bolshevists" in London and had sent a letter from there addressed to all mission blacks (a letter translated into the vernacular, somewhat shortsightedly as it proved, by an obscure Salvation Army missionary) urging them to rise up and kill the missionaries. These Bolshevik agitators were everywhere. In the mid-1920s the Belgian consul for East Africa revealed to all listeners that he was "obsessed with a conviction" that African unrest was inspired by communistic propaganda spread around by American Negroes; his obsession was proclaimed despite the patient explanation of the American consul that there had not been an American Negro in East Africa for more than two years. Once in 1924 the British succeeded in actually capturing a mysterious Czechoslovakian whom they termed a "bolshevik propagandist." American consulates in Africa were on the alert for such activities in the early 1920s, for it was widely understood that the Third International in Moscow had called for subversion of American and African blacks.[7]

Revolutionary agitation obviously had to be coming from the outside; most travelers and writers were agreed that the Africans themselves were incapable of initiating anything so novel and complicated as a rebellion. "The native . . . ," declared Vice-Consul Thomason, was "too dull, too lethargic" to think up such things "for himself." Lord Lugard observed in *Foreign Affairs* that "the agitator for 'self-determination' " in British West Africa was always a lawyer on the local legislative council, who knew less of the black masses than the British official in the field. An American missionary writing in 1931 gently but firmly rebuked those "excellent" but misguided persons who were urging the Africans of Kenya to believe themselves despoiled by their white benefactors; such persons were unwittingly playing Moscow's game, and their ideas would cause "unmeasured suffering to both races." W. S. Van Dyke confounded suggestions of a "native rebellion" with his own considered opinion that it was "a lot of 'bunk.' " Official American consular reports from Africa contained just such conclusions: in each, native unrest was attributed to localized economic conditions, mysterious intratribal dissension, or outside agitators with a grievance against the colonial power in control. Never did these reports, ranging over many years between the wars, suggest that the brief strikes, the disturbances at carnivals and festivals, and the occasional, isolated attacks on black government agents were the manifestations of an irreconcilable conflict between the masses of Africa and their white rulers. Such disturbances were rare, and so easily adjusted that any challenge to the basic structure of African empire could be dismissed as visionary nonsense.[8]

American public opinion—and almost everyone responsible for forming it—was oblivious to weaknesses inherent in African imperialism. The United States government had little access to information about Africa other than its consulates, which regarded imperialism as permanent, and the State Department made no disquieting pronouncements on the durability of African empires. Some popular writers regarded Africa as an agreeable, long-term alternative to life in the United States; so far from entertaining any serious notion that the system of white rule over Africa was shortly to collapse, these Americans sought to escape into some comfortable retreat within that system, some congenial, tranquil little nook somewhere within the reassuring, enfolding arms of empire. Many of the most widely read American authors on Africa expressed such desires.

Martin and Osa Johnson frequently expressed their preference for the "real Africa we had come so to love" to "the turmoil of a troubled world." One can wonder how much of the "turmoil of a troubled world" the couple had seen in the dreary corner of southeastern Kansas from which they had fled at the first opportunity, but one cannot question the sincerity of Osa's moving announcement during a speech she was delivering at the Explorers' Club in Chicago less than a week after her husband's funeral: "I want to get back to the jungles. I could never stand to stay here in civilization very long."[9]

Escape was a common theme in much popular writing about Africa. Delia Akeley claimed that the tumult of World War I had driven her to Africa, and Carl Akeley's secretary declared that whenever she was "crowded into a subway," then "visions of Africa—the freedom, the thrill of exciting moments, the fascination of unspoiled nature, of game—appear to me and blot out the unattractive scenery before my immediate vision." A. J. Kloin had turned to "lion hunting as the one business with variety and excitement enough to keep him out of civilization's familiar ruts." Llewelyn Powys declared that "however much" he "might be submerged by the vulgar modern world," he would never forget the scenery of Africa. Jean Kenyon Mackenzie, the gentle and literary missionary, reminisced about Africa and the wild moonlit dances and silent forests of "that other world" while riding along "shut up so safely in the guts of Manhattan." And even Du Bois, who perhaps longed to escape for different reasons, was not immune. "One of the great and glorious joys of the African bush," he said in 1924, "is to escape from 'news.' "[10]

"Thousands of miles from civilization—close to nature as God made it!" enthused a character in the 1939 movie version of *Stanley and Livingstone*. Theodore Roosevelt prefaced his *African Game Trails* with an oft-quoted tribute to the allure of Africa where still exist "the wide waste spaces of the earth, unworn of man, and changed only by the slow change of the ages through time everlasting." An animal collector for the American Museum returned to Africa after a dozen years as much to "experience again the thrill of living in unspoiled country" as to shoot lions. Paul Hoefler was entranced by the White Nile Province of Uganda; it was "Africa at its darkest—the Africa that the early explorers knew, unspoiled by the semicivilization that has arisen in so many parts. . . ." Zoologists longed to find some spot that had not been carefully picked over by other whites; Edmund Heller combed such a find late in the war years and proudly produced fifteen species "new to science." Anthropologists were equally anxious to roam in virgin territory; W. D. Hambly wrote in 1929 that in Angola he "was delighted to find that there were people so absolutely unaffected by civilization." Mary Hastings Bradley, an early associate of Akeley, spent days searching in the Belgian Congo for some "lost village" that was "untouched by . . . white influence." Many travelers felt they had found such a place in the Kivu and Ituri forests of that colony, where lived several groups of pygmies. These engaging people were described as "Nature's most unspoiled children," whose "outlook on life" was "that of a sunny ten-year-old."* Ivan Sanderson, an American animal collector, called Africa "a veritable paradise on earth" where a man could find "never-ending restfulness" enveloped "by towering walls of greenery, like a microbe in a pile carpet. . . ."[11]

"It is not easy," noted a popular travel handbook published for the German African Lines in 1932, "to express in words in just what the charm of East African travel consists." Perhaps it was one thing, perhaps another. "Rather it chiefly dwells in the vastness of unspoilt Nature, in the romance with which the country is still surrounded, that self-same country which our fathers knew only as a blank space upon a map. . . ." But what catalog of African charms was complete without including the services of an army of blacks; the delightful nostalgia of colonial pomp; the excitements of hunting with gun and camera; the exotic creatures of darkest Africa; the lure of treasure, both real and imagined, of vast, untapped markets; the experience of martyrdom and noble

* The Kivu-Ituri pygmies became something of a tourist attraction, and did not remain unspoiled for long. See Attilio Gatti, "Lilliputians of the Epulu Forests, *Travel* 70 (1937): 15.

uplift, and of simply escaping from a tense and hurrying world.[12]

In June, 1932, the American consul at Nairobi received a note from an employee of the United States Weather Bureau at Wausau, Wisconsin. It is as fitting an epitaph to this period in American relations with Africa as any single incident can be. The employee, one A. E. Osborn, wished to purchase a small piece of ivory, or maybe a little rhino horn, to make a pair or two of six-shooter handles. At the bottom of the letter was a penciled postscript reflecting Osborn's exposure to a decade of popular publicity on Africa: "P.S. Cheer up Congress is going to give us time off or a pay cut. . . . I wish I could take on some hunting in the colony at that time." There was Africa: a passive land, ready to welcome anyone drawn there to hunt its colorful animals; there were no people to be considered except the government; there was no danger, just excitement—to be lightly engaged in; and there was escape, escape from a jobless Wisconsin winter, escape from a whole world where six-guns could not provide solutions to a mounting flood of economic problems.[13]

The historian who is gratified to find hints of prescience in the past will seize upon predictions borne out by later events. He would no doubt end this account with Lord Lugard's statement in 1931 that "the historian of the future will perhaps recognize more clearly than the politicians of today the magnitude of these racial problems. . . ." Or he might cite Lothrop Stoddard's warning in 1935 that another "shattering death-grapple of rival white imperialisms," such as the First World War had been, would give Africans a chance to shake off European control forever. These are thrilling insights, but their effect as predictions is seriously weakened by their irrelevance to either their authors' general principles or to the overwhelming majority of contemporary opinion. Such quotations serve the dishonest function of a verse of Scripture taken out of context. Rather, we shall close with Africa as Americans believed it to be between the two world wars: a land of lions and scenery and black children. Daniel Streeter returned from Africa to Fifth Avenue in the mid-1920s, but he was still thinking of the Africa he had left behind:

My mind was full of white coral beaches fringed with tousled palm fronds, and echoing to the pounding surf of azure seas. . . . I heard the roar of a lion, followed by a deathlike stillness, a hyena's wail, natives singing in the light of the full moon barbaric chords full of sad melody. Before my eyes the snow-cap of Kilimanjaro floated in an opalescent dawn.[14]

notes

abbreviations

AFSJ *American Foreign Service Journal*
AJPA *American Journal of Physical Anthropology*
AJS *American Journal of Sociology*
AM *American Magazine*
AMNH The American Museum of Natural History, New York City
Annals, AAPSS *Annals of the American Academy of Political and Social Science*
AR *Annual Report*
AS *American Scholar*
BAI The Bureau of Animal Industry
BEA British East Africa
BFDC The Bureau of Foreign & Domestic Commerce
BW *Business Week*
BWA British West Africa
CAS California Academy of Sciences, San Francisco
CC *Christian Century*
CH *Current History*
CSMWM *Christian Science Monitor Weekly Magazine*
CW *Catholic World*
DS U.S. Department of State
EFC Emergency Fleet Corporation
FA *Foreign Affairs*
FEA French Equatorial Africa
FMNH The Field Museum of Natural History, Chicago
FR *Foreign Relations*
FR, PPC *FR, Paris Peace Conference*
FRC Federal Records Center, Suitland, Maryland
FS U.S. Foreign Service
FWA French West Africa

GH *Good Housekeeping*
GPO U.S. Government Printing Office
GR *Geographical Review*
IRM *International Review of Missions*
JG *Journal of Geography*
JNH *Journal of Negro History*
LA *Living Age*
LCMD Library of Congress, Music Division
LD *Literary Digest*
LM Lourenço Marques, PEA
MFC Merchant Fleet Corporation
MH *Missionary Herald*
MRW *Missionary Review of the World*
NA National Archives
NAR *North American Review*
NH *Natural History*
NFTC National Foreign Trade Convention
NGM *National Geographic Magazine*
NR *New Republic*
NZP National Zoological Park, Washington, D.C.
PEA Portuguese East Africa
PR [Consulate] Post Records
PSM *Popular Science Monthly*
PSQ *Political Science Quarterly*
RG Record Group
RofR *Review of Reviews*
SA *Scientific American*
SAPFT Special Advisor to the President on Foreign Trade
SEP *Saturday Evening Post*
SI The Smithsonian Institution, Washington, D.C.
SIA Smithsonian Institution Archives
SIAR *Smithsonian Institution Annual Report*

SIMC *Smithsonian Institution*
   Miscellaneous Collections
SM *Scientific Monthly*
SMC *Smithsonian Institution,*
   Miscellaneous Collections
SRL *Saturday Review of Literature*
S&S *School and Society*
USDA U.S. Department of Agriculture

USIA U.S. Information Agency
USMC U.S. Maritime Commission
USNM U.S. National Museum,
   Washington, D.C.
USSB U.S. Shipping Board
VQR *Virginia Quarterly Review*
WW *World's Work*
YR *Yale Review*

introduction

1. May Mott-Smith, *Africa from Port to Port* (New York, 1930), 173–174.

2. Frank B. Kellogg to U.S. embassies in London and Brussels, Washington, Aug. 10, 1927 Loanda DS 032/489B–C.

3. Walter Lippmann, *Public Opinion* (New York, 1922), 18.

4. Clifford Haley Scott, "American Image of Sub-Saharan Africa, 1900–1939" (Ph.D. dissertation, University of Iowa, 1968); Phillip Percival, "Adventure Land," *NH* 27 (1927): 570.

5. James Lippitt Clark, "The Image of Africa," in AMNH, *The Complete Book of African Hall* ([New York], 1936), 73. FMNH, *AR 1933; Report Series* 10 (Chicago, 1933–1935), 11. W. Reid Blair, *In the Zoo* (New York, 1929), 7.

6. See index, *MRW* 59 (1936): 622–623. This observation is, of course, not original with me. The same tendency in missionary writing to describe "the righting of wrongs and the eradication of paganism" has been noted in several recent studies. See Philip D. Curtin, *The Image of Africa: British Ideas and Action, 1780–1850* (Madison, 1964), 325–329 (quotation in note, 325), and J. F. Ade Ajayi, *Christian Missions in Nigeria, 1841–1891: The Making of a New Elite* (Evanston, 1965), 162–163, 165, 263–264.

7. Jay Marston, "Uganda, 'Land of Something New,'" *NGM* 71 (1937): 100–129; A. S. Hitchcock, "A Botanical Trip to South Africa and East Africa," *SM* 31 (1930): 481–507.

8. W[oodbridge] S. Van Dyke, *Horning into Africa* (n. p., 1931), 30.

9. Geoffrey Gorer, *Africa Dances: A Book about West African Negroes* (New York, 1962), introduction to new edition.

10. Walter LaFeber, *The New Empire: An Interpretation of American Expansion, 1860–1898* (Ithaca, 1963), 52–53; James D. Richardson, ed., *A Compilation of the Messages and Papers of the Presidents,* 11 vols. ([Washington], 1909), 8: 175–176.

11. Population statistics are for the years 1930–1931, from *The Statesman's Year-Book . . . for the Year 1934* (London, 1934).

12. Kenneth Kirkwood, *Britain and Africa* (London, 1965), 40 (1st quotation); Michael Crowder, *West Africa under Colonial Rule* (Evanston, 1968), 19 (2nd quotation).

13. On the factors that prevented access to the interior, see R. H. Whitbeck and V. C. Finch, *Economic Geography* (New York, 1924), 503,

and J. Russell Smith, *Industrial and Commercial Geography,* new ed. (New York, 1925), 380–381.

14. May Lamberton Becker, "The Reader's Guide," *SRL* (April 18, 1931): 763.

15. George Louis Beer, *African Questions at the Paris Peace Conference,* ed. and with an Introduction by Louis Herbert Gay (New York, 1923), 71–75; Raymond Leslie Buell, *The Native Problem in Africa,* 2 vols. (New York, 1928), 1: v; Lord Hailey, *An African Survey,* 2nd ed. (London, 1945), xxi–xxii; Parker Thomas Moon, *Imperialism and World Politics* (New York, 1926), 75–76; Marion I. Newbigin, *A New Regional Geography of the World* (New York, [1930]), 240, 251–252.

16. Dr. Treille, "L'hygiène de européen," in *Préparation aux carrières coloniales,* ed. Le Myre de Vilers et al. (Paris, 1904), 42; Karl J. Pelzer, "Geography and the Tropics," in *Geography in the Twentieth Century,* ed. Griffith Taylor (New York, 1951), 313–314.

17. Moon, *Imperialism,* 8.

one: europe in africa

1. Frank J. Magee, "Transporting a Navy through the Jungles of Africa in War Time," *NGM* 42 (1922): 355.

2. Parker Thomas Moon, *Imperialism and World Politics* (New York, 1926), 83–84, 89; Quincy Wright, *Mandates under the League of Nations* (Chicago, 1930), 21–23; Walter Lippmann, *The Stakes of Diplomacy* (New York, 1915), 133–135; Report of Inquiry, May 10, 1918, *FR, PPC,* I, 89 (2nd quotation); Lippmann to Baker, May 16, 1918, *FR, PPC,* I, 97–98.

3. George Louis Beer, *African Questions at the Paris Peace Conference* (New York, 1923), 255; see also 255–258, 279–286; *FR, PPC,* I, 70–71; Lawrence E. Gelfand, *The Inquiry: American Preparation for Peace, 1917–1919* (New Haven, 1963), 227–228; Moon, *Imperialism,* 478–479.

4. *FR, PPC,* III, 785–796, 758–771; V, 473, 506–508; III, 722–723, 743–745; Seth P. Tillman, *Anglo-American Relations at the Paris Peace Conference of 1919* (Princeton, 1961), 85–98; Quincy Wright, "The United States and the Mandates," *Michigan Law Review* 23 (1925): 717 and 723; Moon, *Imperialism,* 478–485; Wright, *Mandates,* 23, 64–65.

5. Wright, "U.S. and Mandates," 729–736; Beer, *African Questions,* 471–472; Wright, *Mandates,* 611–616; *FR* 22, II, 317–322; Wright, *Mandates,* 77; Charles F. Mullett, *The British Empire* (New York, 1938), 714: "To date [1938] that arrangement has not revealed itself more than a euphemism for annexation."

6. Wright, *Mandates,* 135–136.

7. *FR, PPC,* III, 433; Beer, *African Questions,* Annex E, F, and G, 483–499, 500–506, 507–514, for the three conventions.

8. Beer, *African Questions,* 103–110 and 67; *FR, PPC,* V, 492; Quincy Wright, "Sovereignty of the Mandates," *The American Journal of International Law* 17 (1923): 693; Wright, *Mandates,* 476–480, 580–581.

9. The U.S. position is set forth clearly in a note from Secy. of State

Charles Evans Hughes to Myron T. Herrick, U.S. Amb. to France, Aug. 7, 1921, in *FR 21*, I, 922–925; see *FR 22*, II, 316; *FR 21*, II, 111–115; *FR 22*, II, 315–317; *FR 22*, II, 322–325; *FR 25*, II, 199–203, for negotiations with Britain on this subject. For negotiations with France, see *FR 21*, II, 106–109; *FR 22*, II, 138–139; *FR 23*, II, 8–13, and with Belgium, *FR 22*, I, 624–625; *FR 22*, I, 633; *FR 23*, I, 433–440; Wright, "U.S. and Mandates," 739–747.

10. Herbert Ingram Priestley, "Lighting Darkest Africa," *SRL* (May 12, 1928), 857 (1st quotation); John Carter, "Round About the Congo," *The Commonweal* (April 2, 1930), 610 (2nd quotation); Kellogg to U.S. embassies in London and Brussels, Aug. 10, 1927, DS 032/489B–489C; Kellogg to Mrs. Blair Flandrau, Washington, Aug. 10, 1927, DS 032/489A (3rd quotation); Robert Fernald to State, Lagos, Sept. 17, 1928, DS 600.1117/15a over 523; Moon, *Imperialism*, 8. Some Americans believed the new policy of "world trusteeship" represented an advance over crude European sovereignty. See Mabel Janet Byrd, "The League of Nations and the Negro Peoples," *Crisis* 35 (1928): 223–224, 242; "A New Colonial Policy," *Public* (Feb. 8, 1919), 127.

11. Richard Harding Davis, *The Congo and Coasts of Africa* (New York, 1907), 66; Moon, *Imperialism*, 513; Uthai Vincent Wilcox, "The March of Civilization in Africa," *CH* 18 (1923), 784–785.

12. Halford Lancaster Hoskins, *European Imperialism in Africa* (New York, 1930), 102–103; Carter G. Woodson, *The African Background Outlined, or Handbook for the Study of the Negro* (Washington, 1936), 146.

13. See the editorial in the *RofR* 92 (1935): 11–14; Nathaniel Peffer, *The White Man's Dilemma: Climax of the Age of Imperialism* (New York, 1927), 21; Genevieve Mason, " 'Free' Slaves in West Africa," *Nation* (March 4, 1931): 254–256; Richard Thurnwald, "Social Transformations in East Africa," *AJS*, 32 (1932): 181. See also Hans Coudenhove, "African Folk: A Further Consideration," *Atlantic* 128 (1921): 463.

14. Julian Huxley, *Africa View* (New York, 1931), 173; Graham Greene, *Journey without Maps* (New York, 1961), 38; Harry Johnston and L. Haden Guest, *The Outline of the World Today*, 3 vols. (London, n.d.), 3: 598; Evelyn Waugh, *They Were Still Dancing* (New York, 1932), 227; Carveth Wells, "In Coldest Africa," *WW* 58 (1929): 36.

15. Anne Dundas, *Beneath African Glaciers* (London, 1924), 59 (1st quotation); the Gold Coast government, *The Gold Coast Handbook* (Worcester, [1937]), 177–179 (2nd quotation); clipping from *East Africa*, May 24, 1928, enclosed in C. Albrecht to State, Nairobi, June 20, 1928, DS 848t. 911/7; Lillian Oyler, "Missionary Life in Africa and America," *MRW* 54 (1931): 841 (3rd quotation); Herbert Best, "These African Explorers," *Harper's Magazine* 165 (1932): 58 (last quotation).

16. Wells, "Coldest Africa," 36.

17. Eric Reid, *Tanganyika without Prejudice* (London, 1934), 60 (1st quotation); May Mott-Smith, *Africa from Port to Port* (New York, 1930), 177; Isak Dinesen, *Out of Africa* (New York, 1952), 10–12; Karl Mac-Vitty to State, Nairobi, July 9, 1930, PR Nairobi 840.1 (2nd quotation); [illegible], secy., English Club, LM, to Honaker, U.S. consul, March 22, 1921, PR LM 840.6; Oscar Thomason to D. Scoates, Texas A&M, Nairobi, July 6, 1932, PR Nairobi 840.5.

18. Huxley, *Africa View*, 223–224; Robert Delavignette, *Freedom and Authority in French West Africa* (London, 1950), 78–82 (2nd quotation); Seward B. Price, Ball Bros., Co., Muncie, to U.S. consul, Lagos, May 23, 1932, and G. Willson to W. J. Russell, pres., Plateau Horticultural Society, Lagos, July 9, 1932, filed together in PR Lagos 840.6; R. Livingston to Ball Bros., Nairobi, July 9, 1932, PR Nairobi 869.11; Mary Hastings Bradley, *Caravans and Cannibals* (New York, 1926), 19 (3rd quotation); Waugh, *Still Dancing*, 257 (4th quotation); Stewart Edward White, *The Land of Footprints* (Garden City, 1913), 41; Huxley, *Africa View*, 173.

19. Grace Flandrau, "What Africa Is," *RofR*, 83 (1931): 63–64 (1st quotation); Richard Upjohn Light, *Focus on Africa* (New York, 1941), 65–66; A. S. Hitchcock, "A Botanical Trip to South and East Africa," *SM* 31 (1930): 494, 496 (2nd quotation); C. Cross to State, LM, Nov. 23, 1922, PR LM 840.6 (3rd quotation); Light, *Focus*, 51–57.

20. Martin Johnson, *Safari: A Saga of African Adventure* (New York, 1928), 289–293 ("Kenya" quotation); H. R. Ekins, "African Grab Bag," *CH* 44 (1936): 108 (2nd quotation); Bailey Willis, *Living Africa: A Geologist's Wanderings through the Rift Valley* (New York, 1930), 26–27; Raymond Leslie Buell, "Chieftains Enthroned: British Rule in Nigeria as a Significant Colonial Experiment," *Asia* 28 (1928): 56–62, 73, 74–75, 76; Moon, *Imperialism*, 514, 520–521. Paul Knaplund, *The British Empire: 1815–1939* (New York, 1941), 550–606.

21. Moon, *Imperialism*, 131–132 (quotation).

22. S. W. Eells to State, Nairobi, July 24, 1920, DS 848t.01/4; "Kenya Colony: British East Africa under a New Name," *CH* (October, 1920): 25; "Native Labor in East Africa," *Nation* (Nov. 24, 1924): 600–602; Raymond Leslie Buell, "The Destiny of East Africa," *FA* (April, 1928): 408–426; idem, "Two Lessons in Colonial Rule," *FA* (April, 1929): 440–446; idem, "The Crisis in East Africa," *Nation* (Nov. 6, 1929): 533–534; Baron Lugard, "Native Policy in East Africa," *FA* (October, 1930), 65–78; Reginald George Troller, *The British Empire-Commonwealth: A Study in Political Evolution* (New York, 1932), 104–105; Lord Hailey, *An African Survey*, 2nd ed. (London, 1945), 742–755, 820–822; Knaplund, *British Empire*, 601; Johnston and Guest, *Outline of the World Today*, 2: 270. See as well, Elspeth Huxley, *White Man's Country: Lord Delamere and the Making of Kenya*, 2 vols. (London, 1935), 1: 77–79; 2: 158–159; Charles Eliot, *The East Africa Protectorate* (London, 1905), 150–174; Margery Perham, *Colonial Sequence: 1930 to 1949* (London, [1967]), 35–46.

23. Buell, "Two Lessons," 443 (1st and 2nd quotations); Buell, "Crisis in East Africa," 533 (3rd quotation); Llewelyn Powys, "Britain's Imperial Problem in Kenya Colony," *CH* 18 (1923): 1004–1005 (4th quotation); and Lugard, "Native Policy," 71–76. See also "Trouble Brewing in Kenya," *LD* (June 30, 1923); Walter Phelps Hall, *Empire to Commonwealth: Thirty Years of British Imperial History* (New York, 1928), 436–449; Daniel W. Streeter, *Denatured Africa* (New York, 1926), 136; Buell, *The Native Problem in Africa*, 2 vols. (New York, 1928), 1: 298–304; Moon, *Imperialism*, 132; Mary Evelyn Townsend, *European Colonial Expansion Since 1871* (Chicago, 1941), 198–199.

24. "The White Man's Burden," *Nation* (July 13, 1923): 31; Stanley

Rice, "The Indian Question in Kenya," *FA* (Dec. 15, 1923): 260–261, 266–269; MacVitty to State, Nairobi, Feb. 24, 1931, DS 848t.4016/17; E. T. Smith to State, Nairobi, June 14, 1938, DS 848t.52/19; Smith to State, Nairobi, Sept. 14, 1938, 848t.52/20; Smith to State, Nairobi, Jan. 5, 1939, DS 848t.00/83. See as well, Albrecht to State, Nairobi, Dec. 20, 1926 [filed in 1927 volume], PR Nairobi 822, for comment on Indian incitement of local native unrest.

25. Charles W. Coulter, "Problems Arising from Industrialization of Native Life in Central Africa," *AJS* 40 (1935): 583; Woodson, *African Background*, 146; Leslie Reade, "Ethiopia and Kenya," *New Republic* (Oct. 2, 1935): 211–212; "The Singular Importance of Kenya," *Current Opinion* 75 (1923): 150; Ralph J. Bunche, "The Land Equation in Kenya Colony (As Seen by a Kikuyu Chief)," *JNH* 24 (1939): 33–44; "Kenya and the White Man's Honor," *CC* (Feb. 22, 1933): 244–245; see also, Nairobi, Aug. 4, 1927, DS 848t.00/27, for the bimonthly political report on British East Africa, and "Indians in Kenya," *Nation* (Oct. 31, 1923): 497–500.

26. Townsend, *European Colonial Expansion,* 4–5; Derwent Whittlesey, "British and French Colonial Techniques in West Africa," *FA* 15 (1937): 362, 363–365, 366–369; Townsend. *European Colonial Expansion,* 188–191; see also Paul S. Reinsch, *Colonial Administration* (New York, 1905), 17: "France is the classical land of assimilation"; Clinton Stoddard Burr, "Franco-British Rivalries in Tropical Africa," *CH* 22 (1922): 414; A. H. Young-O'Brien, "Brothers to the Gods: Germans, Englishmen, and Frenchmen as Colonists," *Harper's* 177 (1933): 424–425; W. E. B. Du Bois, "The Negro Takes Stock," *NR* (Jan. 2, 1924): 144; idem, "France's Black Citizens in West Africa," *CH* 22 (1925): 559–564; Hoskins, *European Imperialism,* 54; Herbert Ingram Priestley, *France Overseas: A Study of Modern Imperialism* (New York, 1938), 244–304.

27. W. E. B. Du Bois, "Black Africa Tomorrow," *FA* 17 (1938): 100; Vachel Lindsay, "The Congo," in *Selected Poems of Vachel Lindsay,* ed. Mark Harris (New York, 1963), 48; Mott-Smith, *Africa from Port to Port,* 254; Attilio Gatti, *Hidden Africa* (London, 1933), 236; Paul L. Hoefler, *Africa Speaks: A Story of Adventure* (Chicago, 1931), 329–330, 358; "Progress in the Belgian Congo," *JG* 18 (1919): 171 (3rd quotation); Helen M. Rolleston, "Light along the Congo," *CSMWM* (Oct. 5, 1938): 6 (4th quotation); Dorsz to State, Léopoldville, June 5, 1937, DS 811.43 DAV/8.

28. Robert Gale Woolbert, "The Future of Portugal's Colonies," *FA* 15 (1937): 374 (quotation); Moon, *Imperialism,* 118–120, 514; Wynant D. Hubbard, "What Europe Sees in Africa," *RofR* 94 (1936): 50; "Portugal; Cinderella Colony," *Time* (Aug. 8, 1938), 17.

29. Albert W. Kimber, *Kimber's Record of Government Debts and Other Foreign Securities, 1925,* 9th ed. (New York, 1925), 764.

30. Peter W. Rainier, *My Vanished Africa* (New Haven, 1940), 59.

31. Edward Alsworth Ross, *Report on Employment of Native Labor in Portuguese Africa* (New York, 1925); Wilfrid D. Hambly to Dir., Lobito, May 8, 1929, FMNH Archives, "Rawson West African Exp. I" file (2nd quotation); Ray to State, LM, Dec. 31, 1919, DS 800.114/256;

Samuel Foraker to State, LM, May 4, 1921, DS 853g.001/1 (fm); J. W. Bailey to State, Loanda, Jan. 20, 1928, DS 853m.00/17 (fm) 4.

32. Ray Atherton to State, London, March 19, 1929, DS 031.11 FMNH Nigeria/13 (1st quotation); State to Consul at Nairobi, Washington, April 6, 1929, DS 031.11 Coulter/12; J. Butler Wright to [Charles D.] Walcott, secy., SI, March 6, 1926, DS 031.11 Sm 6/-; Atherton to State, London, March 19, 1929, DS 031.11 Coulter/8; Atherton to State, London, March 19, 1929, DS 031.11 AMNH Straus/18; Atherton to State, London, March 19, 1929, DS 031.11 AMNH Straus/14; on the Kenya privileges, see Jenkins to State, Nairobi, April 9, 1924, DS 848t.6202/-; Wilfrid D. Hambly, "Culture Areas of Nigeria," *FMNH Anthropological Series 21* (Chicago, 1935), 373 (2nd quotation); [Rudyerd] Boulton to G. Whitely, chief secy. to the gov., Lagos, Aug. 16, 1934, FMNH, Curator of Birds, dept. files, "Straus West African Exp., Plans and Projects" file (3rd quotation); Willis, *Living Africa,* 19; W. S. Van Dyke, *Horning into Africa* (n.p., 1931), 122, 138–139.

33. Willson to State, Lagos, April 27, 1932, DS 800 63/962; Members of the Straus West African Exp. of 1934 were given letters of introduction to local French officials by the American ambassador to France. See letter, addressed "A Qui De Droit," Paris, Jan. 22, 1934, in FMNH, Curator of Birds, dept. files, "Straus Exp. Plans and Projects" file; Walter E. Edge [amb. to France] to State, Paris, April 24, 1931, DS 031.11 Cleveland Mus. (Cameroons) 7; Hambly, "General Report," dated Jan. 10, 1930, p. 11, in FMNH, Curator of Anthropology, dept. files, "Rawson West African Exp., file.

34. Director, FMNH, to Vernon L. Kellogg, Secy., Nat. Research Council, Chicago, Nov. 2, 1923, and to Baron E. de Cartier de Marchienne, Chicago, Nov. 3, 1923, in FMNH Archives, "Field Central African Exp." file; F. Trubee Davison [pres., AMNH] to Count Robert Van der Straeten-Ponthoz, Belgian amb., New York, May 15, 1935, DS 031.11 AMNH Congo/4; Edmund Heller to FMNH, Kissenyi, Lake Kivu, Belgian Congo, Feb. 18, 1924, FMNH Archives, "Field Central African Exp." file (quotation); W. E. Davis, M.D., "Riding the Jungle Circuit," *SEP* (Oct. 8, 1938): 17.

35. Cross to Hubbard, at Choma, No. Rhodesia, LM, March 25 and March 28, 1924, PR LM, 862.3. There is a large and complete series of correspondence on Hubbard's activities in PEA, filed together between two whole endpapers marked [PR LM, 1924+] 862.3 Hubbard, Wynant D., —Hunting; Stanton to Haagner, LM, June 10, 1939, PR LM, 862.3; [Alexander P.] Magruder, chargé d'affaires, Lisbon, to State, Lisbon, Sept. 14, 1929, report of conversation Arthur S. Vernay and Dir. Gen., Aug. 31, 1929, in DS 031.11 FMNH Angola/31; Fred Morris Dearing to State, Lisbon, March 26, 1929, DS 031.11 FMNH Nig./16 (quotation); see also Theodore J. Marriner to Dir., FMNH, Washington, April 18, 1929, in FMNH Archives, "Rawson West African Exp. (1)" file.

36. Styles to State, Loanda, Feb. 4, 1926, PR Loanda 850.4 Ross Report [in vol. "Confidential Corresp."] (1st quotation); L. Gourley to R. L. Buell at Nairobi, LM, Jan. 14, 1926, PR LM, 800 ["Conf. Corresp."] (2nd and 3rd quotations); Hambly to Dir., Lobito, May 8, 1929, FMNH Archives "Rawson West African Exp. (1)" file (4th and 5th quotations);

Hambly to [Stephen C.] Simms, dir., FMNH, Lagos, Oct. 15, 1929, FMNH Archives, "Rawson West African Exp. (2)" file (last two quotations); Simms to H. E., high commissioner of Angola, Chicago, Nov. 23, 1929, FMNH Archives, "Rawson West African Exp. (2)" file.

37. *FR, PPC,* I, 407, 408–409; "Shall We Take German Africa?" *LD* (Dec. 14, 1918): 18–19; see Evans Lewin, *The Germans and Africa* (London, 1915), 264–266, for comments on British proposals to invite U.S. to take an African mandate; "An Empire Closed and Opened," *NAR* 209 (1919): 735–736 (1st quotation); "New Frontiers in West Africa," *CH* 11 (1920): 485–486; "The Mandate for South-West Africa," *Nation* (June 22, 1921): 877; "The New Partition of Africa," *LD* (May 14, 1921): 12–13; *FR, PPC,* VI, 841–844, 951–953; *FR, PPC,* XII, 133; "The Future of Germany's Colonies," *LD* (Feb. 15, 1919): 21, for quotes from the *Rheinisch Westfälische Zeitung* and the Socialist Berlin *Vorwärts;* "Africa in World Politics," *RofR* 71 (1925): 100, article from the *Deutsche Rundschau,* Nov., 1924; Evans Lewin, "The German People and Their Lost Colonies," *Atlantic* 136 (1925): 265–266; "German Colonial Aims," *RofR* 74 (1926): 441–442; Katharine J. Gallagher, "The Problem of the Former German Colonies," *CH* 25 (1927): 666–668; Mary E. Townsend, "The Contemporary Colonial Movement in Germany," *PSQ* 43 (1928): 64–65; Heinrich Schnee, "The Mandate System in Germany's Lost Colonies," *CH* 32 (1930): 77–80. Ernst Ambrosius, *Andrees Allgemeiner Handatlas* (Helefeld and Leipzig, 1922), 178–179; see also H. Haack, *Stilers Hand-Atlas,* 1932/33 (Gotha, n.d.), 77–78, 86; Musée du Congo Belge, *Bibliographie Ethnographique du Congo Belge et des Regions avoisinantes, 1925–1930* (Brussels, n.d.), 30, 148; for a summary of German activity on behalf of colonial restoration, see Wolfe W. Schmokel, *Dream of Empire: German Colonialism, 1919–1945* (New Haven, 1964), 1–45, 188–193.

38. "Mine and Thine in German Colonies," *Nation* (Oct. 18, 1919): 514–515; "Africa at the Peace Conference," *RofR* 59 (1919): 86; "German East Africa Divided Up," *CH* 12 (1920): 350–351; Lewin, "German People," 264–272; "England and Belgium in Africa," *Independent* (April 10, 1920): 59–60; "British Imperialists and German Colonial Policy," *Nation* (Oct. 19, 1919): 530–534. Americans had praised German colonial rule before the war, too; see Davis, *Congo and Coasts,* 154–161; Alpheus Henry Snow, "The Disposition of the German Colonies," *Nation* (Oct. 18, 1919): 528; Mary Evelyn Townsend, *The Rise and Fall of Germany's Colonial Empire: 1884–1918* (New York, 1930), 246–270; Heinrich Schnee, *German Colonization, Past and Future: The Truth about the German Colonies* (London, 1926), 172–173; *FR 38,* II, 446–451; New York *Journal of Commerce,* Sept. 2, 1932, quoted in G. Kurt Johannsen and H. H. Kraft, *Germany's Colonial Problem* (London, 1937), 58. See also Herbert Adams Gibbons, *The New Map of Africa* (New York, 1917), 228–243, 486.

39. Townsend, "Contemporary Colonial Movement," 66–68; Hjalmar Schacht, "Germany's Colonial Demands," *FA* 15 (1937): 226–227, 228; Philip Snowden, "Give Germany Her Colonies," *Nation* (July 21, 1926): 56–57; Franz von Papen, "Germany's Place in the Tropical Sun," *SEP* (Sept. 30, 1933): 23; "Germany: Nazis Blame Lack of Colonies for Fat

Shortage," *Newsweek* (Dec. 26, 1936): 10–11; *FR 37,* I, 76–77; Willson Woodside, "Colonies for Germany," *Harper's* 176 (1938): 522–525; Frederick Kuh, "Should Germany Have Colonies?" *Nation* (May 19, 1926): 564, 566; Curt L. Heymann, "Germany's Colonies," *CH* 45 (1937): 40 (1st quotation); Franz Ritter von Epp, "Germany's Case for Colonies," *CSMWM* (April 29, 1939): 5 (2nd quotation); William L. Langer, "A Critique of Imperialism," *FA* 14 (1935): 118; Moon, *Imperialism,* 552–553, 554–555; Ida C. Greaves, "A Modern Colonial Fallacy," *FA* 14 (1936): 638; see also Winston Churchill, "The Colony Racket," *Colliers* (Nov. 19, 1938): 11–12, 41–42; "What Deal Will Hitler Accept?" *BW* (Dec. 18, 1937): 30; and "Africa—Continent of Colonies," *BW* (Nov. 5, 1938): 47; Schacht, "Germany's Colonial Demands," 228.

40. Wright, "Sovereignty of Mandates," 698–703; Robert Shaw, "Africa: Back on the Chopping Block," *CH* 49 (1939): 20 (1st quotation); "Strategy in Africa," *Fortune* 12 (1935): 84; Alpheus Henry Snow, *The Question of Aborigines in the Law and Practice of Nations* (Washington, 1919), 21–22 (3rd quotation); Lippmann to S. E. Mezes, April 17, 1918, *FR, PPC,* I, 73.

41. Beer, *African Questions,* 40; Townsend, *Rise and Fall,* 233–235; Willis, *Living Africa,* 55 (2nd and 3rd quotations). See also H. L. Shantz, "Urundi, Territory and People," GR 12 (1922): 356–357; Gallagher, "Former German Colonies," 663; Willson to J. R. Minter, Lagos, March 19, 1932, DS 862q.01/63; Lugard, "Native Policy," 78; R. H. Whitbeck and V. C. Finch, *Economic Geography* (New York, 1924), 503–505; C. B. Fawcett, *Political Geography of the British Empire* (Boston, 1933), 306; "Will Lost Colonies Satisfy Hitler?" *Scholastic* (May 20, 1939): 18–S; "Where There Is No Peace," *CC* (Dec. 15, 1937): 1552–1553; see also Jessie W. Hughan, *CC* (Feb. 26, 1936): 531–532; Woolbert, "Portugal's Colonies," 379–380, also 375–376, Albert Guerard, "The Next War and How to Nip It," *Scribner's* 81 (1927): 399.

42. [Illegible], German consul to American consul, LM, Aug. 8, 1924, with *Kaiserlich,* etc., PR LM 845; Lawrence G. Green, "Shipwrecked in the Heart of Africa," *Travel* 70 (1938): 46; Albrecht to State, Nairobi, May 9, 1927, DS 848t.01/64; MacVitty to State, Nairobi, Aug. 12, 1930, DS 862.3348t/1.

43. Callanan to State, Nairobi, Oct. 9, 1933, DS 862.015/36; Wasson to State, Lagos, July 28, 1939, DS 862.014/478.

44. Shaw, "Africa: Back on the Block," 20; Woodside, "Colonies for Germany," 520; Mary E. Townsend, "The German Colonies and the Third Reich," *PSQ* 53 (1938): 186–195; *Time* (Feb. 28, 1938): 21; Hubbard, "What Europe Sees," 46; *Life* (Dec. 7, 1936): 28; Jan H. Hofmeyr, "Germany's Colonial Claims, A South African View," *FA* 17 (1939): 793–794; Ebling to State, LM, Nov. 2, 1938, DS 862.014/413; Smith to State, Nairobi, July 6, 1939, DS 862.4016/2116, on "Deutsch Ost Afrika"; Wasson to State, Lagos, March 9, 1939, DS 851T.20/6. Although South-West Africa is beyond the purview of this study, the reader may be interested in Nazi activities in that mandate as well; see Benjamin Bennet, *Hitler over Africa,* 2nd ed. (London, 1939), 1–5, 15–17, 19–20, 27–44, 157–179.

45. Smith to State, Nairobi [n.d., ca. 1937], DS 862S.01/88; on the

Seventh-day Adventist incident, see Smith to State, Nairobi, March 31, 1939, July 8, 1939, Aug. 26, 1939, DS 362S.1163 Seventh-day Adventists/1–3; Smith to State, Nairobi, April 14, 1939, DS 862S.00N/4; Smith to State, Nairobi, Feb. 8, 1939, DS 862S.00N/2; a report on "Nazi Activities in Tanganyika": filed with covering note, from Wallace Murray to "Mr. Messersmith, Mr. Welles, Mr. Secretary."

46. Keogh to State, Nairobi, Sept. 16, 1936, DS 862.014/170: an excellent discussion of antirevisionist sentiment among the non-German settlers of BEA; Wasson to State, Lagos, Nov. 8, 1938, DS 862.014/422; Townsend, "German Colonies," 206; "British Prepare to Dicker with Germany on Colonies," *Newsweek* (Nov. 7, 1938): 16–17; *FR* 38, I, 96–97, 136, 432, 714–715; Smith to State, Nairobi, July 13, 1938, DS 862.014/372; Smith to State, Nairobi, Jan. 12, 1939, DS 848t.01/123; idem, Nairobi, Jan. 30, 1939, DS 865d.00/44; idem, Nairobi, March 13, 1939, DS 865d.00/46; idem, Nairobi, March 20, 1939, DS 865d.00/47; idem, Nairobi, April 24, 1939, DS 862S.00N/5; Wasson to State, Lagos, Aug. 9, 1938, DS 841.20248k/1; Smith to State, Nairobi, Nov. 16, 1939, DS 862S.00/6; idem, Nov. 23, 1938, DS 862S.00/7; Dorsz to State, Léopoldville, Oct. 19, 1938, DS 855a.014/5; idem, Oct. 22, 1938, 855a.014/6; idem, Nov. 25, 1938, DS 855a.20/6; idem, Nov. 14, 1938, DS 851u.415/1; idem, Dec. 3, 1938, DS 855a.014/7; Ebling to State, LM, Dec. 5, 1938, DS 853n.00/39; Smith to State, Jan. 3, 1939, DS 862S.00/10; idem, Nairobi, May 31, June 8, June 28, 1939, DS 862S.00/14–16; Wasson to State, Lagos, March 8, 1939, DS 862.014/457; Smith to State, Nairobi, March 25, 1939, DS 848t.00/88; Wasson to State, Lagos, July 21, 1939, DS 862.014/477.

47. Smith to State, Nairobi, Aug. 4, 1939, DS 862.014/484 (1st quotation); idem, Sept. 6, 1939, DS 848t.00/95; Wasson to State, Lagos, Sept. 22, 1939, DS 848L.20/5 (2nd quotation); Patrick Mallon to State, Léopoldville, Nov. 14, 1939, DS 855a.415/2.

two: america in africa

1. Martin Johnson, *Safari: A Saga of African Adventure* (New York, 1928), 4.

2. Brockholst Livingston to Mrs. Olga Watkins, Nairobi, May 2, 1932, PR Nairobi 310; guest list of July 4 reception, 1933 (undated) in PR Nairobi 845; E. Talbot Smith to State, Nairobi, July 6, 1939, DS 811.503/Near East/334.

3. Sol Bloom to the U.S. consul at LM, Washington, June 28, 1932; A. D. Cameron to Bloom, LM, Aug. 11, 1932, both filed in PR LM, 841.5.

4. S. W. Eells to L. L. Shoemaker, Nairobi, Oct. 16, 1919, PR Nairobi 840.5; Paul W. Kelly, capt., Co. "F," 309th Engineers, AEF, Montoir, France. April 3, 1919, to consul, Zanzibar, "German East Africa," PR Nairobi 822; Eells to Kelly, Nairobi, August 13, 1919, PR Nairobi 822.

5. R. P. Clark to State, Loanda, Jan. 23, 1922, DS 353m.11/7; Clark to State, Loanda, Jan. 8, 1924, DS 161.35/131. Also Clark, memorandum for State Dept., Loanda, Feb. 25, 1924, and Clark to managing engineer,

Forminière, Tshikapa, Kasai [the Belgian Congo], March 20, 1924, both filed in PR Loanda, 130; L. Gourley to State, Quarterly Report on Passenger Traffic, June and Sept. quarters, LM, Oct. 14, 1925 (1st quotation) DS 195/470a over 551; Samuel Ebling to State, LM, Jan. 7, 1935, PR LM, 300 (2nd quotation); Ebling to State, LM, Oct. 13, 1937, DS 811.5031 Near East/197.

6. E. T. Smith to State, Nairobi, Sept. 15, 1938, DS 300.11 General Program/127; Smith to State, Nairobi, Dec. 31, 1937, DS 811.5031 Near East/207; E. T. Smith to State, Nairobi, Nov. 16, 1938, DS 811.5031 Near East/290.

7. Fred Morris Dearing, min., U.S. legation, Lisbon, to Cecil M. Cross, consul at LM, July 24, 1924, and J. D. Pointer, Methodist Episcopal Church, Inhambane, to Cross, Inhambane, Nov. 6, 1924, and several related items in PR LM 862.3; Thomas C. Wasson to State Dept., Jan. 21, 1938, Lagos DS 811.5031 Near East/209; Wynant D. Hubbard to secy.-gen. of province, LM, Feb. 26, 1924 in PR LM 862.3; "Raising Babies with Wild Beasts for Neighbors," *LD* (Sept. 12, 1925): 36–42. See pages 140–142 for a more detailed treatment of specimen collecting and animal dealers.

8. Theodore Roosevelt, *African Game Trails,* 2 vols. (New York, 1923), 1: 130–155; Stewart Edward White, *The Rediscovered Country* (Garden City, 1915), 376–406; K. MacVitty to J. T. Smith, Nairobi, Dec. 30, 1930, PR Nairobi 862.2.

9. Roosevelt's tent, styled "My Boma," appears in his *African Game Trails,* 2: facing 332.

10. DS *Register,* Dec. 23, 1918 (Washington, 1919), 64; Clark to State, Loanda, April 5, 1920, DS 123 541/23 [index card only]; Clark to State, Loanda, Feb. 24, 1920, DS 125.5461/-; S. W. Eells to State, Nairobi, Jan. 2, 1919, DS 123 ES/7 [index card only]; DS *Register,* May 1, 1922 (Washington, 1922), 63, 70, 78, 79, 80, 84.

11. Robert Fernald to State, telegram, Lagos, March 29, 1928, DS 125.523/8; Fernald to State, Lagos, May 15, 1928, DS 125.5237/2; State to U.S. consul at Lagos, Washington, Oct. 25, 1929, DS 125.536 H/5; A. F. Tower to State, Léopoldville, Nov. 26, 1929, DS 125.536 h1/2; DS *Register,* Jan., 1929 (Washington, 1929), 54, 64; DS *Register,* Jan., 1930 (Washington, 1930), 30, 53; State to consul at Léopoldville, Washington, Aug. 16, 1930 (telegram), and William R. Castle, acting secy. of state, to consul at Lagos, both filed DS 125.536h/9a and /9b; State to John S. Richardson, Washington, Aug. 4, 1934, DS 125.536h/12a. G. Willson to State, Lagos, Jan. 19, 1931, DS 125.536h7/4; DS *Register,* Oct., 1939 (Washington, 1939), 42, 43, 45; DS, *Foreign Service List,* Jan. 1, 1938 (Washington, 1938), 32, 36, 40, 41, 42.

12. Standard consular forms from all over tropical Africa were returned from African posts with empty columns. See, for instance, W. L. Peck to State, Lagos, July 29, 1933, DS 300.1115/120 over 523, and F. Styles to State, Loanda, Oct. 10, 1924, DS 164.12/1150. Between July 1, 1933, and June 30, 1934, the U.S. consul at LM performed only one visa service. Ebling to State, LM, Dec. 3, 1934, DS 811.111 Quota 53 p/3. W. L. Peck to Hotel Shenley Co. in Pittsburgh, Lagos, Nov. 30, 1932, PR Lagos 850.2, advised the company in response to an inquiry

that it was "very seldom that anyone proceeds from here to the United States."

13. Brockholst Livingston to State, Nairobi, Oct. 10, 1932, DS 125.-0055a/22 (1st quotation); G. R. Willson to C. C. Roberts, agent for the Barber West African Line at Lagos, Lagos, Jan. 15, 1931, PR Lagos 840.6 (2nd quotation); R. Livingstone to State, Nairobi, April 22, 1932, DS 811.111 Quota 62s/2; Livingstone to State, Nairobi, Nov. 21, 1932, DS 125.6427/9. On the French Equatorial Africa controversy, see the department's assignment of the colony to the Léopoldville district in State to consul at Léopoldville, Washington, Dec. 22, 1937, DS 125.-536H7/9, and the consul's attempt to squirm out of it in Edmund Dorsz to State, Léopoldville, Feb. 1, 1938, DS 125.536h7/11. Consuls also tried to trim their districts by placing distant points on the "no-consul" list, and these requests were frequently honored.

14. Apparently the consul had very limited confidence in either Portuguese defense forces or their medical facilities. Regardless of what form the "emergency" might assume, Ebling's plan called for immediate evacuation. Ebling to State, LM, March 20, 1937, DS 300.11 General Program/199.

15. A. M. Warren to State, dispatch and telegram, Nairobi, Dec. 15, 1926; Warren to State, Nairobi, Dec. 30, 1925; F. A. Sterling, U.S. embassy, London, to State, London, March 23, 1926; Warren to State, Nairobi, Dec. 15, 1926; C. Albrecht to State, Nairobi, Feb. 17, 1927, all in DS 811.015248t/ and (same)/-, 1,2,3,5.

16. Mrs. A[vra] M. Warren, "Nairobi Celebrities," *AFSJ* 2 (1925): 338; "Suggestions and Notes that may be of interest to the new Vice Consul in Charge, succeeding H. A. McBride at Boma, Kongo," undated [ca. August, 1916], in PR Loanda 000; Fred Morris Dearing, U.S. legation, Lisbon, to J. W. Bailey, at Loanda, Lisbon, May 24, 1928, PR Loanda 820 (quotation).

17. Memorandum, Div. of Western European Affairs, Aug. 13, 1930, files with covering note to Personnel Board, U.S. Foreign Service, in DS 125.536H/11 (1st quotation); G. Willson to Chief, Div. WEA, Lagos, March 19, 1932, DS 862 Q.01/63 (2nd quotation).

18. Clark sent in a fascinating series of dispatches from points along the way on his long trip in the summer and fall of 1920, all of which are filed in PR Loanda 030; Louis M. Duval, secy., African Mission to the Southern Baptist Convention, USA, Lagos, to the U.S. consul in Lagos, Jan. 16, 1928, PR Lagos 811.11E; Livingston to Mrs. O. Watkins, Nairobi, May 2, 1932, PR Nairobi 310.

19. *AFSJ* 3 (Dec. 1926): 395; Gilbert Grosvenor to consul, LM, Washington, May 12, 1921, PR LM 020; Frank Tose (chief preparator) to Leslie Simson in Nairobi, San Francisco, Sept. 18, 1931, in files of Exhibit Dept. 141, in Archives Division, Library, the California Academy of Sciences, San Francisco.

20. On congressional visits, see W. Jenkins to State, Nairobi, July 17, 1923, DS 033.1148t T39; A. M. Warren to State, Nairobi, July 5, 1925, DS 123 W25/63 [index card only]; J[ames] P. Buchanan to Warren, Washington, Jan. 6, 1924 [1925], and Warren to Buchanan, Nairobi, Feb. 26, 1925, both filed in PR Nairobi 862.3.

21. State to consul, LM, Washington, June 16, 1919, DS 102.73/1454, and State to LM, Washington, April 4, 1929, DS 853p.62222/1; J. B. Keogh to State, Nairobi, Oct. 12, 1935, DS 102.77/1258; R. B. Streeper to State, Nairobi, March 6, 1936, DS 102.7/2283; J. P. Moffitt to State, LM, Nov. 22, 1926, DS 853n. 6132/31, and L. H. Gourley to State, LM, June 13, 1925, DS 853n. 61321/27. On the USDA expedition to the Belgian Congo, see copy of mimeographed instructions, State, Sept. 23, 1935, and letter from P. Ryckmans, gov.-genl. of the Belgian Congo to consul at Léopoldville, Jan. 23, 1936, both in PR Léopoldville 861.2 Research Expedition-U.S. Dept. of Agriculture.

22. See, for instance, G. Willson to State, Lagos, April 13, 1931, DS 166.525 Cocoa, and April 15, 1931, DS 102.81 Palm Oil/523; State to consul at Lagos, Washington, Aug. 15, 1933, DS 166.523/85; C. Albrecht to State, Nairobi, Aug. 4, 1927, DS 165.—6/4405; R. Livingstone to State, Nairobi, May 6, 1932, DS 165.015/1303; W. Peck to State, Lagos, Sept. 27, 1933, DS 110.78 Coordination/129.

23. Albrecht to State, Nairobi, Aug. 11, 1927, DS 196/551; E. T. Smith to State, Nairobi, June 7, 1939, DS 023.642; G. Willson to State, Lagos, May 26, 1932, DS 103.8/476; State to consul at Lagos, Washington, Nov. 9, 1928, DS 158.48ml/6; consul at Nairobi to State, March 18, 1919, DS 848T.9423/-; A. Tower to State, Léopoldville, Aug. 26, 1930, DS 800.515/111 over 536h; Willson to State, Lagos, Sept. 4, 1930, DS 800.515/111 over 523; L. J. Callanan to State, Nairobi, Feb. 25, 1933, DS 103.7/2551.

24. R. P. Clark to State, Loanda, May 11, 1923, DS 811.114N16/164; W. Jenkins to State, Nairobi, May 15, 1923, DS 811.114N16/179; C. Cross to State, LM, April 19, 1924, DS 811.114N16/513.

25. J. W. Bailey to State, Loanda, April 25, 1927, DS 102.5216/800 over 546; A. Warren to State, Nairobi, Jan. 3, 1926, DS 848t.206/2; E. T. Smith to State, Nairobi, July 13, 1939, DS 848t.20/17. Navy Dept., AR 1923 (Washington, 1924), 7.

26. Navy Dept., AR 1920 (Washington, 1921), 25. Aside from these ARs, which are far from inclusive, the only record of fleet, squadron, or vessel movements is by individual log book. That the Atlantic Fleet did not make the South African trip is demonstrated by the 1921 log book of the flagship U.S.S. Pennsylvania, which indicates the ship never left American waters In that year. Log of the Pennsylvania, Jan. 1–Dec. 31, 1921, Bureau of Naval Personnel, Log Book Series, NA, Record Group 24. Log of the Richmond, July 2, 1923–Dec. 31, 1923, 4, 130, 144–148, 154, 181, Log Book Series, RG 24.

27. Log of the U.S.S. Concord, Nov. 3, 1923–Dec. 31, 1924, 35, 41, 63–81, 85, 115–191.

28. Navy Dept., AR for 1925 (Washington, 1926), 8; log book of the U.S.S. Trenton, April 19, 1924–Dec. 31, 1924, 257–261, Log Book Series RG 24; Leo Toch to State, LM, Jan. 11, 1934, DS 811.3343p/1.

29. Kalton C. Lahue, Bound and Gagged: The Story of the Silent Serials (South Brunswick, 1968); Jerry Wald and Richard Macaulay, eds., The Best Pictures 1939–1940 (New York, 1940), 466–467, 506–509; Leslie Halliwell, The Filmgoer's Companion (New York, 1967), 741–742;

Beth Day, *This Was Hollywood* (Garden City, 1960), 141–148; Gabe Essoe, *Tarzan of the Movies* (New York, 1968), 67–75.

30. Robert W. Fenton, *The Big Swingers* (Englewood Cliffs, 1967), 1; Pierre Couperie et al., *A History of the Comic Strip* (New York, 1968), 57; Richard A. Lupoff, *Edgar Rice Burroughs: Master of Adventure* (New York, 1965), 161–163; David Manning White and Robert H. Abel, *The Funnies: An American Idiom* (Glencoe, 1963), 92.

31. Quoted in Fenton, *Big Swingers,* 149; Montgomery Ward & Co., *Catalogue, 1925–1926,* 333 (by 1925 Ward's offered seventeen Burroughs' books at sixty-eight cents); *Life* (June 7, 1937): 94; Charles Roeder to Mrs. Straus, New York City, Jan. 22, 1934, in FMNH Archives, "Straus West African Exp. File" (quotation).

32. R. W. Van Horn, Van Horn & Sons, Inc., Theatrical & Historical Costumes, Philadelphia, March 21, 1927, to consul, Loanda, PR Loanda 840.5; J. W. Bailey to dir. of research, M-G-M Studios, Loanda, April 9, 1928, PR Loanda 840.6; Emory Ross, "Why Study Africa?" *MRW* 59 (1936): 452; Albert D. Helser, *In Sunny Nigeria* (New York, 1926), 17 (2nd quotation); Eric H. Louw, "The Union of South Africa and Its Trade," *Official Report of the 14th NFTC* (New York, 1927), 215.

33. Felix Shay, "Cairo to Cape Town, Overland," *NGM* 47 (1925): 123 (1st quotation); John A. Miller to consul, Swarthmore, Pa., Feb. 26, 1925, PR Nairobi 892.2 (2nd quotation); J. Russell Smith, New York, to consul, May 27, 1929, PR Lagos 892.43 (3rd quotation).

34. For a sampling of geographies poor on African material, see [Hendrik Willem] Van Loon, *Van Loon's Geography: The Story of the World* (Garden City, 1940), 409–453; Albert Perry Brigham and Charles T. McFarlane, *Essentials of Geography: Second Book* (New York, 1920)— with less than one page on equatorial Africa; Frank M. McMurray and A. E. Parkins, *Advanced Geography* (New York, 1924), 453–460; J. Russell Smith, *Human Geography: Book One: Peoples and Countries* (Chicago, 1921), 705–714; R. H. Whitbeck and V. C. Finch, *Economic Geography* (New York, 1924). *The Literary Digest Atlas of the World and Gazetteer* (New York, 1926), 3, contains the population figure of 180 million for Africa; Lord Hailey in his *African Survey* (London, 1938) attributed the figure to Stanley before 1881 (104). Robert Shaw, "Africa: Back on the Chopping Block," *CH* 49 (1939): 20 (quotation).

35. Wynant David Hubbard, "Is Africa Going White, Black or Brown?" *Nation* (Sept. 14, 1927): 249 (1st quotation); Hubbard to Cross, Mazoe River Drift, near Shamva, So. Rhodesia, May 12, 1924, PR LM 862.3; Hambly to Dir., Elende, Angola, May 31, 1929, in FMNH Archives, "Rawson West African Exp. (I)" file. For examples of writers locating places for their readers, see William T. Hornaday, *Tales from Nature's Wonderlands* (New York, 1924), 201; Edmund Heller, "Mount Lolokwi the Unknown," *Harper's* 140 (1920): 147; W. S. Van Dyke, *Horning into Africa* (n.p., 1931), 68. See Ralph Stockman Tarr, *College Physiography* (New York, 1923), 591; Wilfrid D. Hambly, *Source Book for African Anthropology* (FMNH Anthropological Series, vol. 26, Parts 1 and 2; Chicago, 1937), 28; Hailey, *African Survey,* 4–5; D. S. Whittlesey, "Geographic Provinces of Angola," *GR* 14 (1924): 114.

36. See, for instance, Alexis Everett Frye, *New Geography: Book One*

(Boston, 1920), 242, 243, 245; J. Paul Goode, *Goode's School Atlas: Physical, Political and Economic* (Chicago, 1925), 94–95; C. S. Hammond to consul, Loanda, New York, July 21, 1922, PR Loanda 850.1 and William Johnson, chief, Dept. of Cartography, Rand McNally & Co., Chicago, to consul, Lagos, Jan. 22, 1935, PR Lagos 892.51; *1923 Atlas of the World and Gazetteer* (New York, 1923), 44–47; *Literary Digest Atlas,* 58–59; 60–61; *Our Planet: The Blue Book of Maps* (New York, 1935), 94, 95, 124–125; for Williams Co. maps, see McMurray and Parkins, *Advanced Geography,* 450, 451; Hambly, *Source Book,* 29, recommending the *NGS* map; Gilbert Grosvenor, "The National Geographic Society's New Map of Africa," *NGM* 67 (1935): 731–752.

37. Ernst Ambrosius, *Andress Allgemeiner Handatlas* (Helefeld, 1922), 170–171, 172–173, and 174–191; Van Dyke, *Horning into Africa,* 19; Revel B. Frost, Dept. of Geology and Geography, Oberlin College, to Dir., Dept. of Agriculture, Entebbe, Uganda [Oberlin, O.], June 23, 1932, PR Nairobi 892.3 and O. Thomason to chief secy., Entebbe, Uganda, Nairobi, July 8, 1924, PR Nairobi 892.3; A. Samler and G. Gordon Brown, *The South and East African Yearbook and Guide* (London, 1920), sixty-four pages of good maps following 922; Hailey, *Survey,* 3, n. 1; Whittlesey, "Geographic Provinces," 113; Carveth Wells, "In Coldest Africa," *WW* 58 (1929): 76.

38. Van Dyke, *Horning into Africa,* 29–30 (1st quotation); H. L. Shantz and C. F. Marbut, *The Vegetation and Soils of Africa* (New York, 1923), 23–49, esp. 27 (2nd quotation) and 19; Preston E. James, *An Outline of Geography* (Boston, 1935), 59–60; Marion I. Newbigin, *A New Regional Geography of the World* (New York, 1930), 227–228; Martin Johnson, "Martin Johnson's Story, and His New Pictures of Wild Animals in Africa," *WW* 49 (1925): 605; "Raising Babies with Wild Beasts for Neighbors," *LD* 86 (Sept. 12, 1925): 36.

39. J. Russell Smith, *Human Geography: Book Two: Regions and Trade* (Chicago, 1922), 350–352; Charles H. Seevers, *Trailing Animals around the World* (one of the *Wonder Books,* ed. Glenn Frank, Chicago, 1938), 41–42 (2nd quotation); *Van Loon's Geography,* 542; Whitbeck and Finch, *Economic Geography,* 503; Parker Thomas Moon, *Imperialism and World Politics* (New York, 1926), 76.

40. Carl and Mary L. Jobe Akeley, *Adventures in the African Jungle* (New York, 1930), 1; E. Alexander Powell, "Drums on the Lualaba: A Journey Across Africa," *Century* 109 (1925): 630. Joseph Conrad, "Heart of Darkness," in *Great Short Works of Joseph Conrad* (New York, 1966), 187; Jakob Wassermann, *Bula Matari: Stanley—Conquerer of a Continent* (New York, 1933), 135 (3rd quotation. C[ecil] S[cott] Forester, *The African Queen* (New York, 1940), 210.

41. Uthai Vincent Wilcox, "The March of Civilization in Africa," *CH* 18 (1923): 782 (1st quotation); Vilhjalmur Stefansson, "Are Explorers to Join the Dodo?" *The American Mercury* 11 (1927): 18 (2nd quotation).

42. Mrs. Horance Tremlett, *With the Tin Gods* (London, 1915), 41 (1st quotation); Alfred Aloysius Horn and Ethelreda Lewis, *Trader Horn: Being the Life and Works of Alfred Aloysius Horn* (New York, 1928), 241; Paul L. Hoefler, *Africa Speaks: A Story of Adventure* (Chicago, 1931), 19. See also Graham Greene, *Journey without Maps* (New York, 1961), 34.

43. Roosevelt, *African Game Trails,* 1: 23 (1st quotation); the Gold Coast government, *The Gold Coast Handbook 1937* (Worcester, 1937), 180; Gustave Reynaud, "Petit Manuel d'Hygiene," in Le Myre de Vilers et al., *Préparation aux Carrières Coloniales* (Paris, 1904), 436–437; Smith, *Human Geography: Book Two,* 355; Raymond Garfield Gettell, *Political Science* ([Boston], 1933), 34–35 (2nd quotation); S. S. Murray, *A Handbook of Nyasaland* (London, 1922), 226 (last quotation).

44. Van Dyke, *Horning into Africa,* 83; Forester, *African Queen,* 176–177; R. L. Garner, "Adventures in Central Africa," *Century* 100 (1920): 132, 126–127; Albert C. Ingalls, "A Fly versus a Civilization," *SA* 132 (1925): 402 (last quotation).

45. Reynaud, "Petit Manuel," 407–415; Harry Johnston and L. Haden Guest, *The Outline of the World Today,* 3 vols. (London, n.d.), 2: 273; Van Dyke, *Horning into Africa,* 85, 87–88; "Isolated in Central Africa, by a Missionary in Rhodesia," *MRW* 53 (1930): 350–353; State to consul at LM, Washington, March 16, 1926, DS 125.5512/62 (2nd quotation); L. Gourley to State, LM, Aug. 24, 1925, DS 123G74/64 (index card only).

46. Greene, *Journey without Maps,* 42–43; E. Dorsz to State, Léopold-ville, May 4, 1937, DS 158.51T3/27.

47. R. P. Clark to State, Loanda, April 8, 1921, DS 125.5462/10; O. Thomason to State, Nairobi, Nov. 22, 1923, DS 158.48t1/26; R. Fernald to State, Lagos, Nov. 15, 1928, DS 158.48m1/8; J. W. Bailey to State, Loanda, [Jan., 1928], PR Loanda 812 Sanitary Reports; R. Streeper to State (telegram), Nairobi, March 26, 1936, DS 158.48T1/30.

48. James P. Chapin, "Up the Congo to Lukolela," *NH* 31 (1931): 600 (1st quotation); Delia J. Akeley, "The Little People," *SEP* (March 3, 1928), 17; Conrad, "Heart of Darkness," 207.

49. Forester, *African Queen,* 3 (1st quotation); Jean Kenyon Macken-zie, "Exile and Postman," *Atlantic* 150 (1932): 634 (2nd quotation).

50. W. D. Hambly to S. C. Simms, aboard S.S. *Waganda* near Madeira, April 8, 1929, in FMNH Archives, Records of the Director's Office, "Rawson West African Exp. (1)" file; Marius Fortie, "On Foot through Tanganyika," *SM* 46 (1938): 529. See dispatch from LM to State, Dec. 6, 1919, DS 811.607 AK/24. R. P. Clark, to American Telephone & Telegraph Co. in New York, Loanda, May 2, 1923, PR Loanda 875; F. Styles to State, Loanda, Sept. 24, 1924, DS 119.2/1504 (last quotation).

51. Carveth Wells, "In Coldest Africa," 41, 106; John W. Vandercook, "The African Big Game," *Forum* 83 (1930): 184 (quotation).

52. J. E. Hughes, *Eighteen Years on Lake Bangweulu* (London, n.d.), 63; "Painting Africa in Lighter Hues," *LD* 96 (March 10, 1928): 44 (quotation).

53. A. D. Cameron to E. J. Wunneke, LM, Dec. 20, 1932, PR LM 891; Julian Huxley, *Africa View* (New York, 1931), 162; W. Peck to State, Lagos, Dec. 4, 1934, PR Lagos 840.6 (3rd quotation); G. Willson to Ely Culbertson, Lagos, Jan. 12, 1932, PR Lagos 840.6 (last quotation).

54. S. W. Eells to State, Nairobi, April 1, 1920, DS 848t.5017/-.

55. May Mott-Smith, *Africa from Port to Port* (New York, 1930), 32–33; A. F. Tower to Grigsby-Grunow Co., Chicago, Léopoldville, July 16, 1930, PR Léopoldville 866.16/866.31; Daniel W. Streeter, *Denatured*

Africa (New York, 1926), 31. On the residence tax, see C. Cross to State, LM, Feb. 3, 1922, DS 853n.512/-.

56. Richard Upjohn Light, *Focus on Africa* (New York, 1941), 59. See photograph 45.

57. Mott-Smith, *Africa Port to Port,* 1.

58. Streeter, *Denatured Africa,* 56–72.

59. See, for instance, R. H. Lee, "The Titanic Cataract of the Zambesi," *Travel* 37 (1921): 23–25; Stella Court Treatt, *Cape to Cairo: The Record of a Historic Motor Journey* (Boston, 1927), 103–117; Evelyn Waugh, *They Were Still Dancing* (New York, 1932), 255.

60. Jean Kenyon Mackenzie, "Of Luxuries and Hardships," *Atlantic* 132 (1923): 329; idem, "The Unforgotten Journeys," *Forum* 71 (1924): 20–30.

61. Van Dyke, *Horning into Africa,* 59.

62. Osa Johnson, "My Home in the African Blue," *GH* 78 (1924): 167–168.

63. Mary L. Jobe Akeley, *Carl Akeley's Africa* (New York, 1929), 41; Stillman Eells to State, Nairobi, April 1, 1920, DS 848t.5017/-. Osa Johnson, *I Married Adventure* (Philadelphia, 1940), 198; the Gold Coast government, *Handbook,* 71–72.

64. Osa Johnson, "Home in African Blue," 167–168 (1st quotation); Ruth Q. McBride, "Keeping House on the Congo," *NGM* 72 (1937): 660 (2nd quotation).

65. Mott-Smith, *Africa Port to Port,* 147; Mrs. A[vra] M. Warren, "Nairobi Celebrities," *AFSJ* 2 (1925): 338–339.

66. James L. Clark, "On Safari in British East Africa," *Asia* 28 (1928): 363; Garner, "Adventures," 600.

67. Martha Miller Bliven, "Africa: The Impressions of a Modern Woman, After Two Years Spent Among the Natives in the Jungle," *SA* 137 (1927): 325; FMNH, Curator of Birds, dept. files, packet marked "Straus West African Expedition—Financial," small record book, 47. Stewart Edward White, "Nyumbo," *SEP* (Sept. 12, 1925): 225; Martin Johnson, "Lions Roar and Hippos Yawn," *WW* 60 (1931): 39; idem, "Extracts from the Diary of Martin Johnson," *NH* 25 (1925): 578; Osa Johnson, " 'At Home' in Africa," *NH* 27 (1927): 561 (next to last quotation); idem, *I Married Adventure,* 297.

68. Ernest Hemingway, *Green Hills of Africa* (New York, 1935), 122–123; Emily Hoffman Dalziel, "From Arusha to the Blue," *GH* 75 (1922): 35; Powell, "Drums on the Lualaba," 627.

69. Eleanor de Chetelat, "My Domestic Life in French Guinea," *NGM* 67 (1935): 698; McBride, "Keeping House," 650 (2nd quotation); Dalziel, "Arusha to the Blue," 148; Bliven, "Africa," 326 (last quotation).

70. Wells, "In Coldest Africa," 38; [George Eastman], *Chronicles of an African Trip* ([Rochester], 1927), 25; Van Dyke, *Horning into Africa,* 59.

71. Delia J. Akeley, "Monkey Tricks," *SEP* (Sept. 18, 1926): 107; Jan Verhoogen, "We Keep House on an Active Volcano," *NGM* 76 (1939): 542 (last quotation).

72. Caroline B. Parker, "Off to New Adventures," *St. Nicholas* 57

(1930): 189 (1st quotation); Mrs. Akeley *did* know a few words of French. See "No Feminism in Darkest Africa," *LD* (May 15, 1926): 54; Clark, "On Safari," 363; Stewart Edward White, *The Land of Footprints* (Garden City, 1913), 174; Hubbard, "Is Africa Going White?" 251; Maurice Samuel, "Flight Across Africa," *Harper's* 169 (June, 1934): 30 (last quotation).

73. Osa Johnson, "Home in African Blue," 49; Johnson, *Safari,* 4.

74. Hemingway, *Green Hills,* 31.

75. [Illegible 1st name] Duhaga, Omukama [King] of Bunyoro, Kibanda, Busindi, Bunyoro [Uganda] to "Mr. Jenkins" (U.S. consul at Nairobi), Jan. 19, 1923, PR Nairobi, 845. The omukama apologized for missing the consul's visit, having been "away for my tour"; Jenkins was flattered. Streeter, *Denatured Africa,* 89.

76. Moon, *Imperialism,* 566; Margery Perham, *Colonial Sequence: 1930–1949* (London, [1967]), 233. From *The Times,* March 12, 1942 (2nd quotation).

77. Forester, *African Queen,* 33.

78. Llewelyn Powys, *Black Laughter* (New York, 1924), 190.

79. Mott-Smith, *Africa Port to Port,* 182–183; White, *Rediscovered Country,* 200; Clark, "On Safari," 363; Van Dyke, *Horning into Africa,* 136–137.

80. W. L. Peck to Modern Film Corp., Lagos, Dec. 17, 1934, PR Lagos 840.6 (1st quotation); S. W. Eells to Robertson–Cole Co., Nairobi, Jan. 6, 1921, PR Nairobi 840.6 (2nd quotation).

81. Gov.-gen. of the Belgian Congo, to U.S. consul, Léopoldville, June 23, 1930 (1st quotation); idem to consul, Léopoldville, March 31, 1930; vice gov.-gen. to consul, Léopoldville, Nov. 21, 1934, all PR Léopoldville 845; dist. com., Nairobi, to consul, Nairobi, March 13, 1926, PR Nairobi 845; priv. secy. to gov.-gen., Léopoldville, to consul, Jan. 3, 1930, PR Léopoldville 845; K. MacVitty to State, Nairobi, July 11, 1931, DS 848t.463/1; A. Cameron to State, LM, DS 811.415 Washington Bi-Centenary/1513 (2nd quotation).

82. Charles Burke Elliot, "The German Colonies and Their Future," *RofR* 59 (1919), 76.

three: american commercial penetration of africa

1. J. Russell Smith, *Industrial and Commercial Geography* (New York, 1925).

2. "The New Partition of Africa," *LD* (May 14, 1921): 12; Walter Henry Overs, "The Secret of Peace for Africa," *MRW* 44 (1921): 31 (quotation).

3. George Louis Beer, *African Questions at the Paris Peace Conference* (New York, 1923), 96–100, 213–220; *FR* 25, II, 214–216; *FR* 28, I, 433–436; State to Richardson, Dec. 17, 1936, DS 560.Z1/27 (quotations at end of paragraph); *FR* 39, II, 323–324.

4. "The Commercial Outlook in West Africa," *RofR* 62 (1920): 102–

103; S. W. Eells to State, Nairobi, July 24, 1919, DS 848t.463/1 (1st quotation); William L. Saunders, "Why Direct Selling?" [National Foreign Trade Council] *Official Report of the Seventh Annual Foreign Trade Convention* (New York, 1920), 318; report on West African trip to Dakar, Bathurst, Accra, of first American merchant steamer (SS. *Beatrice*), Feb. 7, 1919, to April 30, 1919, submitted Edgar H. Berry, May 17, 1919, Records *USSB,* general file 595–5 NA RG 32 (3rd quotation); Ray to State, LM, July 7, 1929, DS 125.5513/39 (4th quotation).

5. J. Klein to Stephenson, Washington, Jan. 18, 1929, 480.1 East Africa (2509), BFDC, general records, NA, RG 151 (1st quotation); Fred M. Dearing to Klein, Lisbon, Jan. 2, 1929, 480.1 East Africa (2509), Records BFDC (2nd quotation); Thomason to State, Nairobi, Dec. 19, 1921, DS 166.642/15 (3rd quotation).

6. Raymond Leslie Buell, "The Struggle in Africa," *FA* 6 (1927): 22 (1st quotation); Ellsworth Huntington and Frank E. Williams, *Business Geography* (New York, 1922), 296 (2nd quotation); John Carter, "Round About the Congo," *Commonweal* (April 2, 1930): 612 (3rd quotation).

7. Much of the information here is gleaned from reports in records of the USSB, RG 32, and in records of the USMC, RG 178, particularly Report 275, "Imports and Exports by Commodities by United States Coastal Districts and Foreign Trade Regions," for fiscal years 1926–1935; Chamber of Commerce of the United States, *Our World Trade,* annual volumes for 1920–1932 (Washington, 1921–1933); *Exporters' Encyclopaedia, 1927* (New York, 1926), map 146, 147–153, 161–186, 293–298, 857–858; Clark to State, Loanda, April 5, 1920, DS 855a.6363/1; *Moody's Manual of Investments* (New York, 1927), 591; Raymond Leslie Buell, *The Native Problem in Africa,* 2 vols. (New York, 1928), 2: 442–443, 445; Clark to State, Loanda, March 26, 1923, DS 853m.6347/2; Clark to State, Loanda, Jan. 8, 1924, DS 161.05/101; William Phillips, under secy. of state, memorandum of conversation, Washington, July 6, 1922, DS 853m.51/4 (fm); State to Cross, Washington, July 29, 1924, DS 853n.51/4; Cross to State, LM, April 13, 1925, DS 811.503–153n/-; Buell, "Struggle," 39–40; Ulrich B. Phillips, "Azandeland," *YR* 20 (1930): 294.

8. Eugene Staley, *Raw Materials in Peace and War* (New York, 1937), 251–318; James Sommerville, Jr., U.S. embassy, London, to BFDC, Dec. 28, 1927, 480.3 West Africa (2509), Records BFDC; Parker Thomas Moon, *Imperialism and World Politics* (New York, 1926), 546–549; Smith, *Industrial and Commercial Geography,* 479–481; "Radium from the Kongo," *LD* (March 13, 1926): 21–22; Phillip A. Hayward, *Wood, Lumber and Timbers* (New York, 1930), 274–276, 330–335; J. O. Ware, "Plant Breeding and the Cotton Industry," *USDA Yearbook 1936* (Washington, 1936), 729; Artemas Ward, ed., *The Encyclopedia of Food* (New York, 1929), 117–122, 372–373; Nels A. Bengsten and Willem Van Royen, *Fundamentals of Economic Geography* (New York, 1937), 414–416; Evans Lewin, "Africa in the Twentieth Century," YR 17 (1927): 90; Spencer Trotter, *The Geography of Commerce: A Text-Book* (New York, 1911), 348; Charles R. Toothaker, *Commercial Raw Materials: Their Origin, Preparation and Uses* (Boston, 1905), 21–24, 53; Richard Upjohn Light, *Focus on Africa* (New York, 1941), 55; William J. Miller, *An Introduction to Physical Geology* (New York, 1941), 424, 428–429, 440; Lewin, "Africa in Twen-

tieth Century," 78 (1st quotation); "Exporters Watch Africa," *BW* (April 13, 1935); Wynant D. Hubbard, "Africa Emerging from Darkness," *CH* 28 (June, 1928): 442; idem, "What Europe Sees in Africa," *RofR* 94 (1936): 47; comparative tonnage figures from "Report on Volume of Waterborne Foreign Commerce of the United States by Ports of Origin and Destination, Fiscal Year 1924," and USSB Report 275 for 1927, both in Records USMC; U.S. Chamber of Commerce, *Our World Trade*, 1929, 29; Carter, "Round the Congo" (2nd quotation); Klein to Dearing, Washington, Jan. 26, 1929, 480.1 East Africa (2509), Records BFDC (3rd quotation), George C. Chisholm, *Handbook of Commercial Geography* (New York, 1928), 580 (4th quotation). An indication of the collapse in U.S.-African trade in agricultural products is given by George N. Peek, "American Agriculture and Foreign Trade," Report of SAPFT, March, 1935, 41–42, in SAPFT records, NA, RG 20.

9. C. R. C. Nixon, "American Advertising in British Possessions," *NFTC Official Report*, 1938, 91–94; Lloyd W. Maxwell, *Discriminating Duties and the American Merchant Marine* (New York, 1926), 166; Moon, *Imperialism*, 529–531; Arnold Wright, *The Romance of Colonisation* (London, 1923), 370 (quotation).

10. Darrell Hevenor Smith and Paul V. Betters, *The United States Shipping Board: Its History, Activities and Organization* (Washington, 1931), 41, 42–46, 109–110; National Industrial Conference Board, *The American Merchant Marine Problem* (New York, 1929), 36–39, 56–57.

11. J. B. Morrow, Pensacola Chamber of Commerce, to T. V. O'Connor, chmn., USSB, Pensacola, Dec. 6, 1924 (quotation); L. C. Palmer to A. J. Higgins, Washington, Dec. 31, 1924; L. C. Palmer to Sen. Royal S. Copeland, Washington, Dec. 13, 1924; O[scar] W. Underwood to T. V. O'Connor, Washington, Dec. 10, 1924; Duncan U. Fletcher, to L. C. Palmer, Washington, Dec. 10, 1924; all in file 595–5, Records USSB. Palmer was pres. of EFC, USSB.

12. Bridge log, S.S. *West Lashaway*, June 7, 1929–Nov. 5, 1929, entry Aug. 1, 1929, Addah, the Gold Coast, and bridge log, same vessel, Oct. 6, 1931–Jan. 4, 1932, entry Oct. 29, 1931, Akassa, Nigeria, in ship's log books, RG 178, FRC, hereinafter cited as FRC Records USMC; "Condensed Statement, American West African Line," Feb. 29, 1928, 582–25 (Part 6), Rt 32; Ernest M. Bull to T. V. O'Connor, New York, Oct. 26, 1927, 582–25 (Part 6), Records USSB; A. C. Dalton, v. p. and gen. mgr., USSB MFC, to A. H. Bull & Co., Washington, July 10, 1928, 582–25–1, Records USSB; Charles Barthold, American West African Line, to H. Morse, New York, March 16, 1935, 1091–4832 (Part 5) *West Lashaway*, Records USSB (quotation); letter to author, Myer Trupp, dir., Office of International Affairs and Relations, USMC, Washington, Oct. 7, 1969.

13. Material on the S.S. *West Lashaway* is largely drawn from a study of thirty-three volumes of her log books (fifteen bridge logs, seventeen engine-room logs, one chief officer's log), covering voyages from March, 1929, to April, 1935, FRC Records USMC; Charles Barthold to H. Morse, New York, March 16, 1935, 1091–4532 (Part 5) *West Lashaway*, Records USSB; "Quarterly Report on the Employment of American Steam and Motor Merchant Vessels," various quarters, 1921–1939, USSB Report 300, Records USMC. For a summary of U.S. commercial relations with

sub-Saharan Africa, exclusive of the slave trade, see: Robert Collins and Robert Duignan, *Americans in Africa, 1865–1900* ([Stanford], 1966); Robert Emerson, *Africa and United States Policy* (Englewood Cliffs, 1967), 15–20; Clarence C. Clendenen and Peter Duignan, *Americans in Black Africa up to 1865* ([Stanford], 1964), 1–44.

14. MFC interoffice memorandum, March 19, 1929, 1091–4532 (Part 4) *West Lashaway,* Jan. 1, 1927, to Dec. 31, 1933, Records USSB; bridge log, *West Lashaway,* June 7, 1929, to Nov. 5, 1929, entire; J. Caldwell Jenkins, v.p., MFC, to USSB, Washington, Sept. 19, 1930, 1091–4532 (Part 4) *West Lashaway,* Records USSB.

15. B. K. Ogden to MFC pres., Washington, Aug. 16, 1930, 1091–4532 (Part 4) *West Lashaway* (1st and 2nd quotations); R. S. Sparrow, AWAL, to EFC dir. of operations, Brooklyn, March 26, 1935, and Sparrow to EFC dist. rep., Brooklyn, April 4, 1935, in 1091–4532 (Part 5) *West Lashaway,* RG 32; Elmer Crowley, MFC pres., to USSB, Washington, June 1, 1931, 1091–4532 (Part 4) *West Lashaway* (3rd quotation); Oakley Wood, v. p., AWAL to USSB, New York, March 5, 1935, 1091–4532 (Part 5) *West Lashaway* (4th quotation); Huntington Morse, chief, div. of oper., EFC, to USSB Board of Trustees, Washington, March 18, 1935, 1091–4532 (Part 5) *West Lashaway,* all in Records USSB; USMC, Report 1500–8–A, "American Flag Services in Foreign Trade and with United States Possessions, as of April 1, 1939," 10–11, Records USMC.

16. See Ernest M. Bull to Elmer Crowley, New York, Nov. 27, 1927, for an estimate that converting ships on the East-South African route from coal to diesel would lower operating cost per voyage from $22,600 to $7,000, 605–1–1039 (Part 1), Records USSB; Jenkins to State, Nairobi, June 22, 1923, DS 195/470a over 642; J. Harry Philbin to Commissioner Plummer, USSB, Washington, Sept. 12, 1924, 595–5, Records USSB; EFC interoffice memorandum, Nov. 11, 1924, 505–5, Rooordo USSB; USSB interoffice memorandum, Dec. 22, 1925, 605–1–1039 (Part 1), Records USSB; Jenkins to State, Nairobi, Jan. 5, 1923, DS 800. 8880/79 (1st quotation); consul to State, LM, Dec. 1, 1923, DS 195/470a over 551 (2nd and 3rd quotations); see also Cross to State, LM, Oct. 16, 1924, DS 800.–8880/110.

17. Ernest M. Bull to Elmer Crowley, New York, Nov. 27, 1925 (1st quotation); USSB interoffice memorandum, Dec. 15, 1925 (2nd quotation); both 605–1–1039 (Part 1), Records USSB.

18. S. J. Maddock, Seas Shipping Co., to Sen. Hattie W. Caraway, New York, May 11, 1936 (1st and 2nd quotations); Report 1500–8–A, p. 19, Records USMC; [illegible], secy., South African Dispatch Line (SADL) to USSB, San Francisco, Nov. 14, 1930, 625–6–142; Records SAPFT (3rd quotation); W. B. Castonquay, USSB, to SADL, Washington, May 24, 1932, 625–6–142, Records SAPFT; Report 1500–2–A, "American Flag Services in Foreign and Non-Continuous Trades, on Jan. 1, 1931," USSB, 2–3, Records USMC; see also Henry F. Grady and Robert M. Carr, *The Port of San Francisco: A Study of Traffic Competition, 1921–1933* (Berkeley, 1934), 458–459.

19. *Exporters' Encyclopaedia, 1927,* 149–153, 163–165, esp. 165; Otto Martens and O. Karsedt, eds., *The African Handbook and Traveller's Guide* (London, 1932), 1–2; *The Delagoa Directory* (LM, 1921), 38–39

(quotation); Cameron to State, LM, Feb. 16, 1931, PR LM 600; Report 300, 1929, RG 178; Hinkle to State, LM, March 5, 1928, PR 84 LM 600.

20. *Exporters' Encyclopaedia, 1931,* inside front cover (1st quotation); see also 167, 170, 438, 688, 817, 894, 1129; Moffitt to State, LM, April 5, 1927, DS 195/470a over 551 (2nd quotation); P. J. Stevenson, Trade Comm., Johannesburg, to L. C. Palmer, Johannesburg, Jan. 6, 1925, 595–5, Records USSB; Eric Rosenthal, *Stars and Stripes in Africa* (London, 1938), 267, 270; Martin Johnson, *Over African Jungles* (New York, 1935), 4. For the classic traveler's reminder, "port out, starboard home," see H. Osman Newland, *West Africa: A Handbook of Practical Information* (London, 1922), 426. For comments on traveling along African coasts, see Richard Harding Davis, *The Congo and Coasts of Africa* (New York, 1907), 6; Julian Huxley, *Africa View* (New York, 1931), 41; Murray Marischal, *Union-Castle Chronicle, 1853–1953* (London, [1953]), 281–293; Gourley to State, LM, Oct. 14, 1925, DS 195/470a over 551; Moffitt to State (dispatch cited), LM, April 5, 1927.

21. James C. Wilson, *Three-Wheeling through Africa* (Indianapolis, 1936), 15, 22; May Mott-Smith, *Africa from Port to Port* (New York, 1930), 247–249; Boulton to Mrs. Straus, New York, Dec. 18, 1933 (2nd quotation) and her reply, New York, Dec. 19, 1933, in Curator of Birds, FMNH, "Straus West African Exp.," Plans and Projects files; Warren to State, Nairobi, Oct. 7, 1924, DS 051.48t/orig.; State to Wasson at Lagos, Washington, July 22, 1938, DS 800.8880/225.

22. Charles Barthold to MFC, New York, Aug. 2, 1935, 580–1454–4, Records SAPFT; Genevieve Mason, " 'Free' Slaves of West Africa," *Nation* (March 4, 1931): 254; Hinkle to State, LM, March 5, 1928, PR LM 600.

23. Unsigned and undated report [ca. late 1928], to State, Loanda, PR Loanda 840.6 (1st quotation); S. W. Eells to State, Nairobi, April 28, 1919, PR Nairobi 840.6 (2nd quotation); "Trade Opportunity" report, Lagos, Aug. 11, 1931, PR Lagos 840.6 (3rd quotation); Moffitt to State, LM, Sept. 6, 1927, PR LM 840.6 (4th quotation).

24. Cross to State, LM, April 30, 1923, PR LM 840.3 (1st quotation); Jean Kenyon Mackenzie, "Exile and Postman," *Atlantic* 150 (1932): 634 (2nd quotation); Isak Dinesen, *Out of Africa* (New York, 1952), 226–227; [Lady Mackenzie], "The Gayest Hearted of African Savages," *Travel* 37 (1921): 19 (4th quotation); Frank Townsend Meacham, "Partners: Chevrolet and Phonograph," *MH* 125 (1929): 243. See also Leland Hall, "The French in Lonely Posts," *Asia* 28 (1928): 107.

25. Raymond B. Fosdick, *The Old Savage in the New Civilization* (Garden City, 1929), 70 (1st quotation); Edwin W. Smith, *The Golden Stool* (London, 1926), 31 (2nd quotation).

26. Richard St. Barbe Baker, "Motoring in Equatorial Africa," *Travel* 58 (1931): 36–37 (1st quotation); A. L. Renaud, G. M. Export Co., to consul, "Boma Kongo," New York, Jan. 26, 1920, PR Loanda 850.2 (2nd quotation); see, for instance, such correspondence in PR Loanda 865.15 received 1920–1921; L. H. Kurtz, Dir. of Publicity, G. M. Export Co., to consul, LM, New York, Jan. 15, 1923, PR LM 020; State to consul at LM, Washington, July 16, 1931, DS 102.8102 Lawson, Edward B; Warren to State, Nairobi, Oct. 16, 1925, DS 125.6422/42.

27. Warren to State, Nairobi, Aug. 27, 1924, PR Nairobi 000; Jenkins to State, Nairobi, Aug. 29, 1923, PR Nairobi 879; Styles to State, Loanda, Nov. 2, 1925, PR Loanda 866.16; Constant Southworth, *The French Colonial Venture* (London, 1931), 183 (quotation); Stanton to Samuel H. Day, Trade Comm. at Johannesburg, LM, Oct. 12, 1929, PR LM, 866.16; Ebling to State, LM, March 26, 1934, PR LM 866.16; *Delagoa Directory,* 118; Fernald to State, Lagos, Aug. 22, 1928, DS 166.523/13.

28. Warren to State, Nairobi, May 21, 1925, DS 166.642/57 (1st quotation); Willson to State, Lagos, Nov. 18, 1930, DS 164.12 Studebaker-Pierce Arrow Export Corp. (2nd quotation); Tad Burness, *Cars of the Early Twenties* (Philadelphia, 1968), 109–112; William Ashley Anderson, *South of Suez* (New York, 1923), 147 (3rd quotation).

29. Martin Johnson, "Taming Elephants," *SEP* (Jan. 5, 1929): 135; Frank Hives, *Ju-Ju and Justice in Nigeria* (London, 1930), 247; Huxley, *Africa View,* 131–132 (1st quotation); Mary Hastings Bradley, *Caravans and Cannibals* (New York, 1926), 20 (2nd and 3rd quotations); Huxley, *Africa View,* 71 (on hotel placard); Gerry Bouwer, "Pioneering for a Cape to Cairo Highway," *SA* 141 (1929): 154–156; Attilio Gatti, *Tom-Toms in the Night* (London, 1932), 279–281; Moon, *Imperialism,* 94 (4th quotation, from Belgian booklet); Jan Verhoogen, "We Keep House on an Active Volcano," *NGM* 76 (1939): 522; Southworth, *French Colonial Venture,* 183 (5th quotation); Wilson, *Three-Wheeling,* 15, 22 (last quotation).

30. Florence N. Gribble, "Pioneering in French Equatorial Africa," *MRW* 50 (1927): 427 (1st quotation); John M. Springer, "Wealth in Central Africa," *MRW* 51 (1928): 450 (2nd quotation); Mrs. Chas. P. M. Sheffey, *Congo Tides* (Nashville, 1939), 47–48 (3rd quotation); James Dexter Taylor, "Motors and Missions," *MH* 125 (1929): 240 (4th quotation); Merling Walter Ennis, "A Missionary's Legs—How Long?" *MH* 125 (1929): 250 (5th quotation); William Clark Bell, "An Auto in Angola," *MH* 125 (1929): 251 (6th quotation) and 238–255 (7th quotation); Frank Night Sanders, "Impressions of the Angola Jubilee," *MH* 126 (1930): 331 (last quotation). See also "The Versatile Buick," *MH* 125 (1929): 242; Mrs. John M. Springer, "Following Stanley After Fifty Years," *MRW* 54 (1931): 428, 430; Albert D. Helser, *In Sunny Nigeria* (New York, 1926), 41; Emory Ross, "When You Think of Africa," *MRW* 58 (1935): 594.

31. "Fleet Footed Game of Jungle and Veldt (Photographs of the Snow African Expedition)" *Travel* 40 (1923): 16 (1st quotation—"faith on the flivver"); "Flivvering After Big Game in Africa," *LD* (Feb. 24, 1923): 54 (2nd quotation); H. A. Snow's *Hunting Big Game in Africa* (n.p.; n.d.), 3 (3rd quotation); Keene Sumner, "The Snow Family's Adventures Hunting Wild Animals," *AM* 96 (1923): 14–15, 121; interview by author with Mrs. Nydine Snow Latham.

32. Jenkins to State, Nairobi, July 16, 1923, DS 848t.6231/- (1st and 2nd quotations); Jenkins to State, Nairobi, Sept. 20, 1923, DS 848t.6231/1 (3rd and 4th quotations).

33. Martin Johnson, "Picturing Africa," *NH* 27 (1927): 539; Ernest Hemingway, "Shootism versus Sport: The Second Tanganyika Letter," in *Hemingway's African Stories: The Stories, Their Sources, Their Critics,* ed. James M. Howell (New York, 1935), 69; Stewart Edward White,

"The Moto Car," *SEP* (Dec. 5, 1925): 35. See also, Carl E. Akeley, *In Brightest Africa* (Garden City, 1923), 156–157.

34. J. C. Packer to U.S. consul at Nairobi, Northern Frontier Trading Co., Skuska Camp, [Kenya Colony], [Aug.] 5, 1919, DS enclosed 166.-642/5 (1st and 2nd quotations); Eells to State, Nairobi, Nov. 20, 1919, DS 166.642/5 (3rd quotation): Eells to Edward Frear in Chicago, Nairobi, Aug. 26, 1920, PR Nairobi, 840.

35. Osa Johnson, *I Married Adventure* (Philadelphia, 1940), 204; Martin Johnson, *Safari: A Saga of African Adventure* (New York, 1928), picture facing 104; [George Eastman], *Chronicles of an African Trip* ([Rochester], 1927), pictures facing 36, 44, 53; Paul L. Hoefler, *Africa Speaks: A Story of Adventure* (Chicago, 1931), 432; Arthur S. Vernay, "Angola as a Game Country," *NH* 27 (1927): 592 (1st quotation); Marius Maxwell, *Stalking Big Game with a Camera in Equatorial Africa* (New York, 1924), 178–179 (2nd quotation). See the pictures in Maxwell, facing 121, 123, 124, 126. Huxley, *Africa View,* 71–73; W. S. Van Dyke, *Horning into Africa* (n.p., 1931), 158–159, 202.

36. Hemingway, "Shootism," 69; Mary L. Jobe Akeley, "The Africa Nobody Knows," *WW* 56 (1928): 182 (2nd quotation); White, "Moto Car," 34.

37. Hoefler, *Africa Speaks,* 244; Joseph Rousseaux, "Motor-Car Routes in the Belgian Congo," in *The Story of the Cape to Cairo Railway and River Route: From 1887–1922,* ed. Leo Weinthal, 4 vols. (London, 1923), 2: 185–187; Wilson, *Three-Wheeling,* 330; Jenkins to State, Nairobi, Aug. 29, 1923, PR Nairobi 879.

38. Huxley, *Africa View,* 41; Styles to State, Loanda, Oct. 3, 1925, and March 3, 1926, in PR Loanda 600; Frederick R. Wulsin, "Motor Transport: Automobiles in Exploratory Work," in *Handbook of Travel,* ed. George Cheever Shattuck (Cambridge, 1935), 4–5.

39. Burness, *Cars of Twenties,* 195–197, 247–251; John Bentley, *The Old Car Book* (Greenwich, 1953), 94–99; Douglas C. Fraser, *Impressions —Nigeria 1925* (London, 1926), caption picture facing 20 (1st quotation); Light, *Focus,* 99 (2nd quotation).

40. Van Dyke, *Horning into Africa,* 147–150; James P. Chapin, "Up the Congo to Lukolela," *NH* 31 (1931): 478 (quotation); Curator of Anthropology, FMNH, "Rawson West African Exp. (1)" file, Hambly to Dir., Report on Journey to Esele Country, [Angola], Aug. 13, 1929.

41. H[umfrey] E[wan] Symons, *Two Roads to Africa* (London, 1939), 21–22 (quotation); Georges-Marie Haardt, "Through the Deserts and Jungles of Africa by Motor," NGM 49 (1926): 650–720; "Mid-African Souvenirs: Paintings by Alexandre Iacovleff," *Asia* 27 (1927): 464–467.

42. Stella Court Treatt, *Cape to Cairo: The Record of a Historic Motor Journey* (Boston, 1927), 36 and *passim.*

43. Symons, *Two Roads,* 21–22, 89, 147–148, 213–214, 219–221, 262–263; Bailey Willis, *Living Africa: A Geologist's Wanderings through the Rift Valley* ([New York], 1930), 27 (quotation).

44. Cross to State, LM, Dec. 9, 1922, DS 853n.797/- (fm) (quotation); State to consuls, Washington, March 31, 1928, Loanda, LM, Nairobi, DS 165.026/390; Livingston to State, Nairobi, Sept. 10, 1932, DS 848t.7971/2.

45. Thomas to State, Nairobi, May 12, 1924, DS 648t.1112/2; Curator

of Anthropology, FMNH, W. D. Hambly's "General Report," Jan. 10, 1930, p. 6, 10, in "Rawson West African Exp. (1)" file; Wilson, *Three-Wheeling,* 314.

46. "Motoring through the Heart of Africa," LD (May 22, 1926): 64; White, "Moto Car," 91, 35 (1st, 2nd, 3rd quotations); Mary L. Jobe Akeley, *Carl Akeley's Africa* (New York, 1929), 101; C. C. Martindale, "Rhodesian Holydays," *CW* 134 (1931): 281; Stewart Edward White, "You Never Can Tell About Lions," *SEP* (Jan. 2, 1926): 101–102.

47. Gilbert Grosvenor, "The National Geographic Society's New Map of Africa," *NGM* 67 (1935): 731 (quotation).

four: americans and the animals of africa

1. Mary L. Jobe Akeley, *Carl Akeley's Africa* (New York, 1929), 106.
2. [George Eastman], *Chronicles of an African Trip* ([Rochester], 1927), 15.
3. Horatio Hackett Newman, *Outlines of General Zoology* (New York, 1924), 399–400 (quotation); Wilfrid D. Hambly, *Source Book for African Anthropology,* FMNH Anthropological Series 26 (Chicago, 1937), 52.
4. Mary L. Jobe Akeley, "The Africa Nobody Knows," *WW* 56 (1928): 181 (1st quotation); Julian Huxley, *Africa View* (New York, 1931), 363; G. St. J. Orde Browne, *The Vanishing Tribes of Kenya* (Philadelphia, 1925), 237–257; Leo Weinthal, ed., *The Story of the Cape to Cairo Railway and River Route, From 1887 to 1922,* 4 vols. (London, 1923), 3: 339–400; Albert D. Helser, *In Sunny Nigeria* (New York, 1926), 86 (2nd quotation); Osa Johnson, "My Home in the African Blue," *GH* 78 (1924): 167, and Cherry Kearton and James Barnes, *Through Central Africa from East to West* (London, 1915), 24 (3rd quotation); Hugo H. Miller and Mary E. Polley, *Intermediate Geography* (Boston, 1932), 362–367, esp. 362 (4th quotation—series on "Animal Map," etc.). The animal map also appeared in Alexis Everett Frye's *New Geography: Book One* (Boston, 1920), 247. See also Richard Halliburton, *Seven League Boots* (Indianapolis, 1935), 350; Mary Evelyn Townsend, *European Colonial Expansion Since 1871* (Chicago, 1941), 49 (last quotation).
5. Theodore Roosevelt, *African Game Trails,* 2 vols. (New York, 1923), 1: 13; Roosevelt and Edmund Heller, *Life Histories of African Game Animals,* 2 vols. (New York, 1914), 1: 15–16 (2nd quotation); Huxley, *Africa View,* 364–372; W. S. Van Dyke, *Horning into Africa* (n.p., 1931), 142; S. Honaker to L. Bostock, LM, April 7, 1922, PR LM 840.6 (4th quotation); W. T. Hornaday (dir., N.Y. Zoo) to Mohler, chief, BAI, New York, July 5, 1919, in Central Correspondence, BAI, 1913–1939, Box 482, RG 17, FRC (5th quotation).
6. Cumberland Clark, *The Flags of Britain: Their Origin and History* (Shrewsbury, 1934), 115–119; W. J. Gordon, *A Manual of Flags* (London, 1933), 70–88 (all quotations); George Philip & Sons, Ltd., *British and Colonial Flags* (London, n.d.); R. Courtney Cade, *Handbook of British*

Colonial Stamps in Current Use (London, 1955), 129; Stanley Gibbons, Ltd., *Priced Catalogue of Stamps of the British Empire: 1930* (London, [1930]), 253–255, 446; *Scott's Standard Postage Stamp Catalogue* (New York, 1925), 1406–1407; *Scott's Stamp Catalogue: 1932,* 1769.

7. Ellis Parker Butler, *Young Stamp Collector's Own Book* (Indianapolis, 1933), 19 (quotation); Sigmund I. Rothschild, *Stories Postage Stamps Tell: What We Can Learn From Them* (New York, 1930), 148–149.

8. Paul L. Hoefler, "Land of Bardo Kidogo," *Asia* 30 (1930): 859 (1st quotation); Raymond L. Ditmars and Lee S. Crandall, *Guide to the New York Zoological Park* (New York, 1939), 22; Charles H. Seevers, *Trailing Animals around the World,* one of the *Wonder Books* (Chicago, 1940), 58 (2nd quotation); see frontispiece, E. G. Boulenger, *World Natural History* (New York, 1938); Austin H. Clark, *Animals of Land and Sea* (New York, 1925), 140; Michael F. Guyer, *Animal Biology* (New York, 1931), 55–56 (3rd quotation); A. Radclyffe Dugmore, *African Jungle Life* (London, 1928), 223 (4th quotation); W. Reid Blair, *In the Zoo* (New York, 1929), 10, 65; Martin Johnson, *Safari: A Saga of African Adventure* (New York, 1928), 155–171; Paul Du Chaillu, *Wild Life under the Equator* (New York, [1868]), 54 (5th quotation); Carl E. Akeley, *In Brightest Africa* (Garden City, 1923), 239–243; Mary Akeley, *Akeley's Africa,* 239–255; see also 222–223; Paul Annixter, "Jungle Love—A Drama of Gorilla-land —Where Might is Right," *Collier's* (Sept. 12, 1931): 18; Carl E. Akeley, "Hunting Gorillas on Mt. Mikeno," *WW* 44 (1922): 314–317; "Varieties of Gorillas," *Science* 70 (Nov. 29, 1929): x, xii; H. C. Raven, "Gorilla: Greatest of All Apes," *SA* 146 (1932): 20–21; Martin Johnson, "Great Cats of 'British East,'" *Asia* 23 (1923): 917–918; Marius Maxwell, *Stalking Big Game with a Camera in Equatorial Africa* (New York, 1924), 180–182; C. Emerson Brown, *My Animal Friends* (Garden City, 1932), 64–70; William T. Hornaday, *Official Guide Book to the New York Zoological Park* (New York, 1938), 107–108; idem, *Wild Animal Interviews and Wild Opinions of Us* (New York, 1928), 220; Ernest Schwarz, "The Klipspringers," *NM* 31 (1938); Attilio Gatti, "Congo Bongo," *NM* 30 (1937): 80–82; idem, "Congo Okapi," *NM* 30 (1937): 16–18 (6th quotation); Schwarz, "Aardvark—God of Evil," *NM* 31 (1938): 292; André Gide, "Dindiki," *Asia* 30 (1930): 332; "Animals: Chapin's Peacock," *Time* 30 (Oct. 11, 1937): 38, 40; Walter J. Wilwerding, "With Africa's Feathered Legions," *NM* 16 (1930): 219 (last quotation). See also James P. Chapin, "Up the Congo to Lukolela," *NH* 31 (1931): 600–614; Richard Upjohn Light, *Focus on Africa* (New York, 1941), pictures 102–107, 142, 249–277; Hornaday, *Tales from Nature's Wonderlands* (New York, 1924), 201–228; Julian Huxley, "Some African Animals," *Harper's* 161 (1930): 619–623; Martin Johnson, *Over African Jungles* (New York, 1935), pictures facing 52, 57, 96, 129, 144, 165, 180–181, 217; *Wonder Book,* 28–39, 17–70, 77–83; Malcolm MacDonald and Christina Lake, *Treasure of Kenya* (New York, 1966).

9. Herbert Best, "These African Explorers" *Harper's* 165 (1932): 63 (1st quotation); Mary Akeley, *Akeley's Africa,* 109–111 (2nd quotation); Martin Johnson, "Nice Lion," *Collier's* (May 4, 1929): 12; Talbot Mundy, "Random Reminiscences of African Big Game," *SEP* (Dec. 7, 1929): 237; Maxwell, *Stalking Big Game,* 15–16; Hans Coudenhove, "Nyasaland

Sketches: In the Chikala Range," *Atlantic* 131 (1923): 53 (3rd quotation); *Wonder Book,* 23–24; Paul L. Hoefler, *Africa Speaks: A Story of Adventure* (Chicago, 1931), 44, 247 (4th quotation); Daniel W. Streeter, *Denatured Africa* (New York, 1926), 63–64; George Jennison, *Noah's Cargo: Some Curious Chapters of Natural History* (New York, 1929), 72; J. H. Patterson, "The Man-Eating Lions of Tsavo," FMNH *Zoology Leaflets, 1922–1930,* 12 leaflets (Chicago, 1925), 7: 89 (last quotation); Roger A. Caras, *Dangerous to Man: Wild Animals* (Philadelphia, 1964), 16–18.

10. Llewelyn Powys, *Black Laughter* (New York, 1924), 41; Alfred Aloysius Horn and Ethelreda Lewis, *Trader Horn: Being the Life and Works of Alfred Aloysius Horn* (New York, 1928), 129; Frank Buck, with Edward Anthony, *Bring 'Em Back Alive* (New York, 1930), 290–291; Streeter, *Denatured Africa,* 204 (last quotation).

11. Stewart Edward White, *The Rediscovered Country* (Garden City, 1915), 115; Ernest Hemingway, *Green Hills of Africa* (New York, 1935), 142; White, "Lion Hunting," *SEP* (Oct. 24, 1925): 117; Roosevelt, *Game Trails,* 1: 15; but see 2: 568–570 for a list of his kills; Prince Vilhelm, "In the Animals' Paradise," *Century* 106 (1923): 415–416; Akeley, *Brightest Africa,* 216; Martha Miller Bliven, "Africa: The Impressions of a Modern Woman," *SA* 137 (1927): 324; Van Dyke, *Horning into Africa,* 159.

12. "Kenya: A Key Problem for Britain in Africa," LD 99 (Dec. 1, 1928): 16 (1st quotation); White, *Rediscovered Country,* 15; Hornaday, *Official Guide Book,* 1921, 73; Henry Fairfield Osborn, "The Vanishing Wild Life of Africa," *NH* 27 (1927): 515 (3rd quotation); James L. Clark, "By Motor from Nairobi to the Nile," *NH* 29 (1929): 203 (last quotation).

13. Ignatius Phayre, "Hunting Big Game by Train and Auto," *CH* 28 (1923): 780 (1st quotations), Akeley, *Brightest Africa,* 55; Mary Akeley, *Akeley's Africa,* 106, 303; Daniel E. Pomeroy, "Akeley's Dream Comes True," in AMNH, *The Complete Book of African Hall* ([New York], 1936), 5; Dorothy S. Greene, "Carl E. Akeley Again Penetrates the African Jungle," *NH* 21 (1921): 429; "A Gorilla Paradise," LD (Nov. 8, 1924): 68–72; Osborn, "Vanishing Wild Life," 521; "The Parc National Albert in the Belgian Congo," *Science* 70 (Oct. 11, 1929): 350; Mary L. Jobe Akeley, "Africa's Great National Park," *NH* 29 (1929): 648–650; idem, "Belgian Congo Sanctuaries," *SM* 33 (1931): 289–300; idem, "Africa's First National Park," *SA* 145 (1931): 295–298; Huxley, *Africa View,* 237–255, 382–388; Bailey Willis, *Living Africa: A Geologist's Wanderings through the Rift Valley* ([New York], 1930), 154–155; "A National Park in the Belgian Congo," *Science* 61 (June 19, 1925): 623–624; "The Albert National Park in the Congo," *Science* 74 (July 17, 1931): 63; Mary L. Jobe Akeley, "National Parks in Africa: The Extension of Wild-Life Conservation," *Science* 74 (Dec. 11, 1931): 586; Vernon Kellogg to D. C. Davies, Washington, Nov. 5, 1923, FMNH Archives, "Field Central African Exp." file (2nd quotation); Emil de Cartier de Marchienne, "Akeley, the Conservationist," *NH* 27 (1927): 116.

14. Roosevelt and Heller, *Life Histories,* 1: 149–150 (quotation); Warren to State, Nairobi, Aug. 21, 1924, DS 848t.4064/4; Callanan to Charles Terrence Wilson, Nairobi, March 16, 1933, PR Nairobi 840.6;

Streeper to State, Nairobi, Aug. 12, 1935, DS 848u.623/1; Betty Hone, American Comm. for International Wild Life Protection, Cambridge, Mass., to consul, Nairobi, April 15, 1933, PR Nairobi, 862.3.

15. A. Sambler Brown and G. Gordon Brown, *The South and East African Year Book and Guide,* edited annually (London, 1920), 903a (1st quotation, on "big game shooting" in Kenya); Edward P. Borden to H. J. Coolidge, LM, Jan. 23, 1933, PR LM, 862.3 (2nd quotation); J. L. Pinkerton to Ralph H. White, Loanda, Aug. 1, 1922, PR Loanda, 840.6; Stanton to State, LM, Dec. 10, 1930, PR LM 862.3 (3rd quotation); "Animals: Paradise Lost," *Time* (Feb. 3, 1936); 501; Willis, *Living Africa,* 228–229; Jenkins to State, Nairobi, Aug. 9, 1923, PR Nairobi 862.2.

16. Phayre, "Hunting Big Game," 780 (1st quotation); Hornaday, *Official Guide Book,* 1921, 73; see also Blair, *In the Zoo,* 83; Akeley, *Brightest Africa,* 55 and 253.

17. A typical arrangement between *The New York Times*-Wide World Photo Service and the Field Museum for "exclusive pictures" of expeditions is contained in correspondence in the FMNH Archives. See Howard Corbett (*N.Y. Times*) to D. C. Davies, dir., New York, March 8, 1926, and March 9, 1926, in FMNH Archives, "Conover-Everard African Exp." file. S. C. Simms (*N.Y. Times*) to Hambly, Chicago, April 30, 1929, letters in FMNH Archives, "Rawson West African Exp. (1)" file.

18. J. A. Poynton, secy. to Andrew Carnegie, to C. D. Walcott, Lennox, Mass., July 9, 1919, in SI, USNM Archives, 1907–1924; Edmund Heller, "The White Rhinoceros," *SMC* 61 (Washington, 1913); idem, "New Races of Antelopes from British East Africa," SIMC (July 31, 1913); Ned Hollister, *East African Mammals in the United States National Museum,* 3 parts, *USNM, Bulletin 99* (Washington, 1918–1924), 1: 18–19; 2: 2; 3: 2–3; Roosevelt, *African Game Trails,* 1: 170–171, esp. 233, 315; 2: 577–594; Roosevelt and Heller, *Life Histories,* viii–x; *Wonder Book,* photo and legend, 122; letter to author from Ronald T. Reuther, dir., San Francisco Zoological Gardens, March 23, 1970, with enclosure: "A History of the San Francisco Zoological Gardens from 1920–1970."

19. *SIAR, 1919,* 9 (quotations); *SIAR, 1920,* 20–21.

20. Brand Whitlock to State, U.S. emb., Brussels, Dec. 5, 1919, DS 031.11 Sm 6/42; Charles G. Geisler, [vice consul] to State, Cape Town, Dec. 6, 1919, and Dec. 15, 1919, DS 031.11 Sm 6/52–53; Emil de Cartier de Marchienne to secy., SI, Belgian emb., Washington, Dec. 6, 1919, SIA, SI African Exp. file (quotations); file SI African Exp. (No. 2) largely related to this accident.

21. John W. Davis, U.S. emb., London, to State, Jan. 7, 1920, DS 031.11/Sm 6/50; S. W. Eells to State, Nairobi, July 9, 1920, DS 611.48t 244/- (quotation); Eells to State, Nairobi, Aug. 19, 1920, a 14-page report on the affair, DS 031.11 Sm 6/68; Edmund Heller to C. D. Walcott, Belleclaire Hotel, NYC, June 7, 1921, SIA, SI African Exp. (1921) file.

22. H. L. Shantz to Fairchild, Nairobi, May 15, 1920, SIA, SI African Exp. file; William De C. Ravenel [adm. asst. to secy., SI, in charge of USNM], "Memorandum to the Secretary Relative to the Smithsonian-African Expedition," Washington, June 24, 1920 (3rd and 4th quotations); H. C. Raven to secy., SI, n.p., Oct. 2, 1920, an 11-page report on

the exp.; SIA, SI African Exp., No. 3 (1920), (1919) file; Heller to Wal-cott, Bombay, India, Aug. 19, 1920, SIA, SI African Exp. file (5th, 6th, and 7th quotations); Leonhard Stejneger [head curator, biology, USNM] Expedition (1921) file (8th quotation); C. D. Walcott to State, Washing-ton, Nov. 5, 1920, DS 031.11 Sm 6/69 (last quotation).

23. Stejneger to Revenel, Washington, Nov. 19, 1920, SIA, SI African Exp. (No. 3) file (1st, 2nd, and 3rd quotations); C. D. Walcott to H. M. Berman, Universal Film Manufacturing Co., Washington, Nov. 30, 1920, SIA, SI African Exp., No. 3 (1920), (1919) file (4th quotation); George E. Kann, mgr., Export Dept., UFMC, New York, to Walcott, New York, Oct. 26, 1920, and Walcott to Kann, Washington, Oct. 27, 1920, in SIA, SI African Exp. file; Walcott to Heller, Washington, June 14, 1921, SIA, SI African Exp. (1921) file.

24. Sen. Joseph Irwin France to C. D. Walcott, Washington, Nov. 24, 1920, SIA, SI African Exp. file; George Scott to Walcott, Cairo, Egypt, Oct. 6, 1920, SIA, SI African Exp. No. 3 (1920), (1919) file; "Explorations and Field-Work of the Smithsonian Institution in 1920," *SIMC* 72 (1921): 31–38; J. Russell Smith, *Human Geography: Book Two: Regions and Trade* (Chicago, 1922), 364; idem, *Industrial and Commercial Geography* (New York, 1925), 834; H. L. Shantz, "Urundi, Territory and People," *GR* 12 (1922): 341–346; *SIAR, 1921,* 9 (2nd quotation); "Expl. & Field Wk., SI, 1920," 21–31.

25. Warren to State, Nairobi, Sept. 11, 1925, DS 848u.4064/-; Mary Akeley, *Akeley's Africa,* 3–4; Osa Johnson, *I Married Adventure* (Phila-delphia, 1940), 294–303; Pomeroy, "Akeley's Dream," 8–9; Martin Johnson, "Camera Safaris," in AMNH, *The Complete Book of African Hall* ([New York], 1936), 55–62; Thomason to State, Nairobi, Oct. 19, 1927, "Report of the Death of an American Citizen," Carl Ethan Akeley, 56, of natural causes at Mount Mikeno, Ruthuru, Congo Belge, Nov. 17, 1926.

26. S. C. Simms to Harold A. White, Chicago, Oct. 3, 1928, FMNH Archives, "White-Coats Abyssinian Exp." file, and Stanley Field to White, Chicago, Oct. 8, 1929, same file; Harold L. Madison, act. dir., Cleveland Mus. of Natural History, to Secy. of State Henry L. Stimson, Cleveland, April 11, 1929, and State to Albrecht, Washington, April 20, 1929, DS 031.11 Cleveland Mus. (Tanganyika)/4,6; Daniel P. Quiring, "The Cleveland Clinic-Museum Expedition to Northern Tanganyika," *Tanganyika Notes and Records* 2 (1930), 101–103; Carveth Wells, "In Coldest Africa," *WW* 58 (1929), 37–38; Sen. Samuel M. Shortridge to H. L. Stimson, Washington, July 5, 1929, DS 031.11 May, Wilb. D./1 (quotation).

27. [Eastman], *Chronicles,* 68 (1st quotation); CAS "December [1939] Announcement," in CAS Archives (2nd quotation); Stewart Edward White, "Nyumbo," SEP 198 (Sept. 12, 1925): 225; Mary Akeley, *Akeley's Africa,* 121; Frank Tose to Simson, San Francisco, June 10, 1931, CAS Archives, "Exhibits 141" file; Simson to Tose, Norfolk Hotel, Nairobi, Sept. 12, 1931, same file; Simson to Tose, Nairobi, Feb. 3, 1931, same file; accessions list, Leslie Simson, in CAS Archives, "Exhibits 141" file; interview by author of Mrs. Jean Firby, paleontologist, CAS, at CAS, Jan. 20, 1970; *The Simson African Hall of the California Acad-*

234   the lure of africa

emy of Sciences (San Francisco, 1944), in CAS Archives, Simson photographic albums.

28. Conversation with author, at FMNH, Feb. 10, 1970. Thomason to Edward P. Lawton, Jr., vice consul, at Cairo, Nairobi, Oct. 20, 1926, PR Nairobi 310; W. D. Hambly to Simms, aboard S.S. *Waganda,* April 1, 1929, FMNH Archives, "Rawson West African Exp. (1)" file. O. Van H. Engert, chargé d'affaires, U.S. leg., Cairo, to State, Cairo, Oct. 2, 1934, DS 031.11 Kirby, Harold, Jr./35.

29. Wilbur J. Carr to secy. of commerce, Washington, Jan. 23, 1932, 480 [2508] file, RG 151, (1st quotation); memorandum, DS, Div. of Near Eastern Affairs, Dec. 26, 1928, DS 031.11 AMNH Strauss/12 (2nd quotation); Hugh Gibson to State, U.S. emb., Brussels, July 18, 1928, DS 031.11 AMNH/4 (3rd quotation); George Sherwood [dir., AMNH] to State, New York, May 19, 1930, DS 031.11 AMNH, Congo/1.

30. D. C. Davies, to State, Chicago, March 23, 1928, DS 03.11 FMNH Angola/1 (1st quotation); Hambly to dir., FMNH, Lobito, Angola, May 8, 1929, FMNH Archives, "Rawson West African Exp. (1)" file (2nd quotation); Dearing to State, Lisbon, March 18, 1929, DS 031.11 FMNH (Angola)/20 (last 3 quotations).

31. For a refusal, see Herbert Hengstler, chief, FS Adm., to Horace H. F. Jayne, dir., Univ. Mus., Univ. of Pennsylvania, Washington, Sept. 19, 1936, DS 031.11 Univ. Mus., East Africa/2; Frank B. Kellogg to U.S. emb., London, Washington, Feb. 11, [1926], DS 031.11 Sm 6/; Henry Allen Moe, Secy., Guggenheim Foundation to Feis, New York, May 11, 1934, DS 031.11 Kirby, Harold, Jr./5; Ralph Pulitzer to the President, New York, July 23, 1930, DS 031.11 Carnegie Mus. of Pittsb./1; W. J. Carr to "American Diplomatic and Consular Officers," Washington, July 25, 1930; Carr to Pulitzer, Washington, Aug. 2, 1930, DS 031.11 Carnegie Mus./2, 7; Warren to G. V. Maxwell, chief native com., Nairobi, Feb. 16, 1926, PR Nairobi 310 (last quotation); the details of Snow's letters from author's interview with Mrs. Latham.

32. Enclosure 3, Criminal Case 4 of 1927, Dist. Court of West Nile, Uganda Prot., in Stanley Field to Secy. of State Kellogg, Chicago, undated, recd. July 26, 1927 (quotation); this item, and correspondence on case, in 2 bundles labeled DS. 031.11 F 455, in Archives Box 294, FMNH, AR, 1927, 231; Streeper to State, Nairobi, Nov. 17, 1934, DS 031.11 Kirby Harold/38; Dorsz to State, Léopoldville, June 18, 1937, DS 611.455/23.

33. *Life* (May 24, 1937): 56; Akelev, *Brightest Africa,* 1–15; see "Catalogue of Mammals, Birds, Reptiles and Fishes in Skins and Mounted Specimens, For Sale by Henry A. Ward Natural Science Establishment, Rochester, New York," July, 1822 (Rochester, 1822), in *Ward's Catalogues 1878* in the Univ. of California Biology Lib.

34. *The American Museum of Natural History: An Interpretation* (New York, 1931), 33 (1st quotation); Robert H. Rockwell, "Collecting Large Mammals for Museum Exhibition," *NH* 27 (1927): 583 (2nd and 3rd quotations); see Carl E. Akeley, "The Autobiography of a Taxidermist," *WW* 41 (1930): 177–195; Mary Akeley, *Akeley's Africa,* 301–308; W. R. Leigh, "Painting the Backgrounds for the African Hall Groups," *NH* 27 (1927): 575–582; James L. Clark, "The Giant Eland of Southern Sudan,"

NH 31 (1931): 588; Albert E. Butler, "Transplanting Africa," *NH* 33 (1933): 533–544; Roy Chapman Andrews, "My Museum Complex," *WW* 58 (1929): 58–59; James Lippitt Clark, "The Image of Africa," in AMNH, *African Hall,* 71–73; photos 74–77; "World's Largest Gorilla: Preserved by New Art of Sculpturdermy," *PSM* 132 (1938): 38–41; Albert E. Butler, *Building the Museum Group,* AMNH Guide Leaflet Series 82 (New York, 1934); William T. Hornaday, *Taxidermy and Zoological Collecting* (New York, 1935).

35. For instance, see the series of *Field Catalogs: Mammals,* vols. 1, 2, 5, 8, in Office of Curator of Mammals, FMNH; White to Osgood, Nairobi, Nov. 20, 1930. FMNH Archives, "White-Coats Central African Exp." file (quotation); FMNH, *AR, 1931,* 97–98; FMNH, *AR, 1934,* plate xxi.

36. White, "Nyumbo," 225; *FMNH Handbook* (Chicago, 1933), 42–50; Akeley, *Brightest Africa,* 154; FMNH, *AR, 1932,* plate xxv; FMNH, *AR, 1933,* plate xi; *AMNH: Interpretation,* 33–34; "Speaking of Pictures, Taking Museum Color Shots is Tough," *Life* (May 24, 1937): 10–11, 13, 57–59; "American Museum's New Akeley Hall," *Life* (Jan. 3, 1938): 34–36, 52; F. Trubee Davison, "Letters from Africa," *NH* 33 (1933): 578; James L. Clark, "Image of Africa," 73; Guyer, *Animal Biology,* 54; Hambly, *Source Book,* 53–71; Robert W. Hegner, *Practical Zoology* (New York, 1931), 488; William Andrew Mackay and A. A. Canfield, *The Murals in the Theodore Roosevelt Memorial Hall* (New York, 1944), 4–7, 20; William T. Hornaday, *A Wild-Animal Round-Up: Stories and Pictures from the Passing Show* (New York, 1925); for attendance figures, see *Handbook of American Museums* (Washington, 1932).

37. See a brief entitled "Obstacles to the Development and Maintenance of Zoological Park Collections in the United States" [recd. July 3, 1919], submitted to the USDA by the Philadelphia and New York Zoological societies, 482 N.Y. Zoological Socy. file, Records DAI, (quotations); W. T. Hornaday to J. R. Mohler, New York, Dec. 2, 1919, same file.

38. Hornaday to R. W. Hickman, chief, Quarantine Div., BAI, New York, Dec. 10, 1919, 482 N.Y. Zoological Socy., Records BAI (quotation); Robert Hegner, *Parade of the Animal Kingdom* (New York, 1936), 564–600.

39. Belle J. Benchley, "Mbongo and Ngagi," *NM* 21 (1933): 217–222; *SIAR, 1932,* 51; *SIAR, 1927,* 92.

40. Blair, *In the Zoo,* 8–9 (1st quotation). The archives of the Circus World Museum, Baraboo, Wis., contain much material on animal prices; see, for instance, Louis Ruhe to Hagenbeck-Wallace Circus, New York, June 13, 1919; a Hagenbeck-Wallace winter price list, ca. 1925; Meems Brothers and Ward, Inc., price list dated April, 1939; copies in the author's possession. Belle J. Benchley, *My Life in a Man-Made Jungle* (Boston, 1940), 195 (2nd quotation); "Raising Babies with Wild Beasts for Neighbors," *LD* (Sept. 12, 1925): 36–42; Hubbard to Secy.-Gen. of the province, LM, Feb. 26, 1924, PR LM 862.3; Hubbard to Cross, Tete, PEA, July 21, 1924, PR LM 862.3; Hubbard to Cross, Luia River Camp, Tete, PEA, Oct. 18, 1924, PR LM 862.3 (3rd quotation); Cross to Hubbard, LM, Nov. 14, 1924, same file (4th quotation); A. W. Robinson to J. R. Mohler, San Francisco, Dec. 9, 1924, 488, Buck, Frank H. file, RG 17, FRC; "Gnl.

Business—Animals Quarantine Foreign, rec'd. 1916–1930" file contains list of leading American animal dealers, in SIA, NZP files; "Application for Permit Wild Animals and Birds," USDA Bureau of Biological Survey, March 17, 1939, for Henry Trefflich, in Gen. Correspondence, Records of the Fish and Wildlife Service, Box 459, RG 22, NA; State to Nairobi, Washington, March 7, 1929, DS 611.48t5/12; Albrecht to Richard A. Addison, Nairobi, May 13, 1929, PR Nairobi, 862.3; *SIAR, 1936,* 60; see file 1.521 Chapman, G. Bruce, Box 498, Records BAI, FRC; see "Animals 2 (Wild)" file on Gen. Correspondence, Records, Secy. of Agriculture, NA, RG 16.

41. Benchley, *My Life,* 197; 1.521-Benson, John T., Correspondence 1925–1928, file, Box 498, RG 17; enclosed brochure in 1.521 Benson, John T., Box 514, Records BAI, FRC (1st quotation); Louis Ruhe to Mohler, New York, March 29, 1922, 1.521 Ruhe, Louis, Box 488, Records BAI (2nd quotation); Benchley, *My Life,* 197; John T. Benson to Mohler, Nashua, Dec. 7, 1931, 1.521 Benson, John T., Box 514, Records BAI, FRC (3rd and 4th quotations).

42. *SIAR, 1926,* 29–30 (1st quotation); *SIAR, 1927,* 7–9, 29; B. E. Hutchinson for W. P. Chrysler, to SI, n.p., Feb. 17, 1926, [index card], SIA, secy.'s correspondence; C. D. Walcott to State, Washington, Feb. 10, 1926, 031.11 Sm. 6/; "SI Exp. & Field Wk. 1926," 12 (2nd and 3rd quotations); see also 10–21; *SIAR, 1927,* 92–94.

43. *SIAR, 1927,* 8–9 (1st quotation); *SIAR, 1929,* 81–82; *SIAR, 1930,* 84–85 (2nd quotation); Arthur Loveridge, "Field Notes on Vertebrates Collected by the Smithsonian-Chrysler East African Expedition of 1926," *USNM Proceedings* 73 (Washington, 1929), 11, 20, *passim.*

44. *SIAR, 1921,* 19–20; Roosevelt and Heller, *Life Histories,* 1: 172; *SIAR, 1924,* plate 6; Akeley, *Brightest Africa,* 21; Hornaday, *Wild-Animal Round-Up,* 192; Blair, *In the Zoo,* 57–58, picture facing 58, 96–100; Brown, *Animal Friends,* 15–18; Hornaday, *Official Guide Book,* 36–42, 73–74, 77, 83, 91–95, 97; N. Hollister, "A Modern Menagerie: More about the National Zoological Park," *SIAR, 1924,* 249–261; Ditmars and Crandall, *Guide to New York Zoo,* 62–68.

45. John T. Benson to Mohler, the New Willard, Washington, March 29, 1922, 1.521 Ringling Bros., Box 488, Records BAI; Frank Buck, *Animals Are Like That!* (New York, 1939), 85–89; James L. Clark, "Treed by a Herd of Elephants," *Asia* 28 (1928): 244; Hornaday, *Official Guide, 1921,* 91, and *Official Guide, 1939,* 94–95; Boulenger, *World Natural History,* 72; "Gargantua," *Newsweek* (April 11, 1938): 21; *Time* (April 18, 1938): 32; (quotation) and poster descriptions from posters displayed at the Circus World Museum, Baraboo, Wis.

46. S. W. Eells to Gillespie Bros., Nairobi, Oct. 22, 1919, PR Nairobi 840.6; Keene Sumner, "The Snow Family's Adventures Hunting Wild Animals," *AM* 96 (1923): 12–15; Akeley, *Brightest Africa,* 225; Huxley, *Africa View,* 368.

47. Osa Johnson, *I Married Adventure,* 190–191; Martin Johnson, "In the African Blue," *Asia* 23 (1923): 442–443 (1st quotation); Akeley, *Brightest Africa,* 157–158 (2nd quotation); FMNH, *AR, 1923,* 181; Charles A. Goodrum, *I'll Trade You an Elk* (New York, 1967), 105 (3rd quotation); A. Marshall Harbinson, "Into the Somewhere," *Sunset*

Magazine 63 (1929): 44; Osa Johnson, *I Married Adventure*, 307–317; Richard Dana Skinner, "The Screen: Congorilla," *Commonweal* (Aug. 10, 1932): 371 (4th quotation); Martin Johnson, "Our Next African Safari," *WW* 59 (1930): 47–51; idem, *Over African Jungles*, 3, 125–126; Osa Johnson, "My Home in the African Blue," *GH* 78 (1924): 173; Martin Johnson, *Over African Jungles*, 179–181; obituary, *Newsweek* (Jan. 23, 1937): 29.

48. Martin Johnson, *Safari*, 198–199; idem, "Picturing Africa," *NH* 27 (1927): 543–544; idem, "Lions Roar, Hippos Yawn," *WW* 60 (1931): 39.

49. Maxwell, *Stalking Big Game*, 1–8; FMNH, *AR, 1928*, 406; "Wings over Nature's Zoo in Africa," *NGM* 76 (1939): 527–542; [Hugh S. Davis], photographs in *Nature Magazine* 28 (1936): 295–296; Hoefler to consul, Nairobi, Denver, Colo., May 24, 1931, PR Nairobi 340; Thomason to Metro-Goldwyn-Mayer, Nairobi, March 27, 1928, PR Nairobi 840.6 (quotation).

50. FMNH, *AR, 1933*, 11; FMNH, *AR, 1935*, 300 (quotation); Laurence Vail Coleman, *The Museum in America: A Critical Study*, 3 vols. (Washington, 1939), 2: 261–262; Benchley, *My Life*, 200.

51. Coleman, *Museum in America*, 2: 261–262 (quotation).

five: americans and the people of africa

1. William B. Seabrook, *Jungle Ways* (New York, 1931), 7.

2. F. Trubee Davison, "Future Plans for the Akeley African Hall," AMNH, *The Complete Book of African Hall* ([New York], 1936), 88.

3. Beth Day, *This Was Hollywood* (Garden City, 1960), 59; Wynant D. Hubbard, "Africa Emerging from Darkness," *CH* 28 (1928): 445 (1st 2 quotations); "Africanus" [pseud.], "Awakening Africa," *LA* (Jan. 15, 1921): 152 (3rd quotation); Julian Huxley, *Africa View* (New York, 1931), 14; Eileen Bigland, *The Lake of the Royal Crocodiles* (New York, 1939), 66 (last quotation). See also Maurice N. Hennessy, *Africa under My Heart* (New York, 1965), 30–31.

4. Raymond Leslie Buell to L. Gourley, Maseru, Basutoland, Sept. 14, 1925, PR LM 030 [confidential vol.]; Thomason to the postmaster gen., Nairobi, Aug. 10, 1926, PR Nairobi 340 (quotation); Buell, *The Native Problem in Africa*, 2 vols. (New York, 1928), 2: 996–1000, 1038–1043; idem, "The Struggle in Africa," *FA* 6 (1927): 22–40; Lord Hailey, *An African Survey* (London, 1945), xxiii.

5. Melville J. Herskovits to G. R. Willson, Evanston, Ill., Nov. 18, 1930, PR Lagos 842; Willson to Herskovits, Lagos, Dec. 17, 1930, PR Lagos 842; Herskovits, *Dahomey: An Ancient West African Kingdom*, 2 vols. (Evanston, 1967).

6. Melville J. and Frances S. Herskovits, "The Art of Dahomey: I— Brass-Casting and Appliqué Cloths," in *The American Magazine of Art* 27 (1934): 67 (quotation on "inner life"); idem, "The Art of Dahomey: II—Wood Carvings," *American Magazine of Art* 27 (1934): 124–131;

Frances Herskovits, "Dahomean Songs for the Dead," *New Republic* (Sept. 14, 1935): 95; Melville J. Herskovits, "The Best Friend in Dahomey," in *Negro: Anthology Made by Nancy Cunard, 1931–1933,* ed. Nancy Cunard (New York, 1969), 627–632; idem, *The Myth of the Negro Past* (New York, 1941).

7. Stanley Field to Frederick H. Rawson, Chicago, Jan. 11, 1929, FMNH Archives, "Rawson West African Exp. (1)" file; Nelson Trusler Johnson to S. C. Simms, Washington, Jan. 24, 1929, DS FMNH Nigeria/2; Simms to State, Chicago, Jan. 29, 1929, DS 031.11 FMNH/ Nigeria /5 (quotation).

8. FMNH, *AR 1929,* 15, 49–50; Wilfrid D. Hambly, "The Ovimbundu of Angola," FMNH *Anthropological Series,* 21 (Chicago, 1934), 103 (1st quotation); caption on print 686309, Box 558, Wide World Photos, Records USIA (2nd quotation). See also Hambly's photos in Box 544. Hambly to dir., n.p., n.d., "Report on the Rawson-Field Museum Expedition to Angola," FMNH Curator of Anthropology, dept. files, "Rawson West African Exp. (1)" file.

9. *FMNH, AR 1930,* 320–321 (quotation).

10. Hambly to dir., Lagos, Jan. 10, 1930, a 23-page "General Report," 18, FMNH Curator of Anthropology, dept. files, "Rawson West African Exp. (1)" file (quotations); Hambly, "Serpent Worship in Africa," *SA* 147 (Aug., 1932): 100–101; idem, *Source Book for African Anthropology* (Chicago, 1937).

11. Sen. Theodore E. Burton to State, Washington, Jan. 9, 1929, DS 031.11 Coulter, Chas. W./1; W. R. Castle to Coulter, Washington, Jan. 12, 1929, DS 031.11 Coulter/2; H. U. Hall to Hengstler, Ambler, Pa., Sept. 24, 1936, DS 031.11 Univ. Mus. East Africa/5.

12. See the bibliography, Ralph Linton, *The Study of Man: An Introduction* (New York, 1936), 491–497; also, *Musée du Congo Belge, Bibliographie Ethnographique du Congo Belge et des Regions Avoisinantes, 1936* (Brussels, 1937); H. A. Weischhoff, *Anthropological Bibliography of Negro Africa* (New Haven, 1948), and Robert H. Lowie, *The History of Ethnological Theory* (New York, 1937); for a missionary contribution, see Morris Gilmore Caldwell and Hattie Sheldon, "The Culture of the Baya Tribe of West Africa," *SM* 30 (1930): 320–325; and Frank Thone, "Counting Riches in Wives," *Science News Letter* (June 5, 1937): 362–364; G. Gordon Brown, "Legitimacy and Paternity among the Hehe," *AJS* 38 (1932): 185–193; Robert H. Lowie, *Primitive Society* (New York, 1920), 26, 41–42, 341–342, and *passim;* Alexander A. Goldenweiser, *Early Civilization: An Introduction to Anthropology* (New York, 1922), 83–99; George Peter Murdock, *Our Primitive Contemporaries* (New York, 1934), 508–550; Ruth Benedict, *Patterns of Culture* (Boston, 1934), 27, 268–272; Richard Upjohn Light, *Focus on Africa* (New York, 1941), pictures 108–111; Melville J. Herskovits, "Some Recent Developments in the Study of West African Native Life," *JNH* 24 (1939): 28–29.

13. On physical anthropology, see Eugene Pittard, *Race and History: An Ethnological Introduction to History* (New York, 1926), 34–45; Franz Boas, "Race," in *General Anthropology,* ed. Franz Boas (Boston, 1938), 96–99; Hambly, *Source Book,* 161–254; Hambly to dir., n.p., marked "rec'd Aug. 19, 1929," FMNH, Curator of Anthropology, dept.

files, "Rawson West African Exp. (1)" file; see also Goldenweiser, *Early Civilization,* 3–6.

14. Pittard, *Race and History,* 34–35 (1st 2 quotations); Edward B. Tylor, *Anthropology: An Introduction to the Study of Man and Civilization* (New York, 1920), 59–60; J. Arthur Thomson, *What Is Man?* (New York, 1924), 41–42; Franz Boas, *The Mind of Primitive Man* ([New York], 1938), 102; Frank G. Carpenter, *Carpenter's Geographical Reader: Africa* (New York, 1905), 324; Murdock, *Primitive Contemporaries,* 508; Hans Coudenove, "Feminism in Nyasaland," *Atlantic* 132 (1923): 197 (last quotation).

15. Theodore Roosevelt, *African Game Trails,* 2 vols. (New York, 1923), 2: 432–436; Carl E. Akeley, *Lion Spearing* (Chicago, 1926); Leonard Vanden Bergh, *On the Trail of the Pygmies* (New York, 1921), 148–153, 156–157. See selection of pictures in Box 544, Wide World Photos, Records USIA.

16. F[rederick] D. Lugard, *The Dual Mandate in British Tropical Africa* (London, 1922), 581; Carpenter, *Geographical Reader: Africa,* 11; E. Torday, "Curious and Characteristic Customs of Central African Tribes," *NGM* 36 (1919): 353 (3rd quotation); Frank Hives, *Ju Ju and Justice in Nigeria* (London, 1930), facing 28 (last quotation); see also 36–38.

17. Seabrook, *Jungle Ways,* 123; see also 19–22, 130–132, esp. 150–153, 169, 184–189, 194–197; Seabrook's book was severely attacked by reviewers. See "Week by Week," *Commonweal* (June 3, 1931): 115, and Melville J. Herskovits, "Books about Negroes," *Nation* (July 15, 1931): 68–69.

18. Paul Du Chaillu, *My Apingi Kingdom* (New York, 1871), facing 25; idem, *Wild Life under the Equator* (New York, [1868]), 27; E. Alexander Powell, "Drums on the Lualaba: A Journey Across Africa," *Century* 109 (1925): 634 (1st quotation); Alfred Aloysius Horn and Ethelreda Lewis, *Trader Horn: Being the Life and Works of Alfred Aloysius Horn* (New York, 1928), 29; "Sultan Okwawa's Skull Means Power to the British," *LD* (June 14, 1919): 56–59; W. S. Van Dyke, *Horning into Africa* (n.p., 1931), facing 44 and 137; *Time* (Nov. 30, 1936): 42 (3rd quotation).

19. Cecil M. P. Cross, "The Witch of Lourenço Marques," *AFSJ* 2 (1925): 9; Robert Foran, "Tribeswomen of the 'Dark Continent,'" *Asia* 25 (1925): 255; T. Alexander Barns, "The Long-Headed Mangbettu," *Asia* 28 (1928): 968 (1st quotation); Vanden Bergh, *Trail of Pygmies,* 79–83 (2nd quotation); Hambly, "Serpent Worship," 101; Seabrook, *Jungle Ways,* 53–54; Murdock, *Primitive Contemporaries,* 524–526. See also May Mott-Smith, *Africa from Port to Port* (New York, 1930), 99–100; E. Alexander Powell, "Fringe of the Fantastic: Human Problems in the Congo," *Century* 109 (1925): 810; Jerome Beatty, "Great White Chief of the Congo," *AM* (1939): 151 (3rd quotation).

20. Martin Johnson, "Little Men and Little Women," *WW* 60 (1931): 48 (1st quotation); Powell, "Drums on the Lualaba," 633 (2nd quotation); Daniel W. Streeter, *Denatured Africa* (New York, 1926), 264–265; Mary Hastings Bradley, *Caravans and Cannibals* (New York, 1926), 127–128 (4th quotation); Martin Johnson, "Taming Elephants," *SEP* 201 (Jan. 5, 1929): 37.

21. W. C. Bell, "African Habitations of Cruelty," *MRW* 49 (1926): 285 (1st quotation); John H. Harris, "African Reconstruction After the War," *MRW* 42 (1919): 108 (2nd quotation); Maurice Delafosse, *The Negroes of Africa: History and Culture* (Washington, 1931), xxix (3rd quotation); Mary L. Jobe Akeley, *Carl Akeley's Africa* (New York, 1929), 43 (4th quotation); Ladilas Szecsi, "Primitive Negro Art," *Art and Archaeology* 34 (1933): 132 (5th quotation). See also Stewart Edward White, *The Land of Footprints* (Garden City, 1913), 212–213; R[eginald] Coupland, *The Study of the British Commonwealth* (Oxford, 1921), 21; Paul L. Hoefler, *Africa Speaks: A Story of Adventure* (Chicago, 1931), 1; A. L. Kroeber, *Anthropology* (New York, 1923), 496–501; Georges Hardy, "Les Temps Nouveaux. De 1879 à Nos Jours," in Paul Deschamps et al., *Les Colonies et la Vie Française pendant Huit Siècles* (Paris, 1933), 216–217; and Julian S. Huxley, "What Is the White Man in Africa For?" *YR* 21 (1931): 290.

22. Diedrich Westermann, *The African Today* (London, 1934), 30–43 (1st quotation); Kroeber, *Anthropology,* 500; Evans Lewin, "Africa in the Twentieth Century," *YR* 17 (1927): 82 (3rd quotation); Murdock, *Primitive Contemporaries,* 508 (4th quotation); Griffith Taylor, *Environment and Race* (London, 1927), 111 (5th quotation); Roland B. Dixon, *The Racial History of Man* (New York, 1923), 190–191; Hoefler, *Africa Speaks,* 49; Murdock, *Primitive Contemporaries,* 509; W. D. Hambly, *The Native Races of East Africa* (London, 1920), 10; Parker Thomas Moon, *Imperialism and World Politics* (New York, 1926), 159; Lugard, *Dual Mandate,* 67–70; C. G. Seligman, *Races of Africa* (London, 1932), 18–19; Hailey, *An African Survey,* 20–26; Hambly, "Ovimbundu," 327–330; J. Deniker, *The Races of Man: An Outline of Anthropology and Ethnography* (New York, 1913), 428; Harry H. Johnston, *A History of the Colonization of Africa by Alien Races* (Cambridge, 1913), 450. A summary of modern thinking on this question can be found in Melville J. Herskovits, *The Human Factor in Changing Africa* (New York, 1962), 27–37.

23. Alpheus Henry Snow, *The Question of Aborigines in the Law and Practice of Nations* (Washington, 1919), 7 (1st quotation); M. F. Lindley, *The Acquisition and Government of Backward Territory in International Law* (London and New York, 1926), 24 (2nd quotation); also 34–40, 43, and chap. 5. Ellsworth Huntington and Frank E. Williams, *Business Geography* (New York, 1922), 302 (3rd quotation); Mary Evelyn Townsend, *European Colonial Expansion Since 1871* (Chicago, 1941), 47–55 (last 2 quotations). See also Margery Perham, *The Colonial Reckoning* (London, 1961), 33–34.

24. W. E. Burghardt Du Bois, *The Negro* (New York, 1915), 9; Streeter, *Denatured Africa,* 275; Huxley, "White Man in Africa," 286; idem, *Africa View,* 263–270 (3rd quotation); Charles Darwin, *The Descent of Man, and Selection in Relation to Sex,* 2 vols. (New York, 1871), 1: 191; Aleš Hrdlička, "The Rhodesian Man," *AJPA* 9 (1926): 189–192 (4th and 5th quotations); idem, "The Most Ancient Skeletal Remains of Man," in *Source Book in Anthropology,* ed. A. L. Kroeber and T. T. Waterman (New York, 1931), 65–67; L. S. B. Leakey, *The Stone Age Cultures of Kenya Colony* (Cambridge, 1931), xi, 1; idem,

Stone Age Africa: An Outline of Prehistory in Africa (London, 1936), 178; N. C. Nelson, "Prehistoric Archeology," in *General Anthropology,* ed. Franz Boas (Boston, 1938), 196–199; Hambly, "Ovimbundu," 327–328; Huxley, *Africa View,* 263–270; Streeter to State, Nairobi, Dec. 7, 1934, DS 848t.927/1 (6th quotation); Streeter, *Denatured Africa,* 280.

25. Du Bois, *Negro,* 61 (1st quotation); Carter G. Woodson, *The African Background Outlined* (Washington, 1936), 31–127, 191–202; Ralph Linton, "Civilization in Dahomey," *Nation* (Nov. 5, 1938): 485–486 (2nd quotation); Du Bois, *Negro,* 50–68; Raymond Michelet, "African Empires and Civilizations," in *Negro: Anthology,* ed. Cunard, 585–595; Taylor, *Environment and Race,* 114–116; Delafosse, *Negroes of Africa,* 42–123; W. D. Hambly, "Culture Areas of Nigeria," FMNH *Anthropological Series* 21 (Chicago, 1935), 387–390; Herbert J. Seligman, *Race Against Man* (New York, 1939), 164–166.

26. Hambly, *Source Book,* 87–89; Beira and Mashonaland and Rhodesia Railways, *Guide to Rhodesia for the Use of Tourists and Settlers* (Bulawayo, 1924), 111–113, 109–128; G. Caton-Thompson, *The Zimbabwe Culture: Ruins and Reactions* (Oxford, 1931), 199 (1st quotation); see also 7, 185–199; Du Bois, *Negro,* 80–83; Woodson, *African Background,* 430, see also 9, 129, 442–443; Mary L. Jobe Akeley, *Restless Jungle* (New York, 1936), 3; Attilio Gatti, *Hidden Africa* (London, 1933), 112–119; Stella Court Treatt, *Cape to Cairo: The Record of a Historic Motor Journey* (Boston, 1927), 47; Mott-Smith, *Africa Port to Port,* 337–338; Huxley, *Africa View,* 398–399; R. N. Hall, "The Ruins of Great Zimbabwe," in *The Story of the Cape to Cairo Railway and River Route, from 1887 to 1922,* ed. Leo Weinthal, 4 vols. (London, 1923), 3: 425–433.

27. John W. Vandercook, " 'Voodoo': The Case for Magic Science In West Africa," *Harper's* 156 (1928): 353 (1st quotation); John McKendree Springer, *Pioneering in the Congo* (New York, 1916), 309 (2nd quotation); Frank J. Magee, "Transporting a Navy through the Jungles of Africa in War Time," *NGM* 42 (1922): 357 (3rd quotation); caption on print in Box 558, Wide World Photos, Records USIA (4th quotation); Westermann, *African Today,* 321–322 (last passage).

28. Westermann, *African Today,* 331 (1st quotation); Alexander Jacob Reynold, *From the Ivory Coast to the Cameroons* (London, 1929), 212–213 (2nd quotation); Cherry Kearton and James Barnes, *Through Central Africa from East to West* (London, 1915), 73–75; Paul Du Chaillu, *The Country of the Dwarfs* (New York, [1871]), frontispiece and 45–46; caption on print, Box 558, Wide World Photos, Records USIA (3rd quotation); Osa Johnson, *I Married Adventure* (Philadelphia, 1940), facing 184; Ruth Q. McBride, "Keeping House on the Congo," *NGM* 72 (1937): 661–662; Stewart Edward White, "Sabakaki—and Others," *SEP* (Jan. 9, 1926): 35; Seabrook, *Jungle Ways,* 129; E. Schulz-Ewerth, *Deutschlands Weg zur Kolonialmacht* (Berlin, 1934), pictures following 85; Carveth Wells, "In Coldest Africa," *WW* 58 (1929): 98. See also White, *Land of Footprints,* 37, and Adolphe Louis Cureau, *Savage Man in Central Africa* (London, 1915), 75.

29. [Lady Mackenzie], "The Gayest Hearted of African Savages," *Travel* 37 (1921): 15 (1st quotation); Llewelyn Powys, *Black Laughter* (New York, 1924), 103–104 (2nd quotation); Horn and Lewis, *Trader*

Horn, 59; Hans Coudenhove, "African Folk," *Atlantic* 128 (1921): 167 (4th quotation); Richard Halliburton, *Seven League Boots (Indianapolis,* 1935), 358; Evelyn Waugh, *Black Mischief* (Boston, 1946).

30. Reynold, *Ivory Coast to Cameroons,* 219 (1st quotation); Streeter, *Denatured Africa,* 139–142; Felix Shay, "Cairo to Cape Town, Overland," *NGM* 47 (1925): 217 (3rd quotation) and 201 (4th quotation); Lawrence Copley Thaw and Margaret Stout Thaw, "Trans-Africa Safari," *NGM* 74 (1938): 357, 364 (5th quotation); "Plate-Lipped Flappers of Central Africa," *LD* (June 16, 1923): 24; *Life* (Feb. 15, 1937): 71.

31. Torday, "Curious and Characteristic Customs," 367 (1st 2 quotations); dir. to Hambly, Chicago, Feb. 12, 1929, FMNH Archives, "Rawson West African Exp. (1)" file (3rd quotation); G. R. Willson to Livingston, consul at Nairobi, Lagos, July 13, 1932, PR Nairobi 840.1; John and Alice Durant, *Pictorial History of the American Circus* (New York, 1957), 213; Ripley to Peck, New York, Jan. 31, 1934, PR Lagos 840.6 (all 4 quotations on Ripley); Harold Shantz to Martin Johnson, Nairobi, March 1, 1934, PR Nairobi 840.6; Albrecht to Austin C. Schreffler, Nairobi, June 29, 1927, PR Nairobi 867.6; James L. Clark, "By Motor from Nairobi to Nile," *NH* 29 (1929): 266 (last quotation).

32. W. A. Ray, "Ray's Book, Shell, Curio and Novelty Shop," to consul, Muskogee, Okla., June 30, 1921, PR Loanda 892.7 (1st quotation); Roosevelt, *African Game Trails* 1: viii; Cross to Exhibitors Trade Review of New York, LM, Oct. 22, 1924, PR LM, 840.6 (3rd quotation); Waugh, *Black Mischief,* 49; Carl E. Akeley, "Bill," *WW* 41 (1921): 607; Delia J. Akeley, "Baboons," *SEP* 199 (Jan. 15, 1927): 76; Powys, *Black Laughter,* 29 (7th quotation—"erect hairless apes"); Bigland, *Lake of Royal Crocodiles,* 189 (8th quotation); James C. Wilson, *Three-Wheeling through Africa* (Indianapolis, 1936), 300 (9th quotation); Horn and Lewis, *Trader Horn,* 91; Vanden Bergh, *Trail of Pygmies,* 238 (11th quotation); Paul Schebasta, "Among the Pigmies," *Commonweal* 15 (1931): 127 (12th quotation); George Eastman, "A Safari in Africa," *NH* 27 (1927): 534; Horn and Lewis, *Trader Horn,* 138–319; Van Dyke, *Horning into Africa,* 129–130.

33. Woodson, *African Background,* 146; Halford Lancaster Hoskins, *European Imperialism in Africa* (New York, 1930), 105; Evans Lewin, "German Colonial Administration," *Atlantic* 123 (April, 1919): 465 (1st quotation); Jean K. Mackenzie, "Where the Drum Calls to Sunday School," *MRW* 43 (May, 1920): 350 (2nd quotation); for a similar quotation, see W. C. Willoughby, "A Study of Souls in Central Africa," *MRW* 46 (Jan., 1923): 16–17; "African Giants Who Beat Olympic Records," *LD* (May 15, 1926): 36 (3rd quotation); Nels A. Bengsten and Willem Van Royen, *Fundamentals of Economic Geography* (New York, 1937), 29 (4th quotation); Lothrop Stoddard, "Africa—The Coming Continent," *Scribner's* 99 (1936): 236 (last quotation). See also Stoddard, "Men of Color Aroused," *RofR* 92 (1935): 36.

34. J. Russell Smith, *Human Geography: Book Two: Regions and Trade* (Chicago, 1922), 373 (1st quotation); Snow, *Question of Aborigines,* 100–101 (2nd quotation).

35. Warren to State, Nairobi, March 23, 1925, PR Nairobi 840.1 (1st quotation); John H. Weeks, *Among Congo Cannibals* (Philadelphia,

1913), 81 (2nd quotation); Alexis Everett Frye, *New Geography* (Boston, 1920), 13 (3rd quotation); Douglas C. Fraser, *Impressions—Nigeria 1925* (London, 1926), 49 (4th quotation); Streeter, *Denatured Africa,* 69–70 (5th quotation); B. Livingston to Mrs. Macdonald Douglas, Nairobi, Nov. 10, 1932, PR Nairobi 840.5 (last quotation).

36. Raymond Garfield Gettell, *Political Science* ([Boston], 1933), 34 (1st quotation); Huntington and Williams, *Business Geography,* 77–78 (2nd quotation). See also 79–80. R. H. Whitbeck and V. C. Finch, *Economic Geography* (New York, 1924), 503.

37. Linton, *Study of Man,* 49; Kroeber, *Anthropology,* 182.

38. Eugene Van Cleef, *Trade Centers and Trade Routes* (New York, 1937), 192 (1st quotation); Whitbeck and Finch, *Economic Geography,* 512 (2nd quotation); Paul L. Hoefler, "Land of Bardo Kidogo," *Asia* 30 (1930): 854 (3rd quotation); Llewelyn Powys, "Primeval Paths in East Africa," *Travel* 38 (1922): 14; Gunther Tessman, "Negro Notions in Africa," *LA* (Dec. 4, 1920): 576; Harry Johnston and L. Haden Guest, *The Outline of the World Today,* 3 vols. (London, n.d.), 2: 269; idem, *The World of To-Day,* 4 vols. (New York, 1924), 3: 591; W. E. B. Du Bois, "Black Africa Tomorrow," *FA* 17 (1938): 109.

39. George Louis Beer, *African Questions at the Paris Peace Conference* (New York, 1923), 74; Reginald Wheeler, "First Impressions of Africa," *MRW* 52 (1929): 26–28 (2nd quotation); Roosevelt, *African Game Trails,* 1: 128–129; Cross to State, LM, April 12, 1925, DS 811.503153n/- (last quotation). See also Bailey to State, Loanda, Dec. 31, 1926, DS 853M. 504/5; Tylor, *Anthropology,* 60–113; "Black and White in East Africa," *LD* (March 25, 1922): 19; Paul Du Chaillu, *A Journey to Ashango-Land* (New York, 1871), 436–437; J[an] C. Smuts, *Africa and Some World Problems* (Oxford, 1930), 48.

40. Maurioc Samuol, "Flight Across Africa," *Harper's* 169 (1934): 37 (1st quotation); Mary Akeley, *Carl Akeley's Africa,* 27; Huxley, *Africa View,* 120.

41. Light, *Focus on Africa,* xv (1st quotation); Powys, *Black Laughter,* 196; Albert D. Helser, "Why I like My Missionary Job," *MRW* 50 (1927): 115–116 (3rd quotation).

six: americans and the uplift of africa

1. F[rederick] D. Lugard, *The Dual Mandate in British Tropical Africa* (London, 1922), 18.

2. R[eginald] Coupland, *The Study of the British Commonwealth* (Oxford, 1921), 23–29 (1st quotation); Johannes du Plessis, "Milestones in Africa's Progress," *MRW* 51 (1928): 775 (2nd quotation). See as well Lord Olivier, "Government of Natives in Africa, I," *Nation* (May 30, 1928): 621, for a criticism of the concept of "trusteeship." For favorable comments, see "Africanus" (pseud.), "Awakening Africa," *LA* (Jan. 15, 1921): 152–153; Lugard, *Dual Mandate,* 194; Parker Thomas Moon, *Imperialism*

and World Politics (New York, 1926), 564–566; M. F. Lindley, *The Acquisition and Government of Backward Territory in International Law* (London, 1926), 328–336; J[an] C. Smuts, *Africa and Some World Problems* (Oxford, 1930), 44–69; Lugard, "Native Policy in East Africa," *FA* 9 (1930): 65.

3. Uthai Vincent Wilcox, "The March of Civilization in Africa," *CH* 18 (1923): 788 (1st quotation); Franz von Papen, "Germany's Place in the Tropical Sun," *SEP* (Sept. 30, 1933): 30; Wilson S. Naylor, "Africa Fifty Years Ago and Now," *MRW* 51 (1928): 55 (1st quotation).

4. Dorsz to State, Léopoldville, Sept. 14, 1938, DS 800.8880/233.

5. Simon and Phoebe Ottenberg, eds., *Culture and Societies of Africa* (New York, 1968), 4 (1st quotation); "Africa and the Kingdom of God," *MRW* 51 (1928): 835 (2nd quotation). See also in same issue: "Recommended Books on Africa," 861–863. For "Africa Numbers," see *MRW* 51 (1928); *MRW* 59 (1936).

6. John H. Weeks, *Among Congo Cannibals* (Philadelphia, 1913); Jean Kenyon Mackenzie, *Black Sheep: Adventures in West Africa* (Boston, 1916).

7. Albert D. Helser, "Why I Like My Missionary Job," *MRW* 50 (Feb., 1927): 115 (1st quotation); A. E. Vollor, "African Drums and Their Uses," *MRW* 54 (1931): 911–912 (2nd quotation); Mrs. W. C. Johnston, "Elevating the Women of Africa," *MRW* 43 (1920): 531 (3rd quotation); Albert Schweitzer, "Sunday at Lambarene," *CC* (March 11, 1931): 375; Mrs. John M. Springer, "The Modernized African Women—An Asset or a Liability," *MRW* 52 (1929): 846 (last quotation).

8. William L. Rogers, "New Moving Pictures of African Missions," *MRW* 60 (1937): 250–251; "Dramatizing Missions," *Newsweek* (Oct. 17, 1938): 27–28 (all quotations).

9. Jomo Kenyatta, *Facing Mount Kenya: The Tribal Life of the Gikuyu* (London, 1961), 269; Elmer T. Clark, *The Church and the World Parish* (Nashville, 1929), 146 (2nd quotation); Una Jean Minto, "A Church of Seven Thousand Members," *MH* 131 (1935): 251 (3rd quotation); M. Nysart, "Fighting Superstition in Africa," *MRW* 47 (1924): 421–424.

10. E. T. Smith to State, Nairobi, Feb. 4, 1938, DS 811.5031 Near East/212; "Rome's Great Missionary Activity," *MRW* 58 (1935): 262; "Week by Week," *Commonweal* 14 (June 13, 1931): 115; Sister M. Anna, "African Hilltops," *CW* 141 (1935): 478–482. See as well C. C. Martindale, "Rhodesian Holydays," *CW* 134 (1931): 280–285.

11. W. L. Jenkins [consul] to L. D. Brown at Bunyore Mission, Kisumu, Nairobi, July 25, 1922, PR Nairobi 360 (1st quotation); W. Reginald Wheeler, "One Hundred Years in West Africa," *MRW* 55 (1932): 360 (2nd quotation); Frank Knight Sanders, "Impressions of the Angola Jubilee," *MH* 126 (1930): 331; Charles Hurlbert, gen. dir., Africa Inland Mission, Aba, the Belgian Congo, to State, Aba, July 31, 1923, PR Nairobi 360; Thomas Moody, "Sixty Years in the Congo Belge," *MRW* 60 (1937): 379 (3rd quotation).

12. W. J. W. Roome, "Africa Waits," *MRW* 51 (1928): 822–823 (1st quotation); Henry S. Hollenbeck, "Kandala," *MH* 121 (1925): 70 (2nd quotation); Emory Ross, "When You Think of Africa," *MRW* 58 (1935): 594–595 (3rd quotation).

13. F[rederick] D. Lugard, "The White Man's Task in Tropical Africa," *FA* 5 (1926): 59; Thomas Jesse Jones, "The White Man's Burden in Africa," *CH* 23 (1925): 218, 221.

14. Seymour E. Moon, Kongo Evangelical Training Inst., Kimpese, Congo Belge, March 15, 1920, to Reed Paige Clark, PR Loanda 360; Emory Ross, Disciples of Christ Congo Mission, Bolenge, Coquilhatville, Congo Belge, Oct. 6, 1921, to consul at Loanda, PR Loanda 130. W. J. Carr to Tower at Léopoldville, Washington, Nov. 21, 1929, DS 351t.-1163/5; Peck to State, Lagos, Nov. 7, 1932, DS 355a.116/251.

15. J. L. Pinkerton to State, Loanda, Sept. 15, 1922, DS 353m.116/- (1st quotations, from enclosure). On interpretations of land laws, see J. P. Dysart, American Board Missions in South Africa, to consul, LM, Sept. 28, 1920, PR LM 360. "The Missionary Situation in Angola," *MRW* 44 (1921): 915 (2nd quotation); R. P. Clark to State, Loanda, Dec. 28, 1921, DS 853m.404/- (fm); Hollis, cons.-gen., Lisbon, to State, Lisbon, Feb. 4, 1922, DS 353m.116/1 (3rd quotation).

16. W. C. Bell, "The Plea of Chiquetecoli, King of Galangue," *MRW* 46 (1923): 175 (quotation).

17. See, for instance, Travers Buxton, "Is Slavery Dead in Africa?" *MRW* 44 (1921): 854–855.

18. Cross to State, LM, Dec. 4, 1924, PR LM 030 (all quotations); Edward Alsworth Ross, *Report on Employment of Native Labor in Portuguese Africa* (New York, 1925); G. Pinkney Tuck, consul, Geneva, to State, Geneva, June 23, 1925, DS 853n.504 (fm), enclosing the *Report,* which had been read before the League.

19. Ross, *Report,* 58–61 (1st quotation), and 46 (2nd quotation).

20. D. C. Poole, cons. gen. Cape Town, to State, Cape Town, July 17, 1925, PR LM 840.1 (quotation).

21. J. W. Dailey to State, Loanda, Sept. 4, 1920, PR Loanda 060 Missions Confidential Correspondence (1st quotation); Bailey to State, Loanda, Aug. 20, 1926, DS 353m.006/2 (2nd quotation, from enclosure). *Missao Evangelica,* Dondi, Angola, to consul, Dondi, Bela Vista, Aug. 3, 1926, PR Loanda 360 Missions Confidential Correspondence says many missionaries could remember that the prior Portuguese governor, Norton de Matos, had called Decree 77 their "Magna Charta." J. P. Moffitt to W. C. Terril, supt., Inhambane-Transvaal Dist., MEC, LM, Aug. 3, 1927, PR LM 360; Hinkle to State, AR, LM, March 5, 1928, PR LM 600 (page 9); W. Q. Stanton to State, LM, Aug. 14, 1929, DS 353q.116/2; Stanton to State, LM, Sept. 3, 1929, 353q.116/3 (3rd quotation); Stanton to W. C. Terril, at Inhambane, PEA, LM, Sept. 21, 1929, PR LM 360; *FR* 1930, 111 (Washington, 1945), 785–786, 787; Fred Morris Dearing, U.S. min. to Portugal, to State, Lisbon, Dec. 9, 1929, PR LM 360; Dearing to State, Lisbon, Jan. 2, 1930, PR LM 360; Stanton to State, telegram, LM, Jan. 20, 1930, PR LM 360 (4th quotation); Stanton to State, LM, Feb. 19, 1930, PR LM 360 (1st quotation). The matter lingered a little longer in the backcountry, where officials stalled on the new more liberal rules until the gov.-gen. intervened directly. See Alexander McLeish, "Unoccupied Mission Fields and Their Evangelization," *MRW* 59 (1936): 349–350; Julian S. Rea, "Christian Villages in Mozambique," *MRW* 60 (1937): 525; Lord Hailey, *An African Survey* (London, 1945), 96. Ross remained bitterly

246   the lure of africa

disappointed about the small results of his exposé; see Edward Alsworth Ross, *Seventy Years of It: An Autobiography* (New York, 1936), 190–204, esp. 200, 204.

22. See Lorin Palmer, managing ed., *PSM,* New York, to consul, LM, March 6, 1919, PR LM 020; Mrs. E. E. Crist, Boma, Congo Belge, to consul at Loanda, Boma, Sept. 8, 1924, PR Loanda 842; Wilfrid D. Hambly, FMNH, Chicago, to consul at Loanda, Chicago, May 25, 1927; J. W. Bailey to B. Preston Clark, Loanda, Sept. 13, 1927; A. W. McKinnon of American Presbyterian Congo Mission to consul at Boma, Jan. 30, 1919, PR Boma 360; Hambly to dir., FMNH, undated report, p. 2, in FMNH, chief curator of anthropology, dept. files, "Rawson West African Exp. (1)" file.

23. Moon, *Imperialism,* 558–564; Frederick P. Keppell, "A Comment on Christian Missions to Africa," *IRM* 18 (1929): 503–505; J. E. Agard, "Some Impressions of Uganda," *Crisis* 30 (1925): 23–24.

24. "Better Missionary Methods in Africa," *MRW* 44 (1921): 829–831 (1st quotation); Irene Shields to Louise Westover, Missao Americana, Loanda, July 10, 1924, PR Loanda 842 (2nd quotation).

25. Derwent Whittlesey, "British and French Colonial Technique in West Africa," *FA* 15 (1937): 369, and Georges Hardy, *Histoire de la Colonisation Française* (Paris, 1928), 322.

26. Julian Huxley, *Africa View* (New York, 1931), 59–60 (1st quotation), and 100–102 (2nd quotation). See as well Evelyn Waugh, *They Were Still Dancing* (New York, 1932), 281–282, and Arthur Mayhew, *Education in the Colonial Empire* (London, [1938]), 62–64.

27. Lugard, "White Man's Task," 63–64 (quotation).

28. T. J. Jones to William Phillips, New York, Dec. 8, 1923, DS 032 Ed 8; Wilbur J. Carr to consulates at Nairobi, Johannesburg, LM, and Cape Town, all dated Washington, Jan. 12, 1924, all in DS 032 Ed 8; Cross to State, LM, July 23, 1924, DS 032 Ed 8 (1st quotation); Cross to State, LM, Aug. 1, 1924, DS 032 Ed 8 (2nd, 3rd, and 4th quotations); Anson Phelps-Stokes to Charles E. Hughes, New York, Dec. 18, 1924, DS 032 Ed 8; Jones to A. Phelps-Stokes, New York, Oct. 24, 1924, DS 032 Ed 8 (1st quotation); J. Theo. Marriner, to Jones, Washington, March 3, 1926, DS 031.11 C21.

29. Jones, "White Man's Burden," 219–220 (quotations); [editorial], *MH* 116 (1920): 213; "The Report of the African Educational Commission," *S&S* (Nov. 18, 1922): 573–574; William H. Baldwin, "The Real Africa of Today," *CH* 17 (1923): 608; "Education in East Africa," *S&S* (May 30, 1925): 644; T[homas] J[esse] Jones, *Education in Africa: A Study of West, South and Equatorial Africa* (New York, 1922); idem, *Four Essentials of Education* (New York, 1926), 19–23; idem, *Essentials of Civilization: A Study in Social Values* (New York, 1929), xx–xxii. See also Lugard, "Native Policy," 78, and Jackson Davis, "British Africa and the South," *VQR* 13 (1937): 371–375.

30. Arthur Pound, "American Educators Advise Africa," *Independent* (June 6, 1925): 651 (1st quotation); W. E. Burghardt Du Bois, "Education in Africa," *Crisis* 32 (1926): 87; Melville J. Herskovits, "Some Recent Developments in the Study of West African Native Life," *JNH* 24 (1939): 20–21; William H. Baldwin, "A School System for Africa," *Opportunity*

3 (1925): 202 (4th quotation); Huxley, *Africa View,* 312–333; Seymour E. Moon, "African Education—Old and New," *MRW* 56 (1933): 600–601; Moon, *Imperialism,* 559, n.1; Albert D. Helser, *In Sunny Nigeria* (New York, 1926), 20–21.

31. Ralph E. Diffendorfer, ed., *The World Service of the Methodist Episcopal Church* (Chicago, 1923), 115–121 (all quotations on MEC); Clark, *Church and World Parish,* 138–144 (all quotations on the Southern Methodists).

32. Robert Laws, "Fifty-Three Years in Livingstonia," *MRW* 51 (1928): 952, 955 (1st quotation); Mrs. Edwin Cozzens, "Paying Dividends in West Africa," *MRW* 57 (1934): 578–579 (2nd quotation).

33. Charles E. Pugh, "The Spiritual Conquest of Africa," *MRW* 55 (1932): 335 (1st quotation); Clark, *Church and World Parish,* 142–143 (2nd quotation); H. L. Weber, "A Doctor's Experience in West Africa," *MRW* 44 (1921): 456 (3rd quotation); Albert Schweitzer, *On the Edge of the Primeval Forest* and *More from the Primeval Forest* (New York, 1948), *More,* 174–175; idem, "Busy Days at Lambarene," *CC* (March 14, 1934): 355–357; idem, "Sunday at Lambarene," 374 (4th quotation); Rose Maier Ryter, "Baby Clinics in West Africa," *MRW* 57 (1934): 186–187; Dorothy P. Cushing, "A Galen Goes Gunning," *MH* 131 (1935): 10–12; W. S. Lehman, "The Medical Missionary as a Pioneer," *MRW* 43 (1920): 622–623; May Mott-Smith, *Africa from Port to Port* (New York, 1930), 61.

34. Jenkins to European Hospital, Nairobi, May 8, 1923, PR Nairobi, 862.3 & 814; Louise Pearce, "Tryparsamide Treatment of African Sleeping Sickness," *Science* (Jan. 23, 1925): 90–92; idem, "Tryparsamide in the Control of African Sleeping Sickness," *Science* (July 14, 1939): 39–40; Henry Allen Moe, secy., Guggenheim Fund, to Charles D. Hriles, St. Paul, Minn., July 18, 1928, DS 031.11 Stratton-Thomas/1; [illegible], temp. ohmn., Rockefeller Foundation Yellow Fever Commission, to consul, Boma, Lagos, July 18, 1920, PR Loanda 812; Walter Fitzgerald, "The Impact of Western Civilization on Negro Africa," *GR* 26 (1936): 85–87.

35. Wynant Davis Hubbard, "Is Africa Going White, Black or Brown?" *Nation* (Sept. 14, 1927): 250–251; Salvador de Madariaga, "Our Muddling World: Black Men and White Civilization," *Forum* 80 (1928): 756 (1st quotation); Ernest W. Riggs, "Contrasts in Africa," *MH* 121 (1925): 63 (2nd and 3rd quotations); John E. Geil, "African Leadership for Africa," *MRW* 51 (1928): 974 (4th quotation); Kenneth G. Grubb, "Roman Catholic Activity in Pagan Africa," *MRW* 59 (1936): 582 (5th quotation); "The Recent Congo Conference," *MRW* 57 (1934): 502; A. Bruens, "A Catholic Study of the Pygmy," *CW* 147 (1938): 222–223 (last quotation). See also A. Bruens, "Peddlers of Charms and Amulets," *CW* 149 (1939): 98–99.

36. Kenyatta, *Facing Mount Kenya,* 317–318 (1st quotation); "The Pan-African Congresses," *Crisis* 34 (1927): 263 (2nd quotation); W. E. B. Du Bois, "Black Africa Tomorrow," *FA* 17 (1938): 107; Arthur E. Holt, "Africa Tests Christianity," *CC* (Jan. 20, 1937): 82 (4th quotation).

37. Edward Bowron, "Irish Missionaries in Darkest Africa," *CW* 144 (1937): 737 (1st quotation); Donald Fraser, "Nyasaland Contrasts— Terror and Peace," *MRW* 41 (1918); 900 (2nd quotation); Geil, "African Leadership," 976–978; Mrs. J. M. Springer, "How the African Preacher Preaches," *MRW* 55 (1932): 143; idem, "Modernized African Women,"

848; John Morrison, "Tshisunga Daniel—A Congo Apostle," *MRW* 60 (1937): 197–199; Donald Fraser, *The Future of Africa* (London, 1911), 207–209; H. A. Gogarty, "The Church in Equatorial Africa," *CW* 121 (1925): 675–676 (3rd quotation); John T. Gillard, "Native African Bishops," *CW* 150 (1939): 219–222.

38. W. E. Davis, "I Like the Jungle: A Story of Surgery in the Congo," *SEP* (Sept. 17, 1938): 64; Mott-Smith, *Africa Port to Port,* 61–62; Hans Coudenhove, *My African Neighbors: Man, Bird and Beast in Nyasaland* (Boston, 1925), 51.

39. Eyo Ita, "The Efik and the Bush Soul," *CC* (Dec. 21, 1932): 1573–1574; Gogarty, "Church in Equatorial Africa," 677; William B. Seabrook, *Jungle Ways* (New York, 1931), 6–7 (1st quotation); R. L. Garner, "Adventures in Central Africa," *Century* 99 (1920): 601 (2nd quotation).

epilogue

1. Walter Greenwood, "Langy Road," in *The Old School: Essays by Divers Hands,* ed. Graham Greene (London, 1934), 79 (quotation).

2. *Kimber's Record of Government Debts 1932–1933,* ed. Alfred Nagel (New York, 1933), 424–425.

3. [Frederick D.] Lugard, "Native Policy in East Africa," *FA* 9 (1930): 72; W. E. Bailey to State, Nairobi, Oct. 3, 1938, DS 862s.01/97 ("self-contained" quotation); Raymond Leslie Buell, "The Destiny of East Africa," *FA* 6 (1928): 419.

4. Raymond Leslie Buell, "The Struggle in Africa," *FA* 6 (1927): 40; Wilson S. Naylor, "Africa Fifty Years Ago and Now," *MRW* 51 (1928): 59 (2nd quotation); "Africa in World Politics," *RofR* 71 (1925): 100 (3rd quotation); Richard Upjohn Light, *Focus on Africa* (New York, 1941), Foreword by Isaiah Bowman, xv; Arthur E. Holt, "Africa Tests Christianity," *CC* (Jan. 20, 1937): 80 (5th quotation); *Rotarian* (March, 1939): 39 (6th quotation); George Creel, "Bold Pathfinder," *Colliers* (Feb 27, 1932): 54; Hans Coudenhove, "Nyasaland Sketches: In the Chikala Range," *Atlantic* 131 (1923): 60 (last quotation). See also Diedrich Westermann, *The African Today and Tomorrow;* new rev. ed. (London, 1939), 1.

5. Ferdinand Ossendowski, *Slaves of the Sun* (New York, 1928), 37 (1st quotation; Julian Huxley, "What Is the White Man in Africa For?" *YR* 21 (1931): 291–295 (2nd quotation); H. J. Simson, *British Rule, and Rebellion* (Edinburgh, 1938); J. Frederick Essary, *Reverse English: Some Off-Side Observations upon Our British Cousins* (New York, 1928), 28–29; Leonard Woolf, *Empire and Commerce in Africa: A Study in Economic Imperialism* (London, [1919]), 352–368; Parker Thomas Moon, *Imperialism and World Politics* (New York, 1926), 7; Nathaniel Peffer, *The White Man's Dilemma: Climax of the Age of Imperialism* (New York, 1927), 264 and 288–289; Melville J. Herskovits, *The Human Factor in Changing Africa* (New York, 1962), viii.

6. "Pan-African Ideals," *Nation* (Sept. 28, 1921): 358 (1st quotation); W. E. Burghardt Du Bois, "A Second Journey to Pan-Africa," *NR* 29

(Dec. 7, 1921): 42; idem, "Britain's Negro Problem in Sierra Leone," *CH* 21 (1925): 700; Clinton Stoddard Burr, "Franco-British Rivalries in Tropical Africa," *CH* 22 (1925): 415 (4th quotation). See also Gunther Tessmann, "Negro Notions in Africa," *LA* (Dec. 4, 1920): 583; Halford Lancaster Hoskins, *European Imperialism in Africa* (New York, 1930), 105 (3rd quotation); Carter G. Woodson, *The African Background Outlined* (Washington, 1936), 148; Du Bois, "France's Black Citizens in West Africa," *CH* 22 (1925): 562–564; idem, "Black Africa Tomorrow," *FA* 17 (1938): 110.

7. Johnstone [Jomo] Kenyatta, "Kenya," in *Negro: Anthology Made by Nancy Cunard, 1931–1932,* ed. Nancy Cunard (New York, 1969), 804–805; Jomo Kenyatta, *Facing Mount Kenya* (London, 1961), xix; Thomason to State, Nairobi, March 28, 1930, DS 848t.4016/15. See also L. P. Mair, *Native Policies in Africa* (London, 1936), 96–98, 164–166; Warren to State, Nairobi, Sept. 15, 1925, DS 848t.00B/2; Warren to State, Nairobi, Sept. 4, 1924, DS 848t.00B/- (last quotation); Jenkins to State, Nairobi, Jan. 5, 1923, DS 811.4016/80.

8. Thomason to State, Nairobi, March 28, 1930, DS 848t.4016/15; F[rederick] D. Lugard, "The White Man's Task In Tropical Africa," *FA* 5 (1926): 65; Willis R. Hotchkiss, "Do You Love Yourself?" *MRW* 54 (1931): 599–600 (3rd quotation); W. S. Van Dyke, *Horning into Africa* (n.p., 1931): 176; Lester A. Walton, min. to Liberia, to State, Monrovia, April 24, 1939, DS 848p.00/5; Hickok to State, Lagos, Nov. 20, 1935, DS 800. 4089 Youth Movement/1 over 523; Bailey to State, Loanda, July 27, 1928, DS 853m.-5045/1; Ray to State, LM, Dec. 1, 1919, DS 853p.00/2 (fm); State to consul at LM, Washington, Sept. 3, 1929, DS 8532.504/4; Ebling to State, LM, March 20, 1939, DS 853n.00/42; Warren to State, Nairobi, March 11, 1925, PR Nairobi 840.1; Streeper to State, Nairobi, Feb. 8, 1936, DS 848v.125/2; Streeper to State, Nairobi, Aug. 27, 1937, DS 848t.-09/72.

9. Martin Johnson, *Safari: A Saga of African Adventure* (New York, 1928), 13 (1st quotation—"real Africa"); idem, *Over African Jungles* (New York, 1935), 251 (2nd quotation—"turmoil of a troubled world"). See also Johnson, *Safari,* 293. "People," *Time* (March 15, 1937): 87 (3rd quotation).

10. Delia J. Akeley, "The Little People," *SEP* (March 3, 1928): 16; Martha Miller Bliven, "Africa: The Impressions of a Modern Woman, After Two Years Spent Among the Natives in the Jungle," *SA* 137 (1927): 326 (1st quotation); Arthur Chapman, "He Likes to Face Lions Alone," *Colliers* (Jan. 24, 1925): 9 (2nd quotation); Llewelyn Powys, *Black Laughter* (New York, 1924): 88; Jean Kenyon MacKenzie, "Minor Memories," *Atlantic* 129 (1922): 72; W. E. Burghardt Du Bois, "The Primitive Black Man," *Nation* (Dec. 17, 1924): 676. See also Daniel W. Streeter, *Denatured Africa* (New York, 1926), 14.

11. Theodore Roosevelt, *African Game Trails,* 2 vols. (New York, 1923), 1: ix–x; G. Lister Carlisle, Jr., "The Lion Group and Its Creation," in AMNH, *The Complete Book of African Hall* ([New York], 1936), 17 (6th quotation); Paul L. Hoefler, *Africa Speaks: A Story of Adventure* (Chicago, 1931), 316; Edmund Heller, "Mount Lolokwi the Unknown," *Harper's* 140 (1920): 147 and 158; W. D. Hambly to dir., FMNH, undated "Report on the Rawson West African Exp.," 1, FMNH, chief curator of

anthropology, dept. files, "Rawson West African Exp. (1)" file; Mary Hastings Bradley, *Caravans and Cannibals* (New York, 1926), 39–50; Martin Johnson, "Little Men and Little Women," *WW* 60 (1931): 48 (quotation—"Nature's most unspoiled children," etc.); idem, "Jungle Raids and a Determined Daughter," *WW* 60 (1931), 43. See also idem, *Over African Jungles,* facing 192; Delia Akeley, "Little People," 16; Mary L. Jobe Akeley, "Africa's First National Park," *SA* 145 (1931): 295. Ivan Sanderson, "The Great Forests," *Atlantic* 160 (1937): 290.

12. Otto Martens and O. Karstedt, eds., *The African Handbook and Traveller's Guide* (London, 1932), 185 (quotation).

13. A. E. Osborn, U.S. Weather Bureau, Wausau, Wis., to consul at Nairobi, Wausau, June 7, 1932, PR Nairobi 862.3.

14. Lugard, "Native Policy," 78; Lothrop Stoddard, "Men of Color Aroused," *RofR* 92 (1935): 57; Streeter, *Denatured Africa,* 337.

bibliography

i. archival materials

United States Government Archives, Records of:
  Office of the Secretary of Agriculture, Record Group 16.
  Bureau of Animal Industry, Central Office, Central Correspondence, 1913–1939, Record Group 17, FRC.
  Special Advisor to the President on Foreign Trade, Record Group 20.
  Fish and Wildlife Service, General Correspondence, Record Group 22.
  Bureau of Naval Personnel, Log Book Series, Record Group 24.
  United States Shipping Board, General Files, Record Group 32.
  United States Department of State, Record Group 59.
  Foreign Service Posts of the United States Department of State, Record Group 84.
  Bureau of Foreign and Domestic Commerce, Record Group 151.
  United States Maritime Commission, Record Group 78, Federal Records Center, Suitland, Md.
  United States Information Agency, Record Group 306, Audiovisual Section.

The Smithsonian Institution Archives.

The Field Museum of Natural History, Chicago: The departmental records of the Chief Curator of Zoology, the Chief Curator of Anthropology, and the Curator of Birds, plus the FMNH Archives proper (the records of the Director's Office) provide a wealth of information on all the museum's African fieldwork in the interwar period.

The California Academy of Sciences, San Francisco: The Archives Division of the library contains a number of files from the Exhibitions Department and related materials, notebooks, and photographs concerning the collections in Africa of Leslie Simson, and the subsequent construction of the Simson African Hall.

Interviews and Correspondence: The author interviewed Mrs. Nydine Snow Latham, daughter of Henry A. "Del" Snow, at her home in Oakland, Calif., on Jan. 19, 1970. Mrs. Latham provided a great deal of information about her late father's African expedition of 1919–1920, and the family's subsequent operation of the Snow Museum of Natural History in Oakland.

The author also corresponded on the subjects touched upon in Chapter 4 with Mrs. Latham; Robert L. Parkinson, Superintendent of Historical

Collections at the Circus World Museum, Baraboo, Wis.; R. J. Reynolds III of Atlanta, Ga.; and Ronald T. Reuther, Director, San Francisco Zoological Gardens.

ii. periodicals

Africa
American Foreign Service Journal
American Journal of International
    Law
American Journal of Physical An-
    thropology
American Journal of Sociology
American Magazine
American Magazine of Art
American Mercury
American Scholar
Annals of the American Academy
    of Political and Social Science
Architectural Record
Art and Archaeology
Arts and Decoration
Asia
Atlantic
Business Week
Catholic World
Christian Century
Christian Science Monitor Weekly
    Magazine
Collier's
Commonweal
Crisis
Current History
Current Opinion
Foreign Affairs
Fortune
Forum
Geographical Review
Good Housekeeping
Harper's
Independent
International Review of Missions
International Studio
Journal of Geography
Journal of Negro History
Life
Literary Digest

Living Age
Michigan Law Review
Missionary Herald
Missionary Review of the World
Musical Quarterly
Nation
National Geographic Magazine
Natural History
Nature Magazine
The New Outlook
New Republic
Newsweek
North American Review
Opportunity
Political Science Quarterly
Popular Science Monthly
Public
Review of Reviews
Rotarian
St. Nicholas
Saturday Evening Post
Saturday Review of Literature
Scholastic
School and Society
School Arts Magazine
Science
Science Newsletter
Scientific American
Scientific Monthly
Scribner's
Sunset
Survey
Tanganyika Notes and Records
Theatre Arts Monthly
Time
Travel
Virginia Quarterly Review
Woman Citizen
World's Work
Yale Review

iii. magazine and journal articles, and component parts of larger works

"Adolf Hitler's Lost Colonies." *Life* (Dec. 7, 1936): 28.
"Africa—Continent of Colonies." *BW* (Nov. 5, 1938): 47.
"Africa and the Kingdom of God." *MRW* 51 (1928): 834–835.
"Africa at the Peace Conference." *RofR* 59 (1919): 86.
"Africa in World Politics." *RofR* 71 (1925): 99–100.
"African 'Giants' Who Beat Olympic Records." *LD* (May 15, 1926): 36, 38.
"Africanus" [pseud.], "Awakening Africa." *LA* (Jan. 15, 1921): 152–153.
Agard, J. E. "Some Impressions of Uganda." *Crisis* 30 (1925): 22–24.
Akeley, Carl E., "The Autobiography of a Taxidermist." *WW* 41 (1920): 177–195.
———. "Bill." *WW* 41 (1921): 594–607.
———. "Hand to Hand with a Leopard and Some Experiences with Rhinos." *WW* 41 (1921): 393–402.
———. "Hunting Gorillas in Central Africa." *WW* 44 (1922): 169–183 and (1922): 393–399.
———. "Hunting Gorillas on Mt. Mikeno." *WW* 44 (1922): 307. Above two citations represent a four-part series.
———. "Is the Gorilla Almost a Man?" *WW* 44 (1922): 525–533. The last article in the four-part series.
Akeley, Delia J. "Baboons." *SEP* (Jan. 15, 1927): 13.
———. "The Little People." *SEP* (March 3, 1928): 16. An account of author's collecting trip to East Central Africa in 1924 for the Brooklyn Museum of Arts and Sciences.
———. "Monkey Tricks." *SEP* (Sept. 18, 1926): 36.
Akeley, Mary L. Jobe. "The Africa Nobody Knows." *WW* 56 (1928): 180–188.
———. "Africa's First National Park." *SA* 145 (1931): 295–298.
———. "Africa's Great National Park." *NH* 29 (1929): 638–650.
———. "Belgian Congo Sanctuaries." *SM* 33 (1931): 289–300.
———. "In the Land of His Dreams: The Last Chapter of Carl Akeley's 1926 African Expedition." *NH* 27 (1927): 525–532.
———. "National Parks in Africa: The Extension of Wild-Life Conservation." *Science* (Dec. 11, 1931): 584–588.
"Akeley's Monuments are Bongo, Gorillas, Zebras, Antelopes." *Life* (May 24, 1937): 56–59.
"The Albert National Park in the Congo." *Science* (July 17, 1931): 63.
"American Museum's New Akeley Hall." *Life* (Jan. 3, 1938): 34–36.
Anderson, William Ashley. "Patrolling the African Game Country." *Travel* 34 (1920): 20–25 and (1920): 14.
Andrews, Roy Chapman. "My Museum Complex." *WW* 58 (1929): 55–59.
"Animals: Chapin's Peacock." *Time* (Oct. 11, 1937): 38, 40.
"Animals: Paradise Lost." *Time* (Feb. 3, 1936): 50, 52.

Anna, Sister M. "African Hilltops." *CW* 141 (1935): 478–482.

Annixter, Paul. "Jungle Love: A Drama of Gorilla-Land—Where Might is Right." *Collier's* (Sept. 12, 1931): 18.

Anthony, H. E. "A Pre-View of Eight Groups in the Akeley Hall of African Mammals." In AMNH, *Complete Book of African Hall,* 29–46.

————. "The Water Hole Group." In AMNH, *Complete Book of African Hall,* 81–85.

"An Armistice Anniversary in Central Africa." *LA* (March 12, 1921): 663–670.

"Automobile Section. Dedicated to the Proposition that the Modern Missionary is Motor-Minded in 1929 A.D." *MH* 125 (1929): 238–255.

Baker, Carlos. "The Slopes of Kilimanjaro." *American Heritage* 19 (1968): 40–43.

Baker, Richard St. Barbe. "Motoring in Equatorial Africa." *Travel* 58 (1931): 35–37.

Baldwin, William H. "The Real Africa of Today." *CH* 17 (1923): 603–608. A synopsis of the first Phelps-Stokes Report.

————. "A School System for Africa." *Opportunity* 3 (1925): 201–204.

Barns, T. Alexander. "The Long-Headed Mangbettu." *Asia* 28 (1928): 964–969.

————. "Where Dwarfs and Gorillas Rule Africa's Volcanic Kingdom." *Travel* 47 (1926): 34–37.

Beatty, Jerome. "Great White Chief of the Congo." *AM* 128 (1939): 20.

Becker, May Lamberton. "The Reader's Guide." *SR* (April 18, 1931): 763.

————. "The Reader's Guide." *SR* (July 8, 1933): 697.

Bell, William Clark. "African Habitations of Cruelty." *MRW* 49 (1926): 285–286.

————. "An Auto in Angola." *MH* 125 (1929): 251.

————. "The Plea of Chiquetecoli, King of Galangue." *MRW* 46 (1923): 173–177.

Benchley, Belle J. "Mbongo and Ngagi." *Nature* 21 (1933): 216–222.

Best, Herbert. "These African Explorers." *Harper's* 165 (1932): 55–64.

"Better Missionary Methods in Africa." *MRW* 44 (1921): 829–831.

"Black and White in East Africa." *LD* (March 25, 1922): 19. From the Nairobi *Leader of British East Africa.*

Bliven, Martha Miller. "Africa: The Impressions of a Modern Woman, After Two Years Spent Among the Natives in the Jungle." *SA* 137 (1927): 324–327. Mrs. Bliven was Carl Akeley's secretary, and accompanied him on his last expedition, along with her husband.

Boas, Franz. "Colonies and the Peace Conference." *Nation* (Feb. 15, 1919): 247–249.

————. "Race." In *General Anthropology,* edited by Franz Boas, 95–123. Boston, 1938.

Bouwer, Gerry. "Pioneering for a Cape to Cairo Highway." *SA* 141 (1929): 154–156.

Bowman, Isaiah. "Population Outlets in Overseas Territories." In *Geographic Aspects of International Relations,* edited by Charles Colby, 3–41. Chicago, 1938.

Bowron, Edward. "Irish Missionaries in Darkest Africa." *CW* 144 (1937): 735–739.

Bradley, Mary Hastings. "In Africa with Akeley." *NH* 27 (1927): 161–172.
"British Imperialists and German Colonial Policy." *Nation* (Oct. 19, 1919): 530–534.
"British Prepare to Dicker with Germany on Colonies." *Newsweek* (Nov. 7, 1938): 16–17.
Brown, G. Gordon. "Legitimacy and Paternity among the Hehe." *AJS* 38 (1932): 185–193.
Bruens, A. "A Catholic Study of the Pygmy." *CW* 147 (1938): 22–23.
———. "Peddlers of Charms and Amulets." *CW* 149 (1939): 58–59.
Buell, Raymond Leslie. "Chieftains Enthroned: British Rule in Nigeria as a Significant Colonial Experiment." *Asia* 28 (1928): 56. A complete and informative description of British "indirect rule" in operation in Nigeria.
———. "The Crisis in East Africa." *Nation* (Nov. 6, 1929): 532–534.
———. "The Destiny of East Africa." *FA* 6 (1928): 408–426.
———. "Labor in the Congo." *Nation* 127 (1928): 24–26.
———. "The Struggle in Africa." *FA* 6 (1927): 22–40.
———. "Two Lessons in Colonial Rule." *FA* 7 (1929): 439–446. Concerned with Ceylon and B.E.A.
Bunche, Ralph J. "The Land Equation in Kenya (As Seen by a Kikuya Chief)." *JNH* 24 (1939): 33–43.
Burr, Clinton Stoddard. "Franco-British Rivalries in Tropical Africa." *CH* 22 (1925): 410–415.
Butler, Albert E. "Transplanting Africa." *NH* 33 (1933): 533–544.
Buxton, Travers. "Is Slavery Dead in Africa?" *MRW* 44 (1921): 853–855.
Byrd, Mabel Janet. "The League of Nations and the Negro Peoples." *Crisis* 35 (1928): 223.
Caldwell, Morris Gilmore and Sheldon, Mrs. Hattie. "The Culture of the Baya Tribe of West Africa." *SM* 30 (1930): 320–325.
"Carl Akeley's Africa." *SA* 145 (1931): 86–87.
Carlisle, G. Lister, Jr. "The Lion Group and Its Creation." In AMNH, *Complete Book of African Hall*, 16–24.
Carter, John. "Round About the Congo." *Commonweal* (April 2, 1930): 610–612.
Cartier de Marchienne, Emil de. "Akeley, the Conservationist." *NH* 27 (1927): 115–117.
"Catalogue of Mammals, Birds, Reptiles and Fishes in Skins and Mounted Specimens, For Sale by Henry A. Ward Natural Science Establishment, Rochester, N.Y. July, 1882." In *Ward's Catalogues 1878* [University of California Biology Library, QL 72W3].
Chapin, James P. "Ruwenzori from the West." *NH* 27 (1927): 615–627.
———. "Up the Congo to Lukolela." *NH* 31 (1931): 474–487.
Chapman, Arthur. "He Likes to Face Lions Alone." *Collier's* (Jan. 24, 1925): 9–41.
Chételat, Eleanor de. "My Domestic Life in French Guinea." *NGM* 67 (1935): 695–730.
Churchill, Winston. "The Colony Racket." *Collier's* (Nov. 19, 1938): 11.
Clark, James Lippett. "By Motor from Nairobi to the Nile." *NH* 29 (1929): 261–272. James L. Clark was director of the Arts, Preparation, and

Installation Department of the AMNH, and an important field worker
for the museum.

————. "The Giant Land of Southern Sudan." *NH* 31 (1921): 581–599.

————. "The Image of Africa." In AMNH *Complete Book of African Hall*, 69–80.

————. "On Safari in British East Africa." *Asia* 28 (1928): 362–374.

————. "The Ngorongoro Animal Eden." *Asia* 28 (1928): 267.

————. "Treed by a Herd of Elephants." *Asia* 28 (1928): 175.

"The Commercial Outlook in West Africa." *RofR* 62 (1920): 102–103.

Coudenhove, Hans. "African Folk." *Atlantic* 128 (1921): 159–169.

————. "African Folk: A Further Consideration." *Atlantic* 128 (1921): 463–473.

————. "Feminism in Nyasaland." *Atlantic* 132 (1923): 186–197.

————. "Nyasaland Sketches: In the Chikala Range." *Atlantic* 131 (1923): 50–61.

Coulter, Charles W. "Problems Arising from Industrialization of Native Life in Central Africa." *AJS* 40 (1935): 582–592.

Cozzens, Mrs. Edwin. "Paying Dividends in West Africa." *MRW* 57 (1934): 578–579.

Creel, George. "Bold Pathfinder." *Collier's* (Feb. 27, 1932): 16.

Cross, Cecil M. P. "The Witch of Lourenco Marques." *AFSJ* 2 (1925): 9.

Cushing, Dorothy P. "A Galen Goes Gunning." *MH* 131 (1935): 10.

Dalziel, Emily Hoffman. "From Arusha to the Blue." *GH* 75 (1922): 34.

[Davis, Hugh S.] Untitled series of four game pictures. *Nature* 28 (1936): [295–296].

Davis, Jackson. "British Africa and the South." *VQR* 13 (1937): 362–375.

Davis, W. E. "I Like the Jungle: A Story of Surgery in the Congo." *SEP* (Sept. 17, 1938): 16.

Davison, F. Trubee. "Akeley the Inventor." *NH* 27 (1927): 124–129.

————. "Future Plans for the Akeley African Hall." AMNH, *Complete Book of African Hall*, 86–89. Davison was Director of the AMNH, and a wealthy gentleman-sportsman.

————. "Letters from Africa." *NH* 33 (1933): 577–581.

Du Bois, W. E. Burghardt. "Black Africa Tomorrow." *FA* 17 (1938): 100–110.

————. "Britain's Negro Problem in Sierra Leone." *CH* 21 (1925): 690–700.

————. "Education in Africa." *Crisis* 32 (1926): 86–89.

————. "France's Black Citizens in West Africa." *CH* 22 (1925): 559–564.

————. "The Negro Takes Stock." *NR* (Jan. 2, 1924): 143–145.

————. "The Primitive Black Man." *Nation* (Dec. 17, 1924): 675–676.

————. "A Second Journey to Pan-Africa." *NR* (Dec. 7, 1921): 39–42.

du Plessis, Johannes. "Milestones in Africa's Progress." *MRW* 51 (1928): 773–779.

Eastman, George. "A Safari in Africa." *NH* 27 (1927): 533–538.

"Education in Africa." *S&S* (Dec. 25, 1937): 86–89.

"Education in East Africa." *S&S* (May 30, 1925): 644.

"Education in the Gold Coast." *S&S* (Oct. 18, 1924): 491.

"Education in Uganda." *S&S* (Sept. 10, 1927): 325–326.

"The Educational System in Kenya." *S&S* (April 7, 1928): 413–414.

Ekins, H. R. "African Grab Bag." *CH* 44 (1936): 104–112.

Elliott, Charles Burke. "The German Colonies and Their Future." *RofR* 59 (1919): 72–76.

"An Empire Closed and Opened." *NAR* 209 (1919): 734–736.

"England and Belgium in Africa." *Independent* (April 10, 1920): 59–60.

Ennis, Merlin Walter. "A Missionary's Legs—How Long?" *MH* 125 (1929): 250. Ennis was the veteran missionary in Angola who assisted W. D. Hambly during the latter's expedition in 1929.

"Entertainment: Gargantua the Great: Young Fellow of 7 Is the Star of New Ringling Circus." *Newsweek* (April 11, 1938): 21.

"Explorations and Field-Work of the Smithsonian Institution in 1919." *SIMC* 72 (1920).

"Explorations and Field-Work of the Smithsonian Institution in 1920." *SIMC* 72 (1921).

"Explorations and Field-Work of the Smithsonian Institution in 1925." *SIMC* 78 (1926).

"Explorations and Field-Work of the Smithsonian Institution in 1926." *SIMC* 78 (1927).

"Exporters Watch Africa." *BW* (April 13, 1935): 30.

Fisher, Isaac. "Black and White in Certain Parts of West Africa." *Annals, AAPSS* 140 (1928): 319 330. Fisher was a Guggenheim Traveling Fellow, a black scholar at Florida A&M, Tallahassee.

Fitzgerald, Walter. "The Impact of Western Civilization on Negro Africa." *GR* 26 (1936): 77–87.

Flandrau, Grace. "What Africa Is." *RofR* 83 (1931): 63–64.

"Fleet Footed Game of Jungle and Veldt (Photographs of the Snow African Expedition)." *Travel* 40 (1923): 15–22.

"Flivvering After Big Game In Africa." *LD* (Feb. 24, 1923): 54–58.

Foran, Robert W. "Tribeswomen of the 'Dark Continent.'" *Asia* 25 (1925): 238.

Fortie, Marius. "On Foot Through Tanganyika." *SM* 46 (1938): 529–544.

Fraser, Donald. "Nyasaland Contrasts—Terror and Peace." *MRW* 41 (1918): 897–901.

"The Future of Germany's Colonies." *LD* (Feb. 15, 1919): 20–22.

Gallagher, Katharine J. "The Problem of the Former German Colonies." *CH* 25 (1927): 663–668.

Garner, R. L. "Adventures in Central Africa." *Century* 99 (1920): 842–852; 100 (1920): 125–135.

Gatti, Attilio. "Congo Bongo." *Nature* 30 (1937): 80–82.

———. "Congo Okapi." *Nature* 30 (1937): 15–18.

———. "Lilliputians of the Epulu Forest." *Travel* 70 (1937): 11–15.

Geil, John E. "African Leadership for Africa." *MRW* 51 (1928): 973–978.

"German Colonial Aims." *RofR* 74 (1926): 441–442.

"German East Africa Divided Up." *CH* 12 (1920): 350–351.

"Germany: Nazis Blame Lack of Colonies for Fat Shortage." *Newsweek* (Dec. 26, 1936): 10–11.

Gide, André. "Dindiki." *Asia* 30 (1930): 332.

Gillard, John T. "Native African Bishops." *CW* 150 (1939): 219–222.

Gogarty, H. A. "The Church in Equatorial Africa." *CW* 121 (1925): 674–677.

"A Gorilla Paradise." *LD* (Nov. 8, 1924): 68–72.

Greaves, Ida C. "A Modern Colonial Fallacy." *FA* 14 (1936): 627–638.

Green, Lawrence G. "Angola Is in the News." *CSMWM* (Dec. 1, 1937): 15.

————. "Shipwrecked in the Heart of Africa." *Travel* 70 (1938): 25.

Greene, Dorothy S. "Carl E. Akeley Again Penetrates the African Jungle." *NH* 21 (1921): 429–430.

Greenwood, Walter. "Langy Road." In *The Old School: Essays by Divers Hands,* edited by Graham Greene, 73–84. London, 1934.

Gregory, William King. "In Quest of Gorillas." *SM* 41 (1935): 385–395 and 505–529; 42 (1936): 47–71, 111–128, 258–279, 325–338, 403–420, and 517–531; 43 (1936): 23–32, 130–147, and 211–223.

Gribble, Florence N. "Pioneering in French Equatorial Africa." *MRW* 50 (1927): 423–427.

Grosvenor, Gilbert. "The National Geographic Society's New Map of Africa." *NGM* 67 (1935): 731–752.

Grubb, Kenneth G. "Roman Catholic Activity in Pagan Africa." *MRW* 59 (1936): 579–582.

Guérard, Albert. "The Next War and How to Nip It." *Scribner's* 81 (1927): 396–400.

Haardt, Georges-Marie. "Through the Deserts and Jungles of Africa by Motor." *NGM* 49 (1926): 650–720. An extended account of the Citroën Central African tank expedition.

Hall, Leland. "The French in Lonely Posts." *Asia* 28 (1928): 106.

Hall, R. N. "The Ruins of Great Zimbabwe." In *The Story of the Cape to Cairo Railway and River Routes,* edited by Leo Weinthal, 3 vols., 3:425–433. London, 1923.

Hambly, Wilfrid D. "Culture Areas of Nigeria." FMNH *Anthropological Series* 21: 363–502. Chicago, 1935.

————. "The Ovimbundu of Angola." In FMNH *Anthropological Series* 21: 89–362. Chicago, 1934.

————. "Serpent Worship in Africa." In FMNH *Anthropological Series* 21: 1–85, plus plates. Chicago, 1931.

————."Serpent Worship in Africa." *SA* 147 (1932): 100–101. An abridgment, with nine illustrations from old woodcuts, of the article with the same title above.

Harbinson, A. Marshall. "Into the Somewhere." *Sunset Magazine* 63 (1929): 44, 46.

Hardy, Georges. "Les Temps Nouveaux. De 1879 à Nos Jours." In *Les Colonies et la Vie Française* . . . , edited by Paul Deschamps et al., 191–238. Paris, 1933.

Harris, John H. "African Reconstruction After the War." *MRW* 42 (1919): 103–108.

Heller, Edmund. "Four New Subspecies of Large Mammals from Equatorial Africa." *SIMC* 61 (Pub. 2255, 1914). Results of the Theodore Roosevelt and Paul J. Rainey collecting trip.

————. "Mount Lolokwi the Unknown." *Harper's* 140 (1920): 147–160.

————. "New Genera and Races of African Ungulates." *SIMC* 60

(Nov. 2, 1912). Describes, among other things, six new "races" of antelopes brought back by Roosevelt from his famous expedition for the SI.

————. "New Races of Antelopes from British East Africa." *SIMC* (July 31, 1913).

————. "The White Rhinoceros." *SIMC* 61 (Pub. 2180, 1913). A technical study, with plates, of a great White Nile rhino shot by Roosevelt and mounted in the U.S. National Museum. This type of animal was hitherto almost unknown in American museums, and a technical article such as this one was of enormous value to zoologists.

Helser, Albert D. "Why I Like my Missionary Job." *MRW* 50 (1927): 113–116.

Hemingway, Ernest. "Shootism Versus Sport: The Second Tanganyika Letter." In Ernest Hemingway, *Hemingway's African Stories,* 69–71. New York, 1969. Originally published in *Esquire,* June, 1934.

Herskovits, Frances. "Dahomean Songs for the Dead." *NR* 84 (1935): 95.

Herskovits, Melville J. "The Best Friend in Dahomey." In *Negro: Anthology Made by Nancy Cunard, 1931–1933,* edited by Nancy Cunard, 627–632. New York, 1969.

————. "Books about Negroes." *Nation* (July 15, 1931): 68–69.

————. "Some Recent Developments in the Study of West African Native Life." *JNH* 24 (1939): 14–32.

Herskovits, Melville J. and Frances S. "The Art of Dahomey I—Brass-Casting and Appliqué Clothes." *American Magazine of Art* 27 (1934): 67–76.

————. "The Art of Dahomey II—Wood Carving." *American Magazine of Art* 27 (1934): 124–131.

Heyman, Curt L. "Germany's Colonies." *CH* 45 (1937): 35–41.

Hitchcock, A. S. "A Botanical Trip to South and East Africa." *SM* 31 (1930): 481–507.

Hoefler, Paul L. "Land of Bardo Kidogo." *Asia* 30 (1930): 854. Article covers all of Hoefler's expedition, and is profusely illustrated.

Hofmeyr, Jan H. "Germany's Colonial Claims: A South African View." *FA* 17 (1939): 788–798.

Hollenbeck, Henry S. "Kandala." *MH* 121 (1925): 70. Hollenbeck, of Beloit College in Wisconsin, was a medical missionary at Kamundongo, in the Belgian Congo, and a member of the first Phelps-Stokes Commission.

Hollister, N[ed]. "A Modern Menagerie: More about the National Zoological Park." *SIAR, 1924:* 249–261.

Holt, Arthur E. "Africa Tests Christianity." *CC* (Jan. 20, 1937): 80–82.

Hotchkiss, Willis R. "Do You Love Yourself?" *MRW* 54 (1931): 599–600.

"How Missionaries Work in Africa." *MRW* 62 (1939): 20–28. Extracts from letters of six American missionaries at the American Presbyterian Mission in Elat, Cameroun.

Hrdlička, Aleš. "The Rhodesian Man." *AJPA* 9 (1926): 173–204.

————. "The Most Ancient Skeletal Remains of Man." In *Source Book in Anthropology,* edited by A. L. Kroeber and T. T. Waterman, 43–67. New York, 1931.

Hubbard, Wynant Davis. "Africa Emerging from Darkness." *CH* 28 (1928): 442–445.

———. "Is Africa Going White, Black or Brown?" *Nation* (Sept. 14, 1927): 249–251.

———. "What Europe Sees in Africa." *RofR* 94 (1936): 46–50.

Hughan, Jessie Wallace. Letter to Editor. *CC* (Feb. 26, 1936): 331–332.

Huxley, Julian S. "Missions and the Life of Africa." *Harper's* 161 (1930): 733–744.

———. "Some African Animals." *Harper's* 161 (1930): 619–623.

———. "What Is the White Man in Africa For?" *YR* 21 (1931): 285–295.

"Indians in Kenya." *Nation* (Oct. 31, 1923): 497–500.

Ingalls, Albert C. "A Fly Versus a Civilization." *SA* 132 (1925): 402, 404.

"Isolated in Central Africa, by a Missionary in Rhodesia." *MRW* 53 (1930): 350–353.

Ita, Eyo. "The Efik and the Bush Soul." *CC* 49 (1932): 1573–1574.

Johnson, Martin. "Camera Safaris." In AMNH, *Complete Book of African Hall,* 47–62. A fine series of photos of the Eastman-Pomeroy-Akeley Expedition on 55–62.

———. "Extracts from the Diary of Martin Johnson." *NH* 25 (1925): 571–578.

———. "Great Cats of 'British East.' " *Asia* 23 (1923): 917–923. A selection of excellent game shots.

———. "In the African Blue." *Asia* 23 (1923): 442–446. Three full-page game pictures, warmly commended by Henry F. Osborn, president of AMNH.

———. "Jungle Raids and a Determined Daughter." *WW* 60 (1931): 39.

———. "The Land of Glorious Adventure." *NH* 27 (1927): 545–560.

———. "Lions Roar and Hippos Yawn." *WW* 60 (1931): 36–41.

———. "Little Men and Little Women." *WW* 60 (1931): 42–48.

———. "Martin Johnson's Story, and His New Pictures of Wild Animals in Africa." *WW* 49 (1925): 599–620.

———. "Nice Lion." *Collier's* (May 4, 1929): 12.

———. "Our Next African Safari." *WW* 59 (1930): 47–51.

———. "Picturing Africa." *NH* 27 (1927): 539–544.

———. "Scenes about Lake Paradise." *NH* 25 (1925): 578. A series of photos, with one of Johnson's elephant pictures appearing on the cover.

———. "Taming Elephants." *SEP* (Jan. 5, 1929): 37.

Johnson, Osa. " 'At Home' in Africa." *NH* 27 (1927): 561–569.

———. "My Home in the African Blue." *GH* 78 (1924): 48.

Johnston, Mrs. W. C. "Elevating the Women of Africa." *MRW* 43 (1920): 530–532.

Jones, Thomas Jesse. "The White Man's Burden in Africa." *CH* 23 (1925): 213–221.

"Kenya: A Key Problem for Britain in Africa." *LD* (Dec. 1, 1928): 16–17.

"Kenya and the White Man's Honor." *CC* (Feb. 22, 1933): 224–225.

"Kenya Colony: British East Africa under a New Name." *CH* 13 (1920): 25–26.

Kenyatta, Johnstone. "Kenya." In Cunard, *Negro,* 803–807.

Keppel, Frederick P. "A Comment on Christian Missions to Africa."
  IRM 18 (1929): 503–508.
Kuh, Frederick. "Should Germany Have Colonies?" *Nation* (May 19,
  1926): 562.
Langer, William L. "A Critique of Imperialism." *FA* 14 (1935): 102–119.
  An extended review of a reissue of John Hobson's *Imperialism: A
  Study.*
Laws, Robert. "Fifty-Three Years in Livingstonia." *MRW* 51 (1928): 948–
  956.
Lee, R. H. "The Titanic Cataract of the Zambesi." *Travel* 37 (1921):
  23–25.
Lehman, W. S. "The Medical Missionary as a Pioneer." *MRW* 43 (1920):
  630–632.
Leigh, W. R. "Painting the Background for the African Hall Groups."
  NH 27 (1927): 575–582.
Lewin, Evans. "Africa in the Twentieth Century." *YR* 17 (1927): 78–91.
———. "German Colonial Administration." *Atlantic* 123 (1919): 463–
  473.
———. "The German People and Their Lost Colonies." *Atlantic* 136
  (1925): 264–272.
Linton, Ralph. "Civilization in Dahomey." *Nation* (Nov. 5, 1938): 485–
  486. Review of Herskovits' *Dahomey: An Ancient West African
  Kingdom.*
Louw, Eric H. "The Union of South Africa and Its Trade." In National
  Foreign Trade Council, *Official Report of the Fourteenth NFTC,*
  214–225. New York, 1927.
Lugard, [Frederick D.], Lord. "Native Policy in East Africa." *FA* 9 (1930):
  65–78.
———. "The White Man's Task in Tropical Africa." *FA* 5 (1926): 57–
  68.
McBride, Ruth Q. "Keeping House on the Congo." *NGM* 72 (1937): 643–
  670. This article represents, aside from its contents, a feature of
  many American magazine pieces on Africa: it refers to events with-
  out specifying how recently they occurred. Mrs. McBride, for in-
  stance, describes her residence in Boma, which she had left in 1916.
  She was the wife of the last U.S. consul at the post in that city.
Mackenzie, Jean Kenyon. "Exile and Postman." *Atlantic* 150 (1932):
  633–637.
———. "Minor Memories." *Atlantic* 129 (1922): 68–72.
———. "Of Luxuries and Hardships." *Atlantic* 132 (1923): 329–332.
———. "The Unforgotten Journeys." *Forum* 71 (1924): 26–34.
———. "Where the Drum Calls to Sunday School." *MRW* 43 (1920):
  349–352.
Mackenzie, Lady [Grace Esmee]. "The Blood Drinkers of British East
  Africa." *Travel* 35 (1920): 21–26. Photos of the Masai (who tradi-
  tionally raise cattle to drink their blood as their main source of food).
McLeish, Alexander. "Unoccupied Mission Fields and Their Evangeliza-
  tion." *MRW* 59 (1936): 348–352.
Madariaga, Salvador de. "Our Muddling World: Black Man and White
  Civilization." *Forum* 80 (1928): 754–758.

Magee, Frank J. "Transporting a Navy through the Jungles of Africa in War Time." *NGM* 42 (1922): 331–362.

"The Mandate for South-West Africa." *Nation* (June 22, 1921): 877.

Marston, Jay. "Uganda, 'Land of Something New.' " *NGM* 71 (1937): 109–130.

Martindale, C. C. "Rhodesian Holydays." *CW* 134 (1931): 280–285.

Mason, Genevieve W. " 'Free' Slaves in West Africa." *Nation* (March 4, 1931): 254–256.

Meacham, Frank Townsend. "Partners: Chevrolet and Phonograph." *MH* 125 (1929): 243.

Michelet, Raymond. "African Empires and Civilization." In Cunard, *Negro,* 585–595.

"Mid-African Souvenirs, Paintings by Alexandre Iacovleff." *Asia* 27 (1927): [464–467].

"Mine and Thine in German Colonies." *Nation* (Oct. 18, 1919): 514–515.

Minto, Una Jean. "A Church of Seven Thousand Members." *MH* 131 (1935): 250.

"The Missionary Situation in Angola." *MRW* 44 (1921): 915–916.

Moody, Thomas. "Sixty Years in the Congo Belge." *MRW* 60 (1937): 379.

Moon, Seymour E. "African Education—Old and New." *MRW* 56 (1933): 599–601.

Morrison, John. "Tshisunga Daniel—A Congo Apostle." *MRW* 60 (1937): 197–199.

"Motoring through the Heart of Africa." *LD* (May 22, 1926): 61–65.

Mott-Smith, May. "A Circle of Africa." *Asia* 28 (1928): 444. A complete account of her two-year circumnavigation of Africa on a series of cargo ships, with map and representative photos.

Mundy, Talbot. "Random Reminiscences of African Big Game." *SEP* (Dec. 7, 1929): 12, 234, 237. Certainly one of the most honest big-game articles to appear in the interwar period; describes what motivated some men to undertake such recreation.

"A National Park in the Belgian Congo." *Science* (June 19, 1925): 623–634.

"Native Labor in East Africa." *Nation* (Nov. 24, 1924): 600–603.

Naylor, Wilson S. "Africa Fifty Years Ago and Now." *MRW* 51 (1928): 53–61.

Nelson, N. C. "Prehistoric Archaeology." In Boas, *General Anthropology,* 146–237.

"A New Colonial Policy." *Public* (Feb. 8, 1919): 128–129.

"New Frontiers in West Africa." *CH* 11 (1920): 485–486.

"The New Partition of Africa." *LD* (May 14, 1921): 12–13.

Nixon, C. R. C. "American Advertising in British Possessions." In National Foreign Trade Council *Official Report, NFTC 1938,* 90–98. New York, 1939.

"No Feminism in Darkest Africa." *LD* (May 15, 1926): 54.

Norden, Hermann. "The Pioneer Capital of British East." *Travel* 47 (1926): 22.

Nysart, M. "Fighting Superstition in Africa." *MRW* 47 (1924): 421–424.

Olivier, Lord. "Government of Natives in Africa—I." *Nation* (May 30, 1928): 621–622.

Osborn, Henry Fairfield. "The Vanishing Wild Life of Africa." *NH* 27 (1927): 515–524.

Overs, Walter Henry. "The Secret of Peace for Africa." *MRW* 44 (1921): 29–31.

Oyler, Lillian. "Missionary Life in Africa and America." *MRW* 54 (1931): 841–843.

"Painting Africa in Lighter Hues." *LD* (March 10, 1928): 44.

"The Pan-African Congresses." *Crisis* 34 (1927): 263–264.

"Pan-African Ideals." *Nation* (Sept. 28, 1921): 357–358.

"The Parc National Albert in the Belgian Congo." *Science* (Oct. 11, 1929): 350.

Parker, Caroline B. "Off to New Adventure." *St. Nicholas* 57 (1930): 188–189.

Patterson, J. H. "The Man-Eating Lions of Tsavo." In *FMNH Zoology Leaflets 1–12, 1922–1930*, 7: 88–129. Chicago, 1925.

Pearce, Louise. "Tryparsamide in the Control of African Sleeping Sickness." *Science* (July 14, 1939): 39–40.

Pelzer, Karl J. "Geography and the Tropics." In *Geography in the Twentieth Century*, edited by Griffith Taylor, 311–344. New York, 1951.

Percival, Philip. "Adventure Land." *NH* 27 (1927): 570–574. Percival was a professional "white hunter," a safari guide with twenty-five years' experience and extremely well-known to wealthy sportsmen. Hemingway employed him on his trip to Africa in the early 1930s.

Phayre, Ignatius. "Hunting Big Game by Train and Auto." *CH* 28 (1923): 773–780.

Phillips, Ulrich B. "Azandeland." *YR* 20 (1930): 293–313.

"Plate-Lipped Flappers of Central Africa." *LD* (June 16, 1923): 24–25.

Pomeroy, Daniel E. "Akeley's Dream Come True." In AMNH, *Complete Book of African Hall*, 5–10.

"Portugal: Cinderella Colony." *Time* (Aug. 8, 1938): 17.

Pound, Arthur. "American Educators Advise Africa." *Independent* (June 6, 1925).

Powell, E. Alexander. "Drums on the Lualaba: A Journey Across Africa." *Century* 109 (1925): 626–634.

————. "Fringe of the Fantastic: Human Problems in the Congo." *Century* 109 (1925): 802–810.

Powys, Llewelyn. "Britain's Problem in Kenya Colony." *CH* 18 (1923): 999–1005.

————. "Primeval Paths in East Africa." *Travel* 38 (1922): 12.

Priestley, Herbert Ingram. "Lighting Darkest Africa." *SR* (May 12, 1928): 857–858.

"Progress in the Belgian Congo." *JG* 18 (1919): 161–171.

Pugh, Charles E. "The Spiritual Conquest of Africa." *MRW* 55 (1922): 332–336.

Quiring, Donald P. "The Cleveland Clinic-Museum Expedition to Northern Tanganyika." *Tanganyika Notes and Records* 2 (1936): 101–103.

"Radium from the Kongo." *LD* (March 13, 1926): 21–22.

"Raising Babies with Wild Beasts for Neighbors." *LD* (Sept. 12, 1921): 36–42. An account of Wynant Hubbard and his wife and their wild-animal business.

Raven, H. C. "Gorilla: Greatest of All Apes." *SA* 146 (1932): 18–21.
Rea, Julian S. "Christian Villages in Mozambique." *MRW* 60 (1937): 524–527.
Reade, Leslie. "Ethiopia and Kenya." *NR* (Oct. 2, 1935): 211–212.
"The Recent Congo Congress." *MRW* 57 (1934): 502.
"Recommended Books on Africa." *MRW* 51 (1928): 861–863.
"Religion: Dramatizing Missions: Work of Converting Africans Filmed by Foundation." *Newsweek* (Oct. 17, 1938): 27–28.
"The Report of the African Educational Commission." *S&S* (Nov. 16, 1922): 573–574.
Reynaud, Gustave. "Petit Manuel d'Hygiène des Colons." In Le Myre de Vilers et al., *Préparation aux Carrières Coloniales,* 401–466. Paris, 1904.
Rice, Stanley. "The Indian Question in Kenya." *FA* 2 (1923): 258–269.
Riggan, Byron. "Damn the Crocodiles—Keep the Cameras Rolling!" *American Heritage* 19 (1968): 38–44, 100–103. A complete and well-illustrated account of the *Trader Horn* movie expedition to East Africa, and the subsequent hoopla surrounding the world premiere in Hollywood.
Riggs, Ernest W. "Africa's S.O.S." *MH* 121 (1925): 504–507.
————. "Contrasts in Africa." *MH* 121 (1925): 63–64.
Rockwell, Robert H. "Collecting Large Mammals for Museum Exhibition." *NH* 27 (1927): 583–587.
Rogers, William L. "New Moving Pictures of African Missions." *MRW* 60 (1937): 250–251.
Rolleston, Helen M. "Light Along the Congo." *CSMWM* (Oct. 5, 1938): 6.
"Rome's Great Missionary Activity." *MRW* 58 (1935): 262.
Roome, W. J. W. "Africa Waits." *MRW* 51 (1928): 819–827.
Roosevelt, Kermit. "Akeley, the Explorer." *NH* 27 (1927): 118–119.
Ross, Emory. "When You Think of Africa." *MRW* 58 (1935): 593–595.
————. "Why Study Africa?" *MRW* 59 (1936): 451–452.
Rousseaux, Joseph. "Motor-Car Routes in the Belgian Congo." In Weinthal, *Cape to Cairo,* 2: 185–192.
Ryster, Rose Maier. "Baby Clinics in West Africa." *MRW* 57 (1934): 186–187.
Samuel, Maurice. "Flight Across Africa." *Harper's* 169 (1934): 30–39.
Sanders, Frank Knight. "Impressions of the Angola Jubilee." *MH* 126 (1930): 331–333.
Sanderson, Ivan. "The Great Forests." *Atlantic* 160 (1937): 129–140.
Saunders, William L. "Why Direct Selling." National Foreign Trade Council, *Official Report, NFTC,* 315–318. New York, 1920.
Schacht, Hjalmar. "Germany's Colonial Demands." *FA* 15 (1937): 223–234. An important article: its publication signaled the beginning of an official campaign by Germany to win foreign public support for a recession of her lost African colonies. Schacht was president of the *Reichsbank,* and widely respected in American financial circles.
Schebasta, Paul. "Among the Pigmies." *Commonweal* (Dec. 2, 1931): 127–129.
Schnee, Heinrich. "The Mandate System in Germany's Lost Colonies."

CH 32 (1930): 76–80. Schnee, the last governor of German East Africa (1912–1918), devoted the rest of his life to publicizing the good works Germany had accomplished in her empire, and to furthering German campaigns to regain it.

Schwarz, Ernst. "Aardvark—God of Evil." *Nature* 31 (1938): 292.

————. "The Klipspringer." *Nature* 31 (1938): 592.

Schweitzer, Albert. "Busy Days at Lambaréné." *CC* (March 14, 1934): 355–357.

————. "Sunday at Lambaréné." *CC* (March 11, 1931): 373–376.

"Science: Africa Transplanted." *Time* (June 1, 1936): 52, 54.

"Shall We Take German Africa?" *LD* (Dec. 14, 1918): 18–19.

Shantz, H. L. "Urundi, Territory and People." *GR* 12 (1922): 329–357.

Shaw, Robert. "Africa: Back on the Chopping Block." *CH* 49 (1939): 20–24.

Shay, Felix. "Cape to Cairo, Overland." *NGM* 47 (1925): 123–160. This extended discussion of the route, illustrated mostly from news syndicate and commercial press sources, was the substance of the entire issue.

"The Singular Importance of Kenya." *Current Opinion* 75 (1923): 150–151.

Skinner, Richard Dana. "The Screen: Congorilla." *Commonweal* (Aug. 10, 1932): 371.

"Slavery in English Kenya." *Nation* (Aug. 12, 1925): 196–197.

Snow, Alpheus Henry. "The Disposition of the German Colonies." *Nation* (Oct. 18, 1919): 527–530.

Snowden, Philip. "Give Germany Her Colonies." *Nation* (July 21, 1926): 56–57.

"Speaking of Pictures . . . Taking Museum Color Shots Is Tough." *Life* (May 24, 1937): 10–11, 13.

Springer, John McKendree. "Are Africans Worth Saving?" *MRW* 51 (1928): 781–787.

————. "Wealth in Central Africa." *MRW* 51 (1928): 50–58.

————. "White Fields in Rhodesia." *MRW* 62 (1939): 40–41.

Springer, Mrs. John M. "Following Stanley After Fifty Years." *MRW* 54 (1931): 426–434.

————. "How the African Preacher Preaches." *MRW* 55 (1932): 140–143.

————. "The Modernized African Woman—An Asset or a Liability?" *MRW* 52 (1929): 846–849.

Stefanson, Vilhjalmur. "Are Explorers to Join the Dodo?" *American Mercury* 11 (1927): 13–18.

Stoddard, Lothrop. "Africa—The Coming Continent." *Scribner's* 99 (1936): 234–238.

————. "Men of Color Aroused." *RofR* 92 (1935): 35.

"Strategy in Africa." *Fortune* 12 (1935): 84.

Sumner, Keene. "The Snow Family's Adventures Hunting Wild Animals." *AM* 96 (1923): 12.

Szecsi, Ladilas. "Primitive Negro Art." *Art and Archaeology* 34 (1933): 130. Translated from French by Arthur Stanley Riggs.

"Take Your Gun on This Trip." *LD* (Dec. 4, 1926): 81–82. An account in the N.Y. *Sun* of the opening of the Nairobi-Bulawayo section of the proposed Cape-to-Cairo route.

Taylor, James Dexter. "Motors and Missions." *MH* 125 (1929): 240.

Tessmann. Gunther. "Negro Notions in Africa." *LA* (Dec. 4, 1920): 576–584.

Thaw, Lawrence Copley and Thaw, Margaret Stout. "Trans-Africa Safari." *NGM* 74 (1928): 327–364.

Thone, Frank. "Counting Riches in Wives." *Science News Letter* (June 5, 1937): 362–364.

Thurnwald, Richard. "Social Transformations in East Africa." *AJS* 32 (1932): 175–184. A report to the American Anthropological Association at Andover, Dec. 28, 1931, on the results of a ten-months' study in Tanganyika by a Yale scholar.

Torday, E. "Curious and Characteristic Customs of Central African Tribes." *NGM* (1919): 342–368.

Townsend, Mary E. "The Contemporary Colonial Movement in Germany." *PSQ* 43 (1928): 64–75.

―――――. "The German Colonies and the Third Reich." *PSQ* 53 (1938): 186–206.

Treille, M. "Principes Concrets de l'Hygiène de l'Européen dans les Pays Chauds." In Le Myre de Vilers, *Préparation,* 41–71.

"Trouble Brewing in Kenya." *LD* (June 20, 1923): 22.

Vandercook, John W. "The African Big Game." *Forum* 83 (1930): 183–187.

―――――. " 'Voodoo': The Case for Magic Science in West Africa." *Harper's* 156 (1928): 353–360.

"Varieties of Gorillas." *Science* (Nov. 29, 1929): x, xii.

Verhoogen, Jan. "We Keep House on an Active Volcano." *NGM* 76 (1939): 511–550.

Vernay, Arthur S. "Angola as a Game Country." *NH* 27 (1927): 588–594.

"The Versatile Buick." *MH* 125 (1929): 242.

Vilhelm, Prince of Sweden. "In the Animals' Paradise." *Century* 106 (1923): 414–423.

Voloor, A. E. "African Drums and Their Uses." *MRW* 54 (1931): 911–912.

von Epp, Ritter. "Germany's Case for Colonies." *CSMWM* (April 29, 1939): 5, 15.

von Papen, Franz. "Germany's Place in the Tropical Sun." *SEP* (Sept. 30, 1933): 23.

Ware, J. O. "Plant Breeding and the Cotton Industry." In USDA, *Yearbook of Agriculture: 1936,* 657–744. Washington, 1936.

Warren, Mrs. A. M. "Nairobi Celebrities." *AFSJ* 2 (1925): 338–339.

Weber, H. L. "A Doctor's Experience in West Africa." *MRW* 44 (1921): 455–458.

"Week by Week." *Commonweal* (June 3, 1931): 115–116; (June 10, 1931): 144; (June 1, 1932): 117.

Wells, Carveth. "In Coldest Africa." *WW* 58 (1929): 34–37; 58 (1929): 76–81; 58 (1929): 92–98.

"What Deal Will Hitler Accept?" *BW* (Dec. 18, 1937): 30–32.

Wheeler, W. Reginald. "First Impressions of Africa." *MRW* 52 (1929): 25–30.

————."One Hundred Years in West Africa." *MRW* 55 (1932): 359–360. Wheeler was secretary of Presbyterian Board of Foreign Missions.

"Where There Is No Peace." *CC* (Dec. 15, 1937): 1552–1553.

White, Stewart Edward. "Lion Hunting." *SEP* (Oct. 24, 1925): 15.

————. "The Moto Car." *SEP* (Dec. 5, 1925): 34. The reference is to a Model T Ford camp car, but "moto" was the native word for "hot," not "motor."

————. "Nyama! Nyama!" *SEP* (Sept. 26, 1925): 11.

————. "Nyumbo," *SEP* (Sept. 12, 1925): 3.

————. "Sabakaki—and Others." *SEP* (Jan. 9, 1926): 35.

————. "You Never Can Tell about Lions." *SEP* (Jan. 2, 1926): 26. Stewart Edward White was one of the best-known American professional big-game hunters in Africa, and unlike many writers on African subjects, his articles were immediately contemporary.

"The White Man's Burden." *Nation* (July 11, 1923): 31.

Whittlesey, Derwent. "British and French Colonial Technique in West Africa." *FA* 15 (1937): 362–373.

————. "Geographic Provinces of Angola." *GR* 14 (1924): 113–126.

Wilcox, Uthai Vincent. "The March of Civilization in Africa." *CH* 18 (1923): 782–788.

"Will Lost Colonies Satisfy Hitler?" *Scholastic* (May 20, 1939): 11–S, 18–S.

Willoughby, W. C. "A Study of Souls in Central Africa." *MRW* 46 (1923): 13–20.

Wilson, James C. "Three-Wheeling through Africa." *NGM* 65 (1923): 37–92.

Wilwerding, Walter J. "With Africa's Feathered Legions." *Nature* 16 (1930): 219–223.

"Wings over Nature's Zoo in Africa." *NGM* 76 (1939): 527–542.

Woodside, Willson. "Colonies for Germany?" *Harper's* 176 (1938): 520–529.

Woolbert, Robert Gale. "The Future of Portugal's Colonies." *FA* 15 (1937): 374–380.

"World's Largest Gorilla: Preserved by New Art of Sculpturdermy." *PSM* 132 (1938): 38–41.

Wright, Quincy. "Sovereignty of the Mandates." *American Journal of International Law* 17 (1923): 691–703.

————. "The United States and the Mandates." *Michigan Law Review* 23 (1925): 717–747.

Wulsin, Frederick R. "Motor Transport: Automobiles in Exploratory Work." In *Handbook of Travel Prepared for the Harvard Travellers Club,* edited by George C. Shattuck, 3–20. Cambridge, 1935.

Young-O'Brien, A. H. "Brothers to the Gods: Germans, Englishmen, and Frenchmen as Colonists." *Harper's* 177 (1938): 420–425.

iv. books and dissertations

Ajayi, J. F. Ade. *Christian Missions in Nigeria, 1841–1891: The Making of a New Elite.* Evanston, 1965.

Akeley, Carl E. *In Brightest Africa.* Garden City, 1923. Largely autobiographical, the book covers all of Akeley's extremely important career in Africa, excluding of course, the last great expedition in 1926.

————. *Lion Spearing.* FMNH Special Zoology Leaflet 1. Chicago, 1926.

Akeley, Carl, and Akeley, Mary L. Jobe. *Adventures in the African Jungle.* Illustrated. New York, 1956. Originally copyrighted in 1930; this is a later collection by Akeley's second wife.

Akeley, Mary L. Jobe. *Carl Akeley's Africa: The Account of the Akeley-Eastman-Pomeroy African Hall Expedition of the American Museum of Natural History.* Foreword by Henry Fairfield Osborn. New York, 1929. The complete report on every aspect of this highly important American zoological expedition of 1926.

————. *Restless Jungle.* New York, 1936.

Ambrosius, Ernst. *Andrees Allgemeiner Handatlas.* Helefeld and Leipzig, 1922. A beautiful and detailed German atlas, for many years in the Main Library reading room at the University of California.

The American Museum of Natural History. *The Complete Book of African Hall.* [New York], 1936. A collection of useful articles on the African Hall project, contributed by the leading figures in its construction.

The American Museum of Natural History: An Interpretation. New York, 1931.

Anderson, William Ashley. *South of Suez.* Illustrated. New York, 1923.

1923 Atlas of the World and Gazetteer. New York, 1923.

Barns, T. Alexander. *Across the Great Craterland to the Congo.* New York, 1924. Barns was associated with several important American expeditions, and one of the few popular writers to concentrate on the Belgian Congo and Angola.

Barnum, P. T. *The Wild Beasts, Birds and Reptiles of the World: The Story of Their Capture.* Chicago, 1892.

Beer, George Louis. *African Questions at the Paris Peace Conference.* Edited and with an Introduction by Louis Herbert Gray. New York, 1923. These major reports were prepared by Beer for the Inquiry in 1918; Gray, who was Beer's assistant in Paris, describes Beer's role in the mandates negotiations.

Beira and Mashonaland and Rhodesia Railways. *Guide to Rhodesia for the Use of Tourists and Settlers.* 2nd rev. ed. Bulawayo, 1924.

Benchley, Belle J. *My Life in a Man-Made Jungle.* Illustrated. Boston, 1940. Author was director of the San Diego Zoo.

Benedict, Ruth. *Patterns of Culture.* Boston, 1934.

Bengsten, Nels A., and Van Royen, Willem. *Fundamentals of Economic Geography.* New York, 1937.

Bennet, Benjamin. *Hitler over Africa*. 2nd ed. London, 1939.

Bentley, John. *The Old Car Book*. Greenwich, 1953.

Bigland, Eileen. *The Lake of the Royal Crocodiles*. Illustrated by John Nicolson. New York, 1939.

Blair, W. Reid. *In the Zoo*. Illustrated by Elwin R. Stanton. Foreword by Madison Grant. New York, 1929.

Boas, Franz, ed. *General Anthropology*. Boston, 1938. Boas's work is of fundamental importance in any study of American anthropology; his career at Columbia and as curator for anthropology at the AMNH spanned 40 years.

————. *The Mind of Primitive Man*. Rev. ed. New York, 1938.

Boulenger, E. G. *World Natural History*. Introduction by H. G. Wells. New York, 1938.

Bradley, Mary Hastings. *Caravans and Cannibals*. New York, 1926.

Brigham, Albert Perry and McFarlane, Charles T. *Essentials of Geography: Second Book*. Rev. ed. New York, 1920.

Brown, A. Samler and Brown, G. Gordon. *The South and East African Year Book and Guide*. London, 1920.

Brown, C. Emerson. *My Animal Friends*. Garden City, 1932. Author was director of the Philadelphia Zoo.

Buck, Frank. *Animals Are Like That!* New York, 1939.

Buck, Frank, with Anthony, Edward. *Bring 'Em Back Alive*. New York, 1930. Buck was one of America's few animal collectors, and the most famous, but his work was confined to Asia, whence came many "African" elephants, lions, and tigers.

Buell, Raymond Leslie. *The Native Problem in Africa*. 2 vols. New York, 1928. The result of a year's travel in Africa and exhaustive reading. Buell's book remains a standard contemporary source.

Durness, Tad. *Cars of the Early Twenties*. Philadelphia, 1968.

Butler, Albert E. *Building the Museum Group*. AMNH Guide Leaflet Series 82. New York, 1934.

Butler, Ellis Parker. *The Young Stamp Collector's Own Book*. 1st ed. Indianapolis, 1933.

Cade, R. Courtney. *Handbook of British Colonial Stamps in Current Use*. London, 1955.

California Academy of Sciences. *The Simson African Hall of the California Academy of Sciences*. San Francisco, 1944.

Caras, Roger A. *Dangerous to Man: Wild Animals: A Definitive Study of Their Reputed Danger to Man*. Philadelphia, 1964.

Carpenter, Frank G. *Africa*. Carpenter's Geographical Readers. New York, 1905.

Caton-Thompson, G[ertrude]. *The Zimbabwe Culture: Ruins and Reactions*. Illustrated. Oxford, 1931.

Chamber of Commerce of the United States. *Our World Trade in [Year]; Value and Volume of Principal Exports and Imports between United States and Chief Foreign Markets*. [Years 1920–1929]. Washington, 1921–1929.

Chisholm, George C. *Handbook of Commercial Geography*. 11th rev. ed. Edited by L. Dudley Stamp. New York, 1928.

Clark, Austin H. *Animals of Land and Sea*. New York, 1925.

Clark, Cumberland. *The Flags of Britain: Their Origin and History.* Shrewsbury, 1934.

Clark, Elmer T. *The Church and the World Parish.* Nashville, 1929.

Clendenen, Clarence C.; Collins, Robert; and Duignan, Peter. *Americans in Africa, 1865–1900.* Hoover Institution Studies 17. Stanford, 1966.

Clendenen, Clarence C., and Duignan, Peter. *Americans in Black Africa up to 1865.* Hoover Institution Studies 5. Stanford, 1964.

Coleman, Laurence Vail. *The Museum in America: A Critical Study.* 3 vols. Washington, 1939.

Collins, Robert, and Duignan, Peter. *Americans in Africa: A Preliminary Guide to American Missionary Archives and Library Manuscript Collections on Africa.* Stanford, 1963.

Conrad, Joseph. *Great Short Works of Joseph Conrad.* New York, 1966.

Coudenhove, Hans. *My African Neighbors: Man, Bird, and Beast in Nyasaland.* Illustrated. Boston, 1925. A collection of delightful articles, originally written for leading American monthlies. Dated, illustrative of much contemporary thought.

Couperie, Pierre, et al. *A History of the Comic Strip.* Translated by Eileen B. Hennessy. New York, 1968.

Coupland, Reginald. *The Study of the British Commonwealth.* Oxford, 1921.

Crowder, Michael. *West Africa under Colonial Rule.* Evanston, 1968.

Cunard, Nancy, ed. *Negro: Anthology Made by Nancy Cunard, 1931–1933.* New York, [Reprinted 1969]. Originally published in London in 1934, the anthology contains sharply radical Negro views, with a large section on Africa.

Cureau, Adolphe Louis. *Savage Man in Central Africa: A Study of Primitive Races in the French Congo.* Illustrated and translated by E. Andrews. London, 1915.

Curtin, Philip D. *The Image of Africa: British Ideas and Action, 1780–1850.* Madison, 1964.

Darwin, Charles. *The Descent of Man, and Selection in Relation to Sex.* 2 vols. New York, 1871.

Davis, Richard Harding. *The Congo and Coasts of Africa.* New York, 1907. For many years managing editor of Harper's and famous as a war correspondent, Davis was an inexhaustible source of travel stories, novels, plays, in between wars.

Day, Beth. *This Was Hollywood: An Affectionate History of Filmland's Golden Years.* Garden City, 1960.

Delafosse, Maurice. *The Negroes of Africa: History and Culture.* Washington, 1931. An important and oft-quoted book by a former French colonial governor.

The Delagoa Directory. 23rd ed. Lourenço Marques, 1921.

Delavignette, Robert. *Freedom and Authority in French West Africa.* London, 1950.

Deniker, J. *The Races of Man: An Outline of Anthropology and Ethnography.* Illustrated. 3rd ed. New York, 1913.

Deschamps, Paul, et al. *Les Colonies et la Vie Française pendant Huit Siècles.* Paris, 1933.

Diffendorfer, Ralph E. *The World Service of the Methodist Episcopal Church.* Chicago, 1923.

Dinesen, Isak. *Out of Africa.* New York, 1952. Originally published in 1937, the book is a superbly written account of seventeen years' residence on a farm in the White Highlands of Kenya.

Ditmars, Raymond L., and Crandall, Lee S. *Guide to the New York Zoological Park.* New York, 1939. This guide replaced one by Director William T. Hornaday that ran through twenty-four unchanged editions, the last in 1938, and five hundred thousand copies.

Dixon, Roland B. *The Racial History of Man.* Illustrated. New York, 1923. Badly dated now, indifferently received at the time, Dixon's work represented a system of analysis of race based solely on physical characteristics. He postulated a series of archetypes drawn from skull measurements and facial characteristics.

Du Bois, W. E. Burghardt. *The Negro.* New York, 1915. Du Bois' moving account of black history and culture, both in America and Africa, continued to be of great importance after World War I; it represented a major effort to bring Black African history and artistic attainments to the attention of the American public.

Du Chaillu, Paul B. *The Country of the Dwarfs.* New York, 1871.

_____. *A Journey to Ashango-Land; and Further Penetration into Equatorial Africa.* New York, 1871.

_____. *My Apingi Kingdom.* New York, 1871.

_____. *Wild Life under the Equator, Narrated for Young People.* New York, [1868]. Du Chaillu's books were classics of the Victorian age, and continued to be popular with young readers in the 1920s; they are the source of many African stereotypes dear to the American heart.

Dugmore, A. Radclyffe. *African Jungle Life.* Illustrated. London, 1928. The author, who invented the technique of photographing wild animals at night with a trip-wire flash, was considered to be one of the world's leading game photographers, and was well known to American hunters and game fanciers.

Duignan, Peter. *National Archives.* A reprint from *Handbook of American Resources for African Studies.* Stanford, 1967.

Dundas, Anne. *Beneath African Glaciers.* London, 1924. A useful account of life in Tanganyika by the wife of a British colonial officer.

Durant, John, and Durant, Alice. *Pictorial History of the American Circus.* New York, 1957.

[Eastman, George]. *Chronicles of an African Trip.* [Rochester], 1927. A complete and informative account of Eastman's part in the great East African expedition he financed for the AMNH in 1926; the book contains a beautiful set of prints by Martin Johnson. Eastman distributed copies of the book to old friends and employees, and after his death the Kodak public-relations department gave the rest to libraries throughout the United States.

Eliot, Charles. *The East Africa Protectorate.* Illustrated. London, 1905.

Emerson, Robert. *Africa and United States Policy.* Englewood Cliffs, 1967.

Essary, J. Frederick. *Reverse English: Some Off-Side Observations upon Our British Cousins.* New York, 1928.

Essoe, Gabe. *Tarzan of the Movies: A Pictorial History of More Than Fifty Years of Edgar Rice Burroughs' Legendary Hero.* New York, 1968.

Exporters' Encyclopaedia: 1927. 22nd annual ed. New York, 1926.

Exporters' Encyclopaedia: 1931. 26th annual ed. New York, 1930.

Fawcett, C. B. *A Political Geography of the British Empire.* Boston, 1933.

Fenton, Robert W. *The Big Swingers.* Englewood Cliffs, 1967.

Field Museum of Natural History *Anthropological Series.* Vol. 21. Chicago, 1931–1935.

Field Museum of Natural History Handbook. 4th ed. Chicago, 1933. A complete and useful source book of general information on the museum.

Field Museum of Natural History *Report Series.* Vols. 6–12. Chicago, 1921–1941.

Fitzgerald, Walter. *Africa: A Social, Economic and Political Geography of Its Major Regions.* 6th ed., rev. London, [1948]. First published in 1934 (revised in 1940 and 1948) this was perhaps the finest African geography in English available before World War II.

Forester, C[ecil] S[cott]. *The African Queen.* New York, 1940. This classic was first published in 1935.

Fosdick, Raymond B. *The Old Savage in the New Civilization.* Garden City, 1929.

Frank, Glenn, ed. *Wonder Books.* Chicago, 1938.

Fraser, Donald. *The Future of Africa.* London, 1911.

Fraser, Douglas C. *Impressions—Nigeria 1925.* London, 1926.

Frye, Alexis Everett. *New Geography: Book One.* Boston, 1920.

Gatti, Attilio. *Hidden Africa.* Illustrated. London, 1933.

————. *The King of the Gorillas.* Garden City, 1932. An edited version of Gatti's works listed above and below, based on the Royal Italian Scientific Expedition, Cape to Cairo. Gatti got a lot of mileage out of the expedition, and became a well-known big-game hunter and African publicist.

————. *Tom-Toms in the Night.* London, 1932. An incredible mishmash of "adventure," "Zulus," something called "Bantu-Simba Voodoo," and secret societies.

Gelfand, Lawrence E. *The Inquiry: American Preparation for Peace, 1917–1919.* New Haven, 1963.

Gettell, Raymond Garfield. *Political Science.* Boston, 1933.

Gibbons, Herbert Adam. *The New Map of Africa, 1900–1916: A History of European Colonial Expansion and Colonial Diplomacy.* New York, 1917.

Gibbons, Stanley, Ltd. *Priced Catalogue of Stamps of the British Empire: 1930.* 36th ed. London, [1930].

The Gold Coast Government. *The Gold Coast Handbook 1937.* Worcester, [1937].

Goldenweiser, Alexander A. *Early Civilization: An Introduction to Anthropology.* New York, 1922. The author was a student of Boas's at

Columbia, lectured at the New School for Social Research, 1919–1926, in both sociology and cultural anthropology.

Goode, J. Paul. *Goode's School Atlas, Physical, Political and Economic.* Chicago, 1925.

Goodrum, Charles A. *I'll Trade You an Elk.* New York, 1967. An amusing account of the Wichita Zoo in the late 1930s.

Gordon, W. J. *A Manual of Flags.* London, 1933.

Gorer, Geoffrey. *Africa Dances: A Book about West African Negroes.* New York, 1962. First published in 1935, the book is a highly literate report of the author's trip to West Africa in 1934. Gorer's discoveries led him to undertake serious anthropological studies in the United States, under Ruth Benedict and Margaret Mead.

Grady, Henry F., and Carr, Robert M. *The Port of San Francisco: A Study of Traffic Competition, 1921–1933.* Berkeley, 1934.

Greene, Graham. *Journey without Maps.* New York, 1961. Originally published in 1936.

————. ed. *The Old School: Essays by Divers Hands.* London, 1934.

Guyer, Michael F. *Animal Biology.* New York, 1931.

Haack, H. *Stielers Hand-Atlas, 1932/43.* Gotha, n.d.

Hailey, Lord. *An African Survey: A Study of Problems Arising in Africa South of the Sahara.* 2nd ed. London, 1945. An invaluable source of information on colonial Africa, based on several years' study of the best available scholarship by a distinguished commission; this is a reissue of the 1938 original.

Hall, Walter Phelps. *Empire to Commonwealth: Thirty Years of British Imperial History.* New York, 1928. An institutional study rather than a current local report, done at Princeton and a standard reference for years; Hall's major emphasis was on self-governing dominions, always a subject of interest to students of empire in this period.

Halliburton, Richard. *Seven League Boots.* Illustrated. Indianapolis, 1935. Halliburton was a professional writer of travel books; he was not specifically concerned with tropical Africa, but his books give an insight into travel styles of wealthy Americans en route to everywhere.

Halliwell, Leslie. *The Filmgoer's Companion.* Rev. ed. New York, 1967.

Hambly, Wilfrid D. *The Native Races of East Africa.* London, 1920. An early compilation of well-known facts about several linguistic groups in Kenya and Uganda. Hambly spent his active research period with Chicago's Field Museum, where he arrived in 1926 from a London museum to become curator of African ethnology.

————. *Source Book for African Anthropology.* FMNH Anthropological Series, vol. 26, parts 1 and 2. Chicago, 1937.

Handbook of American Museums. Washington, 1932. A great statistical mine of information, covering every major and minor institution in the country; the work of years, it was funded by a Carnegie grant.

Hardy, Georges. *Histoire de la Colonisation Française.* Paris, 1928.

Harvard African Studies. 8 vols. Cambridge, 1917–1927.

H. A. Snow's Hunting Big Game in Africa. n.p., n.d. A publicity booklet issued along with Snow's notorious film of the same name. Mrs. Nydine Snow Latham kindly provided me with a copy.

Hayward, Phillips A. *Wood, Lumber and Timbers.* Vol. 1 of Chandler Cyclopedia . . . of Commodities. New York, 1930.

Hegner, Robert W. *Parade of the Animal Kingdom.* New York, 1936.

_____. *Practical Zoology.* Rev. ed. New York, 1931.

Helser, Albert D. *In Sunny Nigeria: Experiences among a Primitive People in the Interior of North Central Africa.* Illustrated. New York, 1926.

Hemingway, Ernest. *Green Hills of Africa.* New York, 1935. A description of a hunting trip through British East Africa.

_____. *Hemingway's African Stories: The Stories, Their Sources, Their Critics.* Edited by James M. Howell. New York, 1935.

Hennessy, Maurice N. *Africa under My Heart.* New York, 1965. The report of twenty years' experience with the Royal West African Frontier Force.

Herskovits, Melville J. *Dahomey: An Ancient West African Kingdom.* 2 vols. Evanston, 1967. Originally published in 1938, and based on extensive field work, collections, and interviews, this remains a seminal work.

_____. *The Human Factor in Changing Africa.* New York, 1962.

_____. *The Myth of the Negro Past.* New York, 1941.

Hilton-Simpson, H. W. *Land and People of the Kasai.* Illustrated. London, 1911.

Hives, Frank. *Ju-Ju and Justice in Nigeria.* Illustrated. London, [1930].

Hobson, J[ohn] A. *Imperialism: A Study.* London, 1954. One of the most influential of contemporary anti-imperialist treatises, Hobson's study went through several printings and one major revision (in 1938); first published in 1902.

Hoefler, Paul L. *Africa Speaks: A Story of Adventure.* Illustrated. Chicago, 1931. The author's own informative, if badly overwritten, account of his second expedition to East Africa, the "Colorado African Expedition"; from it came a major sound movie of Africa.

Hollister, N[ed]. *East African Mammals in the United States National Museum.* SI, USNM Bulletin 99, parts 1–3. Washington, 1918–1924.

Horn, Alfred Aloysius, and Lewis, Ethelreda. *Trader Horn: Being the Life and Works of Alfred Aloysius Horn.* Foreword by John Galsworthy. New York, 1928. Supposedly the account of the author's life in French Equatorial Africa in the late nineteenth century, this popular book consists almost entirely of nonsense.

Hornaday, William T. *Official Guide Book to the New York Zoological Park.* Rev. ed. New York, 1938. The last of the many editions of this guide. Hornaday was the long-time director of the N.Y. Zoo and an extremely popular writer on animals and wildlife.

_____. *Popular Official Guide to the New York Zoological Park, 1921.* 17th ed. New York, 1921.

_____. *Tales from Nature's Wonderlands.* New York, 1924.

_____. *Taxidermy and Zoological Collecting.* Illustrated. New York, 1935.

_____. *Wild Animal Interviews and Wild Opinions of Us.* Illustrated by Lang Campbell. New York, 1928.

_____. *A Wild-Animal Round-Up: Stories and Pictures from the Passing Show.* New York, 1925.

Hoskins, Halford Lancaster. *European Imperialism in Africa.* New York,

1930. Written by a professor of history at Tufts, critical particularly of European cultural imperialism and land policies.

Hughes, J. E. *Eighteen Years on Lake Bangweulu*. London, n.d. The book was published in the early 1930s.

Hughes, Thomas. *David Livingstone*. London, 1889.

Huntington, Ellsworth, and Williams, Frank E. *Business Geography*. New York, 1922.

Huxley, Elspeth. *White Man's Country: Lord Delamere and the Making of Kenya*. 2 vols. London, 1935.

Huxley, Julian. *Africa View*. New York, 1931. A beautifully written book, a description of the author's journey through East Africa to study ways of improving colonial African education.

James, Preston E. *An Outline of Geography*. Boston, 1935.

Johannsen, G. Kurt, and Kraft, H. H. *Germany's Colonial Problem*. London, 1937.

Johnson, Martin. *Over African Jungles: The Record of a Glorious Adventure over the Big Game Country of Africa*. New York, 1935. All of Johnson's books are equally illustrative of Africa as he saw it; this one is beautifully illustrated with one hundred of his best photographs, most of them taken from two Sikorsky seaplanes that the Johnsons used in the early 1930s.

———. *Safari: A Saga of African Adventure*. New York, 1928.

Johnson, Osa. *I Married Adventure: The Lives and Adventures of Martin and Osa Johnson*. Philadelphia, 1940. Osa's famous autobiographical account of the Johnsons' life together in tropical Africa from 1920 to 1937.

Johnston, Harry H. *A History of the Colonisation of Africa by Alien Races*. New rev. ed. Cambridge, 1913. A classic by one of the prime movers in the birth of the African empire, Johnston's approach was a little dated even in the 1920s. Johnston was a key figure in the British acquisition of Uganda.

Johnston, Harry, and Guest, L. Haden. *The Outline of the World Today*. 3 vols. London, n.d.

———. *The World of To-Day*. Illustrated. 4 vols. New York, 1924.

———. *The World of To-Day*. Illustrated. 2 vols. New York, 1937. These three works by Johnston and Guest are simply three editions of the same work, the first; widely distributed in the United States, they are semi-scholarly, popular "histories" of the world, with heavy emphasis on the British Empire.

Jones, Thomas Jesse. *Education in Africa: A Study of West, South and Equatorial Africa*. New York, 1922.

———. *Essentials of Civilization: A Study in Social Values*. New York, 1929.

———. *Four Essentials of Education*. New York, 1926.

Kearton, Cherry, and Barnes, James. *Through Central Africa from East to West*. Illustrated. London, 1915.

Kenyatta, Jomo. *Facing Mount Kenya: The Tribal Life of the Gikuyu*. Introduction by B[ronislaw] Malinowski. London, 1961. Originally published in 1938, Kenyatta's book is of timeless value to anthro-

pologists and sociologists, and a notable autobiographical state-
ment by the first President of Kenya. Little contemporary notice
of the book was taken in the United States.
Kimber, Albert W. *Kimber's Record of Government Debts and Other
Foreign Securities: 1925.* 9th ed. New York, 1925.
Kirkwood, Kenneth, *Britain and Africa.* London, 1965.
Kirschshofer, Rose. *The World of Zoos: A Survey and Gazetteer.* New
York, 1968.
Knaplund, Paul. *The British Empire: 1815–1939.* 1st ed. New York, 1941.
Kroeber, A[lfred] L. *Anthropology.* New York, 1923. Kroeber, for dec-
ades the University of California's foremost anthropologist, was an
expert on North American indigenes; his knowledge of Africa was
based on standard sources widely available. Even distinguished
scholars gave credence to African stereotypes.
Kroeber, A. L., and Waterman, T. T., eds. *Source Book in Anthropology.*
Rev. ed. Illustrated. New York, 1931.
Lafeber, Walter. *The New Empire: An Interpretation of American Ex-
pansion, 1860–1898.* Ithaca, 1963.
Lahue, Kalton C. *Bound and Gagged: The Story of the Silent Serials.*
South Brunswick, [N.J.], 1968.
Langer, William L., and Armstrong, Hamilton Fish. *Foreign Affairs
Bibliography . . . 1919–1932.* Council on Foreign Relations. New
York, 1933.
Leakey, Louis. *Stone Age Africa: An Outline of Prehistory in Africa.*
London, 1936.
_____. *The Stone Age Cultures of Kenya Colony.* Cambridge, 1931.
Leakey's books describe the single most important paleontological
research in Africa during the interwar period.
Le Myre de Vilers et al. *Préparation aux Carrières Coloniales.* Paris,
1904.
Lewin, Evans. *The Germans and Africa.* Introduction by Earl Grey. Lon-
don, 1915.
Light, Richard Upjohn. *Focus on Africa.* Foreword by Isaiah Bowman.
New York, 1941. A collection of superb photographs taken on a
Cape-to-Cairo flight in the late 1930s for the American Geographical
Society; the photos are by Mary Light. Both the text and pictures are
exceptionally illuminating on both the reality of colonial Africa and
American reactions to it.
Lindley, M. F. *The Acquisition and Government of Backward Territory
in International Law.* London and New York, 1926.
Lindsay, Vachel. *Selected Poems of Vachel Lindsay.* Edited by Mark
Harris. New York, 1963.
Linton, Ralph. *The Study of Man: An Introduction.* Student's Edition.
New York, 1936.
Lippmann, Walter. *Public Opinion.* New York, 1922.
_____. *The Stakes of Diplomacy.* New York, 1915.
The Literary Digest Atlas of the World and Gazetteer. New York, 1926.
Lowie, Robert H. *The History of Ethnological Theory.* New York, 1937.
_____. *Primitive Society.* New York, 1920.
Lugard, F[rederick] D. *The Dual Mandate in British Tropical Africa.*

London, 1922. The classic statement of British tropical African imperial theory; perhaps the most important book on tropical Africa in the interwar period.

Lupoff, Richard A. *Edgar Rice Burroughs: Master of Adventure.* New York, 1965.

MacDonald, Malcolm, and Lake, Christina. *Treasure of Kenya.* New York, 1966. The animal pictures are wonderful.

Mackay, William Andrew, and Canfield, A. A. *The Murals in the Theodore Roosevelt Memorial Hall.* AMNH Science Guide 119. [New York], 1944.

Mackenzie, Jean Kenyon. *Black Sheep: Adventure in West Africa.* Illustrated. Boston, 1916. A collection of letters from "Gaboon" in the French Congo; the author was a sensitive, sympathetic, and highly literate observer; among the best missionary writing in print.

McMurray, Frank M., and Parkins, A. E. *Advanced Geography.* New York, 1924.

Mair, L. P. *Native Policies in Africa.* London, 1936.

Martens, Otto, and Karstadt, O., eds. *The African Handbook and Traveller's Guide.* London, 1932.

Maxwell, Lloyd W. *Discriminating Duties and the American Merchant Marine.* New York, 1926.

Maxwell, Marius. *Stalking Big Game with a Camera in Equatorial Africa.* Foreword by Sidney F. Harmer. Illustrated. New York, 1924. Almost a technical manual on wild-animal photography, the book contains much valuable data and some fine animal pictures, many of them taken from Maxwell's specially adapted Ford.

Mayhew, Arthur. *Education in the Colonial Empire.* London, 1938.

Miller, Hugo H., and Polley, Mary E. *Intermediate Geography.* New ed. Boston, 1932.

Miller, William J. *An Introduction to Physical Geology.* New York, 1941.

Montgomery Ward & Co. *Montgomery Ward & Co. Saint Paul Catalogue Number 103, Fall and Winter 1925–1926.* [Saint Paul], 1925.

Moody's Manual of Investments. Four per year: *Public Utilities, Governments, Steam Railroads, Industrials.* Edited by John Sherman Porter. New York, 1920–1939.

Moon, Parker Thomas. *Imperialism and World Politics.* New York, 1926.

Mott-Smith, May. *Africa from Port to Port.* New York, 1930. A report on the circumnavigation of Africa by a lady American journalist in 1925 and 1926.

Mullett, Charles F. *The British Empire.* New York, 1938.

Murdock, George Peter. *Our Primitive Contemporaries.* New York, 1934.

Murray, Marischal. *Union-Castle Chronicle, 1853–1953.* London, 1953.

Murray, S. S. *A Handbook of Nyasaland.* London, 1922.

Musée du Congo Belge. *Bibliographie Ethnographique du Congo Belge et des Régions Avoisinantes, 1925–1930.* Brussels, n.d. Vol. for 1933 published in 1935, and those for 1936–1939 in 1937–1941. An excellent bibliography, covering nearly every aspect of tropical Africa; includes materials from Belgium, the other imperial powers in Africa, Germany, and the United States, plus a complete list of journals dealing with African affairs.

Nagel, Alfred, ed. *Kimber's Record of Government Debts, 1932–1933.* 16th annual ed. New York, 1933.

National Foreign Trade Council. *Official Report of the . . . Annual Foreign Trade Convention.* For 1920 and 1927. New York, 1927.

National Industrial Conference Board. *The American Merchant Marine Problem.* New York, 1929.

————. *Report of the . . . National Foreign Trade Convention.* For 1938 and 1939. New York, 1940.

Newbigin, Marion I. *A New Regional Geography of the World.* New York, 1930.

Newland, H. Osman. *West Africa: A Handbook of Practical Information.* London, 1922. Covers British, French, and Portuguese West Africa. Full of little details, the handbook is a useful source on daily life in colonial West Africa.

Newman, Horatio Hackett. *Outlines of General Zoology.* New York, 1924.

Orde-Brown, G. St. J. *The Vanishing Tribes of Kenya.* Illustrated. Philadelphia, 1925. A helpful study of the peoples living on the southern slopes of Mount Kenya; for years one of the few serious studies available in an American imprint. The author was a British colonial officer.

Ossendowski, Ferdinand. *Slaves of the Sun.* New York, 1928. The highly fictionalized account of a tour of French Equatorial Africa; mostly junk.

Ottenberg, Simon and Phoebe, eds. *Culture and Societies of Africa.* New York, 1968.

Our Planet: The Blue Book of Maps. New York, 1935.

Patterson, J. H. *The Man-Eaters of Tsavo, and Other East African Adventures.* Foreword by Frederick Courteney Selous. Illustrated. London, 1908. Certainly one of the best-known African game stories ever written.

Peffer, Nathaniel. *The White Man's Dilemma: Climax of the Age of Imperialism.* New York, 1927. A series of critical lectures delivered at the New School for Social Research; Africa was included, but only as an afterthought.

Perham, Margery. *Colonial Government: Annotated Reading List on British Colonial Government.* London, 1950. An excellent survey of the literature at mid-century. Perham is a major figure in British African studies.

————. *The Colonial Reckoning.* London, 1961.

Philip, George & Son, Ltd. *British and Colonial Flags.* London, n.d.

Pittard, Eugene. *Race and History: An Ethnological Introduction to History.* Translated by V. C. C. Collum. New York, 1926.

Powys, Llewelyn. *Black Laughter.* New York, 1924. Articles from the New York *Evening Post* and the *Freeman* about the author's experiences as a white settler in Kenya; contains much on the reactions of that community to the world around it; well written, but supercilious in tone and insensitive.

Priestley, Herbert Ingram. *France Overseas: A Study of Modern Imperialism.* New York, 1938.

Rainer, Peter W. *My Vanished Africa.* New Haven, 1940. Recollections of the first thirty years of the author's life in southern Africa, ending in 1919.

Reid, Eric. *Tanganyika without Prejudice.* London, 1934.

Reinsch, Paul S. *Colonial Administration.* New York, 1905.

Richardson, James D., ed. *A Compilation of the Messages and Papers of the Presidents.* 11 vols. Washington, 1909.

Reynold, Alexander Jacob. *From the Ivory Coast to the Cameroons.* London, 1929. The reminiscences of an officer in the Gold Coast Regiment, 1910–1918.

Roosevelt, Theodore. *African Game Trails: An Account of the African Wanderings of an American Hunter-Naturalist.* 2 vols. New York, 1914. Probably the most famous and off-quoted game-hunting book ever written by an American; originally published in 1910, it went through many editions, and was a standard reference throughout the 1920s and 1930s.

Roosevelt, Theodore, and Heller, Edmund. *Life Histories of African Game Animals.* 2 vols. New York, 1914. The result of the field work done for the National Museum during Roosevelt's Great Hunt in British East Africa in 1909–1910; Heller was the zoologist; his career in Africa was noteworthy.

Rosenthal, Eric. *Stars and Stripes in Africa.* London, 1938. Written by a South African, and centered almost entirely on his country, this is a journalistic survey of American influences in Africa, from the slave trade in Liberia to the use of American-style stage coaches during the South African gold rush of Kruger's day.

Ross, Edward Alsworth. *Report on Employment of Native Labor in Portuguese Africa.* New York, 1925. The famous polemic that poisoned Portuguese-American relations in Africa for years.

_____. *Seventy Years of It: An Autobiography.* New York, 1936.

Rothschild, Sigmund I. *Stories Postage Stamps Tell: What We Can Learn from Them.* Illustrated. New York, 1930.

Schmokel, Wolfe W. *Dream of Empire: German Colonialism, 1919–1945.* New Haven, 1964.

Schnee, Heinrich, ed. *German Colonization Past and Future. The Truth about the German Colonies.* London, 1926.

Schulz-Ewerth, E. *Deutschlands Weg zur Kolonialmacht.* Berlin, 1934.

Schweitzer, Albert. *On the Edge of the Primeval Forest* and *More from the Primeval Forest.* New York, 1948. *On the Edge* was first published in 1922; *More* in 1931. Although not an American, Schweitzer reached a wide reading public in this country with his occasional articles and books.

Scott, Clifford Haley. "American Image of Sub-sahara Africa, 1900–1939." Ph.D. dissertation, University of Iowa, 1968. Scott does not include archival materials, but his work covers a broad range of published sources.

Scott's Standard Postage Stamp Catalogue: 1926 and 1932. New York, 1925 and 1931.

Seabrook, William B. *Jungle Ways.* Photos by author. New York, 1931.

A lurid and fanciful account of French West Africa—widely read and widely denounced by scholars.

Seevers, Charles H. *Trailing Animals around the World.* One of the *Wonder Books,* edited by Glen Frank. Chicago, 1938.

Seligman, Herbert J. *Race Against Man.* Introduction by Franz Boas. New York, 1939. Almost the official (and violent) reaction of the American Anthropological Association to the "nordic" nonsense of the Nazis; contains extensive references to American race relations, is critical of any sort of colonial "race line."

Shantz, H. L., and Marbut, C. F. *The Vegetation and Soils of Africa.* New York, 1923. The definitive work on African vegetation, the result of research done partly during the ill-famed Smithsonian African Expedition of 1919–1920.

Shattuck, George Cheever, ed. *Handbook of Travel Prepared for the Harvard Travellers Club.* 2nd ed., rev. Cambridge, 1935. Contains several interesting essays of tourist travel in tropical Africa.

Sheffey, Mrs. Chas. P. M., *Congo Tides.* Nashville, 1939.

Simms, Stephen C. *Field Museum and the Child.* Chicago, 1928.

Simson, H. J. *British Rule, and Rebellion.* Edinburgh, 1938.

Smith, Darrell Hevener, and Betters, Paul V. *The United States Shipping Board: Its History, Activities and Organization.* Washington, 1931.

Smith, Edwin W. *The Golden Stool.* Foreword by F. D. Lugard. London, 1926. The standard account of the British subjugation of the Ashanti state of the Gold Coast Colony in the late 1890s, with an excellent treatment, as the author puts it, of "Some aspects of the conflict of cultures in Modern Africa."

Smith, J. Russell. *Human Geography: Book One: Peoples and Countries.* Chicago, 1921.

————. *Human Geography: Book Two: Regions and Trade.* Chicago, 1922.

————. *Industrial and Commercial Geography.* New ed. New York, 1925.

The Smithsonian Institution. *Annual Report of the Board of Regents of the Smithsonian Institution, 1919* through *1939.* Washington, 1921–1940.

————. *Smithsonian Miscellaneous Collections.* Vols. 60, 61, 72, and 78. Washington, 1913, 1914, 1922, and 1927.

————. The United States National Museum. *Proceedings of the United States National Museum.* Vols. 56, 71, and 73. Washington, 1920, 1928, and 1929.

Smuts, J. C. *Africa and Some World Problems.* Oxford, 1930.

Snow, Alpheus Henry. *The Question of Aborigines in the Law and Practice of Nations.* Washington, 1919.

Southworth, Constant. *The French Colonial Venture.* London, 1931.

Springer, John McKendree. *Pioneering in the Congo.* New York, 1916.

Staley, Eugene. *Raw Materials in Peace and War.* New York, 1937.

Stanley, Henry M. *The Congo and the Founding of Its Free State.* 2 vols. New York, 1885.

————. *Through the Dark Continent.* New York, 1878.

The Statesman's Year-Book . . . *for the Year 1934.* London, 1934.
Streeter, Daniel W. *Denatured Africa.* Illustrated. New York, 1926. A breezy quotable travelogue of a trip through colonial Africa by a wealthy American tourist and part-time author. Streeter owned the Buffalo Weaving and Belting Co., and was something of a patron of the local arts and sciences.
Strong, Richard P., ed. *The African Republic of Liberia and the Belgian Congo.* 2 vols. Cambridge, 1930. A major source, based on the Harvard African expedition; includes considerable material on the flora and fauna of the Belgian Congo.
Symons, H[umfrey] E[vans]. *Two Roads to Africa.* London, 1939.
Tarr, Ralph Stockman. *College Physiography.* New York, 1923.
Taylor, Griffith. *Environment and Race.* London, 1927.
————. *Geography in the Twentieth Century.* New York, 1951.
Thomson. J. Arthur. *What Is Man?* New York, 1924.
Tillman, Seth P. *Anglo-American Relations at the Paris Peace Conference of 1919.* Princeton, 1961
Toothaker, Charles R. *Commercial Raw Materials: Their Origin, Preparation and Uses.* Boston, 1905.
Townsend, Mary Evelyn. *European Colonial Expansion Since 1871.* Chicago, 1941. Townsend, an important American political scientist, produced a series of important legal and political studies of European, particularly German, imperialism.
————. *The Rise and Fall of Germany's Colonial Empire: 1884–1918.* Introduction by Carlton J. H. Hayes. New York, 1930.
Treatt, Stella Court. *Cape to Cairo: The Record of a Historical Motor Journey.* Boston, 1927. The colorful account of an English couple's much-heralded attempt to pioneer the length of Africa in two Crossley cars in 1924.
Tremlett, Mrs. Horace. *With the Tin Gods.* London, 1915.
Trotter, Reginald George. *The British Empire-Commonwealth: A Study in Political Evolution.* New York, 1932.
Trotter, Spencer. *The Geography of Commerce: A Textbook.* New York, 1911.
Tylor, Edward B. *Anthropology: An Introduction to the Study of Man and Civilization.* New York, 1920. This 1881 classic went through many editions. A period piece, hopelessly outdated now, but probably taken at face value well into the 1920s.
United States Department of Agriculture. *Yearbook of Agriculture: 1936.* Washington, 1936.
United States Department of the Navy. *Annual Report of the Navy Department for the Fiscal Year* . . . *1919–1931.* Washington, 1920–1932.
————. *Annual Report of the Secretary of the Navy for the Fiscal Year* . . . *1933–1939.* Washington, 1933–1939.
United States Department of State. *Papers Relating to the Foreign Relations of the United States.* 1919–1939, inclusive. Washington, 1936–1956.
————. *Papers Relating to the Foreign Relations of the United States:*

The Paris Peace Conference. 13 vols. Washington, 1942–1947.

————. *Register of the Department of State.* From Dec. 23, 1918, through Oct. 1, 1939. Washington, 1919–1939.

Van Cleef, Eugene. *Trade Centers and Trade Routes.* New York, 1937.

Vanden Bergh, Leonard John. *On the Trail of the Pigmies.* Photographs by George Burbank Shattuck. Foreword by Robert H. Lowie. New York, 1921.

Van Dyke, W[oodbridge] S. *Horning into Africa.* n.p., 1931. A colorful account of the great movie expedition into B.E.A.; the book contains a wealth of information on the expedition, and on the subsequently lavish publicity attending release of the movie.

Wald, Jerry, and Macaulay, Richard, eds. *The Best Pictures 1939–1940.* Illustrated. New York, 1940.

Ward, Artemas, ed. *The Encyclopedia of Food.* Illustrated. New York, 1929.

Wassermann, Jakob. *Bula Matari: Stanley—Conquerer of a Continent.* Translated by Eden and Cedar Paul. New York, 1933. A German biography, representing Germany's renewed interest in the Congo; the book provided a useful summary of Stanley's life, based on his own writings, but Wassermann indulged in large-scale whimsical extrapolations.

Waugh, Evelyn. *Black Mischief.* Boston, 1946. Originally published in 1932.

————.*They Were Still Dancing.* New York, 1932. This cleverly written travelogue and the above novel were based on a trip through East Africa that included a visit to Ethiopia for the coronation festivities of Haile Selassie.

Weeks, John H. *Among Congo Cannibals.* Illustrated. Philadelphia, 1913.

Weinthal, Leo, ed. *The Story of the Cape to Cairo Railway and River Routes, from 1887 to 1922.* 4 vols. London, 1923. A lavish set of elaborately and beautifully illustrated books on every aspect of that portion of Africa covered by the train route; all major Africanists were represented by articles and portraits with biographies.

Weischoff, H. A. *Anthropological Bibliography of Negro Africa.* American Oriental Studies, vol. 23. New Haven, 1948.

Westermann, Diedrich. *The African To-Day.* Foreword by Lord Lugard. International Institute of African Languages and Cultures. London, 1934.

————. *The African Today and Tomorrow.* New rev. ed. Foreword by Lord Lugard. International Institute of African Languages and Cultures. London, 1939. The first edition quickly sold out, and ran in a popular French and German edition as well; the 1939 edition added fresh anthropological data, new maps by Heinz Solken, and illustrations from the German edition. The author's conclusions and running commentary remained unchanged.

Whitaker's Peerage, Baronetage, Knightage, and Companionage, for the Year 1929. London, n.d.

Whitbeck, R. H., and Finch, V. C. *Economic Geography.* New York, 1924.

White, David Manning, and Abel, Robert H. *The Funnies: An American Idiom.* Glencoe, 1963.

White, Stewart Edward. *The Land of Footprints.* Illustrated and with two drawings by Philip R. Goodwin. Garden City, 1913.

————. *The Rediscovered Country.* Illustrated. Garden City, 1915. A report, based on a field journal, of White's penetration into that region of German East Africa later known to hunters as the Serengeti Plains of Tanganyika. White did not view blacks sympathetically, but his books are excellent descriptions of camp life; he was observant, careful, and articulate, and his books are perhaps the best of their type.

Willis, Bailey. *East African Plateaus and Rift Valleys.* Washington, 1936.

————. *Living Africa: A Geologist's Wanderings through the Rift Valley.* Illustrated. [New York], 1930. Two excellent books, the first a technical, the second a popular account of the author's observations in the East African Great Rift Valley, where he went on a Carnegie grant to study conflicting geological theories on what caused it.

Wilson, James C. *Three-Wheeling through Africa.* Illustrated. Indianapolis, 1936. A careful and useful account of a trip made by two young Americans from Lagos, Nigeria, across Africa to Massawa on the western coast of the Red Sea.

Woodson, Carter G. *The African Background Outlined, or Handbook for the Study of the Negro.* Washington, 1936. An important first effort at a bibliographical essay on the "Black race" by a major figure in American black scholarship. From 1922 on, the author was director of the Association for the Study of Negro Life and History and editor of the *JNH.*

Woolbert, Robert Gale. *Foreign Affairs Bibliography . . . 1932–1942.* New York, 1945.

Woolf, Leonard. *Economic Imperialism.* New York, 1920.

————. *Empire and Commerce in Africa; A Study in Economic Imperialism.* London, [1919].

————. *Imperialism and Civilization.* London, 1928. The leading works of one of the most important of the economically minded anti-imperialists.

Wright, Arnold. *The Romance of Colonisation: Being the Story of the Economic Development of the British Empire.* London, 1923.

Wright, Quincy. *Mandates under the League of Nations.* Chicago, 1930.

index

285

286　index

Belgian Congo (Congo Free State)
　animals in, 118, 120, 124, 131, 134
　establishment of, 11–15, 24, 85
　missionaries in, 42, 107, 177–78,
　　180, 185, 188–89
　Parc National Albert, 124
　population of, 15
　preparation for World War II in, 49
　religious movements in, 16, 17
　U.S. attitudes toward, 37, 41–42
　U.S. interests in, 37, 53–54, 57–58,
　　62, 94, 98, 134
Benedict, Ruth, 154
Benguela Railway, 39
Bennett, James G., 9
Benson, John T., 141–42, 147
Bergsten, Robert N., 53
Berlin Conference on Africa (1884–
　85), 10, 12–13, 25, 91
Bismarck, Otto von, 11–12
Black Americans
　African art and, 150–51
　criticism of imperialism by, 26–27,
　　185, 188, 191–94, 199–200
　discontent in Africa blamed on,
　　199–200
Black Mischief (Waugh), 164, 165
Black Sheep: Adventures in West Af-
　rica (Mackenzie), 174
Bliven, Martha Miller, 81
Bloom, Sol, 53
Boloki people, 174
Bolshevik agitators, 199
Bongo, 137, 144
Booth, Edwina, 73
Bowman, Isaiah, 170, 197
Bradley, Mary Hastings, 202
Britain. See Great Britain
British East Africa
　American interests in, 14, 30, 32,
　　51, 53–56
　animals in, 119–20, 123–26, 128,
　　134
　inflation in, 76
　missionaries in, 177, 185
　See also Kenya; Tanganyika;
　　Uganda
British West Africa, 15, 187
　American interests in, 15, 187
　political movements in, 17, 20
Bronx Zoo. See New York Zoological
　Park
Brown, G. Gordon, 154
Brown, Mr. and Mrs. L. D., 53
Bruce, James, 8

Brussels Conference (1889–90), 10,
　13
Buchanan, James P., 63
Buck, Frank, 122, 140
Buell, Raymond Leslie, 18, 33, 43,
　149–50, 196–97
Bulloro people, 153
Bunche, Ralph J., 34
Bura people, 174
Bureau of Animal Industry, U.S., 139
Bureau of Biological Survey, U.S.,
　139–40
Bureau of Foreign and Domestic Com-
　merce, U.S., 64, 92, 95
Burroughs, Edgar Rice, 67
Business, American, 13, 52–55, 57, 64
　automobiles and, 105–16
　government policy toward, 90–93
　obstacles to, 93–96
　shipping and, 96–105
　See also Trade with Africa
Business Week (periodical), 46
"Bwana," use of term, 84–85

California Academy of Sciences Mu-
　seum, 132
Cameron, A. D., 96
Cameroons
　British, 141
　French, 14–15, 24, 189
　German, 12
　U.S. and, 26
Cannibalism, 156, 174
Carnegie Fund, 185
Carnegie Museum, 135, 137
Carpenter's Geographical Reader, 155
Carr, Wilbur, 135
Cartier de Marchienne, Emil de, 42,
　124
Catholic World (periodical), 192
Century (periodical), 156
Ceremonial, imperial, American in-
　terest in, 3, 27, 88–89
Chamberlain, Neville, 49
Chapin, James, 113
Christianity, African forms of, 16, 179.
　　See also Missionaries; Roman
　　Catholic Church
Chrysler, Walter P., 142
Clark, James L., 80, 86
Clark, Reed Paige, 54, 58, 62, 74, 75
Cleveland Museum of Natural History,
　132
Climate, effects of, 70–75, 77–78, 168

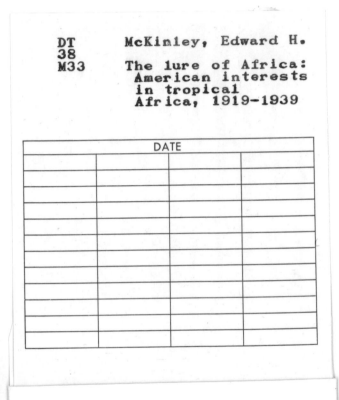

DATE			